The Mystic Fable

RELIGION AND POSTMODERNISM

A series edited by Thomas A. Carlson

RECENT BOOKS IN THE SERIES

Negative Certainties, by Jean-Luc Marion (2015)
Heidegger's Confessions, by Ryan Coyne (2015)
Arts of Wonder, by Jeffrey L. Kosky (2012)
God Without Being, Second Edition, by Jean-Luc Marion (2012)
Secularism in Antebellum America, by John Lardas Modern (2011)
The Figural Jew, by Sarah Hammerschlag (2010)

Michel de Certeau

The Mystic Fable

Volume Two

The Sixteenth and Seventeenth Centuries

Text established and presented by Luce Giard
Translated by Michael B. Smith

The University of Chicago Press
Chicago and London

At the time of his death in 1986, MICHEL DE CERTEAU was a director of studies at the Ecole des hautes études en sciences sociales, Paris. Of his many books, *The Practice of Everyday Life*, *The Writing of History*, and *Heterologies: Discourse on the Other* are available in English translation.

The University of Chicago Press, Chicago 60637
The University of Chicago Press, Ltd., London

Printed in the United States of America

34 33 32 31 30 29 28 27 26 25   2 3 4 5 6

ISBN-13: 978-0-226-20913-5 (cloth)
ISBN-13: 978-0-226-20927-2 (e-book)
DOI: https://doi.org/10.7208/chicago/9780226209272.001.0001

Originally published as *La Fable mystique, XVIe–XVIIe Siècle (II)*, edition établie et présentée par Luce Giard, by Michel de Certeau. © Editions Gallimard, Paris, 2013.

The University of Chicago Press gratefully acknowledges the generous support of the France Chicago Center toward the translation and publication of this book.

Library of Congress Cataloging-in-Publication Data

Certeau, Michel de.
[Fable Mystique. English]
The mystic fable / Michel de Certeau ; translated by Michael B. Smith.
p. cm. — (Religion and postmodernism)
Translation of : La fable mystique.
Includes bibliographical references.
Contents: v. 2. The sixteenth and seventeenth centuries.
1. Mysticism—Europe—History—16th century. 2. Mysticism—Europe—History—17th century. I. Title. II. Series.
BV5077.E85c4713 1992
248.2′2′09409031—dc20   91-4827
CIP

∞ This paper meets the requirements of ANSI/NISO Z39.48-1992 (Permanence of Paper).

Contents

Presentation

After the publication of the first volume of *The Mystic Fable, Sixteenth and Seventeenth Centuries* in May 1982, Michel de Certeau worked indefatigably on the preparation of a second volume, which his illness prevented him from completing. He intended, as was his habit, to include in that work—reworked and with additional material, new developments, and ample modifications—various articles already published as so many milestones in a long-term reflection on mystic texts. To these chapters, the object of an initial version that he would have reread and modified, he intended to add others that were in the process of development. He had gathered the material for these texts, but had not yet committed them to written form. His files contained only disparate preparatory notes. Some notes are ranged under a title intended for a lecture or seminar, in which case they are accompanied by the outline of a plan, although that ad hoc organization does not constitute a coherent format. In their present state these roughed-out manuscripts are not publishable, even as fragments.

When he understood during the last trimester of 1985 that his days were numbered and that he would not be able finish the work in progress, he decided to confide the future publication of his writings to me. I accepted, without thinking through all that this would entail. In the days following his passing in January 1986, I began to realize how difficult that task would be. Being unable and unwilling to take on everything at once, and to give myself time to think things out, I opted to proceed methodically by incremental steps.[1] First I had to establish his complete bibliography in order to track down his many publications in several languages.[2] This survey then gave me the occasion to compile and edit four thematic collections, grouped according to specific interests:[3] *Histoire et psychanalyse entre science et fiction* [History and Psychoanalysis between Science and Fiction] (1987),[4] *La Faiblesse de croire* [The Weakness of Believing] (1987),[5] *La Prise de parole et autres écrits politiques* [The Capture of Speech and Other Political Writings] (1994),[6] *Le Lieu de l'autre: Histoire religieuse et mystique* [The Place of the Other: Religious and Mystic History] (2005).[7] At the same time, in order to make earlier works available in bookstores, I had to take on the task of reediting them, verifying the faithfulness of the texts to the manuscripts, correcting printing errors, completing elliptic references, in many cases writing an introduction, in all cases an index of names, and occasionally some supplementary notes to clarify allusions to contemporary events. Such was the case with *L'Étranger ou l'union dans la difference* [The Foreigner or Union in Difference] (1991),[8] the two volumes of *L'Invention du quotidien* [The Practice of Everyday Life] (1990–94),[9] *La Culture au pluriel* [Culture in the Plural](1993),[10] *L'Écriture de l'histoire* [The Writing of History] (2002),[11] *Une Politique de la langue. La Révolution française et les patois: L'Enquête de Grégoire* [A Politics of Language. The French Revolution and Patois: The Inquest of Grégoire] (2002),[12] *La Possession de Loudun* [The Possession at Loudun] (2005).[13] During the same time period, to inform a new generation of readers, I instigated and edited three collective volumes on Michel de Certeau.[14] In addition to my preoccupations with the French area, I became increasingly involved abroad: I devoted my efforts to networking, increasing the number of contacts, organizing academic conferences and media activity in such a way as to prompt publishers to have this or that work translated. This required verifying the quality of the translations.[15] It was a long-term and time-consuming commitment, demanding patience and tenacity, but one that led to the successful circulation of the work throughout Europe, in North and South America, and even as far as Asia. Of course none of that would have been possible without the intrinsic quality of the work in question, without the strength and originality of these books that continue to attract new readers everywhere, and nothing could have been accomplished without the attentive and effective support of so many friends worldwide.

Having completed this part of my task, I returned to the haunting problem of the second volume of *The Mystic Fable*. I was asked with great insistence to have that volume published, but little did anyone know the difficulty involved. How could I best avail myself of the fragmentary material found in the author's files? How could I harmonize these contradictory plans, how assemble these disconnected notes, these barely identified quotations? For a long time I entertained hopes of finding a satisfactory way to proceed. But all my efforts were in vain. The transmutation of those elements, scattered in heteroclite fragments and elliptic notes, could have been achieved by the alchemist-author who had chosen them, grouped them, separated them into broad themes in his files: for anyone else it is impossible. That is why I have resigned myself to editing this volume the way I have, including only articles published by their author. Only one chapter, the longest, dedicated to Nicholas of Cusa, is partially unpublished, but the author wrote it out in its entirety, and then carefully reread and corrected the typed manuscript.

The choice of texts gathered here (which would have constituted approximately half of the second volume as the author intended it to be), their titles and their arrangement into ten consecutive chapters, framed by an introduction ("Mystic Historicities") and a conclusion ("The Opera of Speech: Glossolalias"), is based on Michel de Certeau's instructions during his last weeks as I carefully noted down at the time. He repeated several times, clearly and firmly, that he did not wish any pseudo "unpublished manuscripts" to be brought forward after his death, taken from recordings of courses and seminars, or based on the notes of his listeners, or made up of an assemblage of manuscript fragments found in his drawers. This refusal is consistent with his exigency with respect to writing, and with the long labor he devoted to putting the finishing touches on his work. He was of the view that there is an intrinsic difference in quality between an oral presentation, albeit prepared with care and based on a series of detailed notes, and a "truly written" text.

The production of one of his writings could extend over time, the composition of a book going through successive versions of its chapters, each considered as provisional. In the meantime, one or another of these versions might be published separately in the form of an article, launched like a trial balloon, and submitted to the criticism of his readers, whose remarks would then inspire an eventual reworking of parts of the text. The goal of the work of rewriting was to clarify the expression and sharpen the analyses. If, by these procedures, the author aimed to enhance the articulation of his argumentation, if he thus succeeded in nuancing his assertions, in further specifying his sources, this process also contributed to the condensation of his thought and the complexification of his style, and it also delayed the completion of his texts. Thus, on the printed proofs of the first volume of *La Fable mystique* [The Mystic Fable], he wanted to make such extensive corrections that the publisher asked him to assume the costs, which he did.

His stringent requirements with respect to his writings explain the long years of gestation of *La Fable mystique*, the subject of which was so important to him. That project, still ill-defined, preoccupied him beginning in 1958, when he began his research on Pierre Favre (1506–46), the mystic and close companion of Ignatius of Loyola.[16] Michel de Certeau was severe with respect to his own texts, and did not hesitate to rework or eliminate perfectly good pages with which he was, for whatever reason, dissatisfied. Here there come to mind his lines from the last page of the first volume of *The Mystic Fable*, so often quoted and paraphrased since then: "He or she is mystic who cannot stop walking and with the certainty of what is lacking, knows of every place and object that it is *not that*; one cannot stay *there* nor be content with *that*."[17] We may therefore be certain that the articles grouped here would also have been reworked by their author before being incorporated into the second volume.

How would that volume 2 have been organized? In the author's files there are various plans, some in the form of typed manuscripts, and replete with handwritten corrections, others handwritten and equally filled with crossed-out words or expressions. Not all of them are dated; their chronology is uncertain, but it is possible to reestablish a plausible succession, as the hypothesis of a volume 3, barely sketched out, emerges—extending from the eighteenth to the twentieth century, containing the Convulsionaries of Saint-Médard, Charcot (and Janet), Freud (and Romain Rolland), Mallarmé and Wittgenstein. As for volume 2, a handwritten letter, sent from Paris on 25 August 1984 to an American friend, Michael B. Smith (later to become the translator of the first volume of *La Fable mystique*),[18] who thoughtfully sent me a copy of it, contains a "résumé" in which Michel de Certeau explains:[19]

> Indeed I am working on volume 2, devoted to the analysis of the "experimental science" of *mystics* from the sixteenth century till the seventeenth. Volume 1 covered the constitution of a new "science"; its central axis, its formal features (enunciation: the speaking subject); and lastly its dissemination ("figures of the savage"). Volume 2 is the presentation of the *content itself* of that science, from Nicholas of Cusa (fifteenth century) to Fénelon and Pascal.

Part 1: from the (mystic) event to history, or the problem of the "foundations" of new historicities, on the basis of four theoretic figures: Nicholas of Cusa (the inductive "look" of society), Teresa of Avila (the autobiography or history of the subject), John of the Cross (the poem generative of a historical "prose") and the "foundations" of societies, orders, convents, etc. (the articulation of experience with a utopian society, societal model: the "constitutions").
Part 2: the "protocols" or *techniques* of that science: a. "spiritual direction," exercise of the dialogue analogous to the psychoanalytic cure; b. corporal and mental "methods," that is, a physics of the soul; c. the reading, or practice of the text (arts of reading, etc., *id est* oral and written); d. the reinterpretation of the past or invention of a personal tradition (the arts of memory).
Part 3: "the economy of the subject," or theoretic unfolding of experience: a. the rhetorics of the speaking body (sensorial experiences, the economy of the body, etc.); b. the problem of the passions (the affective, narratives of passions and their theories); c. folly ("excess" and the relation to the pathological); d. language and angelic manifestations (a poetics of the spoken word or of the soul, the word as "echo" of the other, etc.).
Part 4: the "diaspora" or dispersion of that science with the appearance of the sociopolitical and scientific figures of "modernity." Four essential figures break the mystic science: a. the recovery of the ecclesiastic institution and the pastoral strategies, *id est* the opposition of "theologians" to the "spirituals"; b. political absolutism, and the separation between the public and the private (cf. a few cases of "politician and mystic"); c. the progress of erudition and historicism (case of the interpretation of the Bible, Richard Simon); d. a new logic or art of thinking (cf. the case of Pascal, etc.).
The conclusion will attempt to take stock of the ethical and poetic significance of that literature, of the "art of loving" it develops, and the relation between the "fable" and the problem of God.

This plan corresponds roughly to the one Michel de Certeau had sent a few days earlier, on 19 August, to Pierre Nora, at Gallimard (and which François Dosse included in his biography of him),[20] but it differs in certain subtitles, and with respect to the introduction. It is also more explicit on the content and intention of the announced parts and their various chapters. The manuscript plans that the author wrote in 1985 and commented on during his last days, as he was explaining to me how his files were organized, are somewhat different from the two texts of August 1984. They contain still other chapters for which there is no written version. In any case, compared with the two plans from August 1984, we can see that the thematic gaps in the articles already published are distributed fairly equally across the four projected parts. Thus, for the first part, what is missing is material concerning the autobiography of Teresa of Avila and the foundations of orders and convents. For the second part, the lacunae are the spiritual direction and the "methods" or spiritual exercises, but the very beautiful article of 1973 titled "The Space of Desire, or the Foundation of the *Spiritual Exercises*" might have served as the generating nucleus.[21] In the third part, we do not know what the rhetorics of the speaking body would have been; it is possible that the 1977 article "Le Corps folié" [The Crazed Body] constitutes a rough outline of it,[22] but its tonality seemed to me too different to be included in this volume. Last, as for the fourth part, no existing article focuses on pastoral strategies, but the dictionary entry of 1977 dedicated to Charles Borromée (1538–84) might have been put to good use;[23] as for the question of royal absolutism, the author intended to include his study on René d'Argenson (1596–1651), which dates back to 1963, and in 1985 he asked me to reread it with that in mind and to suggest possible modifications. The difference in the tone of writing and type of sources used led me to leave that text aside as well.[24]

In assembling the present volume, I took as my ultimate authority the oral instructions of Michel de Certeau with respect to the previously published articles that he intended for volume 2. As for the order to be adopted, and the titles to be given to the various chapters, I have followed his instructions and added, when necessary, what was said in the last manuscript plans. As you will see, the included texts are of unequal length; the shortest ones probably would have been completed by the author, if he had had time. None of the included texts have been modified. I have limited myself to checking the previously published version against the author's own printed copy, on which he had occasionally made corrections. When I found in his files a typed version of the published text or even a prior handwritten version, I compared it with the printed version, which enabled me to correct some printing errors and to eliminate a few textual obscurities. Moreover, I have completed certain references in the notes and corrected errors that had slipped in. I have also unified the presentation of the notes, which differed from publication to publication.

Rereading all these texts, we note that among the mystic authors, Nicholas of Cusa, in a very long chapter, and John of the Cross, in three chapters, loom large. Next comes—less than in the first volume—Jean-Joseph Surin, that contemporary of Descartes, into whose writings Michel de Certeau breathed new life.[25] Teresa of Avila is also less present than in the first volume, while Pascal and Angelus Silesius take on much greater importance. The first chapter, the longest, partially unpublished, returns, through Nicholas of Cusa, to the question of seeing, which occupied a privileged position in the meditations of the author, as may be verified in his 1982 article on Merleau-Ponty, "La Folie de la vision" [The Madness of Vision],[26] or in the poetic parable titled in 1983 "Extase blanche" [White Ecstasy], which I included at the end of *La Faiblesse de croire*.[27] With respect to Michel de Certeau's way of proceeding in the present volume, it should be remarked that the historical work is sometimes based on a close analysis of a key text. This applies, in chapter 1, to the preface of Nicholas of Cusa's *De icona*, and in chapter 2 to the prologue of John of the Cross's Cántico, and also, in chapter 10, to Pascal's fourth letter to Mademoiselle de Roannez. This modus operandi was already at work in volume 1; in chapter 6, for example, in the preface to Surin's *The Experimental Science*, and at the beginning of Teresa of Avila's *Interior Castle*.

Here is the list of articles contained in this volume, with their references and original titles:

Introductory. "Historicités mystiques," *Recherches de science religieuse* 73 (1985): 325–54.

Chapter 1. Partial publication in "Nicolas de Cues: Le Secret d'un regard," *Traverses* 30–31 (March 1984): 70–85.

Chapter 2. "Le Poème et sa prose: Le Cantique spirituel," in Michel de Certeau et al., *Le Discours mystique: Approches sémiotiques*, Urbino, Centro internazionale di semiotica e di linguistica, documents de travail, B/150–52 (January–March 1986): 1–19. This text, the outcome of the conference "Le Discours mystique" (Urbino, July 1982), had been sent to Urbino by the author on 3 January 1983.

Chapter 3. "Le Dire en éclats" [preface], in John of the Cross, *Les Dits de lumière et d'amour. Dichos de luz y amor*, followed by *Degrés de perfection. Grados de perfección*, trans. B. Sesé (Sens: Obsidiane, 1985), 13–22.

Chapter 4. "Jean-Joseph Surin interprète de saint Jean de la Croix," *Revue d'ascétique et de mystique* 46 (1970): 45–70.

Chapter 5. A shortened version, modified on several points, appeared with the title "La Lecture absolue (théorie et pratique des mystiques chrétiens: XVIe–XVIIe siècles)," in Lucien Dällenbach and Jean Ricardou, eds., *Problèmes actuels de la lecture* (Paris: Clancier-Guénaud, 1982), 65–80.

Chapter 6. "L'Absolu du pâtir: Passions de mystiques (XVIe–XVIIe siècles)," *Le Bulletin* (Groupe de recherches sémiolinguistiques, EHESS-CNRS) 9 (June 1979): 26–36.

Chapter 7. "Voyage et prison: La Folie de J.-J. Surin," in Bernard Beugnot, ed., *Voyages, récits et imaginaire*, Paris-Seattle-Tübingen,

Biblio 17, Papers on French Seventeenth-Century Literature (1984), 439–67.

Chapter 8. "Le Parler angélique: Figures pour une poétique de la langue," *Actes sémiotiques: Documents* (Groupe de recherches sémiolinguistiques, EHESS-CNRS) 6, no. 54 (1984): 43–75.

Chapter 9. "L'Idée de traduction de la Bible au XVIIe siècle: Sacy et Simon," *Recherches de science religieuse* 66 (1978): 73–92.

Chapter 10. "L'Étrange Secret," *Rivista di storia e letteratura religiosa* (Florence) 13 (1977): 104–26.

In conclusion, "Utopies vocales: Glossolalies," *Traverses* 20 (November 1980): 26–37.

Luce Giard

Mystic Historicities

A historical study on the Christian mystics of the sixteenth and seventeenth centuries is constructed by setting out from archived populations—proliferating, silent—many of whom do not allow themselves to be locked up in libraries and museums. It stands apart, text drawn up, amidst the sway of these myriad memories. But it, too, responds to a twofold attraction. By its method, it aims at finding out how the "mystic" documents are positioned within the society of a time period and what they reveal about it—hence, at situating them in a larger manifold that makes their singularity intelligible, and at configuring, in the form of coherent "tableaux," the correlations established on the basis of the units and rules that a scientific enterprise has set for itself. From this angle, it brings to bear the premise of a social rationality, that is, a possible conjunction between an order and history. But the historian can also hope that his archives will modify the apparatus he uses to analyze them, and that the questions they bring about will unsettle the questions he puts to them. What he expects, then, is not only the means to renew his models in keeping with a process characteristic of all *ars inveniendi*, but also the chance of finding himself on the brink of the unusual. Thus he puts out to sea. The attraction of the elsewhere, like the requirement of rationality, is a part (be it a repressed or a seductive one) of the quest. What he hopes is that in the end, in the countryside of ruins, something will "happen."

These two movements of knowledge are never entirely separable. But the effort to construct a present-day figure of intelligibility from the data pertains to a different "interest" (as Habermas would say) or a different "style" of thought than does an attentiveness to the capacity of things to configure a strangeness within our conceptual patterns. Analysis institutes a locus in which the history we produce enters into competition with the one that may come to us from elsewhere to haunt our territory; its execution will favor either the unveiling of an order, or the interruption of a beginning. Its risk is played out in terms either of understanding or of instauration.

In this respect, the historical study brings to the stage (a scientific stage) the work of memory: it represents—but in a technical way—memory's contradictory operation. Sometimes memory selects and transforms prior experiences to adjust them to new uses, or practices the forgetting indispensable for making room for a present; at other times it allows the return, in the form of the unforeseeable, of things thought to be over and done with (but which are perhaps ageless), and opens up the chink of an unknown in current actuality. Scientific analysis repeats these ambiguous operations of memory in the laboratory. At one moment it reinforces, at others it disturbs the legitimacy of a present order. Between these two styles, the rules of a discipline do not decide. They oversee the correctness and erudition of a study, but they do not decide what interest drives it. The movement underlying the study is, in relation to the technicity employed, the equivalent of meaning in relation to the correctness of a sentence. The grammar of historiography[1] confirms the proper carrying out of the work; it does not determine the direction it takes.

Hence it is permissible, in the field of historiography, to favor one of these directions and to ask under what conditions the mystics of the recent past can continue to pursue their own operations in our laboratories. Such a question may be linked to a banal practice of astonishment. Thus a face, a gesture, or a landscape finds, thanks to the television screen, a space of visibility in which we see, in surprising detail, the sudden beginning of another world. This appearing through the windows of the media no longer occurs, it is true, like "the writing" that "inscribed" the words ME'NE, TE'QEL, and PE'RES,[2] on the walls of the palace of Bel-shaz'zar. The historian cannot count on such a revelation (although psychoanalysis highlights—in dreams, in lapses—manifestations equally terrifying or fantastic, capable of reconfiguring the discourse of reason unbeknownst to itself). He is more like the cameraman or the painter: he builds a scene (a framework of hypotheses and expectations) upon which something unknown can leave its imprint. The very meticulousness of his patience prepares a locus of inscription for what he does not know and the singularity of which shifts an arrangement of the thinkable. This *effect of inscription* is the primary form of what I will call "the historicity" of these old documents: it is the way in which their history begins to engrave itself onto our own, in marking the scientific apparatus with which we produce our fields of knowledge.

The possible intersection of the historian's practices with mystic productions is complicated by an additional difficulty: our scientific queries confront documents that pertain, they say, to a "science," the mystical science.[3] A strange science, to be sure. In the sixteenth and seventeenth centuries, it remains attached to the Christian presuppositions of a medieval theology, but it is henceforth deprived of the rational apparatus that formerly articulated them as objects of thought: therefore, led to exhume the postulates of a belief that is losing its objects, it must support their "foundation" by other means: a pragmatics of the dialogue, a rhetoric of the body subject, a methodology, a "modern" experimental technology even. In any case, if we take that claim of being scientific—which is essential to the purpose of the mystics—seriously, it introduces an ambiguity about the very concept of "science." From what point of view are we then to examine the relationship between their idea of science and ours? This is the problem of a history of the sciences when it considers heterogeneous epistemological systems (a "savage mind") and no longer the development, marked by points of no return, made possible by a common basis of logical postulates. This prerequisite casts doubt on the possibility of defining the research focusing on a "science" constructed outside the presuppositions that found our fields of knowledge.

Successive levels of analysis correspond to different types of inscription of that science within our history: (1) First, there is a *documentation*, attesting in archives and books the many different ways these mystics have been treated and received in the past. (2) Today, *scientific objects* are cut out from this material in order that a part of the information may take on an intelligible form within our thought frameworks. One might therefore inquire into where and how mystic science marks its own practice of history in *specific operations*. These registers, relative to formally distinct inscriptions, should lead from what history has done with the mystics to what they have done with history. To attempt to carry out this reversal (by the mediation of what every science claims to do with history) is to transition from the traces left by a mysticism in our histories to the ways it expresses and fashions itself—to its own historicity. This amounts to asking what "occurs" in these (mystic) documents, that is, how to read them in such a way as to recognize what they "produce," and what, as such, they are capable of inaugurating in the epistemological space of our disciplines of work. Out of their strangeness (or what remains of it) can something be born?

1. A SOCIAL DOCUMENTATION

For the adventurer who expects, based on what he has heard or read, to discover rich treasures of unknown fields of knowledge, the available documentation seems soon destined to bring about a rude awakening. This documentation is the result of the immense labor that has gone into selecting, transforming, and manipulating earlier documents, before classifying them in the repositories in which we discover them. The historian always works second hand, in the sense that he uses what earlier users have already defined, reused, and worked over hundreds of times in their offices and tribunals. He is the last comer in the cemeteries in which the remainders of so many prior operations lie in heaps. He witnesses the end of myriad singular stories. Far from circulating within a kingdom of ancient mystic texts, he silently leafs through a fragmentary landscape of societal leftovers.

This demystifying experience has a positive value. It brings the quest for *mystics*[4] onto the terrain of social realities, in which dreams are taken captive by conflicts, and ideas stricken by time. Taking inventory of a few aspects of these layered archives, victims and witnesses of history, we locate the elementary problems raised by their interpretation. We avoid identifying these documents, which are first of all the result of social activity, with *mystics.* This first "state" of the question undermines the researcher's ideological arrogance or impatience for knowledge with respect to his "hidden" object.[5]

A suspect neighborhood. The chapters in which archival and library classifications house the documents to be studied reflect first of all the classificatory work that, in the sixteenth and seventeenth centuries, cut out the particular region placed under the globally pejorative sign of "mystical." The very grouping of the material raises an issue concerning the function of that socio-ideological identification. To what ends was this designation used in a society organized by rank and status? What arm did it supply against groups and convictions? Reciprocally, to what internalization did it give rise among people described as "mystic," in the name of what "lowering of birth" (as Marie of the Incarnation was wont to say) did they accept it, in the name of what break with the "world" or what ambition, escaping its hierarchies, did they make bold to pursue it? *Mystics* was a stigmatized region, burdened with a denomination as oppressive as those of "inner city" or "immigrant" are today. During the classical age, it was not considered a good thing to reside in that suspect neighborhood, though there are considerable variations—of locale and chronology—in the value ascribed to it. The subsequent fate of the word makes us forget that at that time it belongs to a history of mentalities, that is, to the power relations that intervene to legitimatize cultural qualifications.[6]

Conflicts and violence. Violence reigns in those neighborhoods. The historical evidence relating to "mysticism" comes, for the most part, from disciplinary measures (doctrinal, legal, medical, etc.) intended at the time to exorcise the "dangers" of an emigration (real or imaginary) in relation to the ecclesiastic, civil, or learned authorities. From the beginning of the sixteenth century until the end of the seventeenth, from the Spanish "alumbrados" to the French "quietists," the documents constitute an immense procedural literature, dealing with "plots," "threats," and secret "subversions," to be exposed and repressed.[7] Perhaps they deceive us about what actually took place, but that is what they relate. One massive fact characterizes mystic phenomena in the sources: they are generally inseparable from quarrels and struggles. No mystics without trials. Therefore it is first by trials (regular and public, or internal to a group, or wild) that the mystics become known. A hostility sticks to these texts on love, as if they were unable to get rid of it, and often they themselves are developed in the form of apologias, and as polemics addressed to "the world." These stories haunted by passions appear tied (nailed?) to a violence of history.

This climate of "crisis" probably betokens something essential. The mystic tragedies, great and small, put persons more than statements into question. "Your existence must change," say the voices that raise the challenge, "and not your propositions, which will thereafter conform to your choices." There is no longer any autonomous space in which truths and proofs can be discussed objectively. "Either you convert, or you reject life." The injunction makes either disciples or adversaries. Such a dictate repeats the ancient biblical trial between Yahweh and his people, but the controversy, pitting the opposing wills of the interlocutors against one another, takes, in the archives, the form of legal suits, condemnations, and imprisonments that forbid the (supposed) neutrality of a common law or a reason of state. And yet the countless "affairs" that mark the public appearances of *mystics* constitute no more than a legal and partial aspect of these confrontations, along with the rumors, denunciations, quarrels, and suspicion that fill private chronicles and correspondence and are characteristic of mystic phenomena in towns and cities. A wild everydayness awakens in the vicinity of the "saints." It is as if they touched, in each group, a fragility of the institution or a grief of existence (what self-denials, what nostalgia, what impossible desires?), and as if in disturbing I know not what mute equilibrium, they must undergo an anonymous penalization that constantly tries them in qualifying them. Through them, perhaps an originary "furor," latent in all societies, is revealed—a violence temporarily calmed by the "order" they are criticized for disturbing.[8]

Noises of another body. Parallel to all these social fevers, strange psychic phenomena people the archives. They do not correspond to the sicknesses, the "ideas" of which, known and defined by contemporary medicine, articulate a cosmo- and anthropological knowledge. It is not even a question of bodies undergoing pain or pleasure, but of convulsing organs, aching heads, wounded limbs, local burning sensations or pimples, that is, isolated bodily signatures that take the form of "extraordinary" excess. "Confessions" or "observations" display a phenomenology, dispersed but inexhaustible, of physiological "singularities" (wounds, cuts, blood loss, swelling, levitations, and physical distortions) or sensory ones (internal palpations, disgust, and olfactory, auditory, or visual hallucinations). One document after another shows the thick layer of these bodily fragments, like a sea covered with flotsam—relics of the future, as it were. Indeed, these are not the sacred residues of body that have disappeared, but the local marks of a body to come, a "spiritual" body, which is already implanted here and there, in the form of odd tattoos, like a mute being-there, like the anonymous act of another—a different—body.

This teratology presupposes—invisible—a tireless curiosity of witnesses, biographies, or judges, who take note of the slightest details of physical events and their subtle variations. The bodily excesses stand out before avid eyes. In the convents themselves, an abundant literature of obituaries supplies a detailed inventory of "flaming mortifications," sicknesses and baroque miracles, or agonies observed day after day by the religious family.[9] What suffering grips those onlookers? What fantastic anatomies do they behold? Accumulated from various sources (religious, medical, legal), this multitude of "particularities" leads back to a corporal dramaturgy of society. Collating all the physical signs of "spiritual struggles," what emerges in the form of "coats of arms" that today look like obscenities is a theater of cruelty.

A malaise seizes the researcher (perhaps precisely because of complicities that the documents insinuate into his solitary labor); if he can detach himself from such a physiological vegetation it is thanks to the technical activity he must bring to bear to register and class the material furnished by the "terrain." But what does such corporal inventiveness beneath the sign of *mystics* reveal to him? Probably every jurisdiction, in the past, has taken its revenge on spiritual radicalisms by apprehending them from the angle in which their "sicknesses" (of love or despair) gave it the opportunity for a legal and therapeutic mastery. Especially, the throes and agony and ecstasy of the "saints" seem to have brought out into full daylight an elementary collective sadism that they provided with a language by corresponding too well with it. In any event, in the corporal lexicon of mystic "states" the pathological relationship that a society maintains with itself is played out. The archives introduce a Nietzschean vision of social bodies interrogated on their own identity by internal "sicknesses," that is, by all those dangerous places in which organs cease being silent and emit disturbing noises. Mystic phenomena give form to these insane noises come from elsewhere (is it the angel, is it the devil?) and perceived as questions or threats for the consciousness that the social body has of itself.

Social legitimacies. The documentation holds many other surprises for the visitor who sets out in search of mystic fields of knowledge and gradually discovers the system of intersections between the politics of order and the social "passions" that they express, regulate, and repress without knowing them. It is to discover that the mystic experience might first be well characterized as the taking over of fundamental stakes lurking in the depths of collective life. In any case, to escape these noises of conflict and bodies that an idealist conception of *mystics* considers the muddied byways of history, one might try to separate from them the major works in which a "mystic science" is exposited: Teresa of Avila, John of the Cross, Marie of the Incarnation, Angelus Silesius, etc. There at last the crystal castles of the true science would stand before us. The fact is that these works were granted the status of "mystical" and selected by institutions (a church, a sect, a publisher). They were "brought to light" and defended by pressure groups during guerrilla warfare between organized trends.[10] We know to what silence the texts not benefiting from the support of a religious order or power group[11] were consigned, and also how they were the victims of that support when they did benefit from it.[12] Generally the published work has been revised (with or without the author's permission), and its reincarnations tell the story of the ongoing work that has been done on it by genealogies of disseminators or receivers before coming down to us.[13] This literature has gone through successive "aggregations," or processes of colligation, which have made it conform to social models and imperatives. It is to mysticism what canonization is to saintliness.[14] Just like the contemporary "life stories," far more than them in fact, it is the result of the corrections that have legitimatized it. The theoretical bodies, too, must pay the price of cuts and tortures for their access to an authority that they hold, primarily, from the institution (then dogmatic, now commercial and media-controlled).

But once begun, where does the critical recognition of the social interventions pre- and overdetermining mystic discourse end? Even before being manipulated, censured, and classified, most of these texts had been organized in keeping with the requests and orders to which they responded (those coming from competent authorities, spiritual "families," politico-religious networks). They adopt the language imposed by the interlocutory circumstances of the moment. They obey the sensory, bodily or affective codifications of a milieu. By the very fact of being expressed, they are inscribed in a preexisting system of linguistic rules and programmatic protocols . . .

To sum up, the documentation changes the original given fundamentally. While the researcher may have naively assumed that his work would consist in reintegrating individual phenomena in the social history of the times, he now recognizes at every turn the collective operations that have manufactured his information. What is more, is he not relaying, in the name of a scientific institution, the legal authorities that prepared his material for him, so that with other rules he is doing no more than continuing a socialization already manifest everywhere in the archives? He should wonder, therefore, not how to *connect* these documents to social realities (a question born of an optical illusion), but rather how to *disconnect* them from those realities. What it is difficult to discern in these products of time is not the "social" element (it is everywhere), but the "mystic" one.

2. A NON-PLACE OF PHILOSOPHY

However necessary the material may be for an exercise of astonishment and a practice of control (it surprises expectation and verifies or "falsifies" hypotheses), it does not suffice to define the research. As produced by a past, the material generates alternating effects of difference (a distance) or confirmation (a proof, an illustration) only in relation to an analytic approach. All reading of documents is in reference to an expectation. It unfolds by reason of a codification or "form" which, in advance, determines what the researcher *expects* to find in the texts. It is by its ability to make explicit and to define a code of expectation that a scientific procedure is characterized. Thus it constructs for itself an "object," which is identifiable neither by received information nor by reality itself, and which specifies, in a way that is decisional in principle, a coherent set of criteria that selects the traits to be brought out in a pertinent corpus. By this indirect approach, which allows it to attain a "scientific" status, the analysis *detaches itself* from the terrain organized by the archival or library denominations and by prior social operations. It passes through the information, extracting and combining the elements that relate to its own interests. By this epistemological detachment, the analysis opposes not only the rules—complex and still hidden—of past activities that have produced the material such as it presents itself today; it also opposes the way in which sixteenth and seventeenth century *mystics* also constructed for itself, as a "science," its own object, distinct from the "world" in which it pursued its research. Analysis thus distinguishes itself both from its material and from other sciences.

Regardless of whether this scientific intent is strictly adhered to (in the social sciences, it is difficult to resist adjacent curiosities), it also is inscribed within a history; no longer the earlier (sixteenth- and seventeenth-century) one, the effects of which may be seen in the documents, but the more recent (twentieth-century) one: that of the configuration to which our disciplines belong. It is true that, between these two histories, the one furnishing the research with its material, and the other placing it in the framework of a present-day problematic, there are many points of continuity: a reflection on the sciences has precisely as its task to reveal them, be it in showing, in a historical mode, how the so-called "material"—a past—still determines our analytic procedures unbeknownst to us, or be it in laying bare, in the philosophical mode, a question about the Real that stands above the successive figures of the devices of knowledge. These two modes also concern the status of the "mystic science," as having become a past, and as being an experience of the Real. Thus we can take up the twofold analysis once more, but on the basis of the very gesture by which a scientific ambition is today detached from the data it receives from the past. A set of new social and theoretical interests transforms the way *mystics* appears in the field of our interrogation. To specify that relation is to exhume the present postulates of our analyses and explore the issue of what work that past experience performs in our epistemological sites. It is to "historicize" our research in placing it back into a contemporary configuration on which it is dependent, and to "dehistoricize" *mystics* in showing that one cannot reduce it to a past positivity. In exploring what our sciences *do* with *mystics*, we also recognize what it *writes into* them.

I will limit this examination to two surveys, in order to consider (1) what general *function* has been attributed to mysticism in the system of the social sciences since the beginning of the century; and (2) in which regions of knowledge (psychological, sociological, etc.) and categories (the pathological, the marginal, etc.) the *objects* singled out from within mystic documentation by these sciences are presented. This twofold survey is in answer to two simple questions: (1) *What is involved* in the resurgence of mysticism in the context of the social sciences? (2) *How* is it treated in the context of these disciplines? The one focuses on specifying the interest in the problem; the other on the objective form it may take.

The foundation of the social sciences, an institution aggressively on the rise since the end of the nineteenth century, has brought about a reclassification of all religious manifestations. The traditional struggles between institutions of meaning (a religious clergy, civil or political magistrates), their alliances against inner emigrations (spiritual movements), or the separation that for a long time favored Christian civilization at the expense of the other religions is replaced by the cleavage that initiates a field of knowledge and an opposition between the scientific institution and the "phenomena" (historical, social, or psychological) henceforth under its jurisdiction. The result of a historical process of several centuries, this institution gradually deprives the churches of the intellectual management of their heritage. Specifically, all the different types of "beliefs," brought together into one general category (the "religious" or the "sacred"), are henceforth set in opposition to knowledge and thought of differently by it than they thought of themselves.

The emergence and differentiation of the social sciences also bring about an erosion of philosophy, despite its apparent academic and professional prosperity. With the loss of the state-dominated philosophy advocated by Victor Cousin and the redistribution of the interrogations concerning man between specialized disciplines, a consciousness of a "crisis" in philosophy is expressed everywhere.[15] The "end" of philosophy accompanies, as its counterpoint, the constitution of man as an object of various scientific fields of knowledge. Henceforth "the contrast between the 'scientific' character of this group of sciences and the 'unscientific' character of philosophy is unmistakable."[16] Thus in his *Krisis*, Husserl initiates a critique of scientificity itself, and uses psychology as the strategic basis for a return to "the enigma of subjectivity."[17]

Thus *mystics* becomes one of the places in which the appropriation of the religious by the new sciences and the crisis of philosophy interrelate. From religious phenomena, distributed as "objects" of particular disciplines (historical criticism, pathology, ethnology, etc.), broken up into heterogeneous cultural areas and historical periods, a sort of "residue" or "underlying commonality" is discernable, which receives the name "mysticism" (already used for more than a century). From Renan himself to Henri Bremond, what is indicated thereby is an experience located *on the hither side* of the institutional or historical determinations, freed of all adherence to particular religious traditions or even to objects of belief ("At bottom I am a mystic and I don't believe in anything," as Flaubert already said.)[18] It supplies its utopia to a "spiritualism" freed of all positive and local membership, and is thus distinct from everything that has become the object of the social sciences. This reference obviously harks back to the German romantic development of a philosophical mysticism—of the metaphysical type (in Schelling) or based on immediate "feeling" (*Gefühl*) of the self as "absolutely dependent" (in Schleiermacher),[19] but also (as is too often forgotten) to the "spiritual philosophy" that quietism detached from historical reasons, interests, and institutions. "Pure love" is recognized even in the "free Christianity," "eternal and universal," extolled by Renan[20] and throughout the following century up to Bremond.[21] This spirituality, universal in its essence, affective and experimental in its form, foreign to the positivities of the "world," opposed in advance the rationalist theodicies of the *Aufklärung* and continues, at the turn of the nineteenth century, to support the use of "mysticism" in opposition to the fragmentation of the scientific forms of reason.

Indeed, the only thing that matters here is the epistemological function assigned to this mysticism at the moment when the positive sciences divvy up among themselves the objective treatment of the human "facts" and when philosophy thus seems threatened. This situation leads the pioneers of these sciences, almost all coming from philosophy, to consider the possibility of conceptualizing a unity of the human experience and therefore of surmounting the separations that their disciplines create between the anthropological, historical, or psychological positivities. Within the framework of this differentiation between the sciences and their objects, what place can there be for fundamental questions such as: Are we of the same world? Is there one selfsame human world?

Among other possible solutions (for example, in Durkheim, the overarching intent to found a universal social ethics), mysticism becomes a way of considering these questions. It is the antidote for a scientific positivism. It indicates an "opening" to an invisible essence of Man (an opening free of all objective determinations), whereas scientific observation takes hold of all the visible and cuts it up into heterogeneous unities. It is the non-place of a philosophical requirement within the framework of disciplines that take over all objective places. The concept of "mysticism" [*mysticisme*] is perfectly adjusted to the function it receives.

One work may serve as an example. Indeed, this perspective sheds light on the gradual progress that led Bergson to recognize—in an "experience" that he protected from psychiatric investigations by limiting it exclusively to the "great Christian mystics"—a dynamics of "the open" capable of surmounting the "closure" that shuts each society in on itself. This "closure" is a product of the human sciences. Bergson received it from them as a result (which is also a postulate). In *Les Deux Sources de la morale et de la religion* (1932), he treats, on a psychological basis, a problem analogous to the one Durkheim took up in *Les Formes élémentaires de la vie religieuse* (1912): How to conceptualize "the human" in relation to its fragmentation in positive groups (a problem that was already Lucien Lévy-Bruhl's), and what element can cross the scientific borders established by analysis between individuals or societies. His book is first and foremost a treatise on social philosophy,[22] which, after having set up a law of closure and of heterogeneity, seeks a real principle on which to found a possibility of going beyond that confinement. To him, this principle is not ethical, as in Durkheim, but primarily metaphysical, identifiable by a movement of being: "The mystic love . . . is still more metaphysical than moral in its essence."[23] Nevertheless, it is an empirical given. From the point of view of scientific requirements, recourse to the mystic experience is legitimate since such experience is "experimental" (it is a fact) and consists in "epistemic operations"[24] (they are acts of knowledge), although it still precedes what a science can problematize about it in its own terms.

In many other contemporary works it seems that the same "philosophical" functioning of mysticism can be found: from É. Récéjac to H. Bergson or H. Bremond, via H. Delacroix, R. Rolland, J. Baruzi, and so on.[25] In 1920, Jules Sageret even claimed that all philosophers of stature accede to mysticism.[26] The movement was probably accentuated by the First World War, which revealed—a true epistemological shock—that science serves division, and that an unforeseeable divorce separates its progress from that of societies. Thus "positive metaphysics" abounded apropos of the mystics belonging to each cultural area: Olivier Lacombe and Romain Rolland for India, Louis Massignon and Henry Corbin for Islam, D. Sabbatucci for the Greek world, Alexandre Koyré for German gnostic illuminism, etc.—to limit ourselves to the French domain.

It is worth noting that this "philosophical" function of mysticism reappears at the very place where a scientific enterprise refuses to risk such ventures outside its domain, and considers, in mystic phenomena, only the objects that its conceptual and technical apparatus defines. Here, too, one example will suffice—contemporary with Bergson. The indifference, nay, the allergy of Freud with respect to the "oceanic feeling," which R. Rolland claimed was a "fact," is well known.[27] From *The Psychopathology of Everyday Life* (1901) to *Civilization and Its Discontents* (1930), a psychoanalytic interpretation defines this supposed primary "fact" as a secondary effect due to mechanisms of derivation, to a symbolic use of complexes or to a libidinal investment of the subject in representations: it grasps the phenomenon in the terms it has itself constructed. But in the name "mystic" there is also insinuated in Freud's texts, and even in the final note in his *Complete Works*, a question exceeding that explanation and concerning the relation that the existence of the subject maintains with the limit and with death.[28] That the existence of the subject is instituted by its relation to the exteriority that dictates its limit to it—this would then be a modality of "mysticism." But because this question cannot yet be treated in a scientific manner, Freud thinks he must set it apart, in order to remove it from irrational or dogmatic interpretations. Still, he does not cancel it: "Certain facts absolutely exist that we cannot know at the present time."[29] The mystic fact remains till the end embedded in the work, after the manner of a philosophical interrogation, but an interrogation that no longer has a place.

All these reemployments of *mystics* at the beginning of the century address (1) a "mysticism" *detached* from the objective facts analyzed by the social sciences; (2) an *experimental* datum that therefore possesses, in principle, scientific legitimacy; (3) an element (now primitive, now superior) that makes it possible to transcend the closures created by scientific analysis between its disciplines or between their objects, and to restore the horizon of a human *unity* in symbiosis with *the universe*. A dehistoricization creates the "atopic" space in which a fundamental reflection can be expressed. This "mysticism" is born of what the social sciences seem at the time (and to certain people) no longer able to conceptualize: for one thing, human unity, because it is distributed over closed positivities; for another, the rootedness of the human in a dynamic of vital "energies," because since Kant, the "science of man" isolates a social dialectic from nature.[30] These two "unthoughts" correspond, in short, to the two interrogations that Bergson attempts at the time to interrelate in order to form a metaphysics of *élan vital* (vital impetus) based on the experience of the "great Christian mystics."

Becoming a kind of antihistory in a context in which historiography appears as the ascendant discipline and furnishes, with Fustel de Coulanges, Lucien Herr, Ernest Lavisse, Charles Seignobos, etc., the model of a scientific methodology,[31] this mysticism, by contrast, seduces spiritualist philosophers and, even more, the irrationalist movements that develop in literature. It constitutes as "impregnable"—ecstatic and ineffable—a generalist Reason whose dominance and relevancy are gradually removed by the sciences. It represents, as by a "non-place," a "crisis" or a retreat of philosophy. In this respect, it has a function analogous to the one it had in the sixteenth and seventeenth centuries in relation to a "crisis" or retreat of medieval theology. In both cases, in an experimental mode, it seems to protect or take charge of the fundamental questions borne by a declining configuration of knowledge.

3. UNSTABLE SCIENTIFIC OBJECTS

Mysticism as analyzed by the social sciences appears very different from the preceding. Here, mystic phenomena are treated as "objects" conforming to the rules of each discipline—psychiatry, history, or ethnology. If we examine the transformations undergone by the *mystics* of yore from this point of view , and, conversely, the shifts that, even in that altered form, *mystics* brings about within the new sciences, three processes are particularly noticeable: (a) the localization of mystic phenomena in certain regions of knowledge rather than in others and the effects they have on those regions; (b) the transition mediating the passage of the formal definition of that fleeting "object" from one discipline to another, and lastly (c) the discarding of the mystic experience by the enterprise that takes the task of giving itself a scientific objective seriously. I claim not to draw up a history of the scientific assimilation of *mystics*, a history that would begin with the project of colonizing it and would end with the need for eliminating it (that would be a caricature) or to take the functioning of the "mystic phenomena" as a possible indicator of the recent evolution of the social sciences (that would be a different work), but to suggest a singular "historicity": the *avatars* of *mystics*, products of the contemporary disciplines, have in spite of everything *their own results*, as if, even in the setting that changes them into objects of knowledge, the fragments of a "wild science" retained something irreducible.

Individualist localizations. Mystic phenomena are preferably lodged within the disciplines concerning "individual life." Stephen Sharot observed this recently: "very little attention has been given to the social contexts of mysticism. . . . It is difficult to find a sociology of mysticism."[32] Aside from the well-known analyses of Ernst Troeltsch and Max Weber,[33] born of a confrontation with German historicism, mysticism has generally been cast in individual, especially pathological psychology, the works of which have, moreover, been privileged by philosophy. One may well be surprised at this, not only in light of the documentation, but especially because mystic experience, past or present, presents itself primarily in social forms: "schools" and groups, relations of "masters of truth" to disciples; networks of communication and transmission (oral, written, gestural, itinerant) circulating via family lines, genealogies, milieus, cultural and commercial ties, etc.; models of organization (cenobite or eremitic—eremitism also being a social form) and conversational protocols (confessions, avowals, "spiritual direction"); procedures of trial and recognition (through asceticism, miracles, healings, pilgrimage, etc.); sensory, alimentary, sexual, and linguistic codifications; techniques of representation, of concentration, or of mental "vacuity"; economies of honor, allegiance, or material goods exchanged for symbolic values, and so on. How is it, then, that all this experience has been massively classified in psychology and treated in the form of individual phenomena?

That its accession to the status of scientific objects is associated with its *desocialization* and its *depoliticization* is first a result of history. For a long time, *mystics* was not a private or individual affair. It became so, as the beliefs that it had radicalized by committing itself absolutely to them ceased to define the texture of the lived world. Because it thus isolated the premises of a universe, it probably itself contributed long ago to detaching them from the reality in which they were grounded until that point, or at least to manifesting their progressive exile from daily struggles. That is why *mystics* was often accused of being "atheist," which, in the vocabulary of the time, meant depriving the religious or civil institution of the right to validate itself in the name of its origins or its foundation. In this regard, "atheism," a reproach addressed to early Christianity, is essentially a crime against recognized authorities. It concerns their credibility, far more than the existence of God. Each church, therefore, accuses those who undermine its legitimacy of atheism. *Mystics* has an impact precisely on this point, in a great historical debate on the "authorities." During the sixteenth and seventeenth centuries, the stakes are fundamentally political, and the strategies that organize new power devices spur approaches to knowledge everywhere, serving reform by the production of methods, utopias, and pedagogies. In the imbroglio of the levels of authority that at that time make up a sort of game with three pieces—the prince (a sacred witness to the cosmic order), the civil and religious institutions (a mobile reality of history), and "the soul" (a transcendental principle)—the "saints" practice a reduction, justified in their view by the "corruption" of the institutions, which tends to favor the one-on-one confrontation (already biblical and traditional) of king and prophet,[34] politician and mystic, or "prince" and "soul."[35] In a political situation that fragments and often enslaves the churches, and that disproportionately accentuates (especially in the seventeenth century) the quasi-divine nature of the king,[36] there are innumerable forms of the encounter between these two social figures of ultimate reference, from Teresa of Avila's appeal to Philip II soliciting his support of the foundation of the Carmelite Order against religious authorities[37] to the almost superstitious worry manifested by Louis XIV (though, he says, also favored by "inspirations")[38] with respect to obscure quietist plots. The authority of power, not its reality, is at stake. It is a question of a politics of the believable. Through the mystics' confrontations with the power that connects heaven to the earth, there is sketched out, from England to Spain, a spiritual form of what will become the "citizen," separating from power a transcendental or ethical principle of society.[39] Already quietism and, in its proximity, Fénelon attest to this.

At the beginning of the twentieth century, this politics of *mystics*, or of "the soul," is a thing of the past, at least in Western Europe. It passes into the private realm, and is then relayed to the public sphere by other experiences and other languages. Psychology picks it up where history deports it. Bergson, by the way, was not wrong about this, nor was Husserl: it takes on a dominant role in the fields of knowledge relating to a society henceforth based on the individualist premise. It deals in terms of the units that a liberal economy and democratic institutions combine. If historiography promotes a collective discourse of the nation, the class, or the native land, psychology, a chemistry of the human, scrutinizes the "elementary" mechanisms of social life and focuses on their rationalization. It constitutes the central laboratory of a new politics. And it is on psychology, as well, that the task is incumbent to explain, in the terms of a still pioneering problematic, the now marginal, if not aberrant, phenomena of *mystics*. It is not at all surprising that these phenomena progressively belong to pathology, an elite sector in which one is committed, in the name of scientistic psychology and medicine, to understanding and treating that which "resists" the advance of Reason. In the view of Dr. Michéa, in 1871, it was not so long ago that ecstasy, "which is always a morbid state," "had not completely entered the fold of pathology."[40] At the turn of the following century, it enters that fold completely, with ravishment, levitation, and so many other "disturbances," first in the category of "manias" ("theomania," "demonomania," etc.) that designate abnormal zones yet to be explored in order to reveal first malingering "affections," and then pathogenic "constitutions." It is history that supplies the framework in which increasingly exact "observations" are inscribed, with a remarkable semiology, often unequaled since.

Another determining element in these analyses: their "objective" character. An anatomic cutout of the "facts" makes it possible to locate their combinations and establish "tables," but it takes away their function of being the vocabulary of a *spoken* language and of being inscribed in *interrelational* practices in which the observer himself is involved. It is not surprising that the "pathological" conception of these phenomena, isolated from the interlocutory process, parallels, in many respects, the criticism, so frequent among the mystics of the sixteenth and seventeenth centuries, of the "states" (visions, ecstasies, etc.) at which the spiritual stops, as if "this" were the divine experience, and which, for being thus protected from a necessary going beyond ("it is not this, nor that"), become "sicknesses" of the soul. Reciprocally, it is striking that psychopathological observation, when it is sufficiently long and attentive to allow the results of the exchange between subjects to appear in their movement, resumes the air of a "spiritual direction"—a fact that already struck Freud.[41] Thus, the celebrated work *De l'angoisse à l'extase* (1926), devoted by Pierre Janet to that "Madeleine" whom he has, he says, "followed for twenty-two years." Analyzed as a case of "constitutional asthenia," she is a strange "mystic": born to a bourgeois family of northern France, she leaves home at the age of eighteen to share the life of the proletariat in Germany (in 1872, after the Franco-Prussian War and the Commune); she then becomes a vagrant, a part-time factory worker, and is imprisoned several times in Paris, where she rejects ties with anyone but the "wretched" [*les "misérables"*], and eventually ends up at [the public hospitals] Bichat, Necker, and the Salpêtrière (1896). She fascinates her observer, for whom she writes more than two thousand pages addressed to "my father." Pious, ecstatic, but allergic to priests, she reenacts on the very stage of psychiatry those mystic dialogues in which the "director," be he François de Sales or Fénelon, became the disciple and interpreter of the woman under his spiritual direction. The nine hundred pages that Janet devotes to science and to Georges Dumas betray the conversion of the pathological object into the account of a relation whose dialogical nature is scarcely veiled by the modest reserve of the doctor. It is at the hospital that, as a patient resembling so many heroines of Bremond, *mystics* speaks.[42]

Objects in transit. The phenomenon moves around and transforms in the compartment designated for it. Therefore what is meant by "mysticism" must be formally circumscribed. A Sisyphean task: the object never stops falling out of the theoretical locus to which a definition has raised it. In this respect, the debate that for half a century has occupied Anglo-American reflection is typical. Simplified in the extreme, it attempts to determine which elements can recapitulate so many diverse experiences and at what level of analysis their unifying principle can be recognized. The enterprise begins, of course, with psychological investigations. In an American tradition that has always considered the "religious feeling" to be more fundamental or "elementary" than the various churches in which it can find shelter, a language, and practical applications, William James characterizes "the mystic experience" with four specific traits: ineffability, noetic quality, transiency, and passivity[43]—a description of a more rigorous phenomenology than the reduction later practiced by James Leuba, who traced mystic facts to ecstasy and the latter to an "unconsciousness" compatible with all sorts of secondary ideologizations in conformity with the cultural site of the rapture.[44]

When Robert Charles Zaehner, in 1957, takes up this description, he makes it into the demonstration of a theism, and the experimental emblem of a divine presence. In establishing supposedly constant characteristics, he intends to isolate a phenomenon that spans institutional antinomies, sociohistorical diversities, and even the opposition between "sacred" and "profane." Thus he recognizes the positive manifestation of a universal reality.[45] This is to take an interpretation for the thing itself. The slippage is notable: James's phenomenal description is changed by Zaehner into an indicator and proof of a spiritualism: it ensures the victory of unity over the differences ("abyssal," to R. Otto)[46] that separate the mystic intuitions from one another. The same monistic conception of an experience identified with a "universal nucleus" is found in W. T. Stace[47] and, despite his reservations about Zaehner, in Ninian Smart, for whom mysticism is "phenomenologically everywhere the same," although it is necessary to be conscious of the "extrinsic" variants attributable to the self-interpretation of the visionaries in their own sociocultural contexts.[48] Experience, qua mystic, belongs neither to history nor to sociology. Essentially anti-Babelic, it restores to the One its first language. Psychology has become the instrument of a fundamental theology.

Against this tendency, already criticized by R. Otto and tending to assume mysticism to be "without a country,"[49] Steven Katz has drawn up "a plea for the recognition of differences": he also refutes the possibility, for a comparative study, of assimilating the language of one spiritual tradition to that of another, and for a phenomenology, of postulating that one and the same "linguistic intentionality" in the texts guarantees that they intend the same "intentional object."[50] By means of an analysis of language, he gives mysticism its historical plurality and restores to difference the status of being not "extrinsic" but an essential.

But then what is this *mystics*, disputed between God and history that it pretends to reconcile experimentally? Should we believe it, and how, when it says it is intuition of the absolute in a singular mode? The theoretical debates about it set it, despite itself, now on this side, now on that. According to what criteria? It is in the name of a philosophy of language, and of Wittgenstein, that S. Katz refuses the universalization of which the mystic propositions would be the object. A significant fact: in thirty years, the discussion has moved from the terrain of psychology to that of linguistics, by the mediation of a phenomenology that has been granted the ability to express the very structure of a fundamental experience. But in fact that structure specifies only a *form*, ultimately reduced to two characteristics: the paradoxical and the ineffable. In the end, we thus have two essential rules belonging to a grammar of mystic discourse. They no longer concern either history or ontology. They designate a protocol of linguistics outside of which there appears to be no mystic expression, but which says nothing of what the experience itself is. Necessary but insufficient, that determination attains universal value only when it is detached from the *use* made of it by the mystic subject, that is, from the singular act that he performs. At least, in isolating a form of knowledge that stands out in contrast to our usual ones, it designates, in principle free from a monist or ontological *a priori*, one kind of discourse—a different "gesture of thought" in language. Even if it is not certain that that form belongs uniquely to mystic discourse, it traces a "manner of speaking" at once foreign to our scientific modes of reasoning and verification, and entirely homologous to the essential definition that the "mystic science" of the sixteenth and seventeenth centuries gave of itself by characterizing itself (in a different linguistic register) as a "modus loquendi."[51] Once again, the past "object" seems to return, like a phantom, to the scientific stage, but elsewhere and otherwise than expected.

Necessary omissions. The difficulty in formally circumscribing the mystic experience elicits a different strategy, which consists in eliminating what cannot be processed. Every scientific enterprise must renounce seizing the real in the objects it cuts out from it. Its rigor is based on the limits it assigns itself. Thus an apprenticeship of forgetting supports the production of knowledge. Perhaps, after all, this is just a hunter's stratagem, carefully setting traps where what he cannot grasp comes and is caught. But the reciprocal side of this trick is that things that occur long before we look for them smuggle into the texts (and first of all into a way of writing) a thousand and one ways of overflowing or circumventing what those texts claim to control. It is not so easy to practice forgetting. Nor therefore also to diagnose what is in fact omitted by a scientific study.

A remarkable case is presented to us by the work, monumental in so many ways, of Leszek Kolakowski, *Christians without a Church*.[52] The book, which concerns the Dutch and French figures of a spiritual radicalism, attempts to rearticulate a social history with an intellectual one. It constantly plays on the relation between these two histories represented by two great contemporary models; on the one hand, György Lukács and his Marxist philosophy of culture, on the other, Alexandre Koyré, the most acute erudition at the service of the pioneering works of "modern" science. However it may be with the intellectual systems he exhumes successively (more felicitously in the Dutch part than the French), he gives us a whole methodological reflection on that rearticulation, the principle of which consists in restoring the political and social relevance of spiritual movements. At the beginning, he comes up against a preliminary difficulty that once more bears on the very object of the research: What is *mystics*? How can it be treated? In order to "construct" his "object," Kolakowski's first move is to eliminate *mystics*, which is specified, he says, by experience and by the question of its authenticity, which come within the competency of psychology. On the other hand, he considers what he calls "mysticism," a series of "theological doctrines interpreting the mystic experiences." Its "object" is the variants of the relation between two factors: one "ideological," relative to the religious speculations based on an experience, but considered independently from what that experience is; the other "social," concerning the function of persons or groups who deny a church its authority in doctrinal matters, but claim to bear witness to the true spirit in separating themselves from corrupt institutions.[53]

In the fact that this object transposes onto the stage of a religious past the political situation of the author, a Marxist excluded from the Polish Communist Party and wondering about the possibility of being "a Marxist without a Party," what we should see is not the indication of an undue assimilation (given the extraordinary attention to detail of the historical investigation), but an evincing of the contemporary interrogation from which every important scientific work draws its origin. The "object" of the investigation formalizes a present-day experience that has replaced, in this case, that of the past. The omission of *mystics* marks the spot left to the present, which organizes the problematic (but not the content) of the research and to which another field of operations is offered so that the present interrogation, confronted with different data, can be made explicit and opened up to new hypotheses. In fact, Kolakowski shows rather that the "nonconfessional Christianity" of the seventeenth century was a "failed radicalism," either brought back in line with an institutional conformism, or excluded from history. We may wonder whether the same is not true of the mystics, but whether it is necessarily the sign of a failure for what they bear witness to, and which continues to reappear, like an ethical requirement, like a "song" whose returns defy history. Perhaps Kolakowski's analysis, a victim of what it eliminates, reduces politics too much to its successes.

In any case, the omission that institutes his study may well have in the book itself a curious trace. Indeed, however it may be with respect to debatable points in that study,[54] if the intention that organizes it is to combine the sure techniques of a history of the doctrinal texts with the framework furnished by a theory of social struggles, in fact the marriage does not take place. The work presents rather an interlacing of two heterogeneous approaches. It punctuates, with epistemological remarks on the possibility of treating the doctrines as the "manifestations of social conflicts," a textual analysis whose qualities of precision and acuity correspond to the model of intellectual history furnished by Koyré. In its thickness, it is nonetheless divided, in a tension that is less the sign of a "failed" enterprise than the vibration of a work that opens as a double door—a work of the initial question. How, in listening to the noise made in that work by the elements it cannot reconcile, can one not invoke the experience that is absent from it and that, caught between a violence of history and an excessive practice of each reason, discovers in failure a "mystic" opening?

MYSTIC OPERATIONS

Mystics, analyzed, observed, and treated by so much research, already haunts the scientific work. By the different echoes that it awakens in our fields of knowledge, by the questions for which its study furnishes a language, it reveals, as anamorphoses would do, aspects of what we held to be a past object. We must get out of the epistemology that set a subject of knowledge in opposition to his or her objects of study. The strange "historicity" of *mystics* within the very discourses whose ambition it is to know that historicity obliges us to develop a different model of analysis, to which the examination of contemporary scientific literature would serve as an introduction.

Indeed it seems to me that it is possible to analyze mystic literature itself as a field, defined by a set of historical positivities, in which mystic operations are performed and traced out. In other words, the mystic science would seem to be constituted by the various modes on which these operations are inscribed within the historical networks of knowledge, of body language, and of the specific institutions belonging to an era or milieu. Each text or each document (since we are obliged to work on them) constitutes a theater organized by the vocabulary and syntax of a moment of history, but on which singular actions, as on a touched body, are inscribed. It is to allow the inscription of these operations in the places those documents form, and to try to specify the forms proper to them, that the mystics are devoted when they develop their "science." By this, their science articulates *itself* with history. Therefore we should be able to recognize today, in the texts of that science, a *writing* that is its "way of doing"—just as there are characteristic "manipulations" in the laboratories. Each mystic document is itself also a laboratory in which specific "gestures" are described as those of a dance on a stage. In this respect, a model is proposed to us by G.-G. Granger if, leaving aside the part about "individuation" in his *Essai d'une philosophie du style* (1968), we retain the project of a "stylistics of the scientific practice," that is, the possibility of isolating, in a work, its own "style," that "latent and lived structuration of a scientific activity itself, as constituting an aspect of praxis."[55] Just as there are scientific styles (Euclidean, Cartesian, vectorial), so there are mystic styles—they, too, being indissociable from an esthetics. In this we again see the relevance of the definition that mystic science gave of its inscription in history. *Mystics* does not have its own content: it is an exercise of *the other* in relation to a given *site*; it is characterized by a set of specific "operations" in a field that is not its own—by a way of proceeding or of saying.

Chapter One

The Look: Nicholas of Cusa

Estoy dentro el ojo: el pozo
donde desde el principio un niño
está cayendo, el pozo donde cuento
lo que tardo en caer desde el principio . . .

I am inside the eye: the well where,
from the beginning, a boy is falling,
the well where I recount the time
spent falling from the beginning . . .[1]
Octavio Paz, *Pasado en claro*

"Here, then, very dear brothers, are the explanations I promised you about the ready accessibility of mystic theology," writes Nicholas of Cusa, an erudite, a mathematician, and a diplomat, ever on the move, from Tyrol, more precisely from Brixen, or Bressanone (a German side, an Italian side, like Cusa himself). Named bishop in 1450, he received the mission of reforming this mountainous diocese, a strategic position between a German area and the Italian principalities. He clashed with the majority of the clergy, who were hostile to this foreigner, a Rhinelander imposed on them by the pope, as well as with the forces of Sigismond, the count of Tyrol, who took him prisoner in 1460. Thus, in October 1453, he sent to the monks settled on the banks of their beautiful lake, Tegernsee, in the Bavarian Alps, the treatise he had promised them and that he himself referred to as *The Image* or *The Picture* (*Icona*), but that is known as *De visione Dei sive De icona*.[2]

A memorable year. In the West, the Hundred Years War (1337–1453) ends between France and England. A time of nations begins. In the East, the Eastern Roman Empire crumbles with the fall of Constantinople to the Turks (1453): Nicholas of Cusa, who had been there in 1437, had just brought back the terrifying news from Rome, and amid the rumors of atrocities, violence, and blood everywhere, he wrote, a month before *The Image*, *De pace fidei* (faith creator of peace), an anti-Babelian "vision" of a celestial "theater" in which the delegate of each country, one after the other, rises to bear witness to the movement that supports it. The Greek, the Italian, the Arab, the Indian, the Chaldean, the Jew, the Scythian, the Gaul, the Persian, the Syrian, the Turk, the Spaniard, the German, the Tartar, the Armenian, etc.—each one comes, in the language of his own tradition, to attest to the truth, which is one: this concord of "free spirits" responds to the furies of fanaticism.[3] One history is dying. Another is to be born with the utopian dawning of this new international. During these years, printing begins (1450); Leon Battista Alberti is perfecting his *De re aedificatoria* (1452); Piero della Francesca paints his *Legend of the True Cross* in San Francesco d'Arezzo (around 1453). A new way of seeing gives rise to a way of constructing. Such is the question of Nicholas of Cusa in *The Image:* What does "seeing" mean? How can a "vision" engender a new world?

SCIENCE AND POLITICS

For almost ten years (1451–60), *The Image* is at the center of the regional debate. Between Upper Trentino, southern Bavaria, and Lower Austria, the texts circulate, to the rhythm of the seasons and their associated tasks.[4] They go up the Brenner, come down the Inn or the Danube, and compose a network of places: the abbey of Tegernsee, a seedbed of remarkable men (Gaspard Aindorffer, the abbot, and Conrad of Geissenfeld, Bernard of Waging, etc.), fervent supporters of Cusa, who passed through there at the beginning of June 1453; Melk Abbey, near Sankt Pölten, on the right bank of the Danube, the home of a reformist movement that won over all of southern Germany (and Tegernsee itself, in 1426) and spread Rhenish mysticism; the young Charterhouse in Aggsbach (on the left bank of the Danube), whose prior, Vincent, a prolific author of manuscripts that also eventually ended up in Melk, was engaged in an endless polemic against Gersonian or Cusan intellectualism; the Faculty of Theology in Munich, where the "powerful and well-read" Marquard Sprenger[5] was professor and dean. A local network imposed its own framework of presuppositions, alliances, and struggles on the outsider Nicholas of Cusa: his treatise is a response to a request from Tegernsee concerning mystic theology; his letters are in response to questions or irritations. This style of correspondence is dependent upon "dialogue," which is favored in the Cusan treatises; but here mountains and rivers separate the interlocutors and make visible the nature of the relationships, even those within the same region.

A locus is constituted just as much of conflicts as of agreements. They proliferate around *The Image*. Already in 1448, Nicholas of Cusa was challenged, and *De docta ignorantia* (1440), his major treatise, ridiculed by the good conciliary theologian Johannes Wenck, in an ironic pamphlet whose title, *De ignota litteratura*, might be translated as: "Forget Nicholas of Cusa." This Heidelberg professor, smiter of the "blind" Aristotle, and "opaque" Plato, sent his adversary a remonstrance about what should be considered a "good" theology and what authorities it should be founded on.[6] It was an academic, not a monastic debate. A Rhenish, not an Alpine setting. Nicholas of Cusa, in his response—*Apologia doctae ignorantiae* (1449), an intellectual autobiography in the form of an interview given to a disciple (Italian) shocked by the "insolent" professor—while bringing to bear the thousand suns of his erudition and the vast horizon of his investigations (from Plato to Meister Eckhart), tries to define what he calls the philosophical "hunt" (the *venatio*), a key word that repeatedly, throughout his oeuvre, bespeaks haste and desire. No, he is not one of those "theologians" walled in by a few "authorities" whom they are content to reproduce without thinking them through: "When they know how to speak as do the others whom they have set up as their instructors, they think that they are theologians."[7] Opposed to him around 1448 is a positive theology; around 1453, it is an affective theology. Between these two ways of hypostasizing a particular locus or experience—the Faculty versus the monastery, the literalness of select "authors" versus the feelings of a "devotion"—the Cusan approach, which has justly been characterized as a "theosophy,"[8] ventures to advance.

The German theater of these "affairs" also concerns theory. The "Holy Roman Empire," weakened from within and from without, becomes regionalized. It separates definitively from the pontifical investiture that marked its "universal" character. At the beginning of the century, the official mention of *deutscher Nation*, added to the traditional title, delimits and affirms a nationalism of the *Reichsvolk*, in countries in which Latin had long been replaced by German in administrative and legal texts. The prejudices of the Italian humanists against Germany, against its "barbarous" mores, against its "jargon" (a *gèrgo*, they called it) or against its lack of speculative capacity, as well as their habit of raiding manuscripts from Bavarian and Rhenish monasteries, exacerbated, among the Germanic men of letters, a national consciousness in search of its own legitimacy.[9] Tacitus's *De Germania* was to furnish the reference point and language of an autonomous patrimony for that search for an identity. Nicholas of Cusa, a great expert on archives "mistreated and lost in the cabinets" of thoughtless owners,[10] is "the first man of the modern period" to have knowledge of that still unknown text whose discovery Humboldt would compare to that of America: he made a partial copy of it and apparently stole it (as one once stole relics) from the abbey of Fulda to give to Poggio Bracciolini, an erudite collector and secretary of the Roman Curia, to whom he regularly brought rare manuscripts in 1427–29.[11] Whom does he serve, or whom does he betray, in making off with this "lost" treasure, and in thus securing for himself, by the Italian detour, a role of catalyzer in Germany? He plays upon several regions. He does not identify himself with the law of a place.

But neither does he deny that law. He asserts his allegiance to the Germanic nation. He emphasizes solidarities: thus Hugues of Saint-Victor is for him "our German," "our eminent Saxon."[12] Mosan by birth, he is, to be sure, first and foremost a Lotharingian. As a student, he signed his notes on Gerson's *Mystical Theology* and Proclus's commentary on *Parmenides* as "Nicolas of Treves."[13] His initial formation, his study of the "arts" at Heidelberg, his teaching of law in Cologne, his activities as dean at Koblenz, and even his reading of Meister Eckhart in Mainz[14]—all this experience is Rhenish, haunted by the ever-present Rhine (*stabiliter*), now turbulent, now clear (*jam turbulentior, jam clarior*), a permanence that pervades all the provinces of his work.[15]

After his first sojourns in Italy, he considers himself and identifies himself as "German" (*Germanus*). In the preface of *De concordantia catholica* (1433), he apologizes for a "style" far from the elegance of the "Italians," who are, he says, Latins "by nature" and connected to the Greeks by kinship. "*We Germans*, however, although not far behind in *native ability*—which is not affected by an unfavorable position of the stars—defer to others in the pleasing exercise of eloquence, since we are able to *speak* Latin correctly only with great effort (*labor maximus*), overcoming, as it were, the force of nature." Latin, still an academic language, formerly the norm of a "culture," takes the direction of a Mediterranean "nature" and genealogy. It becomes nationalized. The work presented to "other nations" by a German must, therefore, be judged not by the criterion of its conformity to local rules and a local eloquence, i.e., to the customs of a "nation," but according to the "native ability" that expresses itself in a style "without art" (*incultus*) and "without disguise" (*absque fuco*); "Meaning is the most striking where the way of speaking is the most unobtrusive."[16] Behind the irony of the emigrant who must resort to an alien form of speech there is the affirmation of a difference between the universality of native ability (*ingenium*) and the ethnic diversity of languages ("positivities"). The *humile eloquium* of Nicholas of Cusa, if it still draws inspiration from the Augustinian conception of a *sermo humilis* in the service of the spirit (*spiritus*),[17] already refers to power relations between nations identified by their languages. "A nation, in the Middle Ages, is first and foremost a language."[18] At the beginning of a book dedicated to the political conditions for a "Catholic concord," and therefore to the institutions making possible a universal *populus*, the particularity of the Italian or German *natio* is carved out. The *populus*, a "political" concept in the fifteenth century, is to the *natio*, an *ethnic* entity, what the "spirit" is to the language. This tension defines the work of the oeuvre.

To the "German" activities the Italian or foreign experience is added: the study of law and mathematics in Padua (beginning in 1417); participation in the Council of Basil (1432), diplomatic missions to the Hussites in Bohemia (1433), and to the "Basileus" and the patriarch of the East in Constantinople (1437); the cardinalship in Rome (1448); missions as papal legate throughout Europe (from Austria to the Netherlands) (1451); later, responsibilities as general administrator of the Papal States (1462–64). His tasks give him occasion to become aware of the contradictions between regional strength and the Babelian attrition of unifying institutions. A world is falling to pieces: struggles between popes, or between popes and the councils (the Great Schism, 1378–1449); the awakening of enemy nationalisms (for example, the epopee of Joan of Arc, burned in 1431, or the Hussite movement, until 1434); emancipation of the cities; diversification of language; the breaking apart of doctrines; the birth of a new individualism. By his immense erudition, which "runs," as he says, from the Greeks to the Koran, from law to mathematics, from archival collections to astronomical calculations, or from a thousand and one technical "curiosities" to the great philosophers, as well as by his innumerable journeys, Nicholas of Cusa seems to want to overcome the dissemination of a universe. But he accepts as a premise the *irreducible* character of these different "positions," and he thus introduces the new paradigm of a "modern" philosophical approach. To find and bring to bear a principle that articulates that dispersion without being able to reduce it to unity is, throughout his turbulent life, the *labor maximus* that unceasingly attempts to "overcome the force of nature."

Overall, this work is oriented in two directions: one, institutional, gives rise, in the ecclesial field of deteriorating authority, to the *political* philosophy of *De concordantia catholica*; the other, speculative and taking on the relations of innate ability to the multiplicity of languages, ends up with the *scientific* figure of *Docta ignorantia*. These two major texts, in contrast by their methods and their objects, are in sync by the movement that directs them. The former develops a hitherto unknown way of managing division and proposes models to temper a hierarchy of sacramental "orders" with a system of election by the people and democratic representation.[19] The latter produces a theory of the dialogical relations between the "contradictions" found by philosophical analysis, and of the elusive principle toward which these heteronomous points of view direct the mind.[20] This double task, associating the investigations of the researcher with the career of the diplomat/administrator, is supported by the two essential reference points of his scientific interests, law and mathematics. Already Leibnizian by this constant project and by the multiform modalities of its execution, the Cusan oeuvre ceaselessly intertwines political concerns with scientific speculation.

This is already manifest at the level of general theoretical strategy, with the key concepts that specify the operations of the mind among antinomies in which analysis must recognize the workplace of thinking itself. The "consensus" is the mainspring of the whole institutional organization presented in the *Catholic Concordance*, just as the "coincidence of contraries" is the infinite point around which the philosophy of *Learned Ignorance* is organized. In both cases, the principle of movement cannot be identified with any one of the elements put into play, nor does it hold them at a distance by a process of abstraction; it assumes, in opposite singularities, an internal mainspring capable of actualizing them through mutual relations. In this perspective, each particular positivity is no longer defined by its status in an ontologically hierarchized cosmos (a "stair-step cosmos" or a cosmos in "degrees"), but it is the direct witness of an absolute, like a "point of view," at once "total," "singular," and irreplaceable, whose relation to others manifests its infinite potentiality. In a modality now legal, now speculative, the individual has a value of infinity, whose "impulsion" itself puts him in relation with others. As Cassirer has shown, Nicholas of Cusa inaugurates a *"modern" conception of the individual.*[21] He does so because he devoted himself to *thinking potentiality* in terms of *positions* defined by a *reciprocal determination.* The two points, equally fundamental, also link juridical hermeneutics to a geometrical speculation that already looks like a topology. In any case, since, in a space of social or theoretical sites, oppositions constitute the necessary and insuperable condition of a unifying reciprocity, the decisive moves of that thought have a relation to the "political" that characterizes not only their connection to the immediate socioeconomic circumstances but their formality itself.

1. THE ALL-SEEING

It is in its operations that a scientific and theoretical style can be recognized. Despite the diversity of the techniques to which Nicholas of Cusa has recourse (erudite collation, juridical hermeneutics, geometrical demonstration, etc.), his ways of doing things follow a common problematics. There are Cusan "gestures" that are quite recognizable, even if they take place in different fields. These discursive practices, even better than the concepts resulting from them, trace out, within the immense geography of his travels, his own way of thinking.

The relation that his *localization* as a German speaker holds with his *practice* of Latin, a clerical and academic language, furnishes a first example of this "style." He "allemanicizes" (*alemannizare*) as he says in speaking of the German immigrant arriving in Italy.[22] Indeed, Germanisms haunt his Latin. They are the ghosts of a particular place (the Rhineland or Germany) in a site that is other—Latin, a supposedly "universal" language, but in fact limited to a particular area and genealogy. They also delineate the present of a local speech in a heritage received from the past. The Italian humanists attempt to eliminate this contradiction by making their Latin conform to the model of the ancient *elocutio*: in doing so they replace the geographic or ethnic diversity of languages with the hierarchical privilege of a language of the elite (scholarly Latin) over the "vulgar" dialects. Nicholas of Cusa proceeds otherwise. He passes *from one to the other* by an operation consisting in placing two qualitatively heterogeneous particularities (German, which specifies an ethnic identity, and Latin, which allows for an intellectual communication) *one into the other.* His treatment of Latin is a coincidence of opposites. Linguistic practice already has a theoretical value.

It is noteworthy, moreover, that those transitional operations occasion lexical creations, at times dazzling ones, often marking the decisive moments of thought; then the linguistic *act* becomes itself a *sign* of the theory. These turns of phrase are ways of "turning," of shifting and remodeling the vocabulary by the different ways they are *used*. They give the Cusan style the enigmatic or "obscure" appearance for which he has often been reproved, placing him in the category—a suspect one—of what is "rare" (*rarus*).[23] But they belong in the perspective that during these same years Alberti was developing in Mantua, with his *De trivia* (around 1460) and according to which "the word is no longer the immutable sign of an idea, but a provisional approximation, the support for an ever renewed creation."[24] In Nicholas of Cusa, this creation delineates the very movement of the "concept," that is, of what it conceives and produces (*conceptus*). When he does not let himself be carried away by his own verbal virtuosity and his (very contemporary) taste for the rich surprises of meaning offered by language thanks to alliteration, homophony, and, more generally speaking, phonetic "play,"[25] his turns of phrase are the gestures of thought with and between two bodies of language. "Very often, with *one word*, with a single happily coined term, it [the Cusan's curious Latin] illuminates in a flash the whole speculative depth of the fundamental problems with which he is concerned."[26] The *Blitz*, that lightning flash in discourse, defines both a "way of speaking" (the theory of which will soon focus on mystic science) and a way of thinking the coincidence of opposites. It is not surprising that Latin words are frequently used in accordance with German grammatical rules (the infinitive taken as a noun, the deponent verbs conjugated as passives, the terms *aliud* and *duo* used as invariables, a hundred and one particular constructions, such as the dative after *participare* [*teilnehmen*], etc.), or constructed according to German lexical models (such as *epilogatio*, *improportionaliter*, *inunibilis*, *possest*, etc.), or thought in terms of German analogues (such as *explicatio*, in the sense of *Auslegung*: *complicatio* in the sense of *Mutmassung*, etc.).[27] They represent passages from one particularity to another, but passages that do not eliminate the terms of the opposition. Two antinomic languages, each defined by a "nature," a race, and a genealogy, are brought to points of coexistence: these words mean what they do; they articulate a discourse of coincidence at the same time that they bring about the coincidence of two languages; they are ways of thinking the One in linguistic duality.

By this use of language, we have an indication of what the Cusan "praxis" is. This procedure does not presuppose a language proper to the theory, an autonomous metalanguage that would give speculation a distinct linguistic space—no more than Cusan philosophy presupposes a superior essence that would surmount at a higher level the antinomies of a lower level. A work relative to each singularity frees, so to speak, and develops (*explicat*) "the impulsion" that is interior to each singularity and reveals itself to be infinite by the very impossibility of finding a hierarchical unity between singularities. Awakened by the shock between opposites, the philosophical "praxis" *passes* from one positivity to the other, as from one perspective to the other, in thus "explaining" the "seed of infinity" animating each of them. It is *translatio*, transfer.

In conformity with this sort of operation, but on a larger scale, is the way Nicholas of Cusa treats the scholastic tradition. That way is characterized by new manners of practicing a received corpus. It does not proceed from a rupture, or a detachment, that would permit the construction of a different system. "The powerful *thought-mass* (*Gedankenmasse*) of Scholastic philosophy . . . is not to be thrown aside, but to be drawn into a completely new *movement* of thought."[28] This movement is performed *within* that "mass," in terms of the contradictions opposing certain elements to others, internal or external (Platonic, Arabic, etc.). The vigilance in identifying these oppositions in the indefinite field of available knowledge stimulates the look to which their coincidence is given in a "flash."

The Two "Seeings": A Mathematical Esthetics

An endless erudition, relative to the "positivities" of discursive knowledge, is thus combined with instantaneous vision, which grasps their relationship. The former gives the latter the endless field of particular realities in which to recognize, thanks to their very oppositions, the modalities of a dynamics of infinity. To express the intensity of the visual experience in Nicholas of Cusa, we should speak rather of a combination linking observation and intuition. The former is "developed" in an insatiable quest, captivated by all sorts of daily curiosities (beryl, the game of bowling, the top, the wooden spoon, the clock, etc.),[29] as well as by so many regions traveled through, and by countless books and archives: it creates a *space* for a discourse that often bears the *title* of an object (*beryl*, *bowling*, *painting*, or *the image*, etc.), as if the object "instituted" the space of reflection, in the absence of any other institution, and as if the sight of the thing (at this level of observation or painting) "played the role" of "authorities" that are supposed to create that space but that have become uncertain. Intuition, on the other hand, is "concentrated" in the self-evidence of "views of the mind" (*visus mentis*). These two forms of "seeing" incessantly intersect. Their point of coincidence is the visible figure in which the look grasps the invisible that moves within it. This instrument of passage (*transsumptio*) from one "seeing" to the other is the mirror. Mounted within the texts, it is the equivalent of quotations of poems in the mystic treatises of the sixteenth century. It is in fact to the visual what the illuminatory "word" is to the verbal. It scans the prose of discourse with brisk points of intersection between several spaces.

In Van der Weyden, Van Eyck (for example, the portrait said to be of the Arnolfini, 1434), or the Master of Flémalle (the portrait of Canon Werl, 1434), who are roughly contemporaries of the Cusan, the mirror is a place located *within* the painted framework and often decorated like the monstrance or the reliquary that circumscribes the manifestation of another world. On the inside, it presents to view a *beyond*—another time (death), another dimension (mourning, vice, etc.)—that is not visible in the scene represented by the painting, though it is *already* at work in it. It is the revealer (or the hallucination) of a history that is hidden, but present, the visibility of that which cannot be seen *there.* In Nicholas of Cusa, "mirror" is a concrete object making visible what already animates it, beyond or on the hither side of its appearances. In the display case of explicative prose, things are suddenly illuminated in "mirrors." Thus, the wooden spoon is transformed into "every kind of mirror—viz., concave, convex, straight, and cylindrical. At the base of the handle there is a straight mirror, in the handle a cylindrical mirror, in the concavity of the spoon a concave mirror, and in the spoon's convexity a convex mirror"—when the invisible forms are recognizable in the sensible image.[30] The spoon is perfected in the mirror, in a jewel for the mind, when the spectator, going beyond minute observation, grasps a splendor in it that the eye cannot see. So the former kind of "seeing" yields to the latter. The vision goes from crepuscular to "auroral" (*ut aurora*); in the light of a new day, it sees what comes in the object, transformed into a "heralding" figure, like an angel.[31]

An intellectual intuition has changed all things into possible mirrors. It is noted at the end of *Learned Ignorance*, in the final address to Cardinal Cesarini, in the form of an envoi. The discourse is finished, "Amen." It is followed by this insert: neither conclusion nor proof (the treatise is self-sufficient), it is a signature, that of a received name, the undecipherable of the proper. The evocation is short. And yet it is the founding intuition, like the vision of Ostia for Augustine, but it is born of and in division itself. The scene is played out at sea. The diplomat bringing the patriarch and the emperor back to Constantinople for a meeting with the pope (spring 1438): *In mare ex Graecis rediens.* Between East and West, these two opposites, and in the act of passing from the one to the other, he "believes," he writes, that he has been "led," a journey paralleling the navigation at sea, "by a heavenly gift from the father of lights . . . , to embrace—in learned ignorance and through a transcending of the incorruptible truths which are humanly knowable—incomprehensible things incomprehensibly (*ut incomprae-hensibilia incompraehensibiliter amplecterer in docta ignorantia*)." Despite his desire, he was not able to reach, by "the various paths of the doctrines,"[32] this blinding principle of a coincidence of opposites, a bedazzlement at the heart of unknowing. What he "conceives" is given to him all of a sudden: if he expresses it in Augustinian formulas that already designated the manner in which the Spirit renders our "ignorance" "learned,"[33] he transforms them into the conception that will govern his entire work.

When Johannes Wenck indicts *Learned Ignorance* on the charge of sources adjudged compromising (Dionysius the Areopagite, Eckhart, etc.) and therefore sees the text of his adversary as the repetition of positive expressions that an erudite eye can recognize, Nicholas of Cusa rectifies, before defending the incriminated works: "At the time I received [this] concept from on high I had not seen (*vidisse*) Dionysius or any of the true theologians." He nonetheless "ran" avidly, like a "hunting dog," toward the writings of the teachers (*avido cursu me ad doctorum scripta contuli*),[34] but the "seeing" he speaks of is not reducible to what the documents present to the critical eye; quite to the contrary, it reveals in their visible positivity that which in them comes from further away. It is not incompatible with the indefatigable "running" of an erudition, but from the texts and "curiosities" that the researcher incessantly inventories, it makes "mirrors" of what animates them without being visible in them. The observant and collecting "hunt" (*venatio*) continually supplies new places in which the alchemy that transforms one "seeing" into the other, like lead into gold, is repeated.

Between the two forms of *videre*, Cusan mathematics constitutes a space of coincidence. It is a geometry. The kind of mental operations that defines it begins with compositions of visible places: "Imagine a pyramid . . . ," "conceive a triangle . . . ," "given a circle . . . ," etc. But in this "sensible image" presented to "the eye,"[35] the mind sees formal relations and their possible developments. Geometry links observations or optical constructions to rational evidence. There, the "seeing" of the mind coincides with the "seeing" of the eye: an intellectual intuition with an optical perception; the universality of a "form" with the concrete singularity of a figure. Reciprocally, he who can see in one way, and not in the other, is not a mathematician.

Hence geometry furnishes the model of a *scientificity*, at the very moment (or rather, to the very extent) that it is detached from its ancient ontological function. With the possible exception of what concerns the "one" (the ambivalence of which, for lack of a zero, did not cease being a problem for Nicholas of Cusa), this mathematics is no longer the revelation of forms or truths organizing the universe. It is not epiphanic. Like painting, it is a "construction" of the mind (a *conceptus*) inscribed in the problematics to which Tasso will soon give the beautiful name *fabbrica della mente*.[36] In that it orders coherent sets of "exercises" on elementary figures (the point, the straight line, the curve, etc.) and no longer has the status of a discourse manifesting the structures of being, it becomes capable of formulating and regulating the productions of the mind in all the disciplines. It takes on the value of a privileged language, protected from the ambiguity or polysemy that in other languages permits the play of unforeseeable inventions; it is therefore capable of controlling and developing, as in a laboratory, the intellectual approaches applicable to all the regions of knowledge. "In our science, the only certain thing we have is our mathematics," and nothing "great" has been said "that was not based on the model of mathematics."[37] To each particular research project it presents schemata of constructions and transformations to be carried out on different "positivities."

Geometry's first concern is operations relative to "seeing," since it unfolds entirely in that element and since it makes the visible the very field of intellectual visions. In this respect, it not only presents the formality of procedures that are *also* applicable to visual experience: it has the value of being the model for a science *of* "seeing." This science is in itself an *esthetics.* Whence its status of enigma: "It is an enigma for going on the hunt (*venatio*) for the works of God." Therefore we must "enigmaticize mathematically."[38] The object of this art is not "to see the visible," but "to see the invisible in the visible,"[39] by a movement of the mind that the painting of Van Eyck and of the Master of Flémalle also executes,[40] and that Nicholas of Cusa grounds by referring not to Proclus but to Saint Paul: *Videmus nunc per speculum in aenigmate.*[41] Geometry, an "enigma" in the "mirror" of its figures, becomes a science of the mirror, but only to the extent that it consists in a seeing of the invisible in a visible space, to the extent that it is a praxis of that kind of "seeing." Indeed, such is the characteristic of Nicholas of Cusa the geometer, which he extends to philosophy. He proceeds by theoretic *excesses*: conceptual "bursts" precede, exceed, and reroute the legal course of the reasoning; they have the ability to surprise the analysis and thus renew it; they do not obey the principle of noncontradiction and therefore cannot be submitted to verification. With his genius for invention, he belongs to the category of mathematicians who, in the words of David Hilbert on Georg Cantor, open mathematics to a "paradise" or an irrefutable "theology." The productivity of the inventive imagination is measured solely by the coherence of its results. Nicholas of Cusa begins by "seeing." It is in the formalization or in the demonstration that he proves weaker, often too hasty, or carried away by what he "conceives." This is why he has often been judged in contradictory ways, depending on whether one prioritized mathematical inventiveness (like Moritz Cantor) or the rigor of the reasoning (Pierre Duhem).

Cusan geometry, an art of "seeing" or of transforming figures into mirrors, therefore brings to bear what must be practiced *also* in the reading of authors or in the observation of physical curiosities. A visual language and a conceptual practice, it teaches us to recognize in readable texts and visible objects, as well as in "sensible images," innumerable kinds of mirrors—and a multitude of possible mirrors—forming the wayfaring vision of the universe possessed by "the most gifted" and the most "inventive" mathematician of his day.[42]

The Preface to "The Image"

Nicholas of Cusa was fifty-two when he wrote his treatise. By its placid style, *De icona* seems at first a limpid mirror in which, as Cassirer has already stressed,[43] the focal point of Cusan speculation appears. From the start he proposes as his program the "easy accessibility" of theological *mystics.* A typical program, not only because it defines the style of numerous Cusan texts, conceived of as logical sequences of simple operations, or yet again, already a more central aspect, because in this domain, as in mathematics, one "sees" or "one does not see" (it is not a question of effort), but especially because the treatise postulates a "seeding" of infinity in each of its readers. It gives a language to what is already there. It offers words for what those whom it addresses know somewhere, so that they can be satisfied in answering: "How true! That's it precisely!" The truth is already there, all you have to do is see it—thus begins *De beryllo*; wisdom cries out in the public squares, all you have to do is hear it—thus begins the *Idiota.*[44] The clerics who, by their quibbles, block the access of the "layman" (the *idiotus*) to truth scandalize the Cusan; he has scoffing exorcisms to drive them away, the style of which will be found again in Rabelais: "*A dialecticis libera nos, Domine*—Deliver us, Lord, from the dialecticians."[45] "Easy accessibility" designates an experience unfettered by long, academic preambles, and based on the "impulsion" of every free spirit.

The intention of the preface to the treatise *On the Image* or *On the Picture* is precisely to open a space for the treatise that escapes the long preliminaries of technical competence, as well as the privileging of the "lived," which is ultimately positivistic. Analogous to the geometrical "comparison" (the sphere that is one and plural) that induces, in Teresa of Avila, the innovative discourse *Las Moradas,*[46] the preface serves as a foundation for all the following chapters. It is the zero degree of the treatise. It precedes and permits the word: *prae-fatio.* It presents itself as a "sensible experimentation" (*sensibile experimentum*) that, in dislodging the addressees from their prejudicial positions, creates a space for the Cusan theory. It concerns an "exercise" (*praxis*). A *doing* will make possible a saying. This propaedeutic is, moreover, customary in a spiritual formation and in the relationship between master and disciple: "Do it, and you will understand afterward." The preface also has the significance of a laboratory observation, from which the theoretical interpretation will follow. It plays on the double register of a "spiritual exercise" and a scientific experiment. Here, then, is the entire text of this preface (minus the two last lines).

> If I strive to convey you by human means unto divine things, then I must do this through a likeness (*similitudo*). Now, among human works I have not found an image more suitable to my purpose than the image of someone omnivoyant (*imago omnia videntis*) so that his face (*facies*), through subtle pictorial artistry, is such that it seems to behold everything around it. There are in existence many of these excellently depicted faces—e.g., the one of the archer in the forum at Nuremberg, the one of the preeminent painter Roger [Van der Weyden] in his priceless painting in the city hall at Brussels,[47] the one of Veronica in my chapel at Koblenz, the one, in the castle at Brixen, of the angel holding the emblems of the Church, and many others here and there. Nevertheless, so that you not be lacking in practical experience (*praxis*), which requires such a sensible figure, I am sending you a painting that I was able to acquire, containing the figure of the omnivoyant, which I call painting (*icon*) of God (*icona Dei*)[48]
>
> Hang this icon somewhere, e.g., on the north wall; and you, brothers, stand around it, at a short distance from it, and observe it (*intueri*). Regardless of the place from which each of you looks at it (*inspicere*), each will have the impression (*experiri*) that he alone is being looked at by it. To the brother who is situated in the east it will seem (*videbitur*) that the face is looking (*respicere*) toward the east; to the brother in the south, that the face is looking toward the south; to the brother in the west, that it is looking westward.
>
> First of all, then, marvel (*admirari*) at how it is possible that [the face] behold each and every one of you at once. For the imagination of the brother who is standing in the east does not at all apprehend the icon's gaze (*visus*) that is being directed toward a different region, viz., toward the west or the south. Next, let the brother who was in the east situate himself in the west, and he will experience the [icon's] gaze as fixed (*figere*) on him in the west, just as it previously was in the east. But since he knows that the icon is stationary and unchanged, he will marvel at the changing of the unchangeable gaze. Moreover, if while fixing his sight (*figere obtutum*) upon the icon he walks from west to east, he will find

that the icon's gaze proceeds continually with him; and if he returns from east to west, the gaze will likewise not desert him.
He will marvel at how the icon's gaze is moved immovably (*immobiliter*). And his imagination will be unable to apprehend that the gaze is also moved in accompaniment with someone else who is coming toward him from the opposite direction. Now, [suppose that] wanting to experience this [phenomenon], he has a fellow-monk, while beholding the icon, cross from east to west at the same time that he himself proceeds from west to east. And [suppose] he asks the approaching brother whether the icon's gaze moves continually with him. Thereupon he will be told that the gaze is also moved in this opposite manner; and he will believe his fellow-monk. And unless he believed, he would not apprehend that this [simultaneous opposition of motion] was possible.
And so, through the disclosure of the respondent (*revelatio relatoris*) he will come to know that that face does not desert anyone who is moving—not even those who are moving in opposite directions. Therefore, he will experience that the unmovable face (*immobilis facies*) is moved toward the east in such way that it is also moved at the same time toward the west, that it is moved toward the north in such way that it is also moved [at the same time] toward the south, that it is moved toward one place in such way that it is also moved at the same time toward all other places, and that it observes one movement in such way that it observes all other movements at the same time. And while he considers (*attendere*) that this gaze does not desert anyone, he sees (*videre*) how diligently it is concerned for each one, as if it were concerned for no one else, but only for him who experiences that he is seen by it. This [impression] is so strong that the one who is being looked upon cannot even imagine that [the icon] is concerned for another. [The one who is pondering all this] will also notice that [the image] is most diligently concerned for the least of creatures (*minima*), just as for the greatest of creatures (*maxima*) and for the whole universe.
On the basis of such a sensible appearance (*sensibilis apparentia*) as this, I propose to elevate you, very beloved brothers, through a devotional exercise (*praxis devotionis*), unto mystical theology.[49]

A Symbolic System of the Fantastic

The preface imposes the atmosphere of a place. In the vocabulary, verbs denoting looks (to see, seem [*videri*], look, examine, observe, follow with the eyes, fix one's gaze, etc.). These multiple visual activities gradually extend to all the actors, so that they progressively compose a labyrinth, not of things, but of looks that cross each other—astonished or sustained, immobile or wandering, instantaneous or continuous. A fantastic of the look haunts this closed space, with its accompaniment of surprises, the unimaginable, and the unbelievable. This forest of eyes recalls many ancient visions, among others the famous Rhenish one of Hildegard of Bingen, seized by the apparition of a body covered with eyes.[50] The look fixed on the spectator also has the cultural value of a miracle. Thus, for the feast of "the Invention of the Holy Cross" (3 May), the *Legend of the Saints* (or *Golden Legend*) makes it into the recompense given by heaven to a young "secretary" (*notarius*) who resisted the devil with the sign of the cross (a sign, moreover, delineated by the composition of the Cusan place). Some time after this quasi-sacramental gesture, when, in the Church of St. Sophia, the master and the secretary are standing before an image of Christ, the master notices that the image has "its eyes fixed" (*oculos fixos*) on the young man; he "has him go to the right, then to the left" several times in succession, but the image "turns its eyes" in the direction in which the secretary goes and "keeps its eyes fixed on him."[51] The Cusan exercise bears a close resemblance to the miracle of *The Golden Legend*, including the relation of the master to Nicholas of Cusa, the one who orders the movements of the scene and observes that interplay of looks. Indeed it has its place in a long fantastic, mystic, and miraculous tradition. It stands out against an aura of mystery and secrecy, further enriched by myriad histories of devotion, spirits returned from the dead, and the evil eye. The initiatory operation takes place in the (mythic) climate of a historically fundamental experience.

The examples of the "all-seeing" cited in the text (which there resembles the catalog of a collector or archivist) add an autobiographical dimension to all these looks that structure the space and seem like ghosts of ancestral visions. Nuremberg,[52] Brussels, Koblenz, Brixen: these places mark the stages of Nicholas of Cusa's career; he resided (or still resides) there. A look seems to have followed him across Germany, from north to south, from east to west, despite the diversity of his faces: Sagittarius, the centaur drawing out the arrow that unites earth and sky, in the zodiac; the self-portrait by Van der Weyden, in three-quarters and turned toward the viewer in the middle of the crowd in the right panel of the *Justice of Trajan*; The *Holy Face* shown by Saint Veronica, or Veronica herself;[53] the angel bearing the ecclesial blazon, in the castle (Sigismond's?) that dominates Brixen; finally the painting itself that he has at home, in the bishopric of Brixen, and of which he has a copy made by a painter to send to Tegernsee. It is not only places that are multiple, but also the figured species (centaur, man, woman, angel) and the professional or symbolic sites (the public zodiac, the tribunal of justice, the private oratory, the military castle, the ecclesiastical palace). These are all the successive and diverse appearances of a look, always the same, that "does not leave him." In this sense, the scene constructed for Tegernsee recapitulates, as in a mirror, all of these successive appearances. Just as that scene introduces into a traditional visionary experience an already "modern" optical observation, it inserts a whole series of personal events into a pedagogical exercise. It makes multiple scenes coexist. Heterogeneous places are brought to coincide in this ubiquitous look that no longer has a name or face of its own (it has no identity in the text):[54] the space it organizes thus has the depth of obliterated histories; plural, made up of visual strata that play on one another, it is the anonymous theater of a memory.

The density proper to the image is finally manifested in the relation that the painting maintains with discourse. A dialogical structure. The exercise, says the preface, "requires" the image. In a classical geometrical demonstration, the statement presupposes the figure; similarly, the text, here, requires the painting. Not the one without the other. Sent conjointly, discourse and painting constitute by their very difference the dynamics of praxis. The three rational "moments" that order the experimentation bring back, each time increased, the fantastic quality of the image, and each time the *admiratio*, visual surprise, marks this return. But from the one to the other, from the verbal to the iconic, the relation is inverted in the course of the exercise. At the beginning, it is the painting—a necessary condition—that first generates a space (the semicircle of the observers). At the end, it is an oral testimony (the *revelatio relatoris*) that alone allows one to "believe" what eludes vision, so that the ears give us to understand what the eyes cannot see. Hence the image "requires" discourse; in the space that the former has opened up for the latter and that makes possible the project of "relating marvels" (*enarrare mirabilia*),[55] the treatise will develop into twenty-five chapters. But henceforth of what does this long discourse incessantly speak, what holds it captive, if not the image that is still *there*, that takes from the eyes what it makes visible to the mind and that remains, or even increasingly becomes, at the center of these interwoven words, a presence of absence?

2. A GEOMETRY OF THE LOOK

That the image endlessly becomes the other of the text—this begins when it *appears* ungraspable. Experimentation must ensure this beginning. Its goal is to "convert" one way of seeing into another. It is a "translation" that conforms to the Cusan method, which consists in changing, *in* the received place, the operation that is performed there. The exercise develops within a visual proliferation, but in order to delimit therein a different *practice* of the place.

It belongs to the domain of geometry. Nicholas of Cusa makes this clear in a letter of 14 September 1453 in which he explains the future *De icona* to Aindorffer: in it, a "mathematical figure" will be the object of transformations that extend its significance to "theological infinity" (*theologicalis infinitas*). The "experimental procedure" (*praxis experimentalis*) he intends to develop, he adds, is "very elegant" (*pulcherrimus*) "and very clear" (*clarissimus*)[56]—qualities of a mathematical demonstration. According to this same letter, *De icona* was first a "chapter" of the *Complement* attached to the *Mathematicis complementis* that he sent at the time to Pope Nicholas V, the Maecenas and originator of the humanistic and mathematical renewal in Rome.[57] It therefore belongs to that cascade of "complements," applications of geometry to theology. Detached from this *Complementum theologicum figuratum in complementis mathematicis* of which it was no longer a part, the "chapter" was developed separately, but despite this separateness when it was finally sent in 1453, it remains defined by the program of the *Theological Complement*: "I will endeavor to transform the [mathematical] figures of that book [*Mathematical Complements*] into theological befigurings, in order (to the extent that God grants) to behold with mental sight (*mentali visu intueamur*) how it is that in the mirror-of-mathematics there shines forth that truth which is sought in and through everything knowable—shines forth not only without [it being necessary to use] similes, but with a certain bright-shining nearness. . . . These theological matters are better seen with the mind's eye than they can be expressed in words."[58] It is the privilege of "seeing" to access the true, but by "the mathematical mirror": this conviction of Nicholas of Cusa's last twenty-five years, since *Learned Ignorance*, gives *De icona* its objective, and the preface that introduces it its scientific status.

The privilege of the eye over the ear is not peculiar to Cusa: during this period, predication is replete with it.[59] But the exercise that is to make possible the transformation of "sensible" visual experience into the theory of mystic vision is, for Nicholas of Cusa, a mathematical operation. It is part of the research program of the fifteenth century, which, from Alberti to Piero della Francesca (pending Leonardo da Vinci), closely associates mathematical theory with a theory of art. Mathematics is not only a condition for certainty in knowledge, but also the methodological means of decoding or organizing scientific "observations." At the same time as being a school for rigor, it is a science of seeing (a hermeneutics of figures) and an "architectural" science (an art of constructing reasoned and demonstrative experiments). In the new scientificity, essentially visual, it takes the place that logic held in medieval scientificity, which was essentially linguistic. But, leaving aside these comparisons with his contemporaries, it will suffice to stress that Nicholas of Cusa conceives as a mathematician the exercise that the monks have to carry out not with a compass but with their legs, during a ceremony that also prolongs the "games," mimicry, and "juggling acts" that were a long-standing tradition at the abbey of Tegernsee,[60] and that had the odd audacity of replacing the liturgy with a geometric order, and especially the altar and the Bible with a painting.

This mathematical liturgy stages a space distributed in places by a system of differences between singularities constituted by their reciprocal positions. It seems to correspond to the "geometry of position" whose necessity, three centuries later, Buffon so rightly emphasized. "Everything that has an immediate relation with position is absolutely lacking to our mathematical sciences. That art that Leibniz called *Analysis situs* has not yet been born, and yet that art which would let us know the relations of position among things would be as useful to the natural sciences as—and perhaps more necessary than—the art that has only the greatness of things as its object."[61] Unknown to Buffon, but not to Leibniz, Nicholas of Cusa invents, in his own way, a geometry of the relations of position that anticipates topology, and he applies it to the seeing-seen relation. He constructs his experimental demonstration based on three moments that he distinguishes with precision.

A Simultaneity of Stupors

The painting's gaze constitutes a *point*. According to Nicholas of Cusa's constant theory as he repeats it in the *Theological Complement*, the point itself is a "quasi-nothingness" (*prope nihil*), but it is endowed with an infinite "fecundity"; it is "at the same time" close to nothing from an analytic perspective, and quasi everything from a dynamic one.[62] It is inseparably, being the simplest unit, the epistemological principle of the geometrical definition and, by its fecundity, the genetic principle of spatial construction. There is, therefore, *generation of a space* thanks to the equal lines drawn from a point. The monks, being equidistant from the painting, represent that property. They form a semicircle. They construct a "mathematical figure" from the perspective of mental operations.

With the same gesture, they construct with respect to bodily movements that "theater in the round" that characterizes, in fourteenth- and fifteenth-century Germany, the staging of the mystery and passion plays. The semicircle of the monks, who are at once spectators and actors, as in a liturgy, obeys the primacy of the center and the circumference. It still reflects the form of that theater in the round that is, in the fifteenth century, what the cathedral is in the twelfth and thirteenth:[63] the stage par excellence, the form of visibility given to the representation of what is fundamental and what Nicholas of Cusa will call "circular theology," the symbolic place appropriate to an exercise of meaning.

Finally, the figure is a map, relative to the four cardinal points, in keeping with a dispositive that obeys not a cosmographical symbolism (in which, for example, the center would be the Orient), but the abstract framework presupposed by a geographical construction. Nicholas of Cusa, himself the author of a map of central Europe (the *Tabula cusana*), later commented on by Sebastian Münster,[64] gives his composition of place the significance of an atlas of the world, but a world whose center (the look) *can* be, arbitrarily, placed in the north as well as in any other place, so that, behind the figuration for an instant fixed around this point for the purpose of an experiment, there is the Cusan vision of a universe whose center is everywhere and whose circumference is nowhere.[65] Organized by positions independent of substrata, but actualized in them, the same locus thus functions on three levels: as a "figure" in a geometrical space; as a scene in a theatrical space; and as a map in a geographical or cosmological space. Its genesis allots it a polyvalence. It is a *play of spaces* that are qualitatively different. This first moment can be represented in the schema shown in figure 1.

Foreign to the contemporary studies on colors and chromatics, on kinds of light (radiating, reflected, etc.), and therefore on the eye qua reflective surface,[66] the problematic of the look pertains to a geometrical perspective. The look is a vector—a line and an action in space. Like an

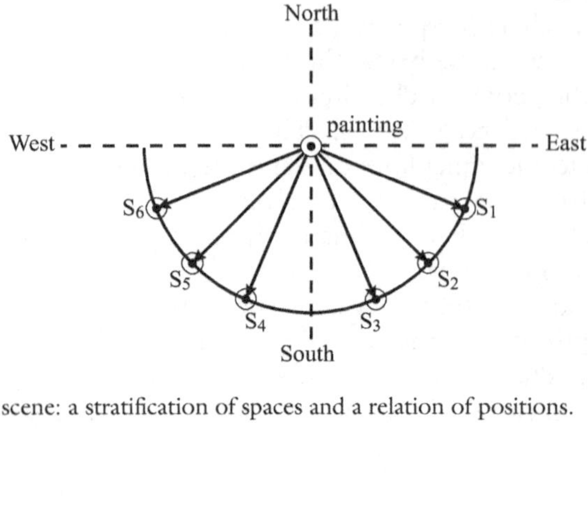

Figure 1. The scene: a stratification of spaces and a relation of positions.

arrow, it penetrates each one of the observers. It thus gives "sensible" form to the theory that makes the point a relationship between what it *contains* within an "almost nothing" (this is the *complicatio*) and what it *develops* from it in the line (this is the *explicatio*). This mathematics of the point agrees, moreover, with the anthropological conception that, in the tradition of Euclidean optics, from William of Conches to Ficino or even Bramante, considers the look as the result of "natural spirits" emitted by the eye and "going out" toward things[67]—a conception of things that is maintained, in a manner that becomes increasingly hesitant and ambiguous, up to and including Descartes's *Dioptrique*.[68] But in the Cusan preface, if the traditional movement remains, its terms are reversed: the supposed object (the painting) looks, and the subjects (the observers) form a tableau vivant. During this first moment, the scene is immobile; the characters, fixed at various points of the semicircle; the eyes of the observers immobilized by the look; the space frozen into pure coexistence of positions relative to the center and without relation to one another.

Fifteen years later, in his *De amore*, Marsilio Ficino was to evoke a look that "drives [one] insane": removed from the opaque and beautiful body that sustains it, the look of the other "strikes" the approaching lover who "stops short."[69] Rapid, this would be the shock of the look of "a passerby," of which Walter Benjamin speaks in commenting on the poem by Baudelaire. A bolt of lightning, taken out of the lively or leisurely travels of vision over bodies and objects. The Cusan composition, in using a painting, removes the body, leaving the eyes of the observers to their movements and their hunts. It retains the look alone. But it does not isolate a dual relationship. It makes *all* these eyes coexist, each of which is captivated by *one* look. It sets the scene for the birth of a space (a multiplicity) at the instant when that one look takes all its inhabitants by surprise. To use Ficino's terminology, what "drives [one] insane" is not being exiled by a look outside social places and connections; it is space itself, the coinciding of the seizures that wear away the collective consciousness of believing oneself to be in a common place; it is the simultaneity of singular stupors.

The Torsion of Space: Movement

Shot through with the astonishment (*admiratio*) that foments and gives its rhythm to the whole of Cusan reflection, the exercise moves to a second stage, which creates movement in this atomized place. An actor must feel the fixity of the look as he moves. His gait also introduces a duration. The trial, still solitary and mute, confronts the look with a succession of actions, with goings and comings from east to west, or

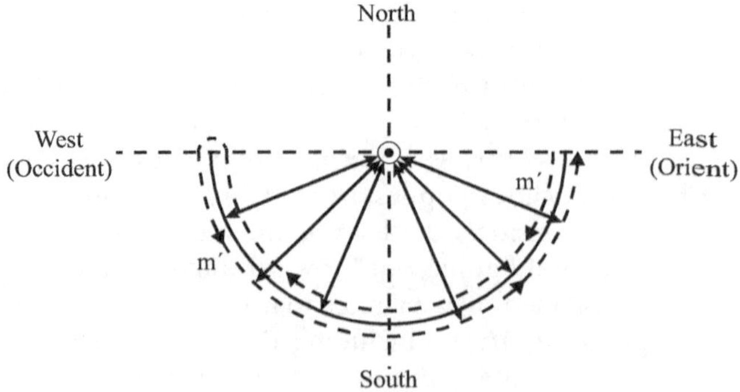

Figure 2. The torsion of space.

from the orient to the occident, physical and itinerant figures of a narrative temporality (see figure 2).

The look "follows" the walker everywhere. It dominates these routes. But it is not external, as if it were "something other" than them; it is immanent in them without being identical to them. Moreover, these successive travels are haunted by the *same* look, though they have *opposite directions.* The discursiveness that they inaugurate, made up of sequences traced successively on the same place, is reversible. These lines, each invested with a meaning, evoke (Nicholas of Cusa himself makes the comparison in chapter 8) those of a book that could be read from right to left, as in Hebrew or Arabic, as well as from left to right, as in Latin or German—or certain Nordic paintings, for example *The Virgin's Wedding*, by the Master of Flémalle, conceived to be read from the right as well as from the left, and thus referencing a space that does not obey the coherence of a visual dispositive.[70] To this compossibility of two directions, two writings or two narrativities that are *opposite*, one might also find equivalents in the palindromes and "juggleries" or linguistic prestidigitations that abound in the fifteenth century, "forbid" linear reading, and multiply the different, or even contrary, meanings by the interchangeability of the routes of decipherment.[71]

These practices consist in outwitting the temporal succession (irreversible discursiveness) that ensures a meaning to the sentence or the text. By transgressing successiveness, they undermine meaning. Hence they replace the law of a *meaning* with a problematic of the equivocal *place.* When they incurve, inverse, and multiply the possible routes in the place where meaning wanted the selection of one of them, they create a proliferation that is polysemic, and ultimately contradictory; the text *becomes an image.* The space traced out, but irreducible to a meaning, is indeed an image. The Cusan experimentation, at this stage, proceeds with the same annulment of discursiveness, and therefore of meaning, by the reversibility of the (physical or narrative) pathways, but its intention in so doing is to show the illegible nature, outside meaning and outside text, of this space insofar as it is *one*. What deprives the pathways—and the painting they depict—of meaning is unicity itself, or the center (which can be situated anywhere). In other words, the look is neither an object, nor an image, nor a concept, and it "lacks its place" (Jacques Lacan):[72] it is everywhere and nowhere. It is an operator that makes "one" by making all the pathways *senseless*. This moment is that of the anti-story. Here the journey is practiced as proof that it changes nothing, and that its time, far from creating points of no return, always returns to the same since each point repeats the same unthinkable, and whether to the east or the west, in one direction or another, it's the same. Beneath the look, time is annulled and movement itself becomes unreal.

A loss of object is also the result of the look. There is no longer any *object seen* for the person *looked at*. The abnormality of this persistent look effaces the possibility of grasping it as an object among others—before or after others. The observer thought he saw. Transformed into an observed, he enters into an "astonishment" that is not accompanied by representation. The experience of the look is a surprise without object. The look of the other excludes the possession of an image. It deprives of sight, it bedazzles, it blinds. Reciprocally, to perceive an object is therefore to ward off its capacity of looking; it is to exorcise its power of bewitching sight. If, as Nicholas of Cusa makes clear further on, *being* itself is a *subject looked at*,[73] then the object seen becomes the alibi of the looked-at being; it serves to fool a look; it diverts the subject from the look and protects it from it. Or else it fills in for a lack of look; it is its substitute and expectation, as if the multiplication of seen objects represented that absence. Seen objects, therefore, reintroduce history and narrative, with their diversions, delays, or expectations; they tell, they spell out in a never-ending myth, the remoteness of a look. At this stage of the Cusan exercise, if the look is the loss of the object, history is born of the loss of the look.

The antinomy between sight and the look, which movement brings into view, is accompanied by an opposition between two kinds of space. The excursions of the eye from east to west and from west to east *should* transform the perceived landscape: as the observer modifies his "point of view," the painting, as he perceives it, is submitted to anamorphoses in keeping with the successive places he occupies. The landscape changes. But as for the look, it does not obey the law of that visual reciprocity that defines a landscape. It "follows" the movements *and* it remains unchangeable. Its ubiquity unifies an *immobile* space whereas the positional shifts of the eye continually change the painting. The movements of the observer differentiate two kinds of space, that of the eye and that of the look, which contradict each other in the same place. More exactly, they impart a torsion on a space in which the fixity of the look defies the law of the landscape. This contradiction plays equally on two historical times of vision: within the framework of Renaissance esthetics itself, in which the analysis of points of view, visual relations between mobile entities, imposes little by little a problematic of perspective (bound to what I call the landscape),[74] the Cusan exercise maintains a medieval problematic of the look, which is universal and stable, overarching all things and each one of them individually. The perambulation of the observer, launching a combinatorial of real and apparent movements, manifests at once the opposition and the coincidence of two visual practices of place which correspond to two historical and anthropological "visions." It maximizes the fantastic of seeing, in the way that de Chirico, in his *The Lassitude of the Infinite*, opens his landscape to a qualitative difference of space by an internal torsion between two kinds of vision.

The Social Space of the Look: Believing

The third moment, marked again by an astonishment (*admiratio*), ensures the passage from the visual to discourse. It does this first by excluding the possibility of imagination's compensating for the insufficiency of sight. The unimaginable (*neque poterit imaginatio capere*), moreover, prolongs the *admiratio* and explicates its "nature": astonishment, deprived of any representable object, becomes the gesture, at once poetic and ethical, of responding to an excess by reaching out toward the ungraspable. It is from surprise that discourse will be born. The absence of a visible or imaginable object serves as a prelude, as yet without content, blank, to the necessity of believing the word of the other. Thus the text-guide rejects the imagination, but on the other hand it appeals to the "will." *Experiri volens: if you want* to pursue the experiment and continue seeking, there is the possibility of a journey no longer physical, but intellectual, by taking a different path that is no longer within the continuity of visual perception, but of *admiratio* itself, surprise without image, opening out on the unknown.

The threshold of sociality appears with recourse to a partner. There is indeed repetition of the movements foreseen at the preceding stage, in one direction by the actor, in the opposite direction by his fellow religious, but the articulation between these two opposite circuits is made in a social mode, first in a coordination in *acting*, then in an agreement at the level of *saying*.

Having done by one's partner what one has oneself executed in conformity with the manual (the preface), the first actor socializes the scene. He introduces into it a transmission and a cooperation. Something happens that is similar to the entry of Friday on the island of Robinson Crusoe. On the Cusan stage, the itinerary of lone and silent man followed by a look is transformed into the genesis of an association. *There are* individuals, but how do they form a group? How do they make *one*? This is the Cusan question. This micro-utopia concerns the problem that will haunt "modern" social thought: on what model are we to envisage the origin of human society, taking as our premise the existence of individuals? In this preface, the model is no longer biblical: the collectivity is not based on sexual difference, that is, on a situation of "nature" (the divine origin of which Nicholas of Cusa recognizes, but the significance of which he relativizes, every human being having both masculine and feminine traits);[75] it is the result of a contract of cooperation and of a division of labor; it is itself the first of the *opera humana*, even if the principle of it is the infinity animating every individual. From a theological schema giving special emphasis to sexual difference, thought passes to a model of political economy, beneath the sign of a production: a community is constructed on the basis of voluntary actions, differentiated or contrary, but coexisting and coordinated. This model subtended the arrangements of representation and cooperation presented just prior to this by *De concordantia catholica*. It is "modern" by its individualist postulate and by its pro-productive perspective, though it is traditional by its theological or mystical foundation, a "seeding" of infinity in each and all.

The style of this cooperation already traces out the form that speech receives when at last it comes forth: a dialogue, the form given to the majority of Cusa's works. It presupposes the irreducibility of each interlocutor in relation to another: lacking common vision, the one must believe the other. The protocol of a verbal agreement between them is made up of successive (but contrary and reciprocal) acts, ordered for the production of a common sentence. The text resumes them in a *"canonic" conversation*, a temporal series, as if it presented a juridical formalization of conversational procedures: the *interrogatio*, the *revelatio* (deposition and revelation made by the witness-interlocutor), the *auditio*, (as much a listening as an audition), and the assent (*credere*) making it possible to "grasp" (*capere*) what one cannot see. At the end, the experience of the look consists in believing without seeing, therefore in living in society, in "understanding one another" (see figure 3).

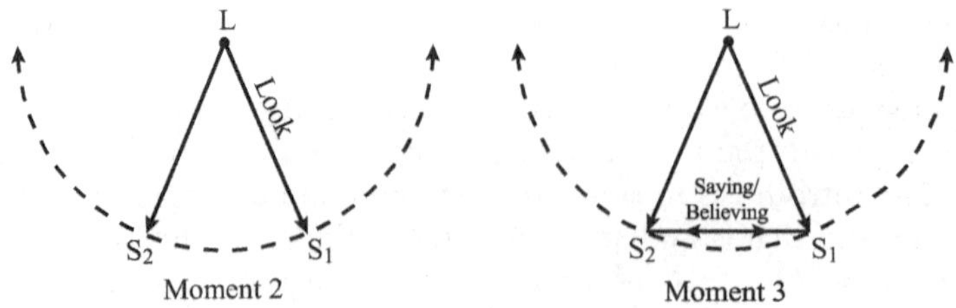

Figure 3. From seeing to believing: saying. The look is for each observer, at moment 2, what believing is between them at moment 3.

The conclusion is abrupt. Being looked at has as its only adequate language the *ex auditu*, that is, what it learns or understands of an other.

In the course of the third moment of the exercise, how did we pass from the *not-knowing* that marks the beginning of it to the *knowing* that is the end of it? This passage is accomplished first by a transposition of the not-knowing/knowing relation to a relation between an initial astonishment ("I don't believe my eyes about it") and a final assent ("I believe what the other says about it"). On this basis, a few elements are decisive.

1. A *will* marks the threshold of an access to a regimen of operations that is other, achieved by several and no longer alone; it makes possible a qualitative change of space, by allowing the introduction of a social field into the visual one. "I want to experiment," "I want to do more," or "I want to go to the very end": these possible transcriptions of *volens experiri* replace the present status of "knowing" with a "wanting to know"; they refer a state of knowledge to the *desire* that is its mainspring; they appeal to the fundamental dynamics that, at the very root of knowing, joins the desire to know (I want to know) with the courage to do (I want to do). To manifest the ethical (or ascetic, or "spiritual") movement that supports a quest, this first element already prepares the form of active hospitality that "believing" will be. It is no longer stupor that responds to the look, but desire.

2. A *torsion between doing and saying* characterizes the site induced by this "wanting the other." The scene of this third moment consists, for the partners, in each one *doing the opposite* of the other (inverse trajectories) and in *saying* to the other afterward the *same thing* ("You too?" "Yes"). The "doing" falls under a contradictory plurality; the "saying," under a unifying coincidence. In the mode of a temporal communication (and no longer just spatial trajectories), we return to the torsion that in the second moment was created by the relation

between the movements of the landscape crossed by traveling eyes and the immanence of the same look in all these trajectories. There is no more reducibility of the "doing" to the "saying" than there is of these movements back to the one and only that haunts them: in these two spheres of operations, the plural ("all and each") is not deleted by the "one." In the social space, the "doing" is to the "saying" what, in the visual space, the eyes are to the look, so that within human relations, "saying" has a function that is analogous to the look.

3. "The look speaks." From the start, Cusa introduces the question of the other, the blind spot of the sight that grasps objects. This look that fixes on him and follows him everywhere is for the supposed observer an interrogation without answer: "So what does he want from me?" No visible or imaginable object can be put in the place of this question. The look annihilates all position that would ensure the traveler a negotiable, autonomous, and protective shelter, an individual and objective "home." Fundamentally, the look *is a saying* that organizes the whole space. "Your look speaks," comments Nicholas of Cusa.[76] It is *enunciative.* But no one knows or can know *what* it means. Nothing articulates or distributes in "articles" and in thinkable objects this unknown will.

To this enunciative conception of the icon, we could find antecedents among medieval esthetic theories[77] or sources in Ockhamist philosophy, which removes from discourse "absolute Power" and the divine will, for which there is no possible veridiction. Whatever the case may be, the all-seeing icon grounds the distinction between an *operator-sign*, the index of a will detached from all effectual place or all "substrate," and *object-signs*, visible images lodged within the landscape. It institutes the question of the subject by an alogical look, or by an absolute wanting that "makes a hole" in representation.[78]

4. The look is inscribed in discourse and in sociality by *a "believing."* Without body and without place, it "drives one mad." But the Cusan exercise, in its last stage, gives the look an appropriate dialogical and social body thanks to the communication whose essential mainspring is a relation of subject to subject: if you do not believe in the other, you remain in the impossible and the insane. Believing corresponds, between the interlocutors, to what the look is for each one of them. Their contradiction is irreducible since every walk bears within itself the solitary secret of its relation to the infinite. No exchangeable element can pass from one to the other. No transformation code can, as with a monetary system, contain their particular exchange with a general system of equivalency. What each can say, qua subject haunted by a look, cannot be seen by the other, but only believed. Thus it would be with a love, or a madness.

The adherence to the "saying" of partners multiplies the relation each one has alone with the look. It articulates it in reciprocal enunciative experiences. In this respect, belief *socializes the insane.* The "madness" of the look becomes a (quasi-)body; yet it is not thereby made controllable, but generative of exchanges that set the initial stupor in movement and metamorphose the solitary *admiratio* into the productive work of a group. Belief is therefore the moment, to be repeated indefinitely, by which the madness of the look is transformed into discourse and history.

3. THE CIRCULAR DISCOURSE: "ALL AND EACH AT THE SAME TIME"

From the preface to the twenty-five chapters of the treatise, there is also the transition from a "doing" to a "saying," from a common exercise to a discourse that demands to be believed by its addressees. But a more brutal dichotomy marks this transition. The scene of "sensible experimentation" closes with the reminder that its status is but the putting in play of an "appearance." "Praxis" is of the order of the "appearance," and therefore separated from the discourse that states the "truth." It falls into the category of an optical illusion, whose effects, techniques of production (for example, the face painted in three-quarter view, etc.), and probably psychological aspects ("we always assume someone is watching us") are well known to contemporaries.[79] Even if the fictive nature of this framework permitted an operation already similar to the "imaginary actions" or, as Ernst Mach would say, the "thought experiments" carried out by sixteenth- and seventeenth-century scientists, consisting, in the absence of the technical means of experimentation and instrumentation, in imagining conditions of perfect isolation for the elements under consideration,[80] a transfer needs to be made, from the "semblance" characterizing the theater of the look, to the "truth" that discourse must express. This transfer takes place, globally, thanks to two transformations of place. On the one hand, the didactic text of the preface (a kind of manual), addressed to the actors of Tegernsee and supplying stage set instructions, is replaced by a meditative text (a "soliloquy," as the addressees will say),[81] addressed to God and going through the cycle of the Christian mysteries. On the other hand, the anonymous, faceless look of the painting (*who* is it? we don't know) is replaced by the proper names of a theology (God, Jesus, etc.), and therefore the polysemy of an ungraspable figure, by the linguistic determination of a referential. While the preface leads to the act of believing, the succeeding chapters specify what must be believed, and how. The articulation of these two parts and the relation of the second to the first will finally reveal the Cusan conception of "seeing." I will discuss only a few elements of it here.

"SUITABILITY"

The discontinuity separating "praxis" and theory does not exclude a *convenance* (suitability) between them, but a *convenance* of a particular kind, that designates, in the Cusan vocabulary, the fact of "coming with," of "going together" (*convenire*), or of "occurring at the same time" (*simul*), which is connected, beyond a spatial metaphor of coexistence or conjunction, with the concept of the "coincidence of opposites." This suitability intervenes in the text at two strategic moments intended to clarify the relation of the preface to the subsequent discourse: the first time, at the beginning of the preface, after the "foreword" that defined the object of the treatise, to ensure the transition from "divine things" to "human" painting ("I have found nothing more suitable . . . ," etc.); the second time, at the beginning of the first chapter, to ensure the return of "appearances" to the statement of "truth" (the "property of seeing at once all and each . . . cannot truly befit the Truth less than it apparently befits the icon, or appearance"). In the two opposite directions—from the divine to the human, and from appearances to truth—the transition is accomplished in the name of suitability. The latter is accompanied by an absence of proportion (an "incomparability," chap. 1). It does not designate a homology and does not refer to an ontological analogy (the *analogia entis*). It rather falls under the category of a *proximology*, in the sense in which Nicholas of Cusa spoke of "a scintillating proximity" of mathematics in relation to the true. In keeping with this typically Cusan move, this suitability is designated by a comparative: one element is more or less "suitable" to another, becomes more or less close to it, up to an unthinkable "maximum" that therefore offers no stable point in a hierarchization, and in which they coincide. The terms *approach*, more or less, *without resembling each other:* thus the polygon and the circle, the straight line and the curve, or the two interlocutors in the exercise. Suitability is treated as a relation between positions, a kind of topology in which the comparative rules the "comparison."

The approximation—be it in suitability or comparison—between the painting's look and that of God is clarified, at the opening of the first chapter, by a very elliptic *praesupponendum* (a flash) that nonetheless aims at defining the function of "true" discourse.[82] "In the first place, I think we must presuppose the following," writes Nicholas of Cusa:

"nothing appears in the painting's sight that is not *truer* (*verius*) in God's true (*verus*) sight." The "apparent" and the "true," the observable phenomenon and invisible existence constitute two levels of being with neither proportion nor resemblance to one another, but "in" the one as "in" the other there is a remarkable "property" (or *perfectio*), the coincidence between all and each—*simul omnia et singula*—which it is "truer" (a category relative to veridiction) to assert of existence than of the phenomenon. Even though, by a play on words characteristic of Cusan alacrity, in the same sentence, the same term (*verus*) receives in turn an ontological value ("veritable") and an epistemological one ("truer"), the thought is clear: it is in the name of the remarkable property demonstrated by each (like the interlocutors of the exercise) that two dissimilar levels of being (the apparent and the existent) come together. But by contrast with the two interlocutors—who represent two heteronomous points of view, but of the same level, neither being consequently "more true" than the other—here the comparative attributed to veridiction refers to a movement of thought that in Nicholas of Cusa takes an essentially mathematical form and is inscribed within a philosophical tradition to which Anselm's "argument" (belatedly considered to be "ontological") already bears witness: a property (or *perfectio*) is all the *more true* the more it *disappears*; the more it escapes vision (that of the eyes, and then even of the intelligence), the more it approaches the "true," so that it is ultimately in a blind bedazzlement of the eyes of the body and of reason—at a point in which the visible vanishes—that it can be the object of a *truth-saying* identical with a nonseeing or a *believing*.

Suitability increases with invisibility. It concerns the resurgence of the same property at two different levels, of which "we must presuppose" that one, less visible, is truer than the other. Experimentation is therefore not the basis of an induction, or the proof or verification of a property. It only causes to appear that which a different "view" allows us to recognize in it. Consider, in geometry, a remarkable property, for example that the sum of the angles of a right triangle is equal to two right angles (a property that can be extended to all sorts of polygons, as has been demonstrated by Georges Bouligand): suitability founds the relation of various concrete representations (or figures) to one another and with the statement of the property; moreover, it defines what the design of a particular figure will also make perceivable by the eye. In the Cusan text, the "property" that the exercise of the preface has "isolated" in an artificial and experimental mode has this double function: it links two disproportionate orders, "sensible" *perception* (*apparenter*) and the "true" (*veraciter*) statement; it defines, as simultaneity between *all and each*, the *formal relation* that is made to appear by that exercise.

In this respect, "seeing" already assumes two meanings. First, to see is to *recognize suitability*, that is, to reveal *one* same thing in *several* heterogeneous places. This first view tends toward another one. For, fundamentally, seeing is the act by which *singularity coincides with the totality*, that is, the very property peculiar to the look. This seeing is "truer"—more sayable—of God, even if (or rather: to the very extent that) it is still less thinkable. "Indeed," the text adds, taking up an etymology dear to Nicholas of Cusa and borrowed from Dionysius the Areopagite (*theos*, "god," supposedly derived from Greek *theōrō*, "I see"),[83] "God is called *theos* because he sees all"—*all and each* at the same time.

The Visible and the Sayable

Subtly, the text plays on three elements: the figure, the statement, and the property. The first is visible; the second is true; the third is not thinkable. The figure makes visible the geometrical relation of the point (or the center) to the circumference—a constant reference of Cusan reflection and the foundation of the scenic construction presented in the preface. The true statement declares the property, simultaneity of "one" and "all." In sum, what is *seen* as the relation of the center to the circumference is *said* as the relation of one to all. But this relation itself, alogical, cannot be thought. It escapes both visual perception and rational discourse.

In other words, the true *statement* is not the truth; it is only a positivity—true, yes, but that we must be able to "see" in order to accede to the truth. A special practice, which Nicholas of Cusa calls "seeing," is the only one that will make it possible to transform the visible figure or the true statement into "mystic theology." The procedure he uses consists in a *mutual referral* of visual perception to the true statement and vice versa, in such a way that they are led to a point of coincidence that in no way diminishes the difference or contradiction between them. If the exercise ultimately transforms circulation within the visible into a dialogical exchange—or the travels of the eye into belief in response to a word—conversely discourse, once begun on the basis of a caesura separating it from the appearance, incessantly returns to the "icon,"[84] in keeping with the declaration of the *Theological Complement*: "These theological matters are better seen with the mind's eye than they can be expressed in words."[85] In itself, the statement of the true is no more the truth of the image than the image is the truth of discourse. What matters is rather the movement by which they "fit together," like two different points of view, or like two actors, in a coincidence without positivity, that cannot be "held" in any visible or sayable place.

We could probably add, on this difference between them, that the visible gives the *form* (the point—the circumference) of which the sayable indicates the *level* (it is neither "sensible," nor localizable). In this respect, to return to a style of thought customary to the Cusan (A is to B as C is to D), and current among the *calculatores* of the time, the figure is to the structure as the discourse is to the symbolic. But that is not the main thing. The essential is played out in the *encounter*, or in the coincidence, between the visible and the sayable, in a way that makes them "testify" to what is neither seen nor known, in the same way the actors of the exercise, stripped of any owned object that they could exchange, must believe one another: "You too?" "Yes."

The combination of the preface (sensible experimentation) with the twenty-five subsequent chapters (the discourse of truth) thus constitutes a scene that is analogous to the one that the third moment of the exercise organized. In the treatise, *the juncture* between its visual moment (a doing) and its discursive one (a saying), characterized by "suitability," is *the effect of the look* to which they attest differently. Like the two observers of the painting, these two "parts" of the text form, by their encounter, the discourse of a look that "follows" them everywhere; they "form a tableau vivant" in relation to this "one" who does not leave them throughout their own, opposite procedures. The gap separating them traces out the flash, the *Blitz* of this look. It *is* not the look itself, which has no place, but its textual effect, a literary equivalent of belief: a presence of absence, the "hole" of the operator.

The Discourse of Coincidence, or Metonymy

This encounter already brings into view how Nicholas of Cusa constructs a "mystic" theology, that is, a discourse organized by a look. It assumes that there is suitability between two systems of expression that go in opposite directions, and that could be represented by the two sides of a right triangle, the vertex of which would be the "hole" of the text, as shown in figure 4.

These two systems of expression, one in the mode of the observable phenomenon (*apparenter*) and the other in that of the true statement (*veraciter*), are mirrors of the same look. Therefore there must be in the discourse as well something corresponding to the torsion generated by the look in visual experimentation. In the field of this look, the succession of true statements can no more be limited to the linearity of a rational order than can observation be limited to the coherence of a

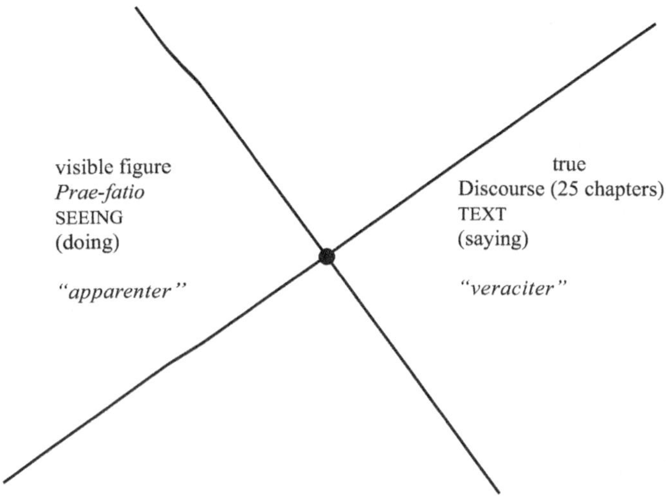

Figure 4. The intersection of the visible and the discursive.

visual plan. Indeed, as the observer sees without seeing (he feels looked at), the interlocutor of the chapters says without saying (he speaks in the place of the other). Relative to a *practice* of discursive space, that is, in the very way of situating oneself in the discourse, a *torsion of the text* involves its enunciation: *Who* speaks, and how? I will retain only the focal point, the functioning of the "I" (ego) throughout these twenty-five chapters.

From the first to the last, they are written in the first person. Hence they have been understood as a "soliloquy," a solitary meditation, a prayer addressed to God. But this "I" is not the same person: it changes along the way. The three first chapters introduce the characters of a pedagogical scene: entries of "I," the teacher (chap. 1), of "you," the disciple (chap. 2, it being no longer the plural "you" [*vos*] of the preface), and of "we" men (chap. 3). It is still a question of theoretical postulates and practical preambles of "truth saying." Chapter 4 switches over. After a brief reminder on experimentation, still addressed to "you, brother," the first paragraph suddenly switches to: "and you . . . will say: O Lord . . . in this image of *you* . . . if *you* do not desert *me*," etc. Then begins the "truth saying," which will be entirely a quotation from the other. Henceforth, and down to the last line of the treatise, "I" is the addressee, and "you" is God. The "soliloquy" is assumed to be a statement by the brother, who is assumed to be addressing the true Seer. We have one *ego* in place of the other. The "true" discourse is entirely conducted by this fictive "I." It also, therefore, is the putting into play of an "appearance" and falls into the category of an enunciative illusion, in the same way that "praxis" was the development of an optical illusion.

To be sure, the author lends this *ego* who replaces him memories or feelings that are his own, for example his experience as an orator, his impressions in the mountains of Brixen or among the trees, his meditation before the clock, etc. But the same is true in all fiction, and the exercise of the preface also had an autobiographical aspect. The problem involves the status of a "true" discourse (statements) in which the interlocutor is "apparent" (enunciation). The work of Nicholas of Cusa arguably presents a number of prior examples of this way of speaking in the place of another, from the very use of the language (German speaking in Latin) to the structure of those many dialogues or "trilogues" (*trialogi*) in which, as in the *Idiotus*, "the other," the "profane," speaks the "truth" to the "philosopher," and in which, consequently, the author speaks in the position of his addressee.

A biographical element exacerbates this paradoxical situation. It concerns mystic theology, whose "ready accessibility" the foreword of *De icona* claims to seek to explain. In writing on 22 September 1452 to Gaspard Aindorffer, whom he met in Tegernsee on the preceding first and second of June, and telling him about the treatise he was soon to write, Nicholas of Cusa confides that he himself has not had the mystic experience. "Someone can indeed show others the path he knows to be true thanks to received teaching (*ex auditu*), even if he has not himself traveled the path. But more certain is one who has seen it (*visu*) for having taken it. As for me (*ego*), if I write or say something about it, it will be the less certain for my never having tasted (*gustavi*) how sweet the Lord is."[86] The allusion is clear: the biblical quotation to which it refers is the traditional designation of mystic experience: *Gustate et videte quoniam suavis est Dominus.*[87] He repeats it, moreover, in *De icona* itself, where, to show the identity between "seeing" and "tasting," he describes precisely what he has not experienced personally: "To taste of your sweetness is to apprehend the sweetness (*suavitas*) of all delights—to apprehend it in its own beginning and by experiential contact (*experimentali contactu*)."[88]

The autobiographical "I" of the letter *limits* itself to a particular place, it *depends* on others to reach the true (*ex auditu*), and it is *separated* from the *gustus* that would create both the "delectation" of the subject and the "certainty" of his discourse. The "I" of the treatise, on the contrary, speaking from a fictive place that is neither his own nor that of his addressee, can believe/cause to believe that he *is saying the same thing* as the interlocutor, a discourse that is "true" for both, including when he describes the "paradise" in which he finds certainty and delight: "I begin to behold you unveiledly and to enter unto the garden of delights."[89] The first *ego* is linked to a story, the "paths" of which diverge and separate, when they do not contradict one another; it belongs to the domain of disjunction (*disjunctive*), which is that of *doing*. The second *ego* is lodged in the non-place of statements about what an interlocutor can believe but not see of the other, and thanks to that belief that declares itself in the name of the other, it speaks of the "look" that generates opposite trajectories; it announces itself in the name of a conjunction (*copulative*), or rather of a coincidence in *one* center that is "everywhere and nowhere." It specifies the field of *saying* itself. The first one is narrative; it belongs to the *relatio*; it relates singular journeys, situations of dependency, and stories of separation. The second is "mystical"; it characterizes the "fable," that "saying" of belief that makes a "suitability" possible.

A similarity with the mathematical "model" is probably unavoidable: Who is the *ego* who speaks in a geometrical demonstration? But even more instructive, in order to grasp the interrelation of the two *egos* in "theosophical mysticism,"[90] is the way Cusa relates his experience of the "gift from on high" at the end of *De docta ignorantia*. Like the *revelatio relatoris* of the partner in the exercise, his personal testimony on the look is located at a crossroads, at the moment when, the treatise finally completed (*Deus . . . qui est in saecula benedictus. Amen*), the author seems to make a three-quarter turn to address the Roman cardinal Giuliano Cesarini, his former "master," three years his senior, a lawyer trained like himself in Padua, also a legate in Bohemia, emissary to the Hussites, also present at the Council of Basel over which he presided, a conciliarist converted to papal primacy like Cusa and like him involved in the union of the Greek and Latin churches in Florence.[91] The "gift from on high," mentioned in passing in that *peroratio* which serves as an insert and envoi to *De docta ignorantia*, is not presented as a "vision," and even less as a "taste." As Cusa repeats in several personal texts (his *Apologia*, for example, or in writing to Gaspard Aindorffer),[92] it is a "concept" (*conceptus*) or a transcendental "principle"—"learned ignorance"—that makes thinking possible without itself being thinkable and that, in keeping with Cusan epistemology, remains a production of the mind, but a "generation" by which the mind produces on the outside the intimate surprise of its own infinite movement, just as the interlocutor of the exercise expressed the shock of his solitary trajectory by a look: "Yes, me too."

This concept can be identified with neither of the opposites whose coincidence he posits outside all rational grasp but in the mind. Inaccessible by "the various paths of the doctrines," it makes it possible to hold their "co-localization" in a point that escapes all intellectual localization. It resembles the site—maritime—of its occurrence: a concept from between two worlds, the eastern and the western, it is the meeting of two opposite histories, each of which accedes to the concept only by the belief in what the other says of itself: a look does not leave me; me neither. It was in 1438, two years before the completion of the treatise. At sea, returning "from the land of the Greeks" with the *Basileus* and the Patriarch of Constantinople for the purpose of a "synod" with the Pope of Rome in Florence, Nicholas of Cusa receives the concept of what the "meeting" of these two long, alien traditions of the same Spirit can be, if on either side one believes what the witness of the other side says about his own history.

At the beginning of *De docta ignorantia*, the dedication, which is also an insert [*hors-texte*], is the counterpart of the final address. It, too, is devoted to a meeting, this time concerning not the west and the east, but "the German" (*Germanus*) with his "wild extravagance" (*barbaras ineptias*) and his "perhaps totally extravagant concept" (*fortassis ineptissimum conceptum*), and on the other hand Giuliano, a cardinal of Rome, a distinguished Latinist and even a Hellenist: Cusa hopes that the "astonishment" (*admiratio*) that is the "source of philosophy" will enable the Roman to "believe" in "something" that "secretly lives in" (*latitare*) the philosophical approach of "the German."[93] In the rhetorical register of the "dedication to the prince," we have here a different variant of the movement itself that, at the other end of the treatise, concerns this concept received at sea.

The important thing, here, is not the assemblage of biographical data, but the homology of gestures that, in very different historical, literary, or speculative modes, permit us to recognize the style of a single way of thinking. In this connection, the dedication to Giuliano Cesarini is comparable to the letter to G. Aindorffer, although the one contrasts the Roman humanist to the "barbaric" German, and the other places the intellectual formed by teaching (*auditus*) at a distance from the Benedictine who has gone through the *schola affectus* (pathway of *gustus*). The explanation of what separates two positions allows each to express its truth in the name of the word of the other. This procedure, presented in the microlaboratory of an exercise, is also valid for the meeting of Byzantium and Rome, and toward the end of his life, in the *Cribratio Alchorani* (The Sifting, or critical examination, of the Qur'an, 1461), Cusa extends it beyond the borders of Christianity to a confrontation between Islam and Christianity, where, after an im-

Table 1. The conceptual mapping of the coincidence of the one and the other in discourse.

	The One	The mark of coincidence in the discourse	The Other
De concordantia,			
dedication	German language →	believing	← Latin language
De icona,			
structure	the visible phenomenon →	the saying	← true statement
exercise, time 3	one-way trajectory →	of the other	← opposite trajectories
discourse	the biographical "I" →		← the addressee
De docta ignorantia,			
dedication	the "barbaric" German →	speaking in the name	← the Roman humanist
peroration	the Christian West →	of what one believes	← the Christian East
Cribratio Alchorani	Christianity →	of the other	← Islam

passioned search for the sources and witnesses, he himself brings the Muslim to expression. Here again, coincidence is not similitude, or assimilation; it assumes a "contradiction" between religions from which each receives the understanding of its own relation to the infinite in believing the testimony of the other.

The cases already encountered may be assembled and their "conceptual" coherence shown in table 1.

Everywhere the coincidence between "the one" and "the other" is marked by an empty place that is at once, in each person, the point of disappearance of his procedure (a "surprise," a "hole") and, between them, the caesura of a "believing." The discourse of the "concept" or of the coincidence is constructed on the basis of that empty place. It pushes into a particular "path" what the belief in the other introduces. *Mystics* (the fable of saying) converts the "narrative" (the "relation" of the operations proper to a path). From this angle, the fictive "I" of the treatise is the inscription, in the text, of what a belief changes in the understanding of the itinerary peculiar to the biographical "I." This is not an eclecticism, as if to give adequate attention to the other it sufficed to introduce a few *additional* statements, namely his, in one's own discourse; as if coincidence were on the order of an addition or an (interminable) acquisition, and obeyed the logic of the "also." It gets played out in a believing, that is, in a relation *from subject to subject*, the one irreducible to the other. It brings *enunciation* into question, which is central to belief, a relation between interlocutors and not between statements.[94] The "I" therefore has a strategic position in the discourse of coincidence. How is it possible to speak in the name of what I believe of the other? The fictive *ego* of the text answers that question. It is a *belief effect* in the position—or in the point of view—of the enunciating subject. It generates a new practice of the way peculiar to the author. More exactly, it represents in the text that effect of the look that is recourse to belief; it is the literary effect of that *effect of the look.*

The discursive or conceptual "I," then, is neither the autobiographical one of the letter to G. Aindorffer, nor that of the addressee. In strict terminology, it speaks not in the name of the other, but in the name of what it believes of the other. In this respect, Cusa remains faithful in his treatise to what he writes in his personal name to the abbot of Tegernsee. In his letter, does he not base "true" knowledge on the *ex auditu*—on what he has heard and believed? But for him, the *auditus* does not designate submission to the textual authorities or the statements of a privileged author (he reminded us of this apropos of J. Wenck);[95] it is a way of hearing and believing, in others, the testimony concerning the relationship of their ways with a "look." Then the *gustus* itself, which does not belong to the personal experience of the author, can probably be *ex auditu*, presented by the fictive *ego* of the treatise.

This conceptual or "speculative" functioning does not erase the rhetorical aspect of the procedure. The technique is a known one. Pascal will use it a lot, taking in charge, in his own discourse, the supposed statements of the other: "The eternal silence of these infinite spaces frightens me."[96] In itself, the art of "saying the other" has well-identified uses: it captures the engagement of the reader, who identifies with this "I"; he makes the text written in the name of this "I" who is an other the novel of the author and of his desire, etc. It is used in a number of genres, particularly in the fantasy novel, which focuses precisely on upsetting, with an uncanny third domain, the distribution of space into the real and the "imaginary."[97] We may also connect its ruses and virtuosities with the flowery developments of rhetoric during the fifteenth century. All this exists in Cusa, who has, moreover, a whole romanesque and fantastic side, although it is caught up in the rapidity of his speculative imagination. The problem does not present itself in terms of an alternative between theory and fiction ("either one or the other"), or in the form of a weak theory falling away into the "literary." It seems rather that the "coincidence" is the "concept" of the "saying one for the other" and that, since this procedure is fundamentally that of metonymy, what we have with his conceptual discourse is *a logic of metonymy.* Considered from this angle, the reflection initiated by coincidence is at once a "metonymic" theosophy and a theory of metonymy. Whatever the case may be with that question, which should be examined further, Cusa's discourse provides itself, by a rhetorical device, the means for *performing the operation* whose theory it *states* in terms of "learned ignorance," and for thus transforming writing itself into a conceptual practice.

Dialogical Circularity

The relation of *one to the other*, such as it appears in the exercise or in the discursive construction of *De icona*, has the (elementary) form of a dual relation: the first actor and the second, the author and the addressee; that is, *one* and *two*. In principle, it is possible to extend this model to the entire number series: 3, 4, 5, 6, etc. The text will proceed to that generalization, but a first difficulty arises. In its binary form, the ambiguity of the term "one" poses a problem of writing. Indeed, in Cusa's texts, the "one" designates either a unit that *belongs* to the number series and for which 2, 3, 4, etc., are the continuation (thus the first actor can be followed by a second, a third, etc.), or the principle that *generates* the series and that therefore "precedes the number"[98] (thus it is with the point, or the look, the generative center of the circumference). Nicholas of Cusa does not have two different signs to distinguish between these two positions, probably because in the fifteenth century he does not have at his disposal an adequate algebraic notation, and because he lacks a theory of zero (he mentions zero only with his conception of the "quasi-nothing" or "near-nothing" point).[99] This distinction, which is not written—he sees it, nevertheless, in geometry, as the relation between the center and the points of the circumference (see figure 5).

The term "other" has the same ambiguity. Either it is the second, in relation to a first point on the circumference; or it is the entire circumference in relation to the center that engenders it, in which case "we call *other* that which is not one,"[100] and "alterity," being opposed to unity,[101] designates "diversity," or yet again the state of what is distinct. As for the passage from the number 1 to the numbers 2, 3, 4, etc., the whole series remains "alterity" or "the other" in relation to the one (or the center). In a philosophy of the One, such as Cusa's (for whom the

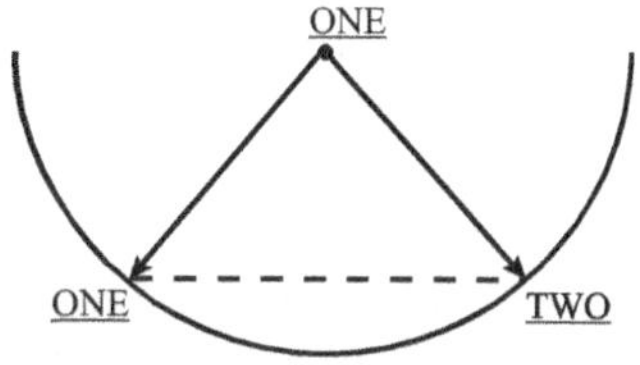

Figure 5. Geometrical representation of the relation of the one to the other(s).

One is superior to Being), the question is particularly important and refers, moreover, to an ancient tradition. Plotinus had already attempted to define the nonquantitative "one," which "does not reside in a multitude" and "is not a minimum."[102] Conversely, inscribing the "one" in a "common genre" and taking it to be "obvious" that "nothing can be said to be *one* and *unique* if we have not previously conceived of an other thing that matches the former," Spinoza was to write: "To say of God that he is *one* and *unique* shows that one does not have a true idea of him or that one is speaking improperly of him."[103] The ambiguity of the term, a dangerous coincidence between the two functions, prompts Cusa to make risky speculations. He would have needed, to denote the "one" qua principle, a sort of zero term, a symbol-index designating an absolute "delocalization" of the reference.[104] Language has its logic.

It is in relation to the "one" qua principle (*unitas*) that the dual relation of the one to the other can be generalized to an indefinite series placed beneath the sign of "alterity." A first example of it is given that will give us an idea of the method. It concerns the names that theology attributes to God. "The whole of theology is circular," or "formed in a circle" (*in circulo posita*), says Cusa, thus designating a form defined by "positions." Indeed, he adds, of these names "one is affirmed of the other" (*unum affirmatur de alio*).[105] The expression itself is ambiguous. It could mean: Unity is affirmed of everything that constitutes its alterity. The fact is that here "one" and "other" relate to the predicates attributed to God: "sight, hearing, smell, touch, feeling, reason, intelligence, and many other points of view (*rationes*) distinguished by the meaning of each word."[106] This list seems to put different degrees of being on the same level: the senses, reason, etc. In reality, it does not obey the order of an anthropological or ontological hierarchy. It follows the *semantic distribution* carried out by language, but it is for the purpose of an *operation* on these units. It corresponds to *a spatialization of meaning by language*. All these heterogeneous "points of view," distributed and separated in linguistic space, opposed to one another by the developments peculiar to each, must, by theology, be "affirmed by one another," according to the model that was valid for a dual relation (see figure 6).

Each of these points of view, irreducible to the others and unfolding in a process relative to the infinity that gives it life, has, then, a relation to the others that is homologous with that of the first actor to his partner, or of the author to his addressee. Comparable to the trajectory of an autonomous procedure, its own development (for example, in the perspective of "reason" or of "intelligence") has a relation with another development (for example, in the perspective of "taste" and of the "af-

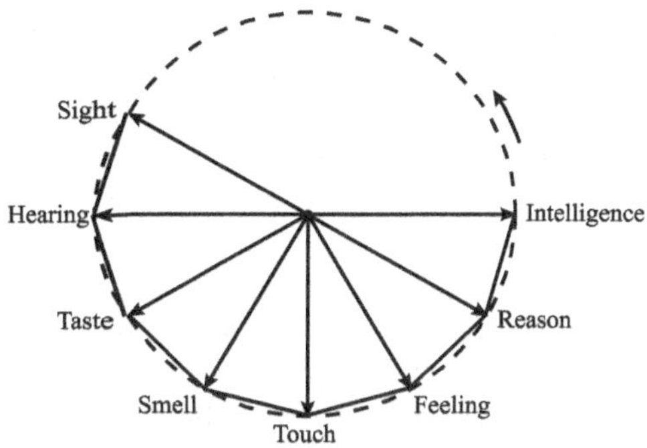

Figure 6. The circularity of theology.

fective") in exhuming from its movement the surprise that builds it and that can be "believed" or recognized by another position. It is in this sense that "one is affirmed by the other," or that each point of view follows its own logic, but in the name of what it believes of the others. The circulation, in becoming more general, keeps the initial dialogical form, the form of the type: "You too?" "Yes." As Nicholas of Cusa often said, this theology is not "negative," nor is it "apophantic": the particular point of view is not denied; it is changed from within, or rather revealed to itself, surrendered to the "impossible" that inhabits it, in recognizing that other ways are built on the same secret. This dialogical and transcendental process also defines, in Cusa, the form taken by his practice of translation (the passage from one system to another, or from one language to another), the method that inspires his interpretation of doctrines, of periods, or of different religions (passages from discursive or historical figures to other ones), or his idea of sociality.

Geometrically, the dialogical figure remains polygonal. The growth in the number of units and the extension of the "transfers" from one to another, however, by multiplying the angles, bring the polygon progressively closer to the form of a circle, which would ultimately be the totalization of the contradictories generated by the center. Does a "maximum," then, make it possible to pass the qualitative threshold separating the polygon from the circle? That would be a mathematical model for conceptualizing "the resolution of all in one." The squaring of the circle. The problem fascinated many minds of the day—painters like Piero della Francesca (who, in his *Flagellation*, contrasts the polygon of the pavement to the circular halo surrounding the face of the Christ figure),[107] every bit as much as mathematicians, Toscanelli, Regiomontanus, etc. Nicholas of Cusa treated it at length, and during the years he was writing *De icona*, he devoted two treatises to it, *De quadratura circuli* (1452) and *Caesarea circuli quadratura* (1457), which, incidentally, do not seem to have convinced the friends he sent them to—the great Florentine mathematician Paolo Toscanelli and, through him, the Austrian astronomer Georg Peurbach, who had once been well-known in Nuremberg.[108] In Cusa's view, "there must exist," in the geometrical order, a way to conceptualize a "circle made up of infinite angles," and thus to move from the angular to "the inangular," or from the straight line to the curve (the perfect *curvitas*).[109] Given "the bright-shining proximity" of mathematics to the true,[110] there must exist in geometry a demonstration that makes visible, in its "mirror," the immanence of the infinite in all parts of the finite. Temerity, but an "inventive" temerity, Moritz Cantor would later comment.[111] Once again, the mathematician and philosopher does not proceed by reasoning or induction; he starts out with a theoretical "excess" (also a kind of belief) from which he tries to develop results that are coherent with one another. The eyes do not lead to the look. It is the look that can find eyes.

Leaving aside the squaring of the circle, it will suffice to recognize the ideal and maximal geometrical form of the "concept" that constructs a "circular" discourse on the basis of opposing points equally testifying to the infinite. This circularity founds a discourse capable of "relating marvels (*enarre mirabilia*) the revelation of which surpasses any sensible, rational, or intellectual view."[112] A fictional program? "Relating" is punctuated by the breaks that "believing" introduces between the contradictory parts of the story, and these "empty spots" insinuate everywhere a look effect that changes the parts into "marvels" for one another. This discourse *relates a look*. By an incessant relation of each procedure to its "contraries," it ensures a becoming, and therefore the possibility of a story of the immanence of the infinite. The mystical is articulated in a narrative. A discursive *time* is given to the initial *stupor*.

Jean-Luc Godard used to say: "The image—that comes from the darkness of the ages."[113] For Nicholas of Cusa, making the contradictory moments that make up the image ("one and all at one time") coincide allows us to see that darkness of the depths of time come into the image. He calls it "cloud" (*caligo*), "dark shadows," unknowing.[114] Such is his mystic theology. But the climate that reigns in this speculation born of *admiratio* and aspired to by the dynamism of another day must bear a more "auroral" emblem. This theology is supported by a surprise that transforms time. In it, the *blitz*, the flash of the look, becomes duration. This discourse "relates" the saying of René Char:

"The flash remains with me." It is "easy" and comes of its own accord, or else it isn't.

"The Idiot"

In *De icona*, the exercise no more presents the position of the second actor than do the chapters envisage that of the addressee in the name of whom they speak. Does the second actor receive the testimony of the first and does he also succeed in "grasping that it is possible"? As for the "brothers" of Tegernsee, do they reciprocate by "listening to" the author and believing the text he sends them? Questions relative to the reception of the treatise. To the question that Cusa asks his addressees—and, in keeping with this own theosophy, he has no choice but to ask them: "You too?"—what answer did they give him and what repercussion does that reception have on his theory?

The debate that, from 1451 to 1460, brought about the writing and circulation of *De icona* can serve as a test. The passion-filled climate of adhesion or rejection is striking. We should probably take into account personal temperaments, the divisions of the times, and the aggressiveness fostered by instability. But the theory itself provokes these reactions. Cusa eludes all problematic of identity. He skirts "positive experience," whether it be erudite or affective, at which a method would stop: he "infinitizes" it by confronting it with other, contrary ones. Nor does he propose a new system: in the name of "learned ignorance," his conceptual operations bring out a "necessary impossible"[115] at the source of every doctrine. Except by way of the places to which the successive missions took him (but he never mentions them), he does not dispose of a stable situation that would give him, as their monastery did for monks, the postulate, the support, and the control of an institution of meaning: he is everywhere the foreigner, the emigrant, the diplomat—a passerby concerned about being "received." And his philosophy does not take for granted the tacit assurance of an order that would be its pillar; it must on the contrary itself take on the "dialogical" construction of a sociality that pertains, moreover, more to communication than to community. By all these aspects, it withdraws from its readers the possibility of an identification, it deprives them of a "safe" point of repair, at the very moment when the degradation of the medieval cosmos is everywhere giving rise to the institution of new social, political, and religious units in search of identity.

Thus it is not for no reason that he has hardly any "disciples,"[116] and that, much later, only a few original thinkers will be seduced at a distance by the stimulation afforded them by his work, such as Charles de Bovelles and Lefèvre d'Étaples during his first period, and Giordano Bruno.[117] Quick and brilliant though it may be, and perhaps because of its celerity, Cusan thought is baffling. It is never where we think it is. The enthusiasts set up places and arrange encounters with it in sites not its own. In Tegernsee, the *Laudatorium docte ignorancie*, written "with love" (*amorose affectus*) by Bernard of Waging in 1451, takes "learned ignorance," the "science of sciences," as the very experience, or the "mystic theology," of the Dionysian tradition—an excessive assimilation that the generous monk continues to maintain, nine years later, in his *Defensorium docte ignorancie* (1459).[118] Often Cusa tries to rectify. No, I am not here; no, I am not that. For example, in his letter to G. Aindorffer, apropos of the mystic "taste." The same holds true for adversaries—for example, the theologian from Heidelberg, Wenck, a convinced conciliarist, as firm in his ecclesiological convictions as he is precise in his professional techniques, and who, already suspecting treason in the conversion of his compatriot jurist to papal authority, catching a whiff of illuminism in that work, acknowledges no legitimate treatment of doctrinal texts in it.[119] No, answers Nicholas of Cusa . . . in vain. He does not succeed in getting rid of the foolishness accompanying the diffusion of his texts.

To this mathematically oriented theosophy that is so coherent, and even repetitive, in its *movement*, but that offers no *object* to the grasp, the response is ultimately hatred or love. It is too closely articulated on the question of the subject, and its style too "passing" and personal, not to get caught up itself in the relations *of subject to subject.* By its reception, the theory is, moreover, led back to what it continually says itself. Fundamentally, even though it is not to be believed (as would be a belief), only an act of *believing* makes it possible to *think* it. An excess without object, an "impossible" that can be "grasped" in itself only by believing it also of the other, is the point at which its own logical rigor has its origin. In the practice of reading, this "postulate of belief" is relative to the author, and it often takes the form of confidence or of suspicion with respect to him.

Characteristic, from this point of view, is the vindictive heat with which the Carthusian Vincent of Aggsbach attacks *De icona* in his *De mystica theologia* (1453) and in a text written against Cusa's apologists, particularly Bernard of Waging, *Impugnatorium Laudatorii* (1454). He blames Nicholas of Cusa, as he does Gerson, of "allying" (*concordare*, a very Cusan word) mystic theology with the "philosophers," thus ruining "the species or act of devotion" (*quedam species vel actus devocionis*) constituted by *mystics.*[120] He mixes everything up a bit, taking "coincidence" for a concordism, and the Cusan "intellectual movement" for the contemporary scholastic *ratio*. Nor is he sure how to define affective *mystics*, but he knows of what *place* he is. He is not wrong about what is at stake, the problematic of identity itself, when he revives the border ensuring the affective against the rational and when he defends the Carthusian tradition of the *schola affectus*, a region protected by the walls of the monastery. The *concordare* is hateful to him. The target is the Cusan gesture of "passing," even though it is treated in terms of content.

In short, the theory does not control its reception. It has the same fate as the divine "face" described by *De icona*: the scorner sees his scorn there; the lover, his love; the young, a youthful face; an old person, an elderly representation; the lion or the ox, a lionlike or oxlike image.[121] The work also becomes the mirror of his readers; it presents them with an object in keeping with what they expect or believe of it. This mobility betrays a weakness, in that the theory should impose itself on its own, in the same way that Spinoza wanted his *Ethics* to appear without him, without his name, without institutional backing, shining forth, like a jewel, by its truth. Paradoxically, the opposite fate befalls Cusa. The pendant of the ambiguity surrounding the work is the promotions granted the man: diplomatic missions, legations, cardinalship, and the general administration of the Papal States. In part, the fragility of the theory and the career success have a common reason: the subtle mobility, the inventive curiosity of the author.

Additionally, there is a greater contradiction in his professional activity. While his theory was conciliarist, his practice from 1437 on served the papacy. He supported the superiority of the council over the pope for reasons that have always remained fundamental. In 1433, in *De concordantia catholica* (especially in book 2, based on the juridical, Roman, and canonic idea of "consent" or *consensus*),[122] he makes "the people" the source for designating power, and election the regular procedure for filling all "presidentiality," including the papacy. "Indeed it is in the people," he writes, "that all powers (*potestates*), whether spiritual or temporal and corporeal, repose potentially (*in potentia latent*) . . ."[123] The necessity for a reform—a permanent conviction—and the creation of institutions guaranteeing the representation of the people coalesced into a theory that was coherent with the entire movement of the work. But under the circumstances of the moment, it was not acceptable. In participating in the Council of Basil, Cusa saw the vanity of the conciliarist project, paralyzed by endless internal quarrels. The assembly of Basel was no longer, in his view, a council *in concordia et consensu*. Then the turnaround occurred. He left for Ferrara, where he joined a minority supporting Eugene IV, and put himself in the service of the papal authority, the only and the last chance for a reform. By his work, he henceforth maintained the traditionalist conception, but a conception relative to the schisms internal to the Church and to the erosion of medieval Christianity.

"Radicalism in theory and conservatism in practice."[124] Despite the doctrinal adjustments it calls for, his activity takes directions contrary to those of the theory. The fact of the matter is, the pope becomes the "conjectural" and historical substitute for the conciliar Church for which the treatise presented the ideal—and ever ideal—model. Thus he is also the (historically absolute) criterion of administrative tasks that retain the religious meaning of being placed within the field of unity and of promoting it in a provisional, but possible, mode. As such, he provides a point of repair, a "center," for the wanderings of the diplomat/reformer. The theory continues to formulate a kind of divine politics, but the practice falls away from it to respond to the imperatives of the circumstances of the moment. The one become *utopian*, and the other *ethical*, even if they remain within the same religious horizon. From the *one* to the *other*, there is no coherence, or even a compromise that would find between the two something in common, but rather a coincidence of opposites of a new kind, escaping theory, which is only one of the end points, but remaining in conformity with the antimonies that Cusan reflection strives to conceptualize. In this relationship between theology and politics, the former becomes a "mystic" theology—a fundamental, founding speculation, but one that announces something fundamental only in the mode of marginalization and secrecy, or of a poetics dislodged from social reality. In this respect, Cusan theosophy articulates the theory of *failure*, that is, of a new, autonomous form of history, and that relationship probably defines the "modern" status of philosophy.

Theory, then, introduces rather a "madness" into practices. A madness marks theory from the beginning of the intellectual movement, not only in the stupor that is its origin, a blank, but in the threshold that makes its discourse possible. If you do not believe the other, as the preface said, you will not be able to grasp that it is possible. This condition, necessary in order to exit the initial mutism, is the folly that makes the theory possible. An irrational initiates the rational. Nicholas of Cusa dares to insist: "It is folly (*stultitia*), they assert, to believe that possible."[125] And he is able to recognize this folly not in an *object* to be believed, but in the very *act* of believing, which poses the possibility of thinking and which one might consider, in him, the *epistemological* form of an *ethical* act, that is, an act that does not depend on the possible. Therefore the "impossible" object of this believing ("You too?"

"Yes." "That's impossible!"), its statement, is but the inscription of that act in discourse; the object believed is *the metaphor of a metonymic act*, or of a change of space, of a displacement of order.

This act is played out not only in the relation of one to the other; it concerns equally all the others—the multitude. How? A Cusan story, one more of them, will suffice to show it. It is told at the beginning of the third book of *Idiota* (1450; Cusa is in Rome for the Jubilee).[126] A "famous philosopher" come from afar (from Trebizond?),[127] a character with a "pale face" and a "long toga," hence exotic and "wild" in the décor of the city, is standing motionless on the bridge of Rome in the middle of the crowd. He "is astonished at the passersby." A man of letters, an orator by profession, accosts him and asks "what reason holds him fixed (*fixus*) in this place." "Astonishment (*admiratio*), says he." Not at objects, but surprise itself. After a moment, he explains: "When I see innumerable populations in great haste come from nearly all latitudes, I am astonished that there is one faith for all in such a diversity of bodies." A personal memory of the Jubilee, that crowd of pilgrims on the Roman bridge, a veritable river, a Rhine of human beings. The surprise is the same one that immobilized the experimenters in painting: all and each one at the same time, witnesses of the "look," always the same. "As for me," the philosopher continues, "I have traveled the world continually and visited the sages" (in relation to the pilgrimage toward the sanctuary, these are travels in opposite directions), to become "more certain" that thought (*mens*) is "conjoined (*conjuncta*) to divine thought, but to this day I have not found through reason a light as perfect as this ignorant people have found through faith." The philosopher must *believe* of the multitude what he cannot *see*, to get out of his uncertainty and grasp that the coincidence of all and each in "one" (a look or a faith) is "possible." The "profane," or "idiot," who is carving out a wooden spoon in a stall in the neighborhood will explain it to him. Thus, *to believe in the saying of the others* is what gives access to *a thought of the One*. That initial folly makes the theory possible. Conversely, that theory is affected, and its social functioning determined, by the folly that authorizes it in the name of a belief in the crowd. The echo of others brought by the testimony of the crowd to the intimate experience of each person, an oceanic rumor of the "me too," changes, to be sure, the private hallucination into a thought of the infinite, but it is not "visible," it is only "audible"; and thus that thought, returned to its own infinite by what it believes of others, has as discourse a theoretical utopia (or an "atopia") separate from the historical "positivities" in which it nonetheless traces out the folly of which it is born.

In the fantastic of *De icona*, there was already a suggestion that Cusan theosophy is ultimately the discourse of a folly. But the whole work, as we consider it from one end to the other, brings out the strange consciousness that the author has of a folly with which he punctuates his texts, as if anticipating an absolute refusal of them. I will limit myself here to revisiting the texts we have already met. In addressing *De docta ignorantia* to Cardinal Cesarini, he insists on the "ineptitudes" of its "barbaric" language and the "completely eccentric" nature of its very "concept." To the readers of *De concordantia catholica*, he stresses the "uneducated" and wild style of his treatise. To Gaspard Aindorffer, the addressee of *De icona*, he points out that he does not have the experience (the *gustus*) that would merit his text's being considered "certain" and accredited in the Tegernsee monastery. Nor do I think that we can view solely as a pedagogical technique or reduce to the personage of the nonspecialist (the "profane" and the unlettered) the "idiot" (*pauper idiota*)[128] in whose name Cusa exposes his own thought in the *trialogus* of the *Idiota*—a work so inseparable from references (primarily Rhenish) to the fools for Christ and the illumination of the illiterate.[129] The text, by all the indications strewn throughout, narrates its relation to a center of darkness circumscribed by an inability, a deficit, a madness.

This black sun haunts the discourse, the solitary experience of a voyager's look. A striking detail: in the preface in which he brings it on stage, Cusa recognizes in this look the flash ("at once all and each one") that does not cease being his own surprise. What he "sees" is his own madness, is himself. Or rather, as he explains apropos of this "preexisting" (*antecedens*) look,[130] it is itself but an "image" (*imago*) of that "model" (*exemplar*). It is the space this folly allots itself in him. His mind is but the mirror in which it appears. To this experience that imposes itself—"easy," but impossible, unthinkable—he seeks, his whole life through, "respondents" who, walking in ways opposite his own, would make it "apprehensible" to him. Hence in a work placed beneath the sign of "ease," he prides himself on only one thing, in his prefaces or his letters: his "immense labor," from archive to archive, from observation to observation, from doctrine to doctrine, or from mission to mission, to "hear" the word of other witnesses, and thus try to open up a trail for that madness in history.

Chapter Two

The Poem and Its Prose

In considering how, in John of the Cross, the poem is coordinated with its prose commentary, I do not concern myself directly with the problem (a classical one) of interpretation; rather I focus on the relations between two discourses, one of which illustrates the opening of a space to beauty (*hermosura*) and the other of which relates to a suffering of history. To begin with, a biographical image may designate the question from a distance: the contrast between the first *canciones* or "canticles" of the *Spiritual Canticle* and the site of their birth, the dungeon of the convent of Toledo in which John of the Cross was placed in solitary confinement from December 1577 to August 1578. Between the glorious body that is the poem and the suffering body of the prisoner, what is the relationship? It organizes the writing of John of the Cross as an exchange between song and history.

With the exception of certain isolated poems, the *Aphorisms*, and the letters, his works are indeed divided from top to bottom into two heterogeneous "halves": the *canciones* (or poems) and the *declaraciones* (or explanations in treatise form). These two discourses, like the two halves of the hermaphrodite described in Plato's *Symposium*, reflect one another: they seek, call out to, mutually change, and embrace one another. The separation that distinguishes them establishes strange links between them. Neither excludes the other, nor is either "the truth" of the work. Their differentiation, a rift between them, initiates a dynamics whose law might be expressed: not one without the other. The operation of the writing brings a dialectic of poetic ecstasy and of historical discursiveness into play. This dialogical structure organizes a creative tension between the adventures of a song and the stages of an ascesis, or between the gift of a spoken Word and a work of the negative. Beauty and suffering thus maintain one another,[1] but a Beauty transformed by suffering and a suffering received and transformed by Beauty.

My hypothesis consists in recognizing in this literary operation the implementation of a historicity, a way that is peculiar to it of articulating time with what escapes it, and hence, ultimately, of thinking time. In other words, the relations between the poem and its prose, in John of the Cross, manifest the formality of a history; on the scriptural stage circumscribed by the text, they produce a model of "spiritual history"—if we understand by this term the relation that a history maintains with "what speaks," that is, with "the Spirit."

1. THE POETIC BEGINNING
Suddenly, the Word

The entire work of John of the Cross as we know it,[2] that is, without the texts he wrote before 1577 and that were destroyed (perhaps when he was imprisoned), has as its point of departure a cry:

> ¿A donde te escondiste
> Amado y me dejaste con gemido?[3]

> Whither hast thou hidden thyself,
> And hast left me, O Beloved, to my sighing?

The *Obras* begin with these two verses. In the beginning, there is what Louis Massignon named "the given word."[4] A Saying advenes suddenly (*repente*), transforming the poet into the "son" of that word. A genealogy is inaugurated with "the symbolic filiation to an unknown creator," the condition of poetic creation.[5] In the seventeenth century, Angelus Silesius's desire for it uplifted and deflated his poetry as its most intense ebb and flow; unfulfilled hopes cradled that night watchman, vigilant to all melodies that might transform him into the "son" of a Word. Silesius was no longer certain of that passing (or past) voice. In him there already resounded the "viduity" [emptiness] that today haunts Dominique Rouche:

Qu'ai-je été, en ces tremblements pâles et conséquents: qu'attente et viduité sans nom?
Rien sinon rien, office d'Un manquant à la lettre. Songe
Et cela qu'encore j'ai pu dire, ou Dire, s'effacera comme le reste,
Qu'il m'arrive d'énoncer quelque fois. En l'Extase.[6]

In John of the Cross, on the contrary, a certainty lives. At the beginning of poetry, there is that which speaks without reason. A melody "gives body to the advent of a measure."[7] It happens between night and day, before the hour of work:

En par de los levantes del aurora
La música callada.[8]
At the time of the rising of the dawn,
The silent music.

Poetry is what nothing authorizes, neither the order of a signified, nor the referent of a reality. The poet obeys an inaugural nomination of which he becomes the speaker. He "belongs to the task for which he is needed." He makes the passage to that "occurrence of an . . . arrival"[9] that is stolen from time. The voice creates that for which it gives space. It is, for John of the Cross, "abundance and impetuosity" in "the saying" of the soul.[10] Similarly, Hölderlin echoes:

A stranger it comes
To us, that quickening word,
The voice that moulds and makes human.
Amazement then took hold of
The souls of all who were struck, and night
Obscured the eyes of the best men.[11]

The poet is abducted by this excess that names and is not nameable. He is "stricken" by what he plays.[12] Here we may mention the portrait Hieronymus Bosch painted of him in his *Garden of Delights*: the artist caught in his harp, his body transfixed by the strings, his arms raised in the sign of the cross. Is it ecstasy or torture? This Icarus transported, imprisoned, and transfixed by his musical instrument—John of the Cross also drew him as a flying crucified form, who falls like a dark bird nailed to the instrument of love and who "swoops down on us";[13] he has described it in the poem of the "little shepherd" (*pastorcico*) whose arms, intertwined with the tree he climbs to die, form with the branches the harp of his sorrows of love:

Y a cabo de un gran rato se ha encumbrado
sobre un Arbol do abrió sus brazos bellos
y muerto se ha quedado asido de ellos,
el pecho del amor muy lastimado.[14]

A long time passed: he climbed the branches of a tree
and spread his lovely arms, and dead lay hanging from his arms;
his heart was sorely hurt by love.

In these figures in which beauty does not separate from suffering, in which the Verb become poet unites in him the spoken word and violence, the origin of discourse shows itself first and foremost, analogous to the "rhapsodic beginning of thought" mentioned by Kant. The leitmotif of the *Cántico* (*salí*, "I went out," said the Bride) designates the poem itself, which comes out, a singular event. This birth, marked by history, is also the beginning of history: there is time only if there is beginning. No history without event. Therefore, far from standing in opposition to historicity, the irruption of a present imparts movement to this last—the same way that the enunciative act (at once model and small change of the poetic act) introduces a temporality into the language.[15] But this beginning is not thinkable in itself. It occurs suddenly, abruptly (*jählings*, says Hölderlin), one knows not whence, for no reason. The originary is related not to what precedes it, but to what it originates. "Poetry is not born: it engenders."[16] It is recognized by what it gives birth to.

The Becoming of the Beginning

The genesis of the poem has its own law. It does not consist in respecting a literary "genre" (symbolic, allegorical, etc.), that is, in following a semantic and cultural rule, which in itself is alien to the nature of the initial word. It attempts to "hold" the first music, to offer it various semantic fields and make them amenable to it, to allow it to haunt and to captivate a language by entering into it as would a dancer. The *Spiritual Canticle* will be the itinerary—journey and account—of the "silent music" in various places. It cannot be defined, as Jean Baruzi thought, by an "allegorical" imagery whose source would be less lofty than the "symbolism" of *The Dark Night of the Soul.* The *Canticle* moves from symbol to allegory; it comes and goes, crossing through various realms of the conceptual imagination, on a route spread over years, to be ultimately left pending, like most of this author's works. This long itinerary of a certain music is endless in its virtual effects; it is a *Divine Comedy* unfinished and unfinishable, to which, after many additions tied to circumstance, an accident puts an end. Valéry will say of his poems, too, that they were never finished, but cut short by some outside intervention (a loan, a request, an editor). The poem of John of the Cross will end the way one dies, after many journeys. A gift begins it and happenstance brings it to a close: these two figures of the event frame its history, like two incisions, two surprises, two modalities of the "sudden" (*repente*).

Of his poetic words John of the Cross says that sometimes God gave them to him, and sometimes he went looking for them.[17] The "looking for" is in step with what is "given"; it is a result of the event, a continuation to be found, that would be "comparable to the verse that was a gift."[18] Dante, in the *Vita nuova*, at the moment of deciding on a new "way of speaking," but without "daring to begin," because the enterprise was "a theme too lofty," above his strength, relates that "walking on a road alongside of which was flowing a very clear stream," he was pressed by the "will to speak." Suddenly, his "tongue spoke as if moved of its own accord." "Words" came, and, as he says, "I placed them in my spirit with great joy, thinking to use them for my beginning." They remained gathered there for several days, before giving birth to the new *canzone* of which they constitute the first verse.[19] The same is true of the *Cántico*, but its genesis, to a longer measure, spans seven years, from 1577 to 1584, from the "beginning," occurring in the prison of Toledo, to the three, then five strophes that John of the Cross adds late, in Baeza and Granada. The music spreads. Making its way through the language of the Spanish *lira* and the biblical *Canticles*, it already hints at what will be traced out in it through the *declaraciones*, in the more distant regions of exegetic or scholastic elucidation, with respect to the demands and tasks that will present themselves.

The *canciones* are characterized by a mobility. John of the Cross does not conceive a marmoreal oeuvre that would escape history. He himself corrects, augments, and modifies his "songs," in the name of the "impetuosity" they are born of and that constantly generates a movement in the existing languages. He no more sanctifies the poem than he does ecstasy or the Bible. He always fought against the fetishism of meaning or of the "revealed" text. He has the same way of treating biblical sayings (*los dichos de Dios*), extraordinary visions or words (*visiones y locuciones*), and poems (*dichos de amor*): in them is "enclosed" (*encerrado*) that which speaks—a "spirit" that "overflows the limits of the letter," a *Saying* that is "more" (*mas abundante*) than the *said*. Without attention to the *Saying*, which "overshadows" the understanding of the *said*, exegesis leads us astray.[20] This "method,"[21] which consists in listening to the Word in its statement, he applies to the biblical revelation as to private revelation; he also applies it in his practice of the *canciones*, continually modified by the music or the spirit that creates them. It is a question more of a poetics than of poems. The "songs" are in continual movement, bodies pliable to the "abundance" in them, that is, to the poetic Beginning.

The textual fluidity of the *canciones* is disconcerting. We have no more than a blurred image of the text. The *Cántico*, like the famous polyglot Bible of Cisneros, has today become the tableau of its successive states, a synopsis in which the number, the disposition, and the content of the strophes varies. This body is in movement, like those whose walk was photographed by E.-J. Marey, and whose limbs are a network of transformations.[22] So it is with the six versions of the poem that are attributed or attributable to John of the Cross. The *Cántico* had no static form. It does not stop. It is true that, opposing or combining their efforts (which also obey the ideology of the "right text"), ecclesiastic authority and the erudite institution have attempted to establish a definitive form and identity for this "walker." It is a lost cause. Variants abound, transitions and symbioses between different states, different movements, and different authors as well. The *one* of the text is disseminated into a plurality. It is not reducible to an object. Its unity is "spirit" or "word" exceeding its instantiations, and manifesting itself by flooding them with literary changes. In place of the dogmatic or historical idea of an "original," an authorized or primitive text, John of the Cross's poetic practice—the work taking place in his *canciones* in the reworking of their "letter"—requires that we substitute the movement and "amplitude" of an "Origin" that in his words "touches (*toca*) from one extremity to the other."[23] His songs are not precious stones to be mounted in a commentary; they move about in the language like the glow of a flame that "touches" and alters it, as the vibration of the touch of a caress spreads out over a body.

The body, here, is not a foreign region from which to import comparisons in the text. Like a language, it is moved by the poetic Beginning. Improvisations on a "given" motif, the *canciones* carry away the saying. But the same "fervor" (*fervor*) moves John of the Cross to other dances, in which the body is carried away. So, during that Christmas Eve in Granada, where "he began to dance and sing," holding the Child in his arms.[24] The body and language respond to the same transports. That effervescence of saying and of gesture orchestrates a *furore* that the sixteenth century connects with the *mania* of the Greeks (a "madness") or with their "enthusiasm." For Ronsard, who refers to Plato's *Ion* rather than to Meister Eckhart's divine *ebullitio*, it is "the effect" of a certain music.

Mon Dieu! que de douceur, que d'aise et de plaisir
L'âme reçoit alors qu'elle se sent saisir
Et du geste et du son et de la voix ensemble.[25]

These "effects," the mainspring of Sanjuanist pedagogy and spiritual transmission, are contingent on a "soundless music" that first affects the articulation of the body itself and language: it touches the voice. Its form is song. From there it extends either to language, in poetic writings, or to the body, in the figures of dance. The oscillation between the writings and dance figures makes the one a metaphor for the other, in both directions. Played on two instruments responding to one another, this fervor is essentially a motion that creates a different spirituality. It is a different practice of places. This madness adds a new dimension to them. Hence it founds the spatial dynamism characterizing an entire Sanjuanist symbolism. The poetic is the invention of space in a prison. It animates, it moves a closed, decadent order from within. It is therefore "mystic" in that it creates movements in the secrecy of a blocked situation, like a burst of Saying at the heart of a closed language. From this point of view, it responds to the historical circumstance of the moment, defined by the reform (a re-creation) needed by a corrupt Church and a time of decadence. The Reformation is first of all a poetics.

But the contrast between dance movements and prison walls also relates to a personal structure. The rigidity of the walls is a psychological trait of John of the Cross; moreover, as the site of poetic birth, it reappears with the very strict and traditional system that frames the commentary of the *canciones*. "Impetuosity" opens the depths of a walled-in world, making it all the more explosive. The intensity of the poetic fervor comes from this extreme tension.

"Amplitude" and Its Framework: A Genesis of Space

If we leave the psychology of the author aside, it is the music of the poem itself that manifests the way the "Awakener," the Breaker of Sleep (*erwecken*), "touches" the regular, even monotonous rhythm that frames it. Adopting in a quasi-systematic way the Italianizing *lira* already practiced by Garcilaso and Sebastián de Córdoba,[26] John of the Cross seems to pacify, or even to check, the escapades and ardor of the new style. With the odd number of verses that characterizes the *lira* (7 or 11 syllables), he combines an accentuation whose stability (2nd, 6th, and 10th syllables) ensures for the strophe as a whole a recitative regularity by a tireless four-time beat. The hendecasyllabic verses, moreover, are thus divided symmetrically into two halves, as follows: "1 **2** 3 4 5 **6** 7

8 9 **10** 11." Furthermore, contrary to the usual practice (in Garcilaso, the discourse often extends beyond the strophe; it has its own rhythm, which escapes that of the music but forms with it an unbreakable network of different tempos), the Sanjuanist *lira* or strophe closes on a complete unit of meaning (such that the hard kernel forms an isolated and easily detachable whole, like an aphorism or a playing card): this indissoluble marriage between auditory and semantic rhythm accentuates even more the hieratic nature of cadence. But this psalmody carries within itself a proliferation of exogenous phenomena: interior rhymes, phonetic repetitions (such as: "a*qu*el *que* yo más *qu*iero," in II, 4; "un no sé *qué que que*dan *b*al*b*uciendo," in VII, 5), glossolalic vocalizations (such as "apártalos amado," in XII, 1, i.e., a-á-a-o-a-á-o). Plays on letters and sound drifts baffle the rhythmic order, like a crazed violin on a harmonic bass executed on the piano. All these "performances," *acti vocali*, escape the underlying cadence that sustains them.

From the narrative point of view, the structure of the poem, acquiescing to the biblical stereotype of the Bridegroom and the Bride, and to the order of its two sequences (first the quest, then the reunion), itself becomes progressively irresolute from within by aberrant procedures: multiple enigmatic addresses (to him, to her, to them . . . one is a bit perplexed); the ambiguous use of personal pronouns (*el suyo* refers to whom, or to what?); exchange of predicates between the actors ("hart," "dove," "wounded," "pining," etc., circulate from one to another). Moreover, the story is devoid of all religious proper names (God, Jesus, etc.) that would give it positive referentiality. It is zigzagged with strange outbursts. Relics of bodies are strewn about: a face, eyes, a neck, arms, a hand, a hair . . . Sensorial intensities are spread about, a desultory concert of smells, sounds of water, the feel of the rustling wind, the savor of pomegranates. It is full of these singular details that an erotic obsession isolates: raped mother, balm of the body, a sole hair on the neck, drunkenness in the caves. Sight, above all, bulges from its orbs to the point of disappearing, in mirrors of fountains where pupils pass, in looks that flee and find each other, in wounds that eyes inflict on other eyes, in blind spaces that exist only for unknown eyes, in an intertwining of disheveled visibilities—ultimately invisible, like words. The traditional story of love carries, with its even pace, perturbing hallucinations. What madness in its lovely folds.

It returns us to the inaugural scene. In his dungeon, John of the Cross "conversed with himself" (*se entretenía*), he occupied his mind, he comforted and sustained himself with *canciones* and "he stored them in his memory to write them."[27] His poems are still unfinished (have they ever ceased being so?) and not yet written (that itinerant orality expresses itself in gestural movements). They inhabit the night of the poet, his body of memory, as did "the beginning" Dante speaks of. From performances to performances, repetitions in dance, they are the operators of a felicitous tension between an order (a psalmodic rhythm and a topos) and excess (inventions and endless drifting). This language, at once "unchained and hieratic,"[28] occupies, or more precisely kills, the closed and desolating time of the historical juncture, replacing it with a *space* to *get out* (*salir*). It is as if the cadenced reprise of the Song of Songs, that ancient love song, were to lull to sleep the oppressive chronicle of current events and, like a dream, make possible a field of freedom and of movement. As for his own ecstasy, John of the Cross sometimes calls it a "dream" (*sueño*),[29] a term that Teresa uses to refer to the elsewhere she is whisked away to.[30] "Dream" is indeed the transformation of temporal relations into spatial ones that serve as a setting for a breakout. But this mutation also corresponds, in the experience of the sixteenth century, to the passage from the closed to the open. In opposition to time as it was then lived and thought of—as a degradation since the "Golden Age," or since the "primitive" Church, down to the contemporary "corruption"—there arose a space of dramatic upsurge, an area of circulation, the proliferating impulse of an "amplitude."

The poem triumphs over historical decadence: it is the genesis of space, spatial animation, a source of movements and itself in motion. It is the velocity of a dance within an old and strictured world.

Pasó por estos sotos con presura (V, 2)

He hastened past these woods

Song circulates like the Word itself. Comparable, too, to the chants and tales that wend their way through groups, implanting possibility, restoring credibility, despite the fateful course of history. Ceaselessly it recommences, in the setting of repetition itself. An animate body is reborn in the tomb of a prison—or of the world. The dancing gesture validates belief. For John of the Cross, belief is the foundation of the entire spiritual itinerary. Faith, he says, postulates that there is always more other: it is to *creer su ser*,[31] to posit the principle of an endless overflowing of being. Now, the poetic act gives rise to that faith. It brings about that excess in a spatial moment that suddenly bursts through, from within, the historical closures of dwelling.

2. A SCENOGRAPHY OF HISTORY: FROM SILENCE TO DISCOURSE

The poetic space foments a mad mobility within a ritual setting. This model, already at work in Hieronymus Bosch's *The Garden*,[32] will also organize the Carmelite monasteries and the reform convents in which the rhythms of a regularity sustain the fugues of prayer: "Despite the narrow enclosure in which you live," Teresa says to the Carmelites, "you can enter" into the delights "at any hour" and "without the permission of superiors."[33] But the *sueño* must be rearticulated on the basis of a historical work, by a movement that specifies the mystic approach and differentiates it from that of the poetic. As Meister Eckhart said: the most difficult is not to go out, but to come in.[34] Overall, the function of the *declaraciones* is to ensure the return to the field of history, by the junction between the ecstatic dance and the labors or the proses of the world.

The relationship between the songs and the commentary—a Sanjuanist equivalent of the relation, in Teresa, between the "comparison" and the narrative or didactic developments—distinguishes this *mystics* from theology, which interrelates a rational commentary with a corpus of "authorities" (biblical, patristic, or magisterial). The replacement of "authorities" by songs dislodges a whole system of interpretation. The to-and-fro movement between poem and prose is what constitutes the gap between this "science" and the discourses constructed on what looks like the same model as commentaries authorized by a speaking body: exegesis, theology, law, and medicine. In John of the Cross, the songs appear according to formalities that become increasingly subtle as we enter further into the work of the oeuvre. This complexity is the result of both the way the *Cántico* developed over a period of at least ten years (1577–87) and the stratification of the levels that converge in it ("intentions" of the author, biblical or scholastic authorities to be brought to bear, textual strategies). The functioning of the commentary can therefore be represented in several scenarios, which interact, moreover, with the successive states of the poem. These models do not obey the law of the alternative—one or the other. Rather they configure together, in the space created by the interplay of the *canciones* and the *declaraciones*, the combinatorics belonging to the animation of a body, that is, a practice of history. Here, I will consider only the first of these scenarios.

The Prologue

The first scenario results from the program that John of the Cross presents in the prologue to the *Cántico*. This declaration of intention (*mi intento*) has only a very distant correspondence with the actual commentary. From one to the other, there is the distance between theory and practice. As usual, the theory does not determine the practices (which yield to rules or various other, often heterogeneous constraints), but it gives them a system of reference that plays the role of creating a differentiation, stimulating and corrective, from usages belonging to various disciplines and traditions. The prologue, then, has a prospective value in relation to an already constituted set of techniques, the logic of which, hidden in their postulates, will continue, but altered by a "law-framework" inspired by different principles. It superimposes the model of a new "science" on procedures that that science reuses—and with which, in sum, that science will measure itself.

The discourse intended to rearticulate the poem in relation to a history is called *declaración*. It was redacted in its entirety outside the prison. To this genre that concerns the content of the text and defines the commentary as a whole, there is added, late, exceptionally, the *anotación*, a "notice" that is addressed to the reader to inform him or her of the right way to make use of the commentary: how to reconcile two disparate sections of the *declaraciones*.[35] The verb *declarar* refers not only to the action of manifesting a hidden truth,[36] but also to that of intending it for an interlocutor, of conducting the discourse before someone and developing its results outside. This explanation traces in a network of personal exchanges the pathways opened up by the poem, more than it aims at explaining a text by other discourses. It is primarily interlocutionary, and not intertextual. It also comes, therefore, from another time and another place than the solitary moment of the *canciones*. It postulates a sociality. A conversation inaugurates it. When, in getting out of prison, at Beas (1578–81), John of the Cross commented on his strophes orally in response to the questions of the Carmelites, those were *declaraciones*;[37] when the sisters, such as Marie de Jésus, addressed him, they "manifested" (*declarar*) their souls to him.[38] That mutual communication between the souls of the religious and the soul of the poem begins the redaction of the first *declaraciones* (on strophes 16 to 31), in 1578–81. Later, in 1584, acceding to the demand of the great *apasionada* of Teresa, Anne de Jésus, and also to the theoretical testament of *Las Moradas* that Teresa wrote just before she died (1582),[39] a continuous commentary takes shape, itself subject to the subsequent modifications that will be called for by other conversations. Here is the beginning of the prologue in which, after having experimented for seven years with the interlocutionary "proper use" of the poem, John of the Cross clarifies his program and the status of the *declaración*.[40]

Forasmuch (*por cuanto*) as these songs, religious Mother, appear to be written with a certain degree of fervor of love for that God whose wisdom and love are so vast that, as is said in the Book of Wisdom, they "touch from one extreme to the other,"[41] and forasmuch as the soul which is informed and moved by him has to some extent this same abundance and impetus in its words, I do not now intend to explicate (*declarar*) all the breadth and plenteousness that the spirit fecund with love produces in them. It would be ignorance, rather, to think that sayings of love of a mystic understanding, such as those of the present songs, can be fairly explicated (*declarar*) by words of any kind. For the Spirit of the Lord, who aids our weakness, as St. Paul says,[42] dwelling in us, "makes intercession for us with groanings which cannot be uttered," pleading for that which we cannot understand or comprehend well enough to manifest it. For who can write down that which he reveals to loving souls wherein he dwells? And who can manifest in words that which he makes them to feel? And lastly, who can express that which He makes them to desire? Of a surety, none; nay, indeed, not the very souls to whom that happens. And it is for this reason that, by means of figures, comparisons and similitudes, they allow something of that which they feel to overflow and utter secret mysteries from the abundance of the Spirit, rather than explicate (*declarar*) these things rationally.

Such similitudes, if they be not read with the simplicity of the spirit of love and understanding embodied in them, appear to be nonsense rather than the expression of reason, as may be seen in the divine Songs of Solomon[43] and in other books of the Divine Scripture, where, since the Holy Spirit cannot express the abundance of his meaning in common and vulgar terms, he utters mysteries in strange figures and similitudes.[44] Whence it follows that no words of holy doctors, despite all that they have said and may yet say, can ever expound these things fully, neither could they be expounded in words of any kind. That which is explicated of them (*declarar*), therefore, is ordinarily the least part (*lo menos*) of that which they contain.

Since these songs, then, have been composed under the influence of a love which comes from abundant mystical understanding, they cannot be explicated (*declarar*) precisely. Therefore I shall not attempt to do so, but only to throw upon them some light of a general kind, as Your Reverence has so desired. And this I think to be best, for the sayings of love are better left in their fullness, so that everyone may pluck advantage from them according to his manner and to the flow of his spirit, than reduced to a meaning to which not every palate can accommodate itself. And thus, although they are explicated after a certain manner, there is no reason why anyone should be bound to it. For mystical wisdom (which comes through love, whereof the present songs treat) needs not to be comprehended distinctly in order to produce love and affection in the soul; it is like to faith, whereby we love God without comprehending him.

> I shall therefore be very brief, although I shall be unable to refrain from extending myself in certain places where the matter requires it, and where occasion offers to explicate (*declarar*) and treat certain points and effects of prayer. Since there are many such in the songs I cannot refrain from treating of some.

Process of Passage

Punctuating its pace with "more" (*más*) and "less" (*menos*), progressing with "rather" (*antes*) or with "better" (*mejor*), supporting itself on postulates that serve as sources of proportional relations (*por cuanto, así como tampoco*, etc.), and taking its bearings through these operations on a "maximum" and a "minimum," the text functions according to comparatives circulating along sliding scales, between inaccessible superlatives. This generalized movement assigns to all the units a "trembling" that is especially marked, as a trace of approximation, an aura of uncertainty surrounding verbal identities, by the indefinite "some" (*algo, algún, algunos*), the almost obsessional use of which is, in John of the Cross, the effect and hallmark of a treatment of things: like the silver rim by which Bosch removes beings from their accustomed universe, this coefficient of indetermination locates mental objects in a second space in which their place is uncertain. The use of the indefinite is, moreover, but the linguistic index of a more general procedure. An "apparent" (*parecer*) also destabilizes the love songs (which "appear" nonsense): the value of both depends on the movement, or the "spirit," of the reader-practitioner, and not on an objective status. The individuals themselves are places of passage, stretched between the "flux" (or flow: *caudal*) of what happens there and the "effects" or outcome, moving toward the outside: like streams, they ex-ist by what they receive and by what they give off; they are at once other than themselves by what they have, and outside themselves by what they do: always "more" or "less" than their supposed identity. All the positivities mentioned (the poem and the commentary, the Bible and the Doctors) are put off balance, set in movement, and put in in-finite, so to speak, by a series of "more" and "less," operators of displacements relative to one another. Thus they appear to have been "touched" by a propulsive "ardor" that is perceptible, however, only by the "effects" of vibration. With this apparatus of comparative dynamics, we therefore have a textual practice of the in-finite.

The burden of the prologue involves not only the object of writing, but the condition of possibility of the writing. At stake is: Can one *speak*? It is accompanied by a corollary: What is speaking? The answer will authorize a writing and circumscribe its field. It rests on a distinction between two states of language: on the one hand, "to speak" (*decir*, *dichos*, but also *manifestar*, *rebosar*, *verter*, etc.), which characterizes the poems and the Bible; on the other, "to explicate" (*declarar*, *declaración*, but also *explicar*, etc.), which designates the commentaries of the poem or those that "the Holy Doctors" have devoted to the Bible. A difference, then, cleaves the apparent homogeneity of the discourse. Because of this, between the ineffable (the Spirit) and the explanation (the treatise), a third place is introduced, which plays the role of passage or mediation: the poetic or biblical "said."

The two registers of language are distinguished as the "more" and the "less." The *said* (or "said out of love") manifests an "immensity" in a limited space. Its content is greater than its container; a "too much" overflows into a "not enough." The said, which belongs to the metonymic group (a part for the whole), presents itself in the form of "similitudes," in statements altered by an excess of the speaker, in "torrents" issuing from a place that has been touched by abundance. It is the beginning of language by the enunciative act of an Unknown. In the prologue, moreover, the term *dicho* [said] modifies at once *canciones*, "amorous souls," and "Divine Scripture."

The *declaración* explicates the relations between these three forms taken by the "said," It no longer refers directly to the ineffable Saying, but to the stirrings it produces in language by tracing out "saids" within it. The *declaración* examines them, compares them, and notes their consequences in existing fields of knowledge. In this respect it explains, within the fields it knows, the effects of what it does not know. By interconnecting them, it also constructs, with "reasons," no longer in "figures," an image of the unity from which these effects derive. The *declaración*, then, links together these places of enunciation, these "said out of love"; it is born of their exchanges and of the wake they leave in the various fields of knowledge; in doing so, it will represent, in the discursive mode, the unity that escapes it. It thus forms the Sanjuanist program of a theological discourse. This first schema corresponds to table 2.

The initial sentence of the prologue specifies the relation between the two states of language. It opens on a first actor, the "said" (the songs of the soul, coupled with biblical sayings), subject of the subordinate clause that provides the discourse with its whys and wherefores, and it moves on to a second actor, the "I" (*yo*), the subject of the main clause, which specifies the project of the commentary. The "spoken" (*dicho*) has priority over the "explained" (*declarado*) of which it is the postulate. The itinerary of the sentence leads from one to the other and characterizes along the way the place and style of the second.

Table 2. The analysis of silence and speech in the prologue.

silence	[inmenso abundancia ímpetu]	*amor* | ▼——▼——▼
language	"*dichos*" (lo más) figuras	canciones almas amorosas escritura divina (religiosa Madre)
language	"*declaraciones*" (lo menos) razones	▲——▲ ▲——▲ [conversar] ▲——▲

First, at the very threshold of the discourse, an apposition places the locus from which the text speaks (the "said out of love") and its addressee (the "Mother" Anne de Jésus) face to face. These are two speaking bodies, two variants of the poetic: the inspired poem and the "amorous soul." Their communications create the field in which the *declaración* can be formed. They make up its landscape. A *conversar*, an interlocutionary network between instances of "said out of love," defines the space in which correspondences between them will be developed. For a *declaración*, there have to be "at least two," the dialogical or ecclesial minimum.[45] *Por lo menos dos*: this is the golden rule of discursive production in John of the Cross. Thereby, as with a ship, the *position* of the commentary is defined.

His approach falls under another textual given. While the *canciones* refer to the verisimilitude of an "amplitude" (an "appearing"), the *declaraciones* are built on the recognition of an inability (the impossibility of explaining). On the one hand, there is a presumption of immensity; on the other, the obvious fact of a limit. At the outset, the two languages are distinguished by the modalities that affect them: the one is probably infinite (in its movement); the other, surely inadequate (to that movement). To infinity, an uncertainty is apportioned, while denial constitutes a statement of certainty. There we have two manners of speaking. The opening to the immense is deprived of certainty, while the limit can be the object of affirmation. These two styles would seem to characterize on the one hand the "believing" word and on the other the "knowing" discourse. They are not incompatible. On the contrary, they are joined, since, set in motion by a commentary that repeats indefinitely that the absolute is "not this," "nor that," the work of the negative will manifest what, of the infinite, eludes certainty and remains merely probable. By his *declaraciones*, John of the Cross chisels in the "appearance" that which *is not* the Saying itself; he manifests in the "sayings out of love" the excess that overflows them; he puts at their service an "inexorable power of discrimination."[46]

PROPORTIONALITY

Between these two unequal languages, which cooperate, nonetheless, in the manifestation of an ineffable, the relations are regulated by the "more" and the "less." As we have seen, the Sanjuanist comparatives designate not a hierarchy of stable states, but a relation of proportion between mobilia. The formula for it would be: y increases as x decreases, toward a maximum for y and a minimum for x. Proportionality, however it may be used in contemporary practices (economic and calculative),[47] and in the speculative tradition (Cusan or Dionysian),[48] is, in John of the Cross, a gesture of his thought. In the relation of the *canciones* to the *declaraciones*, as in other cases (for example, the relation of divine light to human darkness),[49] proportionality reintroduces the continuity of a movement between the languages that a discontinuity of status separates. Their difference of level is transformed into the relation of their "content" (a comprehension) with its appropriation by a discursive knowledge (an apprehension). From this point of view, "the more" of the poem intends an "all" (*todo*) that it "comprehends" in itself, but that remains inaccessible;[50] reciprocally, "the less" of the commentary designates a content that, at the limit, would no longer be anything (*nada*). From maximal comprehension (*en ello se comprende todo*) which yields a minimal apprehension, the diagram of the word goes all the way to its opposite pole, maximal apprehension of a minimal content. The "more" and the "less" move between these two extremes, such that, in the texts, the proportion of the poetic to the explicative varies according to whether content increases toward the "all" or decreases toward the "nothing." This produces an asymptotic curve (see figure 7).

The dynamics of proportionality imposes upon the poem and the commentary a different rule than the separation of genres. It is also dialogical, or, if you like, conversational, but in mixtures in which the proportion of heterogeneous aspects is inverted. The poetic and the explicative are not separated by precise borders; rather they compose alloys in which the relative percentage of the elements that are combined varies. They should be thought of according to the model of Roman Ja-

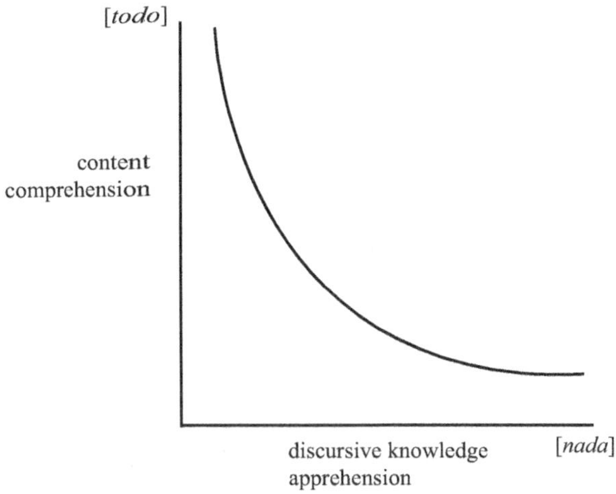

Figure 7. Proportionate analysis of the comprehension/apprehension continuum.

kobson's "functions" (the phatic, the poetic, the metalinguistic, etc.),[51] because they designate not only polarizations inherent in language itself (what is said in it or what it teaches), but also ways of speaking it (to allow to say or to inform). There are therefore transitions from the pure poem, an inaccessible Saying, to the explanation that no longer says anything. A swaying motion introduces the poetic into the prose, and vice versa. The oeuvre (the entire *Canto espiritual*) will present, including the part we isolate today under the term "poem," a series of these alchemic combinations.

After having asserted once more the priority of the inspired Saying (*autoridades de la Escritura divina*) and the deletion of the commentative "I," (*no pienso afirmar cosa de mío*), the prologue ends by describing the operations that progressively introduce "the more" into "the less": the translation of the biblical Latin into Spanish, and the transformation of that Spanish into explanations; and furthermore, the passage from the initial totality of the "songs" (*juntas todas*) to the *declaración* they introduce verse by verse.[52] The water of saying insinuates itself into the prose of discursive knowledge, in a style (*estilo*) that mixes them without making them into one and that tends less to circumscribe "a meaning" than to indicate the "general" movement of a reciprocal mutation of languages on the basis of an ineffable.

Chapter Three

Shards of Speech

A tree standing alone in a field without a proprietor (5),[1] the delicious and durable fruit gathered in a "cold and dry" climate (41), a man dragging his cart uphill (55), a bird caught in birdlime (22), another escaping the hand (31), a fly caught in honey (24) . . . These details—a look has carved them out in the landscape. Singular beings have arrested the attention and remain embedded in the series of John of the Cross's "Thoughts," assembled under the name *Dichos.* They already have the form of fragments. Detached from their everyday environment, in Andalusia or in the province of Jaén, they have the role of quotations, punctuating the discourse of "aphorisms"[2] with visionary beginnings, just as in John of the Cross's treatises, the quotations of his own poems produce echoes in the prose of the commentaries (or *declaraciones*). A few passing images of the countryside or the house are repeated in the thoughts that respond to them. The *Dichos* give a resonance, in the space of reflection, to the flashes of a contemplation pursued through the country in which John of the Cross comes and goes during the years 1578–82. A dialogue with things that "speak" remains etched in the thought that continues to reflect these bits of countryside.

To this resonance of sight in speech another dialogue is added, which involves the addressees of these thoughts and locates their statement within a network of interlocutors. The prologue defines the *Di-*

chos as a relation between the writer who articulates them in language (this is "I") and "other people" to whom they are addressed. The text of the aphorisms itself suggests to us, here and there, the contemporary history serving as the setting of these verbal exchanges—a décor barely evoked, misty, quite different from the well-defined scenes making up the precious implantations of the natural landscape in the discourse. Behind the *Dichos*, through the illusions they condemn, pass the shadows of spectacular experiences ("visions" and "consolations"), ascetic performances ("works"), and solitary adventures that attract a proliferation of "spirituals," "alumbrados," or "blessed" around the Carmel of Beas or the city of Baeza, and whom John of the Cross encountered constantly in his itinerant activity as confessor and spiritual director. The "Sayings of Light and Love" stand out against a background of affective and religious spheres of influence oscillating from the sublime to the diabolical, as related in countless stories of the time.[3] The everyday order of the earth contrasts, then, with that ocean of passions. The "thoughts" are developed between a serene nature and an extraordinary history, as if they moved along the shores where the austere Spanish countryside met the grand waters of mystic desire.

At the junction of these two worlds, the *dicho* has the value of a concept. In contemporary usage, the term designated a remark, a maxim, a saying, even a witty remark or an insult (to have "words" with someone), but also, in the plural, a collection of selected thoughts (*Los dichos de Quinto Curcio*, etc.). For John of the Cross, the "said" includes its statement (the *lengua*) and its operative power (the *obra y virtud*). As the prologue of the *Spiritual Canticle* also explains on the topic of the "sayings of love" (*dichos de amor*) that make up the poem, it is a linguistic locus in which an "impetuosity" occurs that overflows what can be understood or explained about it. It verbally articulates an "abundance."[4] In it, a form and a force of the saying coincide. Therefore that spoken word is affected by the twofold power of clarifying (it is "light") and of animating (it is "love"). It makes it possible to see the road (*luz para el camino*) and to travel it (*amor en el caminar*). It is at once principle of discernment (*discreción*) and of movement (*moción*).[5] It cuts like a double-bladed knife, and it operates. It says what it does. Such, in themselves, are these *dichos de luz y amor*, the definition of which also characterizes the "style" sought by John of the Cross: a way of speaking that strives toward an intense clarity, in an incessant work of distinction and negation at the service of what he calls a "fervor."

But that spoken word (the *dicho*) is always thought of in the plural: for one thing, it is received in its entirety only by a plurality of interlocutors or of exchanges between its listeners; for another, it is given only in a succession of fragments relative to singular situations, which is why John of the Cross speaks of it only in the plural (*los dichos*), just as with the poem (*las canciones*—songs, he calls them). It is essential for the *dicho* to circulate between addressees who address it mutually to one another (it has no autonomous existence, by contrast with the maxim), and to present itself as a singular totality that necessarily elicits others (it grasps all, but from a partial and circumstantial point of view). These two characteristics of the *dicho*, interlocutionary and fragmentary, concern, respectively, its speech-act and what is stated. In clarifying them, we will make more clearly manifest the Sanjuanist concept of an act of "saying" that articulates the *one* who speaks (the Spirit is "he who speaks")[6] with the *plural* of elocutions (a diversity of respondents and thoughts).

DIALOGUES

The prologue placed at the head of the *Dichos* presents their foundation. Even though it does not appear in the autograph manuscript of Andújar and was in actuality sent to a very dear Carmelite, Mother Francisca de la Madre de Dios (Sandoval y Luna), at the beginning of a "little treatise" or "notebook" (*tratadito*) of spiritual advice,[7] it describes the configuration in which the "words" are inscribed. At the beginning of his "work" the writer ("I") declares, on the subject of these *dichos*, that he has its words (*lengua*), but not their effectivity (*obra y virtud*). Partial, his testimony carries him therefore toward "other people" who will be the witnesses for what he does not have. It is not only in the name of what he has, but even more in the name of what "is missing" in him that he addresses "many souls" already moved by the word, but deprived of knowledge capable of allowing them to avoid falling and losing their way. His discourse has the value of discernment for his addressees, just as their progress will be a consolation for him. This excludes, for the writer, the position of master or author, while at the same time a "guide" remains necessary for people inspired by the force of the word.

John of the Cross seems to comply with Teresa of Avila's idea of "spiritual directors": the lettered (*letrados*) of "sure" judgment thanks to their knowledge of Scripture.[8] Writing to a Carmelite nun (who was, moreover, to inspire several strophes of the *Canticle*), he appears faithful, from the point of view of "language," "knowledge," and "certainty," to the mission that the founder assigned to the confessors of her houses. But he integrates it into a larger view. The word circulates between several people, and thus it is interlocution, on the basis of what is lacking in each; it is a *more* for all as a result of being that which its various witnesses have *less* of in relation to one another. Therefore the diversification and dissemination of its statement and its strength initiate collective exchange, thanks to which each receives from the word what he or she lacks. In this exchange, no particular place belongs to the word; it plays on several levels ("many souls," says the prologue), in a network in which the "you" addressed between interlocutors and readers is inseparable from an appeal to "you," "the one who is speaking."

Indeed, after that prologue, the text of the *dichos* presents an intertwining of addresses, sometimes to "you," Lord, sometimes to "you," the reader—with this difference that the first "you" has a proper name (God, Lord, sometimes Jesus) and the second remains without a name. Seen in their entirety, the aphorisms pass briskly from one addressee to the other, so much so that these "turnabouts" appeared to Dom Chevallier "unacceptable" in one and the same collection.[9] The prayers in response to God, "you who first show yourself and go out to meet those who desire you" (2), alternate with the advice given to another "you": "Deny your desires and you will find what your heart desires" (15). But because that other is never named, it could refer to a dialogue of the writer with himself, as one of his *dichos* explains: "What do you ask for and seek, my soul?" (26). Aside from the prologue (but it is not part of the manuscript), this third interlocutor, the soul, substitutable for "other people," might be seen as transforming the text into a meditation analogous to the Augustinian *Soliloquies.* The *Dichos* would then stage the various agencies of the dialogue that make up the life of the solitary: the "I," the "soul," and God. They can indeed be read altogether as the unfolding of an internal dialogue in several voices, like the orchestral volume of a dialoguing interiority. On the alternating registers of invocations of God (prayers), injunctions to the soul (advice), and references to experimental or evangelical truths (maxims), the world of the spirit, in which "I" circulate and write, would unfurl and spread out like a desert haunted by words.

It is historically the case that John of the Cross sent out answers (*respuestas*) to the questions asked to him, and that he addressed advice (*avisos*) or maxims (*sentencias*) to individuals and collectivities in written or oral form.[10] We cannot overlook that obvious fact, nor can we forget that the *dichos* were first formulated in the course of verbal exchanges whose statements themselves often came from a far earlier oral tradition—religious and monastic—still quite recognizable in the aphorisms of Andújar. The question the text raises is of a different order. It concerns the way John of the Cross thinks and lives these relations. The redaction of the *dichos* articulates what he does with these encounters. The text is the form of the experience he has of them. From this point of view, the ambivalence of a text that can be read either as a "soliloquy" or as a guide shows how easy—or secondary—the passage from internal dialogue to external conversation is. The same text is valid for both. There are not two different writings of the dialogue, according to whether it is activated in the animated desert of solitude or in the parlors of convents and on the street. The same *conversar* among several voices is pursued from an inner to an outer décor, and thus John of the Cross can say to "other people" what he says to his soul, and the discourse held with the other is not an exteriority—pedagogical, magisterial—in contrast with the intimate relations between "myself," "the soul," and God. Everywhere the plural advent of the word or *dicho* is deployed. It does not change in nature when it passes from the supposedly solitary *oratio* (dialogue with the soul and God) to speech between interlocutors or writing intended for readers. A network of requests, responses, and advice, a living forest of voices, is the very element—interlocutionary—in which the word "goes out to meet those who desire it." This plurality is the form of "the act of saying."

FRAGMENTS

The changes of address hidden within the same "you" are but the first indication of the movements of this text, organized as a series of variations on words, sounds, and themes. This musical composition can come as no surprise from a writer whose literary subtlety has become more and more apparent since the analyses of Dámaso Alonso.[11] Considering the seventy-eight *dichos* in the autograph manuscript of Andújar alone (they form an isolated whole and were conceived as such by the author, at least at the moment of their writing), the examination of the Sanjuanist procedures enlightens us on the nature of these fragments and the very movement of the thought that wrought them.

The collection, cut off at the end of its first third by the "prayer of an amorous soul" (26), presents itself first as a series of "nuclei," each one dedicated to just one theme and characterized by the repetition of a leitmotif. Thus fragments 5 through 7 treat the master (the master-pedagogue or *maestro*, and the master-owner or *dueño*), a term associated with increasing fertility (*fruta* 5, *beneficio* 6, *virtud* 7), and they are followed by a counterpoint of four fragments (8 through 11) that connect solitude with falling in a sort of refrain:

8. El que a solas cae . . .
9. . . . el caer a solas . . .
10. El que cargado cae . . .
11. Y el que cae ciego . . . solo

A sonorous and semantic rhythm of the same type characterizes fragments 12 through 14, dedicated to the minimum that God loves the most:

12. Más quiere Dios de ti el menor grado de pureza . . .
13. Más quiere Dios en ti el menor grado de obediencia . . .
14. Más estima Dios en ti el inclinarte a la sequedad . . .

The repetition makes differences more noticeable: "in you" (13 and 14), replaces "of you" (12); [God] "values" (14) replaces [God] "desires" (12 and 13); a gradation transitions from "purity" (12) to "obedience" (13) and finally to "dryness" (14), just as, earlier, fertility ascended the hierarchy of "fruit" (5), "benefit" (6), and finally "virtue/strength" (7). Against a background of repetition, subtle shifts are introduced by a series of combinations between the modified elements. As in tales and poems, the transformation of a detail within a host of resemblances creates the instant that strikes: it is nothing, a little hitch in passing, just a slight difference of sound in the melody, but it changes the direction of the rest of the fragment, provoking a drift, and sequels, in that space of meaning, before the following fragment returns to the same refrain and sets off on a new variation.

This is how the aphorisms proceed, often grouped into little poems generally consisting of three strophes (or fragments), sometimes four or six (twice three): 18–20, 22–24, 27–29, 36–37, 43–45, 55–57 and 60–65, 73–76. The modulations made by each poem bear not only on rhythmic and phonetic regularities. They also play on a register of images. For example, apropos of the "lightness" and "freedom" granting the soul its ability to fly, the variation includes the songbird caught in the birdlime (*pájaro*, 22), the bird or plumed flying thing (*ave*, 23), and finally the fly stuck in the honey (*mosca*, 24); these three degrees in ways of remaining attached to the ground are developed according to a procedure analogous to the one used by Teresa of Avila in her *Autobiography*, when she presents the four figures of prayer by inventorying the variable relations between the garden and irrigation, that is, when she treats a "comparison" as a conceptual field.[12]

To these "nuclei," or little poems, it is impossible to give a title (and it would be a misinterpretation), although they do have a strong musical and semantic unity. They form combinations with several entries. A word (for example *solo* or *a solas*, from 8 to 11) is the pivot of the unit; it is the index of both the request and the response, but a rich repertoire of its possible meanings is developed by the use—poetic and aphoristic—to which it is put, and thus the word itself, while remaining a *lieu-dit*, a place marked in the language, is offered to a whole series of circulations. Like a public place, or a commonplace, it creates a space of freedom. It can no longer be fixed in one sole meaning. It *speaks*, i.e., there is something of the other in it. It no longer belongs among the *modos y términos bajos* (26), those "low," literalist, and positive ways of speaking that keep the spirit from "moving ahead" (*pasar adelante*).[13] By the operation that forms the fragment, it is transformed into a "mystic" word. It enters the sway of the *dicho*.

The series of these alchemical units, true spiritual laboratories, is framed by an introduction (1) and a conclusion (78, the longest of the fragments, not counting the "prayer," 26). The introduction asserts, as a postulate, a theological principle of history (the incipit is *siempre*, always); it posits the law of time and therefore of the present; the more wickedness shows its face, the more God shows his treasures of wisdom. A challenge to decadence, the foundation of a reformative proliferation. The conclusion recapitulates the entire spiritual practice by gathering its essential figures beneath the evangelical sign, "he who loses wins." At the beginning, the paradox of theory; at the end that of praxis.

After the invocation of the God who "goes out to meet those who desire him" (2) and the indication (the leitmotif of the whole text) of "good feet," "courage," and "courageous stubbornness" (*porfía animosa*, a self-portrait?) that will be needed along the way (3), comes the series of poems (three, four, or six fragments), but punctuated by isolated aphorisms—hence a succession of long and short segments. Three parts may be clearly distinguished. The first (2 through 25) aims at freeing the "spirituals" from successive illusions that can mislead them within (isolation, consolations, the irrational, narcissism, etc.). It draws the profile of a "purity" of desire in the exalted or anxious profusion of spiritual phenomena: "O little-known love of God!" (16). Here, knowledge is a work of "negation," which makes this part a shortened form of the *Ascent of Mount Carmel*—or perhaps its first form. The third part (53–77) treats essentially relations to external events, the ups and downs of all sorts upon which the event of the Last Judgment sheds light from on high and afar.

Between these two collections, the central part (26 through 52) has an entirely different style. It is interspersed with prayers, confessions, and personal invocations (30, 32–33, 38, 46–47, 49, 52). The long "prayer" that introduces it (26) seems to inundate that region of the text. It slips in everywhere. Aphorisms of the constative type remain here and there: these are the most dazzling (34), the most elliptic (35), or the most daring (39, 51)[14] of this work; they are, moreover, isolated from one another (except apropos of "reason," 36–37 and 43–45), in short irruptions of thought, and it is only in this part of his autograph that John of the Cross separates almost every fragment from the following one by a long dash, as if marking between them the silence of a suspension.[15] On the other hand, fragments 53–54 (beginning of the third part) are connected to fragments 23–25 (end of the first part) by a vocabulary peculiar to them (the "void" in 25 and 53, the "lightness" in 26 and 52): Does the meditation, interrupted by an influx of prayers, resume afterward at the point where it left off? Or do the terms void, excess, and flight that precede and follow the upheaval of the central part trace out its borders, frontier zones already or still touched by the unexpected that supervenes at that point?

Thus the first and third part of the *Dichos* form a whole made up of two equal halves (1 to 25 and 53 to 78), devoted one to inner purification and the other to firmness amid external events, linked to each another by the permanence of a literary genre and also by a succession of references solely to the Gospel of Matthew (4, 18, 74, and 78),[16] a typical trait in Sanjuanist writing.[17] They make up a continuous treatise whose content is classic, even though the poetic and mystic style of John of the Cross metamorphoses each element from within, and whose order obeys an ascetic model that is traditional since the famous aphorisms of the *Praktikos* of Evagrius Ponticus.[18] It is also possible to think that this treatise conforms to the "employ," as the prologue says, that is set out for John of the Cross by his mission as confessor, a work of discernment (*discreción*) accomplished by a man who has the "language" of the Scriptures (he is a *letrado*), but who cannot credit himself with having their "efficacy and virtue."

But now behold how the beautiful edifice cracks beneath the pressure of that force. It is fragmented by it. It opens up—in the middle, rocked by the lyricism of a prayer born of the love that introduces, at the center of the work, complaints, exultations, illuminations, surprises, and "occasions" like birds bursting free—a disorderly space in which the voices of desire well up, along with thoughts that of a sudden are commensurate with God alone in his silence, and even the reckless words that, escaping the subtle "discretion" of the master, have the air of lapses or confessions.[19] "May everything change, just at the right moment" (33): that happens, in the text itself. "Mine are the heavens and mine the earth . . ." (26). The work of liberation that took place meticulously, in the course of the first part (and that repeats in the third), within limited units, comes out onto this inundation, as if the movement traced by the *Dichos* led us into the presence of the relation that the purifying ascesis bears to the sudden excesses of a love hidden until that point in the daily practice of the "nothing else but you."

MELODIES

This discourse reproduces, in its form, the birth of the "songs" of the *Canticle* in the prison of Toledo in 1578. On the basis of an internal critique, it appears to date from the years immediately following the "exodus" from the dungeon. By the contrast between its prudence and its folly, between the astonishing precision of its austerity and the anxious or lyric outpourings of passion, it is a "youthful" text. A greater harmony will be created between the elements coexisting within it. But it is also possible that this tension comes from the function that the contemplative must now perform as spiritual director, once removed from the solitary trials of the "desert" or prison. In any case, the Andújar autograph presents only one version of the *Dichos*. John of the Cross is in the habit of incessantly reworking his texts. He interprets his own works differently; he modifies, reorients, and adds to them, as is proved by the continual revisions of the *Spiritual Canticle* for fourteen years. Thus the autograph is but one moment—a particular performance—of the aphorisms; it should be compared with other executions, as has been done for Bach, in order to follow the artistic and mystic experience delineated by that mobile, combinatory creativity.

Also what should be analyzed in greater detail, in the text furnished by the autograph, is the strange work that is pursued at the musical level of the language: homophonies, internal rhymes, glossolalic repetitions of vowels, linking by repetition of the same word, etc. A play of echoing sounds organizes the ensemble. Words develop sonorous waves around themselves in verbal orchestrations. A musical vitality of the language haunts the order of meaning, though never (this, too, is a trait of Sanjuanist poetics) hiding it. In many ways that art heralds the "Ingenious Aphorisms in End-Rhymes to Divine Tranquility" (*Geistreiche Sinn- und Schlußreime*) by Angelus Silesius.[20] The comparison involves not only the spiritual tradition of the aphorism, or a literary similarity in the procedures of development, but a semantic inaccessibility of the language by its own musicality. The techniques that a literary and linguistic analysis can give an account of put into play, in a sonorous mode, that which is ineffable in the language itself: a *saying* that is not a *said*. It is probably in these orderly and subtle realms of sound—an excess in relation to meaning, an inexpressible in relation to the statement, a ranging of fingers over the keys in relation to the readable—that we should recognize the mystic nature of the language or (to use the terms of John of the Cross) the still linguistic[21] form taken by the "virtue" of the *dicho*, the invisible force of Saying.

By his art, John of the Cross examines these deep reaches of language. There is in him (and others) something that might be called a musical reasoning, a rigorous complexity that is out of the realm of logical reasoning and that follows the labyrinths of a "reason" untethered to words. Perhaps it is about an intelligence more docile and more acute, harkening to what can be heard but not understood of language itself. In any case, attention to the musicality of John of the Cross is an initiation, still from afar, to what he seeks to say.

Chapter Four

Uses of Tradition

Within the entirety of the corpus of seventeenth-century interpretations of John of the Cross in France, I have had to make a choice. Many years ago, in an article with a promising title but a disappointing content, P. Pacheu considered "the mystics interpreted by the mystics."[1] A vast and fascinating confrontation! I will limit myself to what the work of Jean-Joseph Surin, like a mirror, shows us of it, being inhabited by that of John of the Cross.[2]

This problem was taken up by Jean Orcibal in connection with the Carmelites of Bordeaux and the nuns whom Henri Bremond, in his familiar patois, called the "little souls" ["petites âmes"], great by their hidden science.[3] Their reading of John of the Cross remains for us a lost song, however, the secret of itineraries from which only a few traces, found by the historian, that tireless hunter of silences, allow us to suppose a *gait*, a style that continued to be Sanjuanist. The analysis of the "encounter" in the wide-ranging though fragmentary work of Surin is both easier and more formidable. The confrontation is intimidating. It is a vis-à-vis that "astonishes." Moreover, the lucidity of a mystic concerning one of his predecessors (and what a predecessor!), the shifts he brings about in a teaching by revealing it in a different light, bring us back to the problem that polarizes theological reflection today—*interpretation*. The understanding of one mystic by another implies a relation of difference and of continuity, but ultimately of *appropriation* (a term by which Gadamer defines hermeneutics) of the former by the latter. Is not the relation of the tradition with the books of the New Testament, or of the Christian experience with its "sources," a relation of this kind? This is the perspective I have adopted: John of the Cross source of Surin, but also Surin interpreter of the Spanish Carmelite and appropriating him.

1. ON INTERPRETATION AS A "RECEIVED" TEXT

"Father Surin and Saint John of the Cross": the problem was already studied, twenty years ago, by Michel Olphe-Galliard,[4] who has devoted himself particularly to showing the influence of the Carmelite on the "spiritual" Jesuits of the seventeenth century and to drawing up[5] a Sanjuanist topography in Surin's work as it was known at that time.

I will leave aside all question of *influence* here. That problematic risks being misleading, since it considers each work only by the aspect of it that concerns the other. This play of mirrors assumes that each work is what the other sees; it implies that one can judge their relation on the basis of what each has retained of the other. We would thus be led to recognize neither John of the Cross nor Surin, as the direct result of a scrutiny that takes in each work what is alien to it and never grasps it in and for itself. Only their publisher [Desclée de Brouwer] can place John of the Cross's *Complete Works* and Surin's *Correspondence*[6] next to one another on the shelves on which it has assembled the monuments of its series "European Library." But each book, a precious object, is closed upon itself in its box. Each work is a well that holds its secret within it, like a key thrown to the bottom. To retain only what they have in common is either to see in Surin only a *result* of various influences, an experience that is reduced to its outside and its prior materials and that is ultimately nonexistent, or to find in John of the Cross no more than pieces scattered by posterity, often in contradiction with one another, condemning that work to occupy a transitory space of "influences" gathered there by chance and immediately dispersed—in sum, an insignificant space.

In order to understand how the works enrich one another mutually and how experiences (considered in each case in their own coherence and therefore in an essential difference with respect to others) are inscribed in a spiritual reciprocity, we must place ourselves deliberately in *this* or *that* specific place, i.e., open a particular volume, and not eliminate a priori in a work the very thing that constitutes it, namely, the fact that it *exists*. Thus, I take the *Correspondence* out of its box to inventory what is *said* about John of the Cross in the network of "correspondences" that weave the work and milieu of Surin. In other words, it is a question no longer of ascertaining what it is that *remains* of John of the Cross in these seventeenth-century Bordeaux texts, but rather of finding out *who Surin's* John of the Cross is.

This problem has a recto and a verso. On the one hand, it consists in asking what is *received* of the Spanish mystic. But on the other hand, since the first editions, the manuscripts that were first circulated, like the later versions (of the nineteenth century, for example) or the critical editions of the twentieth century, are equally "received" texts, although accredited in different ways (*authenticity* having in each case its own criteria), only the *relation* between these successive "receptions"—between these corpora issued from historical *readings*—makes it possible to answer the question: *who* is John of the Cross?

Only the first aspect will be taken up here. Every reading (Surin's, for example) reuses the text; it invents a meaning and it betrays earlier readings; it is docile to the received text, however, but in the mode of saying either the same thing in other terms, or something else in the same terms. It "receives" this and not that. In doing so it conducts a triage; it reorganizes, judges, checks, and verifies. It thus produces a different *version* of the text. Where is the true text? Perhaps we should put in parentheses the hypothesis (which is a recent postulate in historiography and already yellowed by its brief use) according to which individual experience is *something we can apprehend* behind the texts. In reality, all that is readable of any given spiritual experience is what is received of it. And what is received of it at a given moment is one version of the text.

Let us broaden the problem. All spiritual experience that expresses itself, the moment it is expressed, is "alienated," so to speak, in language. First, it uses the words of others; it therefore is subject to the concomitant constraints. John of the Cross, Surin, or the man of today speaks only a language received from others. The words—and their laws—cannot be freely invented. They are "given" to experience, which does not exist anywhere else than where it is said. Moreover, that expression is submitted to an "obligatory passage," namely, the triage and pressure of a group. Its only existence is by leave of the passport issued it by the community in which it is accepted. Spiritual literature shows this in a thousand and one ways. Strictly speaking there is no such thing as individual experience. That is a mirage. Or rather, it is what the historical work postulates, but never states, since it grasps nothing but signs, that is, facts of communication. Confrontation or critique reaches only "received" texts (and they are all received to some degree).

It refers to someone who remains elusive in the very language he spoke, which is never localizable, never reducible to one of these texts (however "primitive" or "authentic" it may be): a man and a man living from God. A spiritual writing gives only the "I" of experience taken in the "we" of a language; from this point of view, the author or the subject appears only as already subjected to the law of a community. This is what makes his experience into a language. Every writing is therefore of an "ecclesial" structure. Therefore the "primitive" experience is today, in our historiography, what we, for our part, "receive" and what we contrast with what others, in the past, have "received." Every complete edition testifies to a rereading. It explicates the will to establish, on the basis of new criteria, a totalizing and coherent reading.

The reading of Surin is a step, analyzable in itself, in that series of "received texts." It presents itself, to be sure, not as the *Complete Works* of John of the Cross, in a constituted corpus, but as the fragments of a new or "updated" edition. It designates the criteria and organizing points of an interpretation. It announces the articulations of a "translation." In sum, this unfinished "received text," taken in the milieu in which it is elaborated, is a fragment that has been isolated from the tableau of a nonexplicated interpretation.

As far as knowing *who* John of the Cross is or what relation so many readings have to one another—this, quite obviously, I cannot say. What remains is only that each "received text" refers to others and that these references say what none of these interpretations can give or stabilize: the mystic experience of the Carmelite, of which they all nonetheless speak.

2. SURIN, READER OF JOHN OF THE CROSS THROUGH R. GAULTIER

In the sixteenth and seventeenth centuries, interpretations already refer to one another, and these "references" form a wide range of positions, exclusions, or combined orthodoxies. It is difficult to distinguish what the historian calls "currents." There is that of Francisco de Quiroga whose Sanjuanist exegesis has, for the last fifteen years, found in Jean Krynen[7] a defender as lucid as he is impassioned. Close to this reading are those of Juan de Bretón, José Antonio de Sobrino, etc. Another tendency, hitherto better known, is that of Luis de León, Thomas de Jésus, Agustín Antonilez, etc. And one may wonder what the position of Innocent de Saint-André was, and of others. Between these currents, holy wars show that one went to war out of faithfulness to a source shared, the moment it was expressed, by the divergent representations that so many *Explications* and Carmelite *Théologies mystiques* gave of their origin.

Where is Surin's exegesis situated? It must first be noted that he was an astonishing reader. This is striking in his interpretation of Ignatius Loyola, centered on the discernment of spirits. I will add that, considering the whole of his work, one is surprised at the rank given to John of the Cross in this literary and mystic space—a rank higher than I had thought at first, being too impressed (I say this by way of *retractatio*) by the mark left by Teresa of Avila, a wake fanning out over the surface of so many texts addressed to women or to Carmelites.

Surin read John of the Cross. He read him early, and this is important, because this great reader and hunter of "mystics" remained, almost to the end of his life, in the language formed by his studies and youthful discoveries; he worked the soil of a first and determinant vocabulary in endless ways, as if in him the prodigious mutations of experience were carried out with the same material. From the start, traumatic and ecstatic moments organize, from a topography of words and "places," everything that will come later. A psychological characteristic, to be sure,[8] but one that is also intellectual, literary, and spiritual. This elementary geography allows us to see, despite the often tragic ruptures or the ultimate "expansions" of his work, the bedazzlement and "halt," as it were, brought about by the encounter with John of the Cross. At the beginning of his universe there is, I believe, that earth and that sun.

From a historical point of view, one is less astonished at this after J. Orcibal's study of a French translation of the *Ascent of Mount Carmel*, and of the *Living Flame of Love* (but not of the *Spiritual Canticle*) prior to 1616 and "prepared for printing by the ecclesiastics of Bordeaux," according to Mother Isabelle des Anges.[9] Carmelite friars and nuns, but also and primarily "some religious of another Order," a Franciscan, etc., are involved in the enterprise of the *señores eclesiásticos* of Bordeaux. There, functioning networks were in place. And among the characters involved, one of the main ones, the dean of the chapter, if he really was Jacques des Aygues, was the uncle of Jeanne des Aygues, who was to become one of the most faithful among the women directed by Surin.[10]

Isabelle des Anges, the founder of the Carmel of Bordeaux and associated with that work, played a decisive role in the life of young Surin while he was still a high school student. He saw her, on days off, behind the bars of a mystic empire. He heard her speak of God in Spanish, a foreign language that became for him the sign of the ineffable. And there, in the chapel of the Carmelites, he was only "thirteen or fourteen" (i.e., in 1613 or 1614) when, in his words, he received an indelible "inner impression of the divine attributes one after the other."

Still more important, for the elaboration of his language, was the translation by René Gaultier published in 1621 by Sonnius in Paris.[11] It contains a mystic vocabulary that would be transplanted in Surin—that same vocabulary that had kept me from thinking, at one time, that there was a proximity between the two mystics, because I was comparing Surin's text to the translation by Cyprien de la Nativité (1641). Moreover, Gaultier's work seems like an ending. It refers back, and explicitly so,[12] to a whole body of earlier work, as attested by the manuscript of Lyon as well as the writings of the Bordeaux Carmelites. It closes and bears witness to a period of transcription. It is to this first layer of the Sanjuanist text "received" in France that Surin belongs, as shown by myriad details to which I will return: thus the use of "song" to designate the mystic teaching, or the translation of *noticia* by "notion," etc.

More broadly, we should probably pause at Gaultier as at a decisive date, too much forgotten thereafter and down to our own time, obscured by the sinuous and brilliant translation of Cyprien de la Nativité. The rising tide of a new text has obliterated the preceding one. But it is the first that, little by little, we retrieve in the libraries and works of the seventeenth century. That primitive Sanjuanist layer in France preceded the work to which Paul Valéry not long ago awarded a poetry prize.[13] I believe the former profoundly marked the spiritual encounters with John of the Cross; it organized the mode of their meeting, while the precious monument of Cyprien is rather the product of all those "communications."

To keep within the Bordeaux region, numerous indications reveal the importance and permanence of Gaultier during the entire seventeenth century, as if, to use Surin's vocabulary, he remained for a very long time the only "pipe" through which the Sanjuanist teaching entered France. As late as the eighteenth century, the College of Guyenne library contained just one translation, that of Gaultier (the 1628 edition).[14] I do not wish to enumerate further indications, though there are many. And if they do not make it possible to give a response (which would require a more extensive survey than the one I have carried out), they at least require that we ask questions about the empire constituted in secret by this forgotten translator.

Gaultier, in his innocence, did not think it necessary to arm the Sanjuanist doctrine with theological defenses. Being himself overwhelmed with admiration for it, he is content with offering those marvels to the public, like an explorer returning from goldmines. Nor is he any less vigorous and specific. He also places everything in a system of expression that he finds appropriate, and that reappears in Surin: that of a space. His sentence creates "regions," is punctuated with "openings" and issues onto "horizons." When John of the Cross writes that such and such occurs "in contemplation," Gaultier translates "in the space of contemplation," etc. His prose invents oceans, vast "expanses," immeasurable "latitudes," and "immense deserts"; it makes the text become an articulation of spaces, a trait equally characteristic of Surin, but also of the Bordeaux translation prior to 1616.[15] A symbolic material, a "style" of the mystic language, something more structuring than ideas—organize the experience just beginning to appear in print with the work of Gaultier. Surin belongs to that "space."

As a bookish people, we are always inclined to emphasize the influence of books and to take the literary indices that we *still have* of the past as *the origin* of the experiences of which they speak. In many cases it is the opposite that is true: exchanges, encounters, a shared endeavor, end up being a book. This is what we see at least in these Bordeaux milieus, as our ignorance, like a receding wave, exposes a surface replete with traces, particularly those of networks in which a mystic language was elaborated. Convents, religious, ecclesiastics, women tainted (as it will be put subsequently) by "mystiquery," the "pious" of all sorts were able, bit by bit, to work the verbal and mental material suitable to communicate their experiences.[16] Related to this material and this living laboratory, though in different ways, are the labors of Gaultier and the oeuvre of Surin. One cannot not be impressed, in this respect, by the literary quality and spiritual lucidity of the texts produced by these Carmelites or these ladies, though it be in the form of *Recreations* and *Portraits*, a genre in fashion at the time.[17] Henri Bremond was right to become the knight in the service of the pious woman of the seventeenth century. She has a decisive role. She is the Amazon of *mystics*, and "the Catholic renewal is largely the work of women."[18] It is also impossible to write a history of John of the Cross in that beginning of the seventeenth century without passing through the ruelles[19] and [convent] parlors of Bordeaux, places in which the "received text" attested by Surin was largely formed.

3. JOHN OF THE CROSS, A "SAINT" WHO WIELDS AUTHORITY

Apropos of Surin, it must be noted that for him, John of the Cross intervenes as an authority, first because he is a "saint" or, at least, almost a "saint." The word at the time denotes more a kind of knowledge and experience than virtues. In other words, it refers to the *sapientia sanctorum*, a constellation of "maxims," of "saids," of "doctrines," but also of "conquests," opposing in countless ways the scholasticism of the professional theologians with a "science of the saints" or a "mystic science."[20] But the "saint" also benefits from a public recognition on the part of the Church: he has received a patent. His authority is situated at the articulation between what he has said of his experience, and what the Magisterium has made him into. Surin, a polemicist and crusader of *mystics*, resorts to the saints to oppose the attacks of the "philosophers." He seeks, through them, to defend a "science" against the "machines of theology."[21] He opposes their "authorities" with other authorities, selecting from within the tradition what he needs to refute the selection that scholasticism, too, had made in the vast and complex treasure of the same tradition.

Thus he uses John of the Cross, but in a somewhat embarrassed way. "A very illustrious man," he writes, "who is about to be canonized."[22] There is a lack of official recognition. This bothers him. He adds: "Father John of the Cross, the companion of Saint Teresa."[23] Saint Teresa—is she not the irrefutable? Better known, easier, already coronate, she is read even by high school students, who have her *Life, written by herself* in their pockets and have received as their dissertation subject the story of her romantic and stellar existence.[24] "Companion of Saint Teresa," is, then, a good reference for a man for whom the beatification process began in 1613, but who will remain "about to be canonized" until 1726. For all that, he is no less of an "authority," later to embarrass Bossuet, after having been difficult to challenge for the "examiners of mystic theology" with whom Surin comes into conflict.

But he is a "saint," and it is as a saint that the "blessed John of the Cross" has authority. The frequency in Surin of references to *La Vie du bienheureux Père Jean de la Croix* by Quiroga (José de Jesús María), translated by Élisée de Saint-Bernard and published in Paris in 1638, is characteristic. This is shown by many allusions. I will mention just one trait, because it has become quasi-mythical and has organized the Sanjuanist legend and iconography:[25] the *Pati, Domine, et contemni pro te*. It is one of the stereotypes of reference to John of the Cross. Thus it also plays a polarizing role in Surin's oeuvre: in it, it designates less ascesis, pain, or martyrdom than the "mad" passivity of the mystic and the violent "inaction" of the God who enters the soul like a robber. The preference given to the *pati et contemni* here is an event, an indelible mark in actual life as a result of which Surin identifies what he calls "suffering love."[26] It is a divine seal similar to the blow indistinctly given and received by Jacob, in the course of his nocturnal struggle. The *pati* is a moment in time, but it inaugurates a new mode of existence. It is at once a hiatus and a structure in the relation with God, for him who, henceforth "bears such a strong wound of his love."[27] "Havoc" and "gentleness," "deprivation" and "abundance" characterize this blow: it opens "the door to a new country."[28] It reaches "the substance of the soul," "whence there comes to him a beatitude and a death, as it were, which ordinary terms can neither declare nor make known. . . . And were it not for the fact that God wants us to hold onto reason, which obligates the soul to hide its astonishment, we would have to abandon the helm and be felicitously shipwrecked in God."[29]

The *pati*, receiving that sort of transposition that assimilates it to the "wound of love," becomes the *Llaga* (wound) of the *Cántico*. But it remains nonetheless a particular episode in an itinerary. A rent in the tissue of time specifies the science of the saints. Recourse to the biographical reference is essential to it. This articulation of an event with a science rejoins the place occupied by the "rare" fact in the organization of the scientific research of the seventeenth century, or the role played by the "encounters" of the traveler in knowledge of the world. In the expanse of fields of knowledge henceforth subject to suspicion, there are, here and there, points of certainty, irrefutable experiences, and islands of certainty, as it were. Thus the explorer on his return from Brazil or Canada can say to his reader: Believe, if you like, in Ptolemy's maps, but as for me, I know, from having been there, that there is a river at this spot. And others thereafter refer to his testimony. The saints are also explorers, and they speak to the theologians like travelers to geographers: "Your discourses are perhaps true, but as for that point, I have experienced it, I have been there, I know it and bear witness to it." They "jolt" the reasons transmitted by the past, in the same way that the New World would overturn so many traditions. Thus, they are looked upon "as savages or strangers whose language is not understood."[30] But what they saw or relate opens up new possibilities to the ambitious. "True stories" *authorize* spiritual travels made *possible* by encounters, just as leaving for Rio or Amazonia is made *possible* by the *fact* that such and such a person passed by there and described it. The combination of particular (or "extraordinary") experiences and a science normally hidden ("mystic") defines a kind of discourse that is often—unsurprisingly—hagiographic. Whence the importance of the biographies of "saints"—which are forms, and not just vessels, of a "science." Whence also the biographical quality that the doctrinal reference to the authority of John of the Cross retained.

Considered from another angle, that authority presents itself as tied to a Carmelite constellation that may surprise the historian. Surin, perhaps by prudence, probably out of innocence, but even more because he did not distinguish between them, that is, because he did not read them as we do, frequently connected John of the Cross, Thomas de Jésus, and Jean de Jésus-Marie.[31] Of these three names, two are always in Latin, which is an indication that he consults their Latin editions,[32] whereas he reads John of the Cross in the French translation. There is a *French* John of the Cross, a locus of communication between nuns or pious women and priests, and there are *Latin* texts, loci that are, in a sense, cultivated, tamed—advanced regions of the Discalced Carmelite tradition. But where these three names are separated for us by considerable doctrinal distance, Surin sees one sole block. In the battle between mystics and antimystics, he advances that united Spanish infantry over which, I believe, the Teresian standard waves.

This indistinction is not confusion. But what we express in the form of distances between times and different doctrinal "currents," Surin accomplishes through a triage of each of his three authors for a truth whose principle he holds within himself, mobilizing them along the lines of the criteria and debates of his day, regrouping them on the basis of a reading that organizes. The result is a corpus cut out by the look. It is not the one performed by our historical look. This trio would, I think, make Jean Krynen shudder. But it already bears witness to the fact that the John of the Cross of that French seventeenth century has his own status.

4. THE "MYSTIC" LANGUAGE

John of the Cross, because he belongs to that corpus of which he is the choice element, receives a special position from Surin, that of being a "mystic author," that is, the founder of a "mystic language." This is a central issue in seventeenth-century Christian thought, because it gave rise to a new division—or rather partition—of the religious sciences: an epistemological trihedral, coordinating the *positive*, the *scholastique*, and the *mystique* (a word that appears at that time as a noun), and replacing the medieval architecture whose keystone was theology.[33] From this angle, John of the Cross is considered the originator (with a few others) of a "discourse" or a "manner of speaking," of "sentences" (according to a term then used) or of a "style" (says Surin) also described as *mystic*. It is a question of a type of discourse to which one has recourse, without necessarily following the Sanjuanist doctrine, because it allows statements that are *different* from his. It defines the status proper to a new series of texts: it makes possible great variations, even theological divergences, but in implying a continual return to the prototypes. It is, in sum, what a literature sets for itself as its condition of possibility. Surin does not recognize—at least not explicitly—this role as being that of the Rheno-Flemish, perhaps because he is southern and at the doors of the Spanish Eldorado, perhaps as a result of a more general "resistance" to the "Germanic" tradition, of which he would represent just one more witness.[34]

It is possible to approach the recourse to the Sanjuanist mystic discourse by the *content* of this language (before envisaging its constitutive *form*). Words and images passed from one mystic to another, and the systematic study of this would be very revealing if we had lexicological instruments better suited to that examination.[35] The seventeenth century was more attentive than we are to this precious baggage, this material of the spirit.[36]

The Symbolic Units

A few of the great organizing symbols of the Sanjuanist experience can, at the very least, be followed in their migrations, and they are found in Surin, who considered these "pieces of furniture" of mystic language to be essential. It is apropos of "those who have reached perfection" that he speaks of the "goods that fill the imagination": "such souls," he writes, "have the habit of receiving the communication of several truths by illustrious symbols that are like so many rich articles of furniture and exquisite pieces placed in the coffers of their memory."[37]

Of the rich Sanjuanist "memory," many treasures passed over to Surin—by what channels it matters little, except that we must underscore the mediation of Bordeaux milieus. Nor is it important to enumerate possible contacts or the "pieces" transported—such as the symbols constituted by new wine, the ray through the hole in the wall, crystal into which light enters, burnt wood or metal melted in the fire, the drop of water in the sea,[38] or that imagery of night, which fascinates and obsesses the "mystic" experience (hidden by definition), but which is more difficult to isolate from its widespread use in the literature of this period.[39] What is more determinate is the analysis of the differences, because they show a new articulation set out by the same symbols: the experience that explains itself organizes differently the relation between the terms combined by each symbol (iron and fire, drop of water and ocean, day and night) and between the various symbols entering into the constellation composed by the totality of a work. The internal relations of each symbol are, moreover, relative to the "external" relation to other types of expression, that is, to its functioning within the whole of the literary work. When Surin replaces the Sanjuanist relation of the drop of water to the sea with recourse to the fish "citizen of the Ocean" or to the swimmer drowned in the sea,[40] he is designating a different experience: in the "abyss" of fusion and loss of self, he is maintaining a qualitative distinction between man and God (the swimmer and the sea). And that difference is posed by the homologous correctives presented by other symbols, that is, by the symbolic organization of the doctrine.

What is "pertinent" in the analysis of the images is therefore the differential, provided that what is grasped in this way are the significant variations within a symbolic language. This language represents, every bit as much as does the language of concepts or that of pictorial figures, a particular regime of expression. In this respect, it is a kind of public institution, but one that has its subtleties and its own laws. Like a change of tone in colors, or like a new use of the words *Geist* or *Vernunft* due to the organization of a philosophical system, the variant, even slight, of one of the terms of the symbol designates a different style. To this subtle play of differences, past or possible, in the relations between the poles of a given symbolic binomial, there corresponds, in the author or reader, a personal sensibility; it reveals, through these minimal shifts, heterogeneous structural creations—without, however, putting into question the symbolism, since on the contrary it is this last that makes those differentiations possible, and in a sense it is the continuity (or repetition) of the same symbols that creates the space in which originalities hew themselves out. Thus the symbolic "concepts" draw their meaning from organic ties with others *within* the work, but can play this role (of becoming meaningful) only by an element of difference (and therefore of comparison) in a relation with their counterparts *outside* that work.

A Psychological and "Technical" Register

The analysis of these displacements from one combinatory to another, that is, from the Sanjuanist symbolic system to that of Surin, would lead us too far—even apropos of particular cases, such as the image of the "well of pain" explicitly taken from John of the Cross.[41] One would have to examine closely how the Jesuit recuts the precious stones borrowed from his predecessor, to make them into a new piece of jewelry. I will merely note two modes among those that characterize the "manner" in which Surin recuts them: he minimalizes the cosmological to the advantage of the affective and the technical.

On the one hand, he *psychologizes* the symbols—and I remove from this word any pejorative sense, since "psychologism" is only a type of language, equal to the "cosmological" or the "abstract," but different, and its value depends not on its status but on what it says. In Surin, the symbol (for example the iron and the fire, the drop of water in the ocean, etc.) turns toward the description of (psychological) states or (moral) conduct in order to point out their internal contradictions and their relation to a "to come" already signified (but invisible) by the tension of the present. This use, moreover, puts pressure on the terms of the symbol. It leads to the metamorphosis of the "drop of water" into "swimmer" (or "fish") in the ocean; of the "fire" into a (quasi-family) "hearth" in which green wood is burned, or into an (artisanal) "furnace" in which metal is smelted. The concept-images, of the cosmological type in John of the Cross, are humanized and civilized—indications of a different time, a different coding, and a different doctrinal perspective.

The slippage from "fire" to "hearth"[42]—and even more so to "furnace" (which leads to "smelting," "metal," "apparatus," the whole lexicon of a profession)[43]—indicates a different dominant feature: technology, and no longer nature, tends to define the register of the imaginary. Not only are the great natural symbols shifted toward the dwelling or the trade (night is formulated in terms of prison, for example, or water in terms of navigation), but they are articulated with *technical activities*: painting, which is not new, embroidery, the various procedures of astronomical calculation, the successive steps in weaving,[44] etc. The crafts and science of the times enter mystic language in a capacity even more important than the mere fact of that introduction: in the capacity not of objects (seen, known, or undergone), but of *operations*, techniques of production and scientific procedures. This represents a new organization whose functioning displaces the symbolic material received from the past.

Prose and Poetry

From a very different angle, in which analogy takes precedence over difference, the relation to John of the Cross is revealed, in Surin, by a shared articulation of prose with poetry. This combination of the poem with commentary is fundamental in the Sanjuanist language. The relationship between them negates all immediate and definitive reading; it refers unceasingly from the one to the other; it forbids reducing expression to either the esthetics toward which the poem would be moved if it were alone, or the moralism to which the commentary would lead if it were not for the poem. A space is created by this movement; the meaning is not fixed here or there; it is stated by this referral itself, which localizes it neither in a silence external to the text, nor in one sole type of statement. In this way, the rich ambiguity that John of the Cross sought in preferring to "leave to the sayings of love their full extension . . . rather than to reduce them (*abreviarlos*) to one sole meaning" is safeguarded.[45] "Open," thanks to that combination of two "symbolic" languages (each one of them is but the half that the other lacks), the discourse will multiply this system of interreferentiality to make connection of opposites a kind of mystic style; thus, at the same time it says what cannot be said in a particular, localizable way, and prevents the illusion of "thinking that that is nothing but what one says about it."[46]

In Surin, this combination prevails. Though less explicitly articulated, it is a resurgence of the Sanjuanist model, and that global organization attests, better than more visible signs, a profound continuity. Indeed, in his treatises, Surin cites his own *Canticles.* He relates his prose to them (at least the prose that treats mystic life) just as he relates it to Ronsard's poetic illumination,[47] that is, to a different "manner" of meaning the *same* thing: two different discourses, but parallel, express, by their very *écart* (which is "proportion") what neither says by itself.

However it may be with the detail of this functioning, we must add that, in both works, the same tropism turns the prose toward the sun of poetry, either because, in John of the Cross, the former comments on the latter, or because, in Surin, the prose quotes fragments of the poems, surrounding them as if it were their jewel box. The topographical result is more or less the same. In the page layout, a privileged place is given to the verses: those strung diamonds create a space around themselves and seem to hold the prose that carries them at a distance. Is it because the master builders are both great poets? Several of Surin's *Canticles* are counted among the masterpieces of universal poetry.[48]

From an external point of view, two details, among many others, are to me indicative of that common preference and of the importance of the Bordeaux environment that has prepared or recognized that encounter. On the one hand, the term *song,* which refers to the Sanjuanist doctrine in the first Bordeaux translation,[49] is also the one Surin uses many times to speak of his own: "my song," he says.[50] A key word: it opens both works. Another point of encounter is no less modest and symptomatic. A manuscript of the *Cantiques spirituels du R. P. Surin* presents us with two "Cantiques spirituels du Bx [Blessed] Jean de la Croix,"[51] the *Cántico* and *La Vive Flamme* [The Living Flame] in a translation that is no longer that of Gaultier and not quite that of Cyprien de la Nativité. This manuscript is marked "de la chambre des Assemblées."[52] Hence it seems to belong to the *Aa*:[53] it serves as a booklet for a group of seminarians who continue the tradition of the "ecclesiastic" translators of the Spanish Carmelite, but add the French mystic poet to it. It is more like a *libretto*. To each chant a "tune" is assigned. As for the *Cántico*, it is performed "to the tune: Ma Philis de tes beaux yeux."[54] The "spirituals" are not so formal: seminarians, Carmelites, "pious" men and women of the time sing John of the Cross and Surin as today one sings the "canticles" of Gelineau. Thus, the "song" is not just a word but a practice. As at the Bordeaux Carmel, it is danced, perhaps.

5. THE "MYSTIC PHRASES": TO SAY AND NOT TO SAY

The "song" leads us from the content to the form of mystic language. By a subtle dialectic between the "tune" and the words, it can often represent a practical, modest, and true solution to the theoretical problem that preoccupied John of the Cross[55] and haunted Surin: How can we speak of a "thing that has no name and that cannot be expressed?"[56] How can we find the right words for the "unknown language" that God "himself forms by his Spirit?"[57] The question of a *modus loquendi* (Lessius), of a *façon de parler* (Anne de Jésus) mobilizes the reflection of the "mystics" during the first half of the seventeenth century, and it tends to define the status of a discourse or a science in its own right that will be referred to by a new noun, *la mystique* [*mystics*].[58] Now is not the time to demonstrate that this question is central in Surin's work, but by its starting point and by the terrain it sets out for itself, it refers, in his work, to John of the Cross and the interpretation given to him in the seventeenth century. At the beginning, there is the contradictory injunction of the Spanish mystic, implicit or explicit in many texts of his French reader: "Souls, *say it*. Oh, no, *do not say it*."[59] How to say? How to not say? Between these two poles, between the impossible and the necessary, language vacillates, breaks, and is reborn. By the sixteenth century, this dramatic linguistic setting, tied to the dissemination of theological nominalism, polarizes the reading of Pseudo-Dionysius around his *Mystic Theology* to the point of making us forget the other aspects of his work in favor of everything concerning possibility, nature, and the modalities peculiar to a mystic discourse—in sum, what Piero Scazzoso has analyzed with great acuity.[60] A systematic use of the "dissimilar," in the uninterrupted text, and a combinatorics of terms resolutely taken to be inadequate would be the equivalent here, in the use of words, to the way Kierkegaard organizes fictive discourses in a rigorous theater of "masks" and turns it into a system of cross-references between his pseudonyms.[61]

But in the exegesis of John of the Cross in the seventeenth century—the one (most often apologetic) on which Surin relies—the problem is focused on the verbal *object*, on that precise point of contention represented, in the vocabulary, by "extraordinary terms." All the weight, and all the contradiction, of the *to say and not to say* are concentrated on that micro-unit designated alternately as the "phrase" or the "word." How is it *mystic*? Surin's discussions and analyses of this topic constitute one of the leitmotifs of his work. They often appeal to the authority of John of the Cross.[62] In reality, they are articulated on more proximate Carmelite exegeses. This is particularly true of the very beautiful *Notes et remarques en trois discours pour donner l'intelligence des phrases mystiques et doctrine des œuvres spirituelles du B. P. Jean de la Croix . . .* [Notes and Remarks in Three Discourses to Provide an Understanding of the Mystic Phrases and Doctrine of the Spiritual Works of the Blessed Father John of the Cross . . .] by the Reverend Father "Iaques [Diego] de Jesus."[63] Without entering here into the details of the demonstration, I believe the role of this text in the debate on Surin's mystic language and teaching to be very important.

It closes the Sanjuanist discourse. Placed at the end of the *Œuvres*, its object is to defend the work: What you have just read, it says to the reader, is perfectly orthodox and in conformity with good theology. Leaving the palace, we come upon the ramparts and moats. But Father Diego, far from reducing John of the Cross to scholasticism as does Nicolas de Jésus,[64] justifies the autonomy of this new language—the mystic language. He does so by relying on its antecedents, Dionysian in particular, since (contrary to what will be the case at the end of the seventeenth century) "new" is still a way of being labeled as "suspect." Still, he does distinguish, in the sources, two groups and two different traditions, "Saint Denis with his mystics and Saint Thomas with his theologians."

Nicolas and Diego represent two systems of interpretation that will divide Sanjuanist exegesis during the whole century. The former denies the separate specificity of the mystic "terms," reduces their intellectual content to classic theology by *resolutiones scholastico-mysticas*, and assigns to *mystics* the role of being an appendix added and linked to "speculation" as a set of "practical" applications. So Antoine du Saint-Esprit (1677), Godinez (1681), and finally the *Cursus theologiae mystico-scholasticae* of Andalusian Joseph du Saint-Esprit. The other current strengthens and "steadies" the position of the mystic language in supplying it with a tradition of its own; it repartitions the past in keeping with the newly constituted units of discourse. This will still be the approach of Honoré de Sainte-Marie in 1708, following Sandaeus (1640) and, in some respects, the Portuguese Joseph du Saint-Esprit (1684), prudently faithful to the *Apologia mistica* of Quiroga. Diego is of this lineage.[65]

He concentrates his reflection on the "words," in a perspective that still polarizes the recent research on the language of the mystics in Jean Baruzi, H. Chandebois, etc.[66] How will the micro-unit of the term express "these matters that are so without matter," he wonders. He answers: by a repetition of the deficit proper to each one of them; the insufficiency of the one term will be compensated for by the addition of its opposite, so that the *relation* itself between opposite (but equally "wanting") signifiers designates the signified. The discrepancy between inverse "figures" is the locus of meaning, because they "do not permit us to repose in them," and because the broken unit, articulated in symbolic halves, forbids our coming to a definitive halt at one of its two elements. The "proportion" between two contrary "lacks" defines the mystic "word." The smallest unit of discourse is therefore constructed according to the law that organizes the whole (for example, as we have seen, the relationship between prose and poetry). It is the locus of a tension characterized by an expression of "Saint Denys": *per dissimiles formationes manifestatio.* It is the manifestation of something else, thanks to "dissimilar forms" or, better yet, by "dissimilar similarities." Diego gives as an example the way Pseudo-Dionysius speaks of the "peace" of the mystics:

"He says: *immanem quietem.* That they have a cruel repose. The most dissimilar and contrary thing to tranquility that can be. Yet he did it with divine counsel, since by what he said of *tranquility*, he removed the imperfect of *fury*, and in saying *cruel and furious quietude* he declared the perfection and excellence of this repose. For whoever understands *tranquility* alone seems to offer himself something idle, half-hearted and cold, careless, of doubtful quality and mediocre perfection. But he who adds that it is *cruel and furious*, already removing the imperfection of fury by *tranquility*, intimates the strength, perfection, and intention, and, as it were, the unbearable and incomprehensible excellence of that *tranquility*, and the excess that it has over the imperfect that passes into us."[67]

This "model," such as it is written, replaces the singular of a localization (one sole "word") with the plural of a relation (two contrary terms). It forces the basic unit to represent what the whole discourse means, namely, the *coincidatio oppositorum* dear to Surin. Perhaps it also bears witness to an incapacity to think as a norm or an organization of discourse as a whole what must thus be found in each one of its elements, that is, in "words." In any case, one sole central view concerns both the "extraordinary terms" and spiritual experience. It is determinative in Surin, perceptible in his theory of mystic science, in what this keen man of letters called the "style" of experience, in his verbal mannerisms themselves or in his most personal pages, such as this description—still so close to Diego's commentary:

> This peace entering (into the soul) produces something that is not of its nature: very great impetuosities. It is this peace alone that can keep pace in this company, like the sound of the sea coming not to ravage the land, but to fill the space of the bed that God gave it. That sea comes as fierce with roaring though it is tranquil. . . . Thus comes peace into the soul, when the grandeur of peace comes to visit her after her sufferings. . . . It comes like an element of the other life, with a sound of celestial harmony and with such rigor [*raideur*][68] that the soul herself is swept off her feet, not by any opposition to her well-being, but by abundance.[69]

6. FROM EXTRAORDINARY GRACES TO THE "UNIVERSAL AND CONFUSED NOTION"
A Disputed Place

The dossier of a long debate over the interpretation to be given to the passages of the *Ascent of Mount Carmel* concerning "visions" and "supernatural" words (II, 16–22), already partially examined by Ferdinand Cavallera, is too bulky to be taken up here. May a few orienting remarks suffice.

For four years (1656–60) Surin and his correspondents argued passionately,[70] and the discussion was to continue until 1663.[71] The question concerned both the meaning of the Sanjuanist teaching and the personal life of Surin. For he was at the time sustained by "extraordinary" graces that came to him as though through "the breaches made in [his] soul"[72] by twenty years of dilapidation. For him, "repaired" by the "visits" of God, recourse to the texts of John of the Cross is almost indissociable from the support that his "destroyed soul" finds in those graces. The "suit" brought against him in particular by Father Bastide, for a time his spiritual director, is, he says, "the harshest opposition I have ever seen," "one of the rough [*sic*] things that I have ever borne."[73] In "the country of divine love," these pages are a vital place, in which, he says, "this saintly person," John of the Cross, "must be understood as referring to the entire abnegation that is in the depths" of the soul, "and not to actual separation" from the extraordinary graces:[74]

> For my part, I believe that what Father John of the Cross and others say: that we must distance ourselves from gifts and reject them and separate ourselves from them should be understood as applying only to the depths of the soul; that the latter should have God alone, but that such gifts are necessary to it and have good effects; that the effort to push them away is in fact damaging; that all that can be said is that we must carefully see to it that we go to God alone and seek him alone.[75]

To which Father Bastide answers: "I say nothing at all that is not taught by Father John of the Cross, unless it is that I soften and explain what he seems to say a bit crudely."[76] Let us just add to the dossier the text of *The Ascent* itself, the authority under dispute. John of the Cross writes:

> But, with respect to what has been said, it must be pointed out that, although we have insisted so much that such things should be set aside, and that confessors should not incite their penitents to discuss them, it is not well that spiritual fathers should show displeasure in regard to them, or should seek to avoid them or despise them, or give their penitents cause to show reserve and not to venture to speak of them, for it would be the means of causing them many inconveniences if the door were closed upon their relating them. For, since this is a means and manner whereby God guides such souls, there is no reason for thinking ill of it or for being alarmed or offended by it; but rather there is a reason for proceeding very quietly and kindly, for encouraging these souls and for giving them an opportunity to speak of these things; if necessary, they must be exhorted to speak; and, in view of the difficulty that some souls experience in describing these things, this is sometimes quite essential. Let confessors direct their penitents in faith, instructing them frankly to turn away their eyes from all such things, teaching them how to void the desire and the spirit of them that they may make progress, and giving them to understand how much more precious in God's sight is one work or act of the will performed in charity than are all the visions and communications that they may receive from Heaven, since these imply neither merit nor demerit. Let them point out, too, that many souls who have known nothing of such things have made incomparably greater progress than others who have received many of them.[77]

To this firm and nuanced position, John of the Cross in his practice gave a rather restrictive interpretation, as proven, for example, by his intervention concerning Gratian.[78] Surin does the opposite, out of a personal reaction, to be sure, to survive among the ruins into which a "celestial" springtime is suddenly infused, but also to defend *mystics* against the minimizing exegesis of his milieu.[79] In that milieu, the "extraordinary" is suspect, not only for reasons of prudence or discernment, but by the very effect of a doctrine, of nominalist origin, that exiles the "supernatural" from language, constitutes the "natural" as an autonomous order, and thus considers everything experiential to be necessarily natural.[80] Thus a definition of the norm creates, as that which it makes unthinkable, an "extraordinary"—an abnormal. That is the place to which every Christian is consigned who reports an "experience" of the truth. He finds himself deprived of words (which have all been ascribed "natural" meanings), consigned to the secret ("mystical"), and imprisoned by the very logic he struggles against. Perhaps the *form* of the "mystic words" is partially dictated by that original theological determination that, excluding all true designation of the spiritual, forced the search for an expression in the relation between contraries. Perhaps also the localization of experience in the psychological realm or in the night of the ineffable is due, to a large extent, to its elimination from the rational or verbal order.

Nevertheless, in the singular disagreement pitting Surin against Bastide and others, John of the Cross becomes a factor in a new problematic. His text vacillates between two interpretations (that of Surin and that of Bastide) that depend more on each other than on it. The fact of its being "received" changes it and relocates the question. In this debate, it is less a question for us of determining which of these two interpretations is most faithful to it than of knowing, in terms of the role to which it is assigned on either side, what it *became* for these readers in Bordeaux.

The "Sanjuanist" Model

From this debate that takes up hundreds of pages in the *Correspondance* and in *La Science expérimentale*, I will retain only one other lesson. In that altercation, Surin's exegesis is more revelatory of the nature of the triage he carries out in the Sanjuanist oeuvre, and of the personal turn he lends to what he quotes from it. He retains two poles from it—either the denial of self to which he opposes the "torrents of grace," or the hell he opposes to paradise—as accentuating the extremes whose "coincidence" alone signifies the truth of spiritual life. In each case also, he accentuates the affective character of the reference; he dramatizes it or hardens it, but in order better to show, through these antinomies, that the truth is but more "other" thereby, not only more mad and more miraculous, but of a different order; that the "happy drowning" is birth of being in the loss of having. Here John of the Cross is giving the blueprint of the mystic experience. Hence he takes on the appearance of a quasi-abstract reference. His doctrine posits the opposing end points of a tension. It furnishes the spiritual life with a theoretic schema, just as the Sanjuanist "style" gives mystic language a model.

A systematic study of the vocabulary and quotations of Surin makes it possible for us to establish that the mention of the Carmelite comes in as if at both antipodes of the experience analyzed: at the point where darkness is total, and where light is blinding. He evokes the cross,[81] abnegation[82] and especially the hell of the soul to which "the blessed John of the Cross devoted a special book"[83]—or "the living flame of pure love,"[84] the "possessions of the soul," and "riches of the spirit,"[85] and finally the "spiritual marriage" spoken of by "the blessed John of the Cross in an entire book he wrote on that."[86] The work of John of the Cross is divided into opposite "places," ultimately constituted by two categories of titles and books. The text as received by Surin is much more antinomic than the "primitive" text. This seventeenth-century reading applies the same treatment to the "mystic" doctrine and to its language; it interposes between those two extremes an "essential," their paradoxical relationship, their beyond that is impossible to say immediately, their spiritual meaning, their truth that is not localizable in a particular experience: the "universal and confused notion."

That is perhaps, in Surin's teaching, the invisible center in relation to which everything is organized, the black sun of his oeuvre. The "universal and confused notion" illuminates the last years of his correspondence. With its appearance, we see his style, which had for a long time been more armed, precise, and rapid, become more placid or rapturous (which should we say?). Having left for a distant "region" of love, the adventurer seems to let go of his sword and finally let himself, there where he is, be seduced by this country born of an unhoped-for sun. What "happens" to the mystic is not an elsewhere, not a "here," nothing particular, but, opened up by a circulation that has touched so many extremes, a space without space, an "amplitude" compatible with the "common life" without being identical with its particularities, an experience in which "the chasm of faith" includes no further privileged or "extraordinary" places.[87] The "universal notion" relativizes so to speak the terms that already announced it by their opposition. In experience, meaning prevails over the signs that it was necessary first to negate in order to focus on it.

If we do not pause to analyze the many texts in which Surin explains "that universal notion of God known in silence and peace," "the confused idea of that divine silence," "that indistinct cloud of peace," "that secret word that is spoken in the heart with no sound of sensible and distinct words, without the expression of any created thing,"[88] we return to pick up the trail of John of the Cross, that of his *noticia general y oscura*. Once more it is by the intermediary of René Gaultier. The 1621 translator uses "notion," and not "notice" (as does Cyprien de la Nativité), to translate the Sanjuanist *noticia*.[89] He even multiplies the use of this term. He uses it, for example, to translate the *cosas distintas* with which the truth can no longer be confused (*The Living Flame*, III, 2). He prepares and refines the instrument that will allow his mystic reader to express the goal of his journey. It is in the beautiful and rough transcription of Gaultier that Surin meditated on this page—decisive to him—of *The Living Flame*:

> In the space of contemplation of which we are speaking, in which God pours into the soul, there is no need for any distinct notion (*noticia*), nor for the soul to make several discourses, because at that time God communicates to it loving notions (*noticias*) that are like light and heat without distinction, and at that time as the understanding is, so is also love in the will: for as the notion (*noticia*) is general and obscure, the understanding being unable to understand distinctly what it understands, so also the will loves in general without any distinction.[90]

How can one go beyond that "indistinct" silence? It brings us back, in the end, to the discreet presence of René Gaultier, justly introduced by André Rayez into the *Dictionnaire de spiritualité*.[91] To the worker who lost himself and made himself indistinct in the text of others this note on the interpretation of John of the Cross by Surin should have been dedicated. Erudition, which is also hard-working and hidden, discovers little by little, beneath the mountains that fascinate the look, great subterranean layers, deep circulations, and secret discoveries: pious translators, Carmelites or ecclesiastics of Bordeaux covertly ensure the transmissions that emerge in the great works. With these faceless *mediocre* ones, shifts are brought about, meetings prepared—a common experience is elaborated. The mystic work of history.

Chapter Five

Absolute Reading

In pondering the reinterpretation of the tradition in the sixteenth and seventeenth centuries, I will pause to consider a historical figure of reading that I will call "absolute" reading, because it frees itself from the text and, in so doing, absolves itself from its law. It involves a paradoxical relation to the book, to this garden of ordered signs, this body tattooed with graphemes. It is not, properly speaking, a "reading," in the sense of an interpretation, but rather a practice of reading: a *modus lectionis*, a *modo di leggere*, as it was called, a way of reading, that shows how to circulate in a space of signs, and how to use that space, in the same way that during the same period "guides" were intended to instruct the traveler more than to describe the visited countries.[1] Beginning at the end of the sixteenth century, hence late (as is frequently the case) and after many treatises had been dedicated for over a century to specifying its rules, protocols, and principles, that art of reading was called "spiritual reading," *lettione spirituale*.[2] The term deserves to be underlined right away because the "spirit" thus designates "that which speaks," and it refers here to that which speaks in the text or that which lets itself be heard in the text, in sum to the orality of the text, or to the text insofar as "it speaks to" its reader and thus becomes for him or her the "fable" of an initiative and unknown voice.

The new term ("spiritual reading") circumscribes a set of behaviors that gradually becomes distinct from the medieval tradition it comes from, the *lectio divina*, and that is characterized, in a first approximation, by being less interested in the nature, authority, or even meaning of the book than in its use. The "method" it isolates is part not of a "hermeneutics," relating to meanings, but of a pragmatics, attentive to the operations of the reader. Such a shift moves from the "truths" that the text is assumed to contain to the activities by which its user constitutes (or "edifies") himself qua speaking, desiring, and answering subject. Thus it profoundly modifies the relation to works received from the past, at the same time as it reveals, in a figure perhaps exotic, but technical, of modernity, a postulate of all reading activity: a voice of the text.

Taking as my corpus the voluminous dossier of treatises, guides, descriptions, etc., that belong to a mystic literature and that, from the fifteenth to the seventeenth century, define the rules or conduct specific to the "spiritual reading," I would simply like to show, thanks to that history (perhaps less singular than it seems at first), what contribution it makes to a phenomenology or to a theory of reading, and how it posits in different terms the relation, apparently docile, that the reader has to books, those monuments assumed to be stable, like recumbent statues sculpted by a past.

1. THE BOOK OF THE "SPIRITUALS": A HISTORICAL FRAMEWORK

The mystic treatises of the sixteenth and seventeenth centuries promote, as we will see, a detachment of the reader in relation to the book. This campaign (and it is one) seeks to autonomize the reading subject. It has a scandalous character, if we compare it to the ideology that the *Aufklärung* made the premise of pedagogy for nearly two centuries, and that holds the book itself, its content, to be the privileged agent of education. While during the eighteenth century the reader appears to be the result of the book, like the shadow it casts or its inscription in social history through the mediation of the school and the professor, the mystic conception aims to emancipate the reader-subject and to credit him with an existence of his own, detached from any subjugation or conformity to the book. The history of the readers cannot be reduced to that of their books.

Such a rupture is no less scandalous with respect to a medieval tradition that makes the cosmos the book of which all the others, including the Scriptures, are the more or less authorized revealers, and that considers all human beings to be readers called to make their lives conform to what has already been given to them to understand, by various means, of the fundamental book. Hence the "spiritual" reading of the modern mystics is inscribed within a greater whole in which the book receives a new status. As for the circumstances that brought about the transformation of the book, I will restrict myself to a few reminders. The crisis that took the theoretical form of Ockhamism definitively separates from all discourse the unfathomable Author of the world in which we are, and thus strips the concept "book" of its universal and ontological value. On the other hand, the beginnings, still disseminated and modest, of the "bourgeois" epopee replace the ontological and hierarchized Book with an instrumental book, the product of an operative writing and destined for the fabrication, accumulation, and diffusion of a kind of knowledge capable of ordering a world. An important corollary: Once detached from the cosmic order and from its Author, which in the past it was assumed to make readable, the book also ceases being *the* norm of experience; it acquires an operative value to the extent that it is conjoined with facts that are exterior to it. The one medieval *Codex Naturae* is divided into two figures, sometimes opposing each other, sometimes combinable, but henceforth irreducible—a bookish figure and an experimental one. From this point of view, the innumerable humanist declarations rejecting books in favor of observations[3] attest to the movement to which the mystics also belong, in privileging "the experience," but an experience whose terrain is the subject himself.

In its function within the network of hermits and other Christian groups designated in the sixteenth and seventeenth centuries as "illuminati," "mystics," or "spirituals," the book presents a few characteristics of its own. A brief look at these will serve as a framework for the absolute reading.

The book increasingly replaces institutions, considered as being decadent or corrupt, or their official representatives, adjudged incapable, often by the very fact of their knowledge, of understanding the demand addressed to them by the "spirituals." Scripture compensates for the inability of the ecclesiastical agents. The former is assumed to speak while the latter are mute or deaf. This new role involves not only the holy books but all books capable of supplying a language to love and its anxiety. John of the Cross, at the threshold of his treatises, declares that he writes because the "directors," or representatives of the institution, "do not understand" the desirous appealing to them.[4] His books take the place of the authorized voice that is lacking. Teresa of Avila seeks, in contemporaneous works of spirituality, what the clerics cannot tell her.[5] For a great many others the same is true. The book takes the place of the lacking or decadent institution. It plays its role. It becomes itself the major institution, while, lucidly, the clerical organizations react, with more or less violence, against this diversion.

The *nature* of the book also changes, along with its role. In truth, it is no longer even the same book, even though we are dealing with a selfsame text. In the spiritual practice of the twelfth and thirteenth centuries, the book, in the form of the liturgical Bible, the monastic Rule, or an "authority" coming from the "Fathers," is an organ of the institution, which oversees its interpretation, controls its circulation, and ultimately has the function of "author." From the fifteenth century on, it frees itself from that allegiance, in virtue of a triple autonomy. First, its *printed dissemination*, which ensures the texts a longevity hitherto reserved for magisterial genealogies, makes a personal appropriation possible, and the networks of its commercialization, a book institution independent of the academic or clerical authorities, allow for new relations of individual authors with individual readers.[6] Second, the progressive use of the *vulgar tongues* favors all the shifting ambiguities of daily speech, that "parlance" of love already defended by Dante[7] and that, eluding the semantic preciseness of university or theological Latin, infiltrates everywhere with its possible plays of free interpretation. Third, with the growing diversification of literary genres, a literature termed "spiritual" proliferates, already resembling the *novel* by its narration of passions and extraordinary journeys in the lands of desire. This new book procures an insularity for its readers. It gives every individual story its own place. It is autobio-graphical by nature.

It is no less a book for all that, a *space* external to the perusing eye, a "theater" of the mind (what we call an "atlas" was then known as a "theater") and also, as many of these authors say, a "mirror" opening up within the visible a scenography of the invisible, but, by contrast to the parchment, which is rare and forbidden, this theater is transportable, manipulable, and available for all sorts of intellectual or phantasmagorical operations. Everyone thus has a laboratory for experimentation, the possibilities and rules of which will be explicated by the "ways of reading." To be sure, these spaces available for "productions" (that is, for the performances of actors, for all the movements of the subject on a different stage) are connected to the spaces that were already produced by an "art of memory" for the purpose of mental activities, but the imaginary theaters of old are henceforth characterized by a twofold difference that in turn transforms the *ars memoriae* itself.[8] First, the inner place that imagination created for itself is objectified, transformed into the spatial and cartographical reality of the book. Second, this exteriorization of the terrain on which the combinatory activities are carried out increases the possibilities of invention; it facilitates more complex possibilities of signs, and, in particular it gives more flexibility to the relations between "ideas" and the places in which they were stored in memory to retrieve them. While the art of memory presupposed a fixed "locale" for each type of figure, the book transgresses that order of definite places; it mixes with virtuosity "locales" and "figures," and it refers to the old taxonomy only in the form—alphabetical—of a final *index locorum*, a relic of the traditional practice. In this perspective as well, the theater of the book individualizes and multiplies the operations possible for readers.

Still, and here its institutional character becomes clearer, the book circumscribes a *place in which there must be a word to be heard*. In the chaotic and mendacious space of the world, it cuts out, marks, and makes present, like the temples or sacred stones of yore, a place in which we may expect meaning to speak. What matters, more than the statements it composes, is the fact that it is, or should be, a sign of enunciation, the sacrament of a word to be heard. As such, it is "spiritual" if, and only if, it is inscribed in the problematic of the "dialogue," of the *conversar* or the *oratio* that constitutes the focal point of the mystic approach.[9] Circulating within a landscape of corruption that obsesses all the spirituals, punctuating a Christian history conceived everywhere as having become decadent since its origins, it gives objective form to the expectation that the Spirit of the beginnings must still manifest itself today. It gives rise to that belief that somehow survives the slow attrition of an aging world in which things, and even authorities, fall silent one after another. It safeguards a hope. Mute though it is, like Rabelais's "frozen words,"[10] the book gives form and feature to the waiting that, in the uncertainty or silence of the cosmos, puts its faith in an unknown voice, capable of being that of the divine interlocutor and of the faithful in turn—the voice that speaks and that prompts one to speak a language in the process of disappearing. It supervenes, falling into your lap like a treasure to be opened: a space for voices to be recognized.

2. THE "MOMENTS" OF READING

This conception of the book is part of a "horizon of expectation." It is possible to recapitulate my first point in appealing to that category, developed either by the Soviet formalists, in particular by Yury Tynyanov, as extended by the *Rezeptionsästhetik* of Hans Jauss,[11] or, in a probably more fundamental phenomenological mode, by Maurice Merleau-Ponty, attentive to what he calls "perceptual faith," an expectation that structures all perception.[12] Indeed, the ideological definition of the book of the spirituals refers us to the social expectation that characterizes that milieu of readers. This first exploration does not suffice, however, to specify their reading. In connection with the situation in which the book is placed, and which precedes the activity of reading, we have still to inquire into the product of that activity: the meaning. This second exploration, focusing on the last stage of the process, will consider the effects of expectation on the understanding of the book and the discrepancies or alterations that a "resistance" of the text introduces into what its readers expect to find there. The interplay between the readers' expectation and the resistance of the text forms what we call the "meaning."

But this study itself examines only one partial aspect of reading. The book is no more reducible to its meaning than a statement is reducible to its content. Like the statement, it is embedded in a holistic manifold of practices, or "directions for use," that give it quite other values than its semantic definition. These practices of the book, moreover, modalize the interest directed to its meaning, sometimes to exaggerate it or isolate it, sometimes to relativize or depreciate it. Today the object of a "pragmatics" and of an "ethnography of speech" or "of communication,"[13] the sociocultural uses made of language constitute a mediation between the expectation of the reader (which concerns a history of mentalities) and the identification of a meaning (which comes under hermeneutics). They give rise to a third exploration, relative to a third function, differing from the two others, and involving the behaviors or intentional practices of the reader. These last were the basis of the distinction formerly established by Roland Barthes between reading for pleasure, reading for instruction, and reading for the purpose of writing:[14] this classification was in reference to instructions for use. Borges already said that "one literature differs from another less by the text than by the way it is read."[15]

Now this question is privileged by the spirituals, who are, moreover, conscious that this point, and not a problem of meaning, is what contrasts their way of reading with the theological or academic one. There is nothing surprising about this. From "the way of speaking"[16] to the way of reading, their strategy consists in specifying which uses of language allow us to say, to confess, or to hear what escapes language, namely, the Other or God. In theory, this strategy has as a consequence the priority, sometimes obsessive, that the spirituals grant modalities (for example: can, should, know, believe). In practice, it consists in specifying the behaviors by which an "intention" can be expressed in instructions for use. This is what we find in the texts devoted to ways of reading, on the basis of the principle posited, already in the twelfth century, by a major work of the spiritual tradition, the *Lettre aux frères du Mont-Dieu* by Guillaume de Saint-Thierry: "Intentioni enim servit lectio" (reading is subservient to intention).[17] This transgressive principle, which imposes the law of the reader/listener on the book/teacher, is in keeping with the ways of doing things that frame "the intention of the reader"[18] in terms of operations. In order to present them, I could analyze the "Notice to the Reader" texts that open these works of spirituality by referring to the practices of their intended readers. With variations, they repeat and develop the "envoi" sent by one of them: "Amy, lecteur, *utere et fruere.*"[19] Use this book and profit from it. These two words say the essential, which focuses on a use of the book. I will, instead, in order to describe this art, sketch out the ideal schema of a few essential "moments" as found in numerous documents that tell us the story of the relations of the reader with the book. These relations are not stable. They vary with the itinerary of the reading subject; they mark his progress and are transformed or reiterated in keeping with his comings and goings. I will retain only four figures: the positing of the beginning, the mutation of the book into a garden of affects, the fabrication of a speaking body thanks to a "mastication," and the interruption that detaches from the text.

A beginning. The book acts as a threshold: a border is needed, so that there may be an other in relation to a quest on the part of the subject. Its first status is that of object. It marks an exteriority. It cuts an otherness out in the vast field of language in which there roams a desire that does not know itself. Essentially it is intended not to furnish knowledge, but to trace out, in an uncertain landscape that one supposes to be haunted by the divine and therefore assimilable to a dialogical ("religious") language, the difference of an opaque, separate, *being-there.* Rather than being the statement of a signified, it is a signifier of the Other. The book is a *distinct place* that serves as the index designating the "want-to-say" of another.[20] It creates division, an elementary structure and minimal condition for the initiation of a dialogical praxis: without difference, no relation.

Teresa of Avila relates that "when a book was lacking, her soul was in confusion and her thoughts in disorder": the book is the placeholder of the other and creates distinction. It allows one to "busy oneself" (*ocuparse mucho en leccíon*) during the time of *oracíon;* in that respect, still according to Teresa, it is *recreación*: she says that when, for lack of imagination, she feels a "void," a vacant scattered state, the book appears once more as an ob-ject in that undifferentiated space, casting the little stones of its words into it, as if already offering consonants for the confused vocalization of desire. Therefore she declares reading "necessary, even if one reads little." It is a principle of articulation. "During those years," she concludes, "except after communion"—a characteristic restriction, for the Eucharistic bread (or Host) also plays the role of ob-ject, it is the material signifier of the other—"I never dared to begin to pray without a book."[21] The "dialogue" does *not* begin *without* the book. *Nicht ohne*: the category of "not without" designates the way of beginning.

Most of the spirituals underline this point that the book maintains an essential relation to the void. But its position is characterized, in these beginnings, by the fact that it "occupies" an empty place; it maintains it, it marks it, without filling it. Teresa also points out that this book/object allows her at once to "go out" and to "stay." It takes her "out" of the neutral of the undifferentiated (at times when "nothing comes out of her") and it makes her "stay" there, in the desert of a solitude (at times when her spirit prompts her toward vagabondage and wandering). Organized in keeping with a mental physics of attention, or rather of admiration (that surprise without object—*Betroffenheit* or dazed perplexity), the book keeps a place more than it supplies a meaning. In the extreme case, it suffices to hold that index of otherness in one's hand: "Often," says Teresa, "I would open the book with no need for anything more."[22] Opened, but not read, it embodies what it does not interpret. In a word, like the institution it takes the place of, it constitutes the mute being-there of the twofold assumption on which a believing is based: *there is* otherness; *there is* meaning. But what "other," and what meaning? It says nothing about that. Like a rock in a landscape, it is *there*, as a monument and not a document, a witness but not an interpreter of these assumptions.

In this role, it can be replaced by elements of the countryside: flowing water, flowers, etc., are inscribed in the landscape like the open page in visual surroundings; they "replace the book."[23] A century earlier, Suso, Jean Tauler, and many others counseled the worshiper to support or fix the prayer with those "natural" things, but, for them, the things in question signified the will of a Speaker. They were documents: a teaching. At the end of the sixteenth century, with Teresa, the book is no longer a variant of the great cosmic Book spoken by God; it becomes itself the referent. The flowers refer us to the open setting of the unread page. Like the book, they make up an alphabet of beautiful silent things that guarantee a reality without saying a truth.

The garden of affects. In insisting on a beginning that excludes curiosity and promises admiration, this art of reading prepares a second "moment" that consists no longer in setting the tone for the reading, but in indicating its matter, its stuff: affects. That the readers should change the book into a garden of affectivity—this is affirmed by a long tradition. *Sapor et non scientia*, as Saint Bonaventure said in the thirteenth century. At the beginning of the seventeenth century, Álvarez de Paz repeats: "Non notitiam, sed gustum et affectum," and, at the end of the preceding century, Luis de Granada, a great collector of mystic literature, defines the way of practicing it in speaking of the "charm" and "pleasure" of reading.[24] The *gustus*, *sapor*, *inflammatio*, etc. clearly express a "passionate" use of the book. Furthermore, the "savors," "tastes," "fervors," that occur periodically in it presuppose a reading made of movements: emotion and motion are joined; the *affectus* implies and stimulates a *motus*. Hence *lectio* is considered to be an *actio*. This performance is carried out, it seems, only in order to exit itself. It is drawn out of itself now toward dialogue with the other (*oratio*), now toward the service of the other (*opus*),[25] in the form of quasi-ecstatic and transitory expressions on the frontier of the activities toward which its dynamic tends. An operation of passage, it turns elsewhere, far from the book, what it puts in play in its garden.

Thus there is an essential ambivalence in this mobilization of affects in the enclosure of the open page. What it captures and represents comes from a very old pleasure. As Teresa of Avila testifies: "I always wish I had time for reading, and have always been fond of it."[26] Since the novels of chivalry that she devoured as an adolescent, unbeknownst to her father, or the "lives of the saints," which are but a variant of them, she has read with "pleasure," with "passion."[27] The works of spirituality will take over the same fictional function where the former leave off; they are poems revelatory of affects, just as poems awaken sleeping fairies. This reading resembles the dream, narrating desires day denies. Faithful to the biblical alliance of dream and spirit, Teresa calls the other life she seeks and discovers "dream": "Life gives me the impression of a dream; nearly always I think I am dreaming what I see."[28] Thus *lección* and *sueño* come together. Reading originates, legitimizes, and nourishes dreams. It authorizes the temerity they express: "Take your desires for realities." In the tradition of the monastic paradise (*paradisus claustralis*) and of the gardens of courtly love,[29] the book becomes the covered walk of lovers, a "solitude" in which feelings are declared. It is situated between a dream that has written itself and a writing that one dreams, between the dream that has taken the objective form of a text and the dream that, like a phantom awakened by a passerby, invents other voyages. The Carmel as conceived of by Teresa will, moreover, be the reproduction of what she makes the book into, a place enclosed, in which lovers can walk freely and speak to the Beloved.

But this reading constructs the fiction of a text. By the novel into which it metamorphoses, if it expresses or liberates the real movements of desire, it produces only an imaginary book or objects, a fugitive language constituting nothing appropriable, neither discursive knowledge nor positivity. In going beyond the text, it runs toward the *nothing* of what it represents. It is an exercise of absence. To take things from a different angle, it may equally be said that since the affect refers us back to the speaking subject, this exercise overvalues utterance, the act of saying (oneself), and devalues the said, the semantic content. It excavates, in language, that "empty place" that is, for Émile Benveniste,[30] the "I" of the speaker. Hence, if we do not identify the "spiritual" life with that set of imagery (an illusion against which the mystic authors constantly put their readers on guard), this art of reading tends paradoxically toward something other than the book and other than the reader; it makes the place it institutes untenable. By the very representation of his affects, the reader loses himself in something other than himself. Such is the ambivalence of an expression produced only to sink away in the silence of contemplation or the silence of service, two forms of access to the reality of the other. Reading makes the book a passing thing (it fades away) and a passage (it transports), in short, a metaphor of the subject.

The fabrication of a speaking body. To opinions recommending a reading that is "slow" (that should not read too much, or too quickly, or too many different authors), "interrupted" (segmented by a hundred and one ways of addressing the feelings it awakens to the interlocutors), and "elevated" (detached from the information furnished by the text),[31] and thus considering the book as a "ferryman" or a shifter, there must be added apparently contrary opinions suggesting a "mastication" of the book. "Take and eat": on this traditional theme, a whole series of counsels are developed for "swallowing," then "ruminating," "chewing over," and "digesting" the text. An eating orality replaces a saying one. It has as its model the *ruminatio* of the cow, an alchemy internal to an immobile body, a work performed on itself by that animal, meditating like a Buddha on the grass. Thus, not to go back too far, the rule given in the twelfth century by Guillaume de Saint-Thierry: "Of daily reading, each day something (*aliquid*) must have gone into the belly of the memory to be more surely digested, then brought up to be more frequently ruminated."[32] The words enter into a physiological machinery, owing to "sympathies" that today might receive a psychoanalytic legitimization. Until the seventeenth century, that reading remains an affair of the mouth and the stomach. Surin requests that bookish "nourishment" be "solid" and well "prepared" for the "necessities" of the "stomach."[33] These are not just images. Eating the book can cause illness, portliness, or fitness. Not only that, but the swallowed text irritates or soothes the taste buds and mucous membranes of a spirit that haunts the grottos of the body. It visits, "restores," or wounds an internal sensoriality.

My purpose is not to restore to this digestive reading its medical or chemical setting,[34] but only to stress, first, the relation of the text to the body, and second (to use a term from these authors), what "profit" their readers derive from it. Indeed, these are two essential aspects of mastication.

The first concerns the fabrication of a body by *some* language. To be more precise, fragments of the body are transformed by bursts of language as if lead were changed to gold in those places where the body is "stricken" by a "word." This experience would probably bear comparison with what much evidence indicates today, from the phenomena of hysterization to the varieties of structuration of the body by societal systems, namely, that the body is modeled along the lines of cultural and linguistic codes; it is itself made up of heraldry (or pages) historicized by bits of "ruminated" phrases. It is marked by textual citations as if it had an inner skin on which words were tattooed. There are, in the course of this reading, textual sequels: "intestinal" pains or distention, instances of sudden warmth in the head, heart palpitations, the outpouring of tears. *The Way of a Pilgrim* will restate it once more in the nineteenth century: "What are you crying about?" . . . "she would answer, 'It touches me so, that beautiful writing in the Bible.'"[35] What, then, is this "something" (*aliquid*) of the language that is able to "strike" a part of the body and to metamorphose it into a relic of the other, an erotic sign, a spoken and speaking memorial? Let us ask psychoanalysts—or lovers.

Basically, "profit" designates that "touch" itself, the corporeal response to a textual feature. "A few things penetrated [by us] are of more profit than many [merely] grazed," writes Surin on the subject of those "few books" that one must "espouse" and "familiarize oneself" with.[36] The intensity of the response is measured by the depth of a penetration. To analyze this "profit," we must return to Valentin Voloshinov: "to understand is to respond"; "the sign exists only in interaction."[37] But the interaction here is played out between the body and the text; it is "symbolic" fiction (or fabrication), having the structure of the echo, for the local physical alteration belongs neither to the reader/subject nor to the book read, neither to the body nor to the mind; it is neither the one nor the other, but between them, like a pain of love. Letting happen what he does not know of his stricken body, the reader could say with Marguerite Duras: "I cry for no reason that I can explain. It's as though I were shot through with grief. Someone has to cry, it is *as if* it were me."[38] These anonymous tears present a form of the *aedificatoria lectio*,[39] which "edifies" or produces the fragment of a new body responding to an unknown.

Interruption. In inscribing itself in the body, reading leaves the text. It escapes. The truth is that this moment of detachment begins to form from the beginning: "With your eyes fixed on the book," says Juan de Avila, "do not attach your heart to it."[40] A diffuse attention maintains a horizon of the absolute. It cannot be held within the textual enclosure; it considers the pages of the book as places of transit that must be abandoned one after another. No house is its own: it is not here, not there. The book is a residence that must be left behind: "It is good to interrupt reading."[41] This universal counsel is an invitation to interrupt the text with dialogue and invocation: *Lectionem interrumpat oratio*, repeats J. Álvarez de Paz.[42] The use of the book, daily and regular, is interrupted by periodic separations that forbid identification with the text. This rupture is the only thing that will allow access to a "never spoken" word, perhaps like Don Juan, who continually breaks up with women to seek The Woman who will ultimately have the face of his death. This practice articulates a work of mourning. A commentator will go so far as to say: "The best book is the one that disappears the most."[43]

The text stands under the law of the *not too much.* It rapidly becomes exorbitant, obscene. The reader is claustrophobic; he suffers from an excess of book presence and from being enclosed by meaning. He needs exits. He flees by his way of cutting, the way oral speech oddly leaves the sentence once begun in suspense, the way it comes to a halt, turns away, passes on to other musical patterns—captive, one might say, to a voice that is the hinterland of language. A true reading, according to Tony Duvert, is "discovered from the first utterance of strangeness": this "readability obscures the work because it gives up the socially prewritten communicable for the never spoken language of a never said reality—the body, the object, the nonmeaning."[44]

This pared-down text is related to a great number of *excerpta*: manuscripts collating excerpts, they assemble, in the form of personal notebooks, bits of texts read, "extracts" and quotations that represent not a summary or the gist of the book but the parts that have "touched" or "smitten," and that one retains in leaving it—a few words, as if from a song from one's childhood, debris relating to the history of the reading subject and not to the positivity of a thinking or information, signifiers analogous to those Freud would exhume in the course of an analysis and to which he gives the beautiful name *Stückchen Wahrheit*—a little fragment of truth.[45] But what truth, and whose? These ruins of texts are gathered there, in these collations of enigmas that make up, added to one another, at once scattered and gathered together, the visible linguistic magma through which the invisible location of that which speaks is indicated. With respect to the books themselves, those ruins tell the story of a desertification of the countryside left behind by the mystics. They form the tableau of an impoverishment, or rather of a disorientation due to a willed insecurity in the form of a fragility toward the other. Like a last subway ticket in the pocket of the emigrant, all that is left of a library is a line or two from a poem. And if the worshiper does not fetishize this last word (by a reversal that remains always possible), he ends up forgetting it. He is at sea.

An apparently opposite practice is possible. The fragment "adapts" to an increasing diversity of situations. It is the same, and yet it serves very different intentions. Hence it is emptied of its own content. It ceases being objectifiable, taking on the position of subject. Speaking of the Scripture, which has "several faces" and which "each person can adapt as suits him," a text that is mobile like cloth, Francisco de Osuna compares it to the "people in certain paintings," who "always seem to look at the observer, wherever he stands."[46] The radiance of the text is the look that follows the passersby/readers and changes them into looked-at beings. Thus the broken statue alluded to by Rilke, "Archaic Torso of Apollo," headless and meaningless, becomes this "candelabrum set before his gaze which is pushed back and hid, restrained and shining"; so that

> . . . there is no place
> that does not see you. You must change your life.[47]

Similarly, the textual debris, the ruins of the text and of meaning, no longer says anything true or false; it "signifies" as one makes a sign to leave or come forward; it issues a "summons" to "your life" to appear before it, it judges you. It changes into a word that says nothing and is no longer anything, of the Other, than his look.

The Tomb of a Voice

After having considered the expectation and the practices of reading, we must turn to the meaning to which they give rise. But, precisely owing to these ways of reading, it now becomes a question of something other than meaning. The medieval circuit went from the interpretation given by the master (the *lectio*) to the inner assimilation of the message by the listener (the *meditatio*), and from this last to the response addressed by the faithful to the founding Verb (the *oratio*). It recognized a "reading" at each stage that the creative Word went through in its descent, first through the Book of the World, then through a magisterial and scriptural instruction, down to the listeners/readers called by it to conform to its Law. During the period I am speaking of, that chain broke, even though each of the links remained organized by its prior belonging to the great dogmatic story of the divine locution. The book no longer "speaks," nor does the master. Meditation functions on an automatizing of the understanding and produces fields of knowledge. Thus the word passes through all those corporeal sounds whose speaker is no longer known.

Of this breakup of the theological story I shall, to conclude, retain only its major consequence, because, besides the fact that it is the focal point of the "spiritual" or "mystic" reading, it also became the prerequisite of a "modern" reading: the exegesis that scrutinized the meaning of the statements (or "mysteries") emitted by a bona fide Speaker was replaced—as if assuming a backup position with respect to that exegesis and concerning its premise—by a questioning directed at the enunciation itself. The essential problem is no longer *what* the divine messages are saying, but whether there still is a *saying*, and if so, where and how? The question has shifted from an elucidation of the *meaning* to the search for a *voice.* The new status of the book and the privilege granted to the way of reading are decisive symptoms of this shift—the book ceases to be a "master" and becomes the instrument of a quest, and the way of reading replaces obedience to an instruction with a way of loosening or breaking the book, like a tombstone, to hear the voice it is assumed to contain.

That the book is no longer the master is declared by all the spiritual authors, thus taking up a position in the debate that, on the topic of reading, continues to ask: Who is the master? Indeed, Augustin Baker, in his *Sancta Sophia*, reduces books, those "masters," to being no more than "servants."[48] Modern contemplation abandons them, contrary to the faithfulness maintained in this respect by a whole medieval monastic tradition.[49] To "celestial philosophy" they furnish only "an alphabet,"[50] itself transitory, white stones dispersed where there is no real traceable pathway. Finally, the book is only the fragment, or the index or metaphor of a mystic "Book" whose hidden figures form a litany in the *Pro theologia mystica clavis* of Sandaeus, "Liber Dei," "Liber experientiae," "Liber vitae," "Liber mortis"[51]—and whose utopian definition is the unhoped-for coincidence between a living word and an order of meaning.

This does not mean that the deterioration and/or mythification of the book works toward an individualization of the reader. If this reversal does indeed take place in the course of modernity,[52] it remains foreign to the perspective of the spirituals, attentive to the loss and possible reunion with the Voice presupposed not so long ago by the theological understanding of the world. They do not introduce an individual-master using a book-instrument; they articulate the desire of the Voice capable of founding the subject qua respondent. Relative to the uncertainty of the subject as well as of the book, their way of reading pins all its hopes entirely on the postulate that there is a *saying* that is more essential than the text, and that ultimately *only a voice can make us believe in the text.* In devaluing the book/object, they return to what is presupposed by all human practice of the book and to what it cannot forget, namely, that one way or another it "speaks." Beyond the threshold of the word introduced by the automatization of the book, they expect, they work (in a way that is in turn disappointed and fulfilled) toward the emergence of the voice from the tomb.

That there is no reading without the quest for a voice—this has become the paradox of a modern practice of the book, since, as has been said about E. T. A. Hoffmann, "that voice that the written text continually makes heard, at the same time continually eludes all its [the text's] attempts to grasp it."[53] The question that haunts and organizes the way of reading of the "spirituals" thus survives to this day, in various still recognizable guises. May it suffice to mention the form it takes under the name, equally obsessive, of "the oeuvre" and its relation to the book. "The book is there, then, but the work is still hidden. It is absent, perhaps radically so; in any case it is concealed, obfuscated by the evident presence of the book, behind which it awaits the liberating decision, the 'Lazare, veni foras.'"[54] The story of the ghost told by the absolute reading probably gives reading its mythic narrative. In any case, it illustrates in ways of doing things, an interrogation that effectively concerns, apropos of the voice or the work buried in the book, the possibility of that performative: Lazarus, come forth.

Chapter Six

Stories of Passions

To follow the Christian texts that, in the sixteenth and seventeenth centuries, received the theoretical and/or practical status of "mystics," we must follow the flow of history upstream, from passions to *suffering*. One sole actant stands before us, in whom the passions lose themselves or originate, and whose "emotions" are but signs of things to come, or secondary effects. The body is the stage: a body-theater that suffering "torments" and "tortures," a body that suffering causes to "enjoy" (*gozar*) by "wounding" it (*herir*, *llagar*, *vulnerar*), a body that suffering recreates by what it "touches," tattoos, and writes.[1]

It seems, from reading these texts, that the passions (re)become a suffering when they are no longer linked to classifiable "objects," of which they are no longer the "effects," and that they therefore fall back into a primitive indistinctness, like "sadness for no reason." Thus the characters or "passions" that a philosophical or psychological tradition presented as the "effects" of actors located on a different stage ("objects") merge into just one, suffering, which for its part is an *agent* (subject of actions) at once *originary* (in the beginning is suffering), *blind* (it knows neither whence it came nor whither it goes), and *neuter* (one does not know whether it is pain or bliss, good or bad, etc.). Its action is oxymoronic, the coincidence of opposites. It is a "glorious nonsense" (*glorioso desatino*), a "heavenly madness" (*celestial locura*).

By contrast with Descartes, it is as if the stage were no longer the "little gland" in which he located the "combat" between the soul and the spirits, but rather the whole extension of a broken-up body whose parts, like an organ, are played by suffering, and as if the drama ebbed back even to the hither side of the passion that Descartes placed first, in a category apart, unique in having no "opposite" and in eluding the binary schema—wonder, whose object "astonishes" and "surprises" us "before we in any way know whether this object is agreeable to us or is not so."[2] The mystic stage would seem to be situated at this zero point of passion. "Aurora," as Jacob Boehme says, the nocturnal morning in which "objects" are not yet distinguishable, but in which "surprise" already occurs, a sudden sensation opening to the will the space of broad daylight in which choice is possible. In other words, discourse is fixed on the condition of possibility of the passions and their "review" or subsequent classification. Which he also designates as a return or access to the "indistinct" and the "confused."

A STAGE FOR VOICES: A HISTORICAL SITE

There is, nonetheless, a work of distinction, but it does not carry out a division between the passions; it isolates the places of suffering from the "world"; it delimits a site. *There is* a stage for *that*, a stage for voices that "touch" (*tocar*), write, engrave, and shatter bodies transformed into Tables of the Law broken by these touches. Since the sixteenth century, it is often in a "hospital" that these "sick" with love, struck by an evil of which they are unaware, are lodged. "Love is a sickness," for John of the Cross, and Surin, after many others, locks it up in an infirmary. A prelude to the castles and subterranean theaters of Sade. But this "theater" that, in the language of the era, is a representation and an atlas resembles rather the theater that "possession" constitutes for voices impossible to name and whose touch makes the body delirious: a "pure madness" must circumscribe this stage and distinguish it from its environment.[3] Hence the theater of mystic suffering.

In this respect, it presents a variation of the *Passion*, which, from Monte Cassino (twelfth century)[4] to Handel, J. S. Bach, or Telemann,[5] puts voice (at the beginning, *vox alta*, *bassa*, and *media*) to the evangelical discourse and progressively gives rise to the proliferation and drifting away of these voices in relation to the text: from plainchant it went to chorales, arias, and choruses that overflow, cut, and sometimes eliminate the story of the "narrator" (*cantor* or *historicus*). An intoxication of voices and melodies that elude history, the mystic discourse may be seen as constituting, in this long liturgical, festive, and artistic series, a pocket in which the difference between a *text* without voice (it no longer "speaks") and senseless *voices* (they no longer articulate the orthodox narrativity) is intensified. It is situated precisely in this gap.[6]

One last contextual note: passion is a perturbation. The "passions of the moon," as they say. It is an "agitation." It also designates suffering, colic, or historicity itself ("time is the passion of movement"). It involves both a disorder and the nature of movement.[7] From Galileo[8] to the mystics, *motus* and *motio* are the center of an enquiry into what causes movement, and equally into what moves, behind the signifiers that Ockham isolated from a primordial *Potentia*. The mystic theater is, in a different mode than the Galilean *Discorsi*, the search for a rearticulation of the *motus* by discourse and for a writing reorganized (undone/redone) by the *motiones*. It undertakes at once to think and to represent, hence to "produce," the alteration that inscribes the Other in a body or in a corpus by "agitating" it.

The scene is organized, as by a science, around and in expectation of that agitation. It frames or mounts an "it's coming" within a network of expectations that give an "extraordinary" form in advance to what is hoped for. It will be a dream, an ecstasy, a poem, a vision, etc. The lexicon of expectation programs the miraculous. Patient, a preliminary codification of "places" adumbrates, in order to set it apart, the thing that is to come. A multiplicity of empty places in search of the advent. Finally "it happens": *Se me ofreció.*[9] The act of suffering suddenly shakes the language of expectation. A blow is struck—a wound, a touch, a voice. Then the blows increase. Several striking "spirits," noises, movements. "It's speaking." The Spirit is *el que habla*, it is *made up of* voice. But this occurs in a region apart, which is no longer that of the text.

In this tradition, from Teresa to Angelus Silesius, a historical given organizes the stage on which the voice suddenly appears and strikes. The authorized language, assumed to constitute a world, no longer speaks. The interrogation therefore essentially involves not the truth of statements, but the possibility of a speaking. What is a language when it is no longer spoken? Writing is "nothing," says Angelus Silesius, who rhymes *Schrift* with *nichts*, and seeks a place (*Ort*) for a word (*Wort*). From writing, then, the cry is separated. "It speaks," but off to the side, in a space of fiction, tagged as "foolishness," "madness" [*folie*], or "illness," a place of "pleasures" and "pains," in which the beautiful thing (the *hermoso y deleitoso* diamond and castle of Teresa of Avila)[10] replaces the true thing.

The suddenness of suffering, then, alters a space other, emptied of meaning, deprived of narrativity. No more stories for you, says the text, even though, in fact, it endlessly recites the form of the advent. As an initial first approach, we may say that something else plays itself out there: in a darkness of waiting, a plurality of accidents. Voices zigzag their way through the silence of fiction that has been prepared for them, set apart from everything else.

THE MODALIZING EXCESS

The texts produce an ab-solutization of suffering in detaching it from its possible objects. It is a question of a suffering "for no reason," "without whys or wherefores." Several procedures generate this effect. Among others, I retain two of them.

1. *The defection of actantial roles and syntactic subjects.* At the level of manifestation, the opposition between a passive role and an active one (patient vs. agent) is blurred by the uncertainty touching the authorities of the operation: where is the agent, where the patient, and who is the subject? One does not know (*no sabe, no sé qué*). In the semantic organization, a threefold indistinction blurs, in Teresa of Avila, the description of the subject (does it suffer or enjoy?), its actantial position (is it passive or active?), and its sexual differentiation (is it masculine or feminine?).[11] The binary schema of opposition is undone by the reiteration of a "neither one nor the other." But this exclusion of the poles of the alternative insinuates its opposite: both. From this point of view, the oxymoron (*glorioso desatino*, "happy shipwreck," etc.), the organizing trope of these texts, would serve as a metaphor for the more fundamental procedure that, in *eliminating* subjects (neither one nor the other), also *multiplies* the actors within the same authority.

In John of the Cross or Surin the same phenomenon can be seen, but it occurs in the place of the "I" (*yo*): there, an emptying out of the predicates (the "I" is not rich, not knowing, not reasonable, not this, not that, indefinitely, never that) goes hand in hand with a proliferation of opposites in that same place, for example concerning gender (masculine and feminine), mood (active and passive: I wound and I am wounded), or grammatical position (subject and complement: I wound him and he wounds me).[12] It is a question more of an erosion of the actants than of their erasure. It seems that the "detachment" of the predicates fixing the role of each subject makes it possible to pluralize the subject of each act and to amplify that place disproportionately. *I* is a world of opposites. "I am legion." Thus the space in which an analysis of modalities will unfold is created.

Suffering is a point at once originary and recapitulative in which, in a provisional compossibility, subjects and acts of passion ferment. It overflows the *place* of the subject while eroding the subjects, by an incessant multiplication of its occupants who ultimately are no more than disguised figures of one another, each being replaceable by its opposite. What comes undone is the assumedly operative subject. What swells at the same time beyond its limits is the question of the subject.

2. *The augmentation of modalities and modal sequences.* The proliferation/defection of subjects is relative to a proliferation of modalities. Indeed, the erosion triggering the multiplication of authorities [*instances*] is the indication of an extraordinary development of modalizations, and therefore of modalizing subjects. It is as if mystic literature were positioned essentially between a subject (S_1) and its object (a doing, a having, or a being) in order to analyze the modalities of this relation, that is, its implications, conditions, and possibilities.

Thus mystic literature composes "modal series" or "syntagmatic series" the interest of which would be paramount for establishing, on the basis of particular cases, hypotheses of "modal logics."[13] It seems to posit an imbrication of modalities in the following order:[14]

S_1 ["must/ought to" {want to {know how to (or can)]
Act (to do/make, to have, to be)

Using abbreviations, we obtain:

S_1 [m {w {k c] A

This succession is essential because mystic discourse proceeds in stages ('degrees,' stages, levels, etc.) that treat modalities in the following order:

a. The subject *does not know how to* (noted ~k) and/or *cannot* (noted ~c) do/make, have, or be. At this stage, which is the first in mystic experience, the modalities of knowing how to and being able to change places, or their order varies. Thus we have as a modal sequence:

~k ~c (or: ~c, ~k, ~c~k)

b. The subject *wants* not to know how to or not to be able to (this is, for example, renunciation):

w ~c (or: w ~k)

c. The subject *does not want* not to know how to or to know how to, not to be able to or to be able to (this is, for example, "indifference"):

~wc and ~w~c (or: ~wk and ~w~k, etc.)

d. The subject no longer has a will of his or her own. The law of the Other (should that still be called "must/ought to"?) transforms the series of modalities and gives the relation between the subject and his or her act (to be, to do/make, to have) its "normal" status. The "must/ought to" is incarnated, realized, and possesses. The act *is* what it should be (a state of perfection), and what it is must be (a destiny of being is realized in it). It *does* what it should ("holiness"), and what it does must take place (it is the realization of a justice), etc. We have:

m [w k c] O

Suffering, in the final analysis, is the act of what must be, the identification of the contingent act with the must be, a divine doing or having that seeks a body for itself. The objective of the staggering of the modalities is to "work" the order in such a way as to melt it in its entirety into the pragmatic and everyday act that, without any wanting or being able to or knowing how to of its own, coincides with the founding act. At that moment, says Meister Eckhart, the subject is both me and God. What remains is the doing, with no other modality than its own law. After having been open in its whole extension, the range of the modalities closes into an act without subject, the absolute of suffering.

BREAKAGE AND NOISES

The fact is, discourse only *aims* at that absolute. Most often it analyzes the path leading to it. Debris of bodies and vocal noises mark this path. A splitting up characterizes the itinerary constituted by the *Ascent of Mount Carmel* (John of the Cross), the entry into the center of *The Interior Castle* (Teresa of Avila), or the navigation of *The Lost Child* (Surin). A breaking up or fragmentation stands constantly opposed to the making *one*, that is, the putting into a picture, which is a mirror effect. The unity of pictures (vision, ecstasy, etc. are still that) comes from the fact that they are representations: totalization is an effect of distance, an illusion generated by separation. That is why the image must be broken by what it is content to re-produce. Breakage, wounds, and falls, then, form the writing of a real in its image. Fragments trace in the mirror the shock of what it reflects but does not give.

Parallel, perhaps, to the erosion of the actants, this breaking up allows in turn a metonymization of the body (exorbitation of a detail for the whole), the production of a mystic corpus (fiction of body in place of the body), and the existence, as in suspense, of noises that are the touches of the other—in sum, the dubbing of a discourse of the act by an amorous discourse.

Relics of the body. In the tradition of the "blazons" of the sixteenth century, poems dedicated to parts of the body (the leg, the breast, the neck, the genitals), mystic literature isolates body fragments and makes them into relics of the other, relics of love. A particular part of the body was "touched," like a lexicon or a lute, and this enraptured fragment becomes the metonymy of the impossible body that would in its entirety be the writing of the Other, reassembled and played by him. Memory thus composes, with little bits and pieces, its relics. Singularities string the beads of a language of amorous suffering.

In Teresa (for example *la candela en la mano* of the agony of love in the *Vida*), in John of the Cross (for example the breast, the eyes, the neck, a hair, etc., in the *Cántico*), and in a number of others, this debris of the body is made up of little bits of truth (*Stückchen Wahrheit*) that have the value of metonymy. By means of fragments, a highlighting of the body is accomplished: a metamorphosed double, still globally absent, is already partially there, in these touched parts that make a future present in the actual. The relic is that which, of the body, is already for the Other and belonging to him. Desire thus goes off, crazy (*loco*), toward that fracturing of the body: the "madness" of being a "broken vase" (*quebrado*). A *despedazar* (to put in pieces, to break up) designates suffering. By pieces already changed, what awaits the whole and will not be without death is shown metonymically. The act of tearing apart/being torn apart indicates the mode of production of a body of love. Certain parts already function in it as citations of the Other, as its marks in the opaque, carnal lexicon of a waiting.

Inducing fragments. This process is repeated in the writings where fragments of poems or dreams play the role of inducers of text/commentary. The dream (in Teresa) or the poem (in John of the Cross or Surin) constitutes the atopia of an approaching event. *That* "offers itself," *that* happens like a real occurrence in a space of fiction. But this space, touched ("exposed," like the space of a photograph), already given and traced by an elsewhere, circumscribes the space of a writing that remains iconic and that therefore must be broken (like an image) in order for that theoretic (contemplated: *theōrein*) body to be tailored to fit into the historical, which is a disseminated network of the present contingency. Here, then, the poet shatters his poem, and the mystic dreamer analyzes his dream.

These fragments will leave a trace in the historical. Like a curve of the nape of the neck or a radiance of skin between the body hairs for someone in love, these bits of poem or dream induce writing; they engender endless commentary; they generate a change of history. They are magic stones or relics transforming the successive places where they are transported. Thus, in John of the Cross, the verses of his poems are spread in debris, inducing doctrinal or pedagogical texts relative to demands; they might act in very different circumstances and thus take on very different meanings. In Surin, his own verses are quoted, alien shards of light in treatises whose indebtedness they represent. The poetic debris circulates everywhere as a possible beginning or recommencement of history.

Enunciative noises. This procedure is comparable to that which at this time produces discourses of truth with biblical fragments—the Bible no longer being the totality in which a true elucidation is inscribed, but that of which a relic, a stone torn away from the ruin of a lost world, makes possible the construction of a treatise. But among these mystics what is involved is a relation between *poetic fictions* (the *dichos de amor* of John of the Cross) and their taking apart which produces itineraries or *histories.* Something of these poems or of their fragments does not "fit" into histories and does not allow itself to be told in journeys or initiations. Implanted in prose, with no possible commentary or transitivity from fiction to history, the poetic sound of the quoted fragments remains. Scattered throughout the entire mystic corpus, "there are" (*Es gibt*) these resonances of a body touched, "moans" and sounds of love, cries breaking the text they induce, enunciative lapses in a syntagmatic organization of statements. These are the linguistic analogues of the erection, or of those tears in which Raymond Lull recognized the mystic *saying* itself:[15] voice without language, or rather utterance flowing from the wounded body, but opaque when it no longer has the space offered to the amorous saying by the voice of the other. Tears, the aphasic utterance of suffering, reduce the cry to the murmur, to the light sound of what occurs without one's knowing whence (from what obscure wound?), without one's knowing how *that* could be said without the voice of the other.

The poem itself furnishes marks of its status as enunciative song: for example the use of the interjection (*oh Noche . . .*) or the use of the common noun as a name addressed ("Love, . . ."). Then, like the *ow* of pain, the *said* is reduced to a *saying.* Or, as in the statement/call of a loved first name, the *said* is precisely what *happens* to the speaker: the speaker is damaged by the sound he pronounces; he is seized by the name that a female passerby tears out of him on a street corner. Identity of the statement and the stating? No, because there is an *excess* of sound over sense. The enunciative sound overflows the statement.

From Teresa of Avila to Angelus Silesius, mystic discourse does not cease producing that excess: in alliterations, rhymes, assonances, rhythms, and vocalizations—effects of an excess of saying over the said. This musical continuum, which does not "fit" into the text of the commentary, refers to an enjoyment without discourse (*gozar sin entender lo que se goza*),[16] but not without sound. This saying of suffering survives only in fragments, like the snatches of a refrain or a conversation in memory: lapses of voices without context, "obscene" quotations of a body, and noises in suspense all seem to certify, by this disorder of impressions, that there is otherness, and at the same time they seem to expect indefinitely, from an impossible presence, that it should transform the traces that it has left into its body. Thus the fragments of poems incise themselves into prose that can do nothing, endlessly, but produce their effects.

These poetic noises, in the civilized discourse that protects itself from them by exhibiting them, are perhaps the attenuated and piecemeal echo of what appeared to Jacob Boehme to be the origin in an empty space, without limits, without Logos and still without God: the "furor" of a suffering between the father and the son, the noise of a violence deprived of word and object, the "war" that already articulates, however, the desire to tear or be torn with the act of living.[17]

Chapter Seven

The Experimental Science of Madness

Long confined to the corridors of history on grounds of madness, Jean-Joseph Surin (1600–1665) is nonetheless, according to good judges (from Jean Orcibal and Louis Cognet to Julien Green), a "literary genius" whom they find "worthy of putting on an equal footing with Pascal and Bossuet."[1] But this mystic writer and poet was "locked up" for nearly thirteen years, though intermittently, in the infirmary of the Jesuit College-University of Bordeaux (1637–50)—"his dungeon," as he says—and for almost twenty-three years was practically unable to move. The hero of the exorcisms of Loudun after the death of Urbain Grandier (1634–37), this Jesuit had first manifested on that stage the symptoms of an affliction attributed, at the time, to possession and considered, beginning in 1635, as a "curiosity" that intrigued the erudite (Father Mersenne, Peiresc, the Dupuy brothers, etc.). Shortly thereafter he was "imprisoned" for mental illness. The documents of the time, scattered between Bordeaux, Paris, Rome, etc., report on the physiological and psychological disorders of the "madman": inability to move or difficulty in moving, aphasic periods, inability to write (until 1654), nocturnal wanderings, solitary furors, prostrations, etc.[2] At the center of these "ills" there is, it says, the "thought" that he is "damned," definitively "rejected" by God. Later, he himself related his experiences as a patient in a text that is, in the seventeenth century, the equivalent of Daniel Paul Schreber's *Memoirs of My Nervous Illness*, and that he titles *La Science expérimentale des choses de l'au-delà* [The Experimental Science of the Things of the Beyond]. Redacted in 1663, this account, written "for himself," is among his last works, after the abundant writing during and following his slow "cure" (dated by him from 1651 to 1660): *Catéchisme spirituel*, *Guide*, *Questions sur l'amour*, etc. He heals in writing. It is a strange history: "magna quaestio factus sum," he says.

Here I consider only the story of this "journey," *La Science expérimentale*, and only the two parts (II and III) that concern mental illness.[3] This partial autobiography should be compared not only with the whole work but with analogous cases, less serious and less spectacular, but relatively frequent among the witnesses to the Counter-Reformation, like the long aphasic depression of Jean-Jacques Olier or the four years of neurasthenia of Vincent de Paul himself. More broadly, this "diary of a madman" should be included in a banished literature from which there emerge, only here and there, a few "mad" authors, such as James Carkesse (*Lucida Intervalla*, London, 1679), himself locked up for madness in Finsburg and then in Bedlam, a "self-curing Poet" who wrote songs inspired in him by Apollo in order to "survive" his doctor Thomas Allen.[4] These texts form the other face, correlative and contrary, of a better-known medical literature, from Zacchias to Willis,[5] or from Robert Burton's *Anatomy of Melancholy* (1621) to the medical diary of Dr. Richard Napier (1597–1642).[6]

In *La Science expérimentale*, Surin does not deny his madness. He does not write, he says, "to defend himself against an accusation . . . that is to be considered mad, for he has fallen into this disagreeable situation in a way so authentic that it would almost clash with common sense to deny it, given the strange things that have happened to him." Furthermore, "he was not too frightened of this title," *mad*—"this lovely bouquet on his hat that scarcely anyone would care to have." He thinks of this state of "insanity" or of "dementia" in the wake of the fools for Christ,[7] as the imitation of this Jesus who appeared "before the whole people in the ridiculous equipage of a king of farce." On the other hand, he absolutely denies "that it was madness to believe oneself damned." In his language, it is the "trial" of the spirit and not the "infirmity" of a "hypochondriac."[8] These two "afflictions" are combined, but not of the same nature. The one is a straying of the "imagination," a "debilitation of the head and the senses"; the other concerns "the soul"—the subject himself in his relation to the other, God absolute, who constitutes him qua desirer. These two afflictions, however, "blend" into a madness with two faces, the one psychic, the other spiritual, which the "observers" combine, reducing it all, as most do, to a pure "extravagance," or, as one or two friends who are also wrong do, to a mystic desolation. The "science" will consist in distinguishing them from each other and in isolating, in a patent madness, the part that pertains not to medicine but to *mystics.*

This "mixed" history—"O, matter and impertinency mix'd," said Edgar of King Lear[9]— Surin calls an "apocryph."[10] It is itself a writing in which evangelical revelation, the truth of the subject, is inextricably bound up with the "chimera" of a dementia and spoken by the lie of madness. The differentiation of these two "spirits" is carried out at the very heart of the "adventures" during the course of these twenty years of illness. It is a work whose object is the subject, an "experimental science" that makes madness itself the locus of the "know thyself." The story that, after the fact, traces acquired knowledge beyond borders, in a country "outside the common" and "outside meaning," in a "wild" and solitary life, describes at once the discovery of a world other than the one of "here" ("things of the beyond"), the repeated gestures that "cast" headlong the adventurer seeking an "exit" from his confinement, and the experiments making possible a "science of the spirit."

It is striking that in this threefold mode, the 1663 story respects the *form* of a journey described some twenty years earlier by the poems that Surin, like James Carkesse, composed in his "dungeon":

> I want to go running through the world,
> Where I'll live like a lost child;
> I have taken the humor of a wandering soul,
> Having cast all possessions aside.[11]

The poem already presents increasing hardships of illness as the stages of a science, but it *de-realizes* them, putting them all in the conditional: "If I leave . . . ," "If illness takes me by surprise . . . ," "If my parents call me mad," "If . . . in a ship without sails and without rigging. . . ." He is not referring to any real experience: "My song must not describe." From lived history he takes only its form, abstract as well as poetic. In this *I* that suffering has deprived of all its abilities, an empty space, the last stanza of the "song" at last places

> the madness
> Of this Jesus who on the cross one day
> For his pleasure lost honor and life.[12]

In this respect, the "song" gives a crystal-clear and unadulterated figure of what the story will relate in a historical mode of a "mixture of the spirits." It furnishes an atopic and theoretic model to the experiences that will be taken in charge, long afterward, by the autobiographical narration of *La Science expérimentale*. What is more, in coordinating the stages of a "spending" or a "loss" with the advances of a "pleasure," the poem structures in advance the "journal of a madman" as the relation of the journey to a different science.

Paradoxically, these "Memoirs" of a shut-away represent not just one more variant among the genre of journey narratives; they also involve the nature of the journey. In relation to a certain number of "modern" accounts that I have had occasion to analyze, from Jean de Léry to Bougainville[13], this variant, the result of a physical and mental imprisonment, sheds light on questions that all travel attempts to articulate in the twofold modality, geographical and scriptorial, of the opening of an *other* space. Once again reason, a paradigm that organizes Western consciousness, would seem to have as its secret and revelatory virtue that from which it wrested itself free in constituting it as its "other"—in this case, madness.

1. DISTANCE OR SPACE

The journey takes form only from the starting point of a spatial division: here/there. Jean de Léry, in his *Histoire d'un voyage au Brésil* (1578), distributed places between "on this side" [*par-deça*] and "on the other side" [*par-delà*]. This dichotomy is the condition of possibility of the travelogue as a spatial variant of *heterology*,[14] that is, of a discourse that speaks on/of the other. While being everywhere necessary, it nevertheless presents modalities that change according to the types of spaces that the narrative considers. For example, from the caesura between "here on earth" and "beyond," which structures the ecstatic journeys and circulations from the terrestrial region to the celestial ones (heaven, purgatory, hell), there follows, beginning with the sixteenth century, a more geographic partition between "here" and "there," and when that supposedly physical partition diminishes somewhat in importance with colonizing and scientific expansion, it is replaced by other spatial distributions, such as the opposition between the "real" and the "imaginary" (constitutive of a literature that makes the elsewhere a realm of the fantastic) or the one separating the past or the future from the present (giving the elsewhere the figure of an origin or a prospective utopia). These diverse modalities of spatial cleavage are, moreover, stratified, so that in the texts there is a constant interplay of them and they thus have no pure form.

In considering how the narrative manifests this condition of the journey, we note two contrary movements: the narrative must *posit* the difference (and thus show that it transports one "elsewhere"), and yet *surmount* it (to describe it, symbolize it, and often assimilate it into a text). For example, it posits the difference by recounting the "hardships" of the journey (distances traveled, storms, privations, illnesses, etc.) and by stressing the "extraordinary" nature of what may be seen "over there" (incredible oddities, terrifying monstrosities or indescribable marvels, that is, everything Herodotus, describing the Scythians, already classifies under the general category of *thōma*).[15] Looking at it from this angle, it develops a rhetoric of the other. But at the same time the construction of a text, while developing the motif of what escapes our language ("there are no words for that"), obeys the law of its place. The provisional gap of an alterity ends up bringing a justification or a lesson back to the starting point, that is, in both cases, a legitimization of the place in which the text is written. It permits an *apologia pro domo.* From this point of view, the narrative returns to a logic of the same. Discreetly, it conforms to it and reinforces it. Moreover, must it not respond to the necessity of "thinking *that*," and consequently of reducing the strange to what is "thinkable" within the original frame of reference?

The reconciliation between these opposite tendencies may be observed in several procedures characterizing the travelogue. Let me stress two of the most important ones:

1. The movement of the narrator to different places marks, gradually or suddenly, the passage from a "here" to an "over there." This narrative illustration of the spatial dichotomy is paralleled by a chronological distance between the past of the narrated journey and the today of the writing: behind the scenes, the temporal caesura orchestrates the spatial caesura, and from Léry's *Histoire* to Lévi-Strauss's *Tristes Tropiques*, it adds its own effects of distancing to the series of places traveled. The past reinforces the distant. But in both the spatial mode and the temporal one, speech is privileged: "I was there and I saw." The dissemination of places and the breaking of time work toward the heroizing of the traveler-narrator, ever the same, who comes out qualified by his passage through foreign lands. From this point of view, by increasing the number of places visited, the statements serve to accredit the speaker, who himself constitutes the unity of the text.

2. The extraordinary is produced narratively by enlargements or miniaturizations of units familiar to the reader and by unknown combinations of known elements. Already in this process, the distant reconnects with and comes back to the nearby. Additionally, to portray the exceptional, the descriptions of "marvels" very frequently use the

quantitative: that is, number, dimensions, proportions, etc. Numbers, in particular, construct the representation of alterity. Hence the strange is placed on a common scale, making it assimilable and making it possible to conjoin an effect of "other" and a reduction to the "same." As a speech-act valorizes the narrator qualitatively, so the statements ensure quantitatively a return to the starting point.

La Science expérimentale brings into play a rhetoric of distance by the intensity of its spatial vocabulary ("ways," "regions," "countries," etc.), by the exactitude of the indications of place and movement within the "refuge" in which the patient finds himself as well as during his rare excursions, and finally by the maritime imagery that constitutes the horizon of the entire narrative: on "a sea of rigor and severity," among "the furious squalls of despair," Surin is "a vessel without a helm," "the waves raising the vessel to the heavens and then lowering it to hell,"[16] so that he is surprised "to have escaped the boulders and the sirens and the other perils," monsters, gulfs, straits, winds, and storms.[17] But the seascape seems painted on the wall of the dungeon, like the creations of Outsider Art.[18] Indeed, this Ulysses voyages essentially in "the little room" of the infirmary and "very much alone in that neighborhood." The obsessive décor of the text consists of the bed and "the ruelle of the bed" ("my residence . . . several years") with all "the necessary" around it, the curtains, the food, the sudden irruptions of the nurse, especially the window, in one passage "barred with bars of iron" yet "a way to see a beautiful landscape," "an opening" through which a divine "brilliance" shines, a frame in which the words "Pure Love" are written in capital letters.[19] The patient stays in his bed for a long time "like a board nailed to a door," without "any power to move his feet or hands to find relief."[20]

The fresco of ocean storms does indeed create an effect of distance, but, as opposed to what happens in geographical itineraries, its function is to be *visibly* the metaphor of a different kind of voyage, organized by the distance from self to self. As in other narratives of madness, such as Gérard de Nerval's *Aurelia*,[21] this distance generates a transformation of the narrative techniques. I will comment on two of them, one relating to the "here/there" dichotomy and the other to the extraordinary. The one concerns the relation of the narrator to the character in the narration; the other involves the focalization of the semantic content by the modalities (to know how to, to want to, to need to, etc.) and first of all by the question of the "possible."

"I" and "He"

In *La Science expérimentale*, the caesura between "here" and "there" falls between the narrator and the hero of the autobiography. It concerns less the content of the narrative than the construction of the text itself: the narrator ("I") is "here," and the character ("he," "the Father") is "there." This distance, a literary index of madness, provokes textual swings from one of these positions to the other. Surin relates that one day, in "the hallway of the infirmary," he "would fall sometimes on one side, sometimes on the other."[22] The narrative seems to proceed the same way, speaking sometimes in "I" ("I remember . . . ," "I do not claim . . . ," "I was sent . . ."), sometimes about "him" ("he was sent . . . ," "he could neither think nor speak . . . ," etc.). A lesion of the speaker, divided into writing subject and narrated object: "I speak here sometimes in the first person, sometimes in the third."[23] This "third party" is "a pitiful thing to see"[24]—a "package" "hurled out the window and cast thirty feet from the wall, all the way to the riverbank, with his robe on, his slippers on his feet, and his square bonnet on his head."[25] At a preliminary level, the attempted suicide belongs to the problematic of the object—that which is rejected, cast out.

As the account of the journey regulates the relation of two heterogeneous spaces, the 1663 text is the treatment of the relations between the first person and the third. The first chapter, explaining the legitimacy of the project, posits the writing "I": "I hesitated for a long time as to whether I would commit to writing things . . ."[26] The second chapter posits the other person ("The Father went out . . .") and begins the story with "he." In the course of the text, "I" presents himself as "cured," describes the madness as a "past," analyzes the narrated conflicts as an arbiter, and no longer participates in the exceptional "experience" of the "things of the beyond"; "he," on the other hand, is "mad," gripped by illness, engaged in debates with his contemporaries, but endowed with a knowledge favored with "extraordinary operations" taking place in "him"[27] (see table 3).

Reason, deprived of experience, stands opposite experience, deprived of reason. This structure, analogous to the one organizing ethnological discourse (or the interpretation of dreams), makes the combination of the two poles into an exegesis of these "operations" possible. The accommodation is realized first by the appeal of the present text to an "I" who was already hidden behind the madman, observing his mad acts without being able to control them: "I remember everything, because of the integral reflection and wisdom *at bottom* that I had then."[28] The "I" who writes today can reference an "I" whose reflection was already there, "at bottom," beneath the past extravagancies of the patient. This "I," formerly invisible "in what appeared," can at last appear in broad daylight; it is the one who writes "now." The opposition between "I"

Table 3. First- versus third-person characterization contrasted.

I (narrator)	He (hero)
cured, he has his reason	he is mad
madness *in the past*	madness *in the present*
judges conflicts	is a *participant* in conflicts
no longer has experience-science	endowed with experimental *knowledge*

and "he" is therefore assimilable to the opposition—traditional in the journey narrative[29]—between being and seeming.

The narration becomes the history of the progress of this "I" in the alienated region of the "he." In the first part (*La Science expérimentale*, II), after the introduction, a project of writing in "I" (chap. 1), we have first a little segment in "he" (chaps. 3–4, dedicated to extreme alienation, aphasia, paralysis, attempted suicide), but at the end there are breaks of furtive appearances of the "I." Then comes a zone of alternations (chaps. 5–9) in which one passes from one to the other, the entry of the "I" corresponding on each occasion to the present act of writing or remembering.[30] Finally, there follows a vast zone, pacified, so to speak (chaps. 10–17), involving recovery, in which "I" triumphs, with only three instances of the "he." The following part (*La Science expérimentale*, III), inaugurated by a return to the "he" (chap. 1), confirms the triumph of the "I," even though, like a ghost, "he" still appears frequently, except at the end (chaps. 12–14). This story is that of the writing, a present experience. It leads the foreign country of the self ("there") back to "me," "here." "Intending to write this *for me* alone,"[31] says Surin, in recording his "adventures" in the mode of a return to "communal life" (marked, at the end of each part, by the emergence of the "we"), he performs the act of writing as an operation that we might call therapeutic or psychoanalytic, but that is really the *reconquista* of statements by the speaker, and of the "he" by the "I." This operation gives a space of inscription back to the "I." It rearticulates the subject on the contours of a lost world.

The Modalities: Want, Can, Believe

The extraordinary punctuates *La Science expérimentale* as it does all travel narratives. It contains, Surin says, "strange things, and so incredible . . . that one will take for true fantasies and imaginings," "marvelous hatreds against Jesus Christ," an "incredible oppression," unimaginable experiences ("I have no idea of anything in this world equaling that"), etc.[32]. The "strange" reigns over the first half of the text, devoted to "trials"; the "extraordinary" dominates the second half, devoted to "graces." They are both interspersed with "remarkable" stories having the value of "exempla."[33] It is the rhetoric belonging to the genre, although it unfolds, as we shall see, on a very specific terrain.

But to the extent that the goal of the extraordinary is to make difference believable and promote credence in an "over there," *La Science expérimentale* develops a problematic that concerns rather the possibility or impossibility of belief. More broadly, modalities dominate the text and organize it: to believe, to have to, to be able to, to know how to, to want to. All being placed beneath the sign of what Surin believes he knows and of what "seems" or "appears" to him to be true, thus enveloped in a "seeming" that qualifies the assertions, the narrative becomes a subtle labyrinth of combinations between modalities: to be able to believe, to believe [oneself] to be able, to want to know, to want to believe, etc. This network captures in its threads all the stories, which thus form a narrativization of the modalities.

Without going into detail, the geography of this constellation will suffice to characterize this narrative that declares itself a science. *To know* is what is at stake: at the beginning, it is indissociable from the seeming and the lie,[34] hence from suspicion; its status and nature will ultimately emerge from the whole course of the narrative; they will be its result. On the other hand, *to want* is the permanent mainspring of this course: from one end to the other, Surin "wants" only one thing, to conform to the will of God; he wants the will of the Other. The uncertainty of knowing and the immutability of wanting constitute the two poles of the constellation. The other modalities articulate the relations between these two terms, the central question being: how to procure a knowing (or a "discernment") of this wanting? In this between-the-two there is a proliferation of combinations of believing, being able to, and having to, the intertwining of which forms the fabric of the narrative.

The basic statement seems to be: I *want to* do what I *believe* God *wants*. Between these two wants, believing is a barrier. How can it be replaced by a *knowing* so as to want to do what one *knows* God wants? The "strange" is located precisely here; it is Surin's stopping with the persuasion that he is damned: he *cannot believe* that an opening is given to the *wanting* that carries him toward God; therefore he *must* stick with the place that is set for him in the divine order and act as damned, which he *cannot* do either. The "extraordinary," as opposed to the strange, is the dazzling discovery that it is *believable to believe* and *pos-*

sible to be able: "Yes, that can be."[35] Do you believe that I can hope, that is, believe? Such is the question he asks his advisors. And he asks himself: "Is it really possible that I am capable . . . of hoping" in God? "Is it possible . . . that I am capable of God?"[36] The doubling of modality (to believe that it is believable, to be able to be capable) corresponds to the questioning of the prerequisites of all knowledge or all assertion, at the same time that it brings Surin back to the ordinary order of things. In the mode of believing and in that of being able, the question is one: it concerns the ***possibility of the possible***, a question underlying every poetic or voyaging "enterprise." From this point of view, the narration of *La Science expérimentale* treats the possibility of any journey, or the possibility of a different space. A question as mad as it is fundamental.

The opening of a possible to wanting, moreover, describes the same movement as the inscription of the "I" in the region of the self that has become foreign to it ("he"). In these two forms, we move from the caesura to what Surin calls a "way out." While "I" was separated from its social ob-jectivity (that is, from "what appeared") and wanting seemed definitively deprived of the power to tend toward its object (by the "persuasion" of being "rejected" and "damned"), a "dilatation" is offered to the subject, and a possible given to wanting. For Surin, writing corresponds very precisely to that opening of a space that had been forbidden for almost twenty years. He relates how, still unable to move, in 1654 he came out of the "inability to write" one day when he was deprived of the friend to whom he dictated texts entirely composed in his head, inside: "I felt a great warmth in my spirit to produce[37] my thoughts; it was painful to me that the writer was slow in coming. With impetuosity, I took up my pen and made as if I wanted to write. It had been more than eighteen years since I had written anything. . . . In that warmth I found two or three pages set down, but with such letters that it did not look like anything human, it was so confused. After that I continued to write every day for a month."[38] Born of the relation between a wanting (an "impetuosity") and a simulation ("as if"), this writing is suddenly the "I" itself "laid down," at first "confused" and inhuman, a deformed body, then distinct, on the hitherto-alienated page of "appearing." Six years later (in 1660)—on the model of writing, which remains a simulation, the laboratory of a "way out," the first trial terrain of the "possible"—walking will emerge: "I walked out into the garden . . . I entered the alleys of the wood," no longer "laid down" and "carried," but tracing with his steps the forest of the world.[39] Writing is therefore not extrinsic to experience, as if describing it from without. It is a part of experience. It is itself "experimental science." To the "I" it offers a way to "produce itself" in the illeity of that which appears; to the desire or impetuosity of a wanting, it gives back the *possibility* of a respondent to whom it can address itself.

2. THE OTHER WORLD: THE INVENTION OF A BODY

Writing gives the "I" a body, in that it "produces" that body into the objectivity of that which "appears." But the body is what sends a signal to someone else and marks in the visible (or the legible) the expectation of a respondent. The written, however silent or solitary, is a voice that counts on another voice. As such, it is already a body, or gives body to the subject. The possible ("Yes, that can be"), here, is *the possibility of being expected*, which alone allows a body, physical or scriptorial, to be born.

Thus the existence of writing bears witness to birth. It constitutes the *being-there* of hope or of "being able to believe." But as for its content, it relates the genesis that made the birth possible. The memory[40] of this past fills a text that is the result of that painful gestation. The story develops as if in the shelter of—and inside—the body, which has finally appeared in the light of day. More precisely, it brings to itself that obscure genesis, it leads it to the moment in which it is in the process of appearing (this moment and this place "in which I am at present writing this").[41] The textual interrelating of interiority (which, in its prison, "furiously" sought a way out) with the exteriority of "the air" (which in Surin means at once the breathable, the musical, and the visible)—or the past dungeon with the present ability to circulate—will thus be, if not the birth, at least the exercise of this body, its very working, the model or prototype of the innumerable ways of embodying desire. For that matter, in the writer that Surin is, the written traces the movement of speech; it is a beginning of the speaking body. Essentially, it is the bringing into play of a saying, but in the conditions of simulation (an "as if") and of restriction still imposed on him by an aloneness.

Writing, moving back toward its origins, first rejoins "a sea [*mer*] of rigors and severity": in a word, the mother [*mère*]. Without going over the role of Madame Surin,[42] as opposed to "Mother" Jeanne des Anges (the "daughter" and confidante of "Father" Surin for almost thirty years),[43] without trying, then, to scrutinize the genealogy of a body lost at sea/mother [*perdu en mère*] (a question in which Surin lets slip more than his discretion would have liked, and in which his critics already took a lively interest),[44] it will suffice to follow what the story relates about the genesis of a body, an inner duration that extends from the initial separation to the opening of a space. A phenomenological description: it is not about knowing whether it is "true" or "false," or about making a diagnostic (we are not Surin's doctors), but about listening to what the discourse says about the body. Here, as always, the story not only expresses explorations that preceded it, it models what it narrates, it does what it says; it is performative, it invents as much as it inventories the space it articulates.[45] Three aspects are particularly salient in this invention of a body: the importance given to the details of everyday life, the tactility of the inner body, and the concentration on a physiology of breathing.

The Extraordinary of the Ordinary

The "little necessities of life" are changed into "terrible hardships." The familiar becomes monstrous. It is staggered with "horrible difficulties" and "furious ills."[46] It is not only walking or taking a step that is transformed into the extraordinary, but moving, getting dressed or undressed, undoing a hook of the soutane, changing undershirts (a weekly tragedy that, beginning on Thursday, transforms the end of the week into "anguish" and "torture"),[47] putting the candles out, having lunch, putting a morsel into his mouth, drinking (God, he says, "takes the glass away from his mouth"), tasting even, since—and this was the depths of the bottom of the abyss for a native of Bordeaux—"the taste of wine is taken away from him" ("actually seeming to me as if it were water . . . , it was truly the life of a damned man on earth"),[48] etc.

A world of trivial, banal, obvious details passes into the realm of the strange. The everyday, transformed into a population of unsuspected adversaries and dangerous enemies who threaten to deny Surin his space, also takes on the status of literary subject. It becomes the stake in a war that the madman keeps losing. The insignificant is the essential. It is true that spirituality had long established that law and Surin knew it ("small defects, neglected, end up having great effects").[49] But in this case the familiar objects and gestures change in nature. The wild, the hostile, the impossible lie ready to pounce. Already every unprotected journey discovers the fantastic side of the everyday: the insignificance of the daily routine metamorphoses into adventure; from sleeping to eating, from the usual tenor of life to the "of course," the "taken for granted" of communication; the whole ordinary takes on a strangeness and becomes the theater of operations of the heroic. Surin's madness, in "removing" from him his space of bodily practices, provides the everyday, far before Freud—or Gombrowicz—with a new relevance. It articulates the question of the subject in terms of daily trivialities. In the mode of a hostile invasion, it already evokes the credo of late

Wittgenstein: philosophy has a future only in becoming "a 'synopsis' of . . . trivialities."[50]

The Tactility of the Deep Body

The aggressivity of the ordinary, resulting in a retreat into the interior, gives rise to a structure that was, in the sixteenth century, a figure that was philosophical as well as pathological: melancholy. The melancholic, suffering from being *separated* from the world, *sees* it all the more. The less he is, the more he sees. The eye becomes a subject in relation to innumerable objects. The pain of being deprived of a participation in things is counterbalanced by the pleasure of observing them. In Surin, the shrinking of the place that he occupies and that is reduced to an inner dungeon also overflows vision. But in contradistinction from contemplation given to philosophical "Melancholia," vision becomes a fearsome experience, as opposed to touch, which is an internal enjoyment of the body.

Vision, an organ of exteriority, does not conquer things. On the contrary, the objects and people toward which Surin directs his look—a look of desire and expectation (with "an incredible attraction to go and see . . .")—send a furor of the world back to him. These are the "devastatingly violent" actors of a Last Judgment. On all sides, fearsome and vengeful eyes accuse him. He does not see, he is looked at, and most often from above. He is "slain" by these looks. He therefore tries to commit suicide, to "be seen" hanged before the altar or hurled down on the paving stones.[51] To acquiesce in this way to the divine "command" that forever rejects him and that he considers certain—is this not to second the judgment of his fellow religious, such as his Jesuit provincial, who decided "that he had to be sent away, out of sight from the world"?[52] Is it not above all to unite with the reaction—much more primitive—of someone who could not see him? A characteristic touch: these terrible views "engrave themselves" and "write themselves" on him; they "touch him" in an "indelible" manner;[53] writings, then, like looks that wound, but as if tattooed in stigmata inside the body, they "imprint themselves" on an inner skin whose perceptions have something more archaic and fundamental than visual sensations.

This touch is detected especially by mouth or stomach palpations and mixed reactions of multiple internal papillae; it is the source of pleasures and certainties. The body is a grotto in which a vitality escaping all vision is maintained and restored. While the head is "enfeebled," stricken, broken, and "dismantled," and while the members lie bound and the muscles and nerves are "taut," a euphoric and secret sensoriality animates the regions privileged by the narrated body: palate, diaphragm, chest, stomach—blind places in which pleasures and self-evidence are produced. Surin, closed up in his body, discovers a strange proliferation, autonomous and sure, proper to the internal surface of its walls. In a reversal of the normal account of a journey, which is the epopee of the eye, the description of these sensations of "warmth" and intimate "caresses" suggests rather—as the invention of a living interiority that moves and discerns, enjoys and knows—the history of a pregnancy lasting some ten years.

One scene among many others may serve to elucidate this antinomy between vision, which rejects Surin, and taste, which "repairs" him. "My tongue," he says, "feels God and tastes God as it tastes Muscat grapes and apricots and melons." "Although it is quite contrary to the Schoolmen and philosophers," he has the certainty of sensing "something like a divine being if it were drinkable." Something that is "delight," "royal," and "warmth" in the stomach or the entrails such as what would have been produced by "a drink of Spanish wine or hippocras," "an exquisite restaurant or precious quintessence."[54] Taste, a proximal sense, contradicts vision, a distant one. Tactility guarantees a caressing approach that Surin may have always lacked. In any case, far from referring to a metaphysical affirmation allying the word to being, as in the case of the (Eucharistic) rite or of the (dogmatic) statement, that "effect perceptible to taste and to the inner membranes of the palate and the stomach" joins an *erotics* to a *knowledge*. This experience of the mucous membranes is of the epistemological type (it involves a "certainty"), but an epistemology based on touch and linked to a discernment of pleasures. It attributes to touch, that is, to an erotic function indissociable from a relation to the *other*, a value of knowledge that the visual relation to an *object* does not have.

In any case, the body is born of that experience. In the fantastic that accompanies that birth, and that has, in the *imaginaire* of a madness, the appearance of a mythical story at once certain and fictive, the body appears as a cave occupied by the "lakes of the belly" (Georg Groddeck); it is an immense "mouth." On the banks of these lakes, "delicious" waves of the other come and "kiss" the inner shores constituted by the "inner membranes."[55] Perhaps that touch also obeys the law of the "as if" in the same way writing does. In the scene referenced earlier, Surin "imagines" that he is repeating the sacramental Eucharistic sequence of the bread and the wine, while at the same time taking care to distinguish the Eucharist from the simulation he is carrying out. For him, it is a question of a baroque simulacrum of the "real" rite, symbolic and social, of which he is deprived. But this diversion constructs another stage of science. It marks the passage to a new paradigm, which replaces the assertions of a divine metaphysics with the "effects" of an erotics, and which finds on the basis of sensorial relations that "great principle of life"[56] that the institution of meaning no longer assures the body.

The Physiological Pathos of Breathing

This body living inside is alien to what the physician knows about it; his knowledge is limited to what he can see of it when he opens it up. Surin takes seriously neither the physician, who, to refute his impression of being unable to breathe, reminds him of the "sixty muscles" that "serve to breathe,"[57] nor the learned who claim to cure him by means of good broths, entertainment, and sleep.[58] He sings:

> Physicians, apothecaries,
> I renounce your mysteries.[59]

In fact he does not "renounce" them so radically, since the perception he has of his body remains largely organized by the knowledge of contemporary physicians. He, like them, distinguishes between the "animal faculties," which are injured, and "the vital" ones, which remain "still strong and good;"[60] like them, he refers to that "chemistry of humors" and to a "mechanics of liquids," in a fluid universe in which elixirs reign, and in which the "potable" is mixed with the humors;[61] like them especially, and like the majority of his companions, he grants "the air" a benefic or malefic virtue, decisive in the treatment of melancholy.[62] But the mutation that the internal experience of the body introduces into the intellectual framework that symbolizes it is all the more remarkable.

The clearest example, at the center of the "tragedy" of which the inner body is the theater, relates to breathing, or, as Surin says, to the *respir*. From the outset, experience diverges from the medicine of the day. It relates no longer to a combinatorial of cosmological elements but to a physiological perception, relative to the functions of the living being in relation to the ambient milieu. Two opposite movements specify what might be called the internal biological feeling of the relation to the environment: "contraction" and "dilatation." They have both spiritual and physical significance. Hence the two lexical series describing them are valid at different levels. We have, on the one hand, tightening, grip, constraint, restriction, immobility; or: compact, bound, flattened, stopped, etc. On the other hand, disgorgement, torrent, issue, impetuosity, fury, rage, pipe; or: dilated, released from, pulled out of, etc. This luxuriant vocabulary plays on a whole gamut of registers, for example from physical suffocation to moral despair, but it designates a global experience whose referent is constantly breathing, not facial, but inner, from the chest, the lungs, or the diaphragm.

"My muscles were locked up like padlocks," Surin writes, so much so that for "more than ten years," "I was left without ever having a breath from the diaphragm, but only from the lung, and so narrow at that" that speaking was impossible. Conversely, healing makes him "feel the opening of respiration from the diaphragm" and lets him "dilate his lungs and even his diaphragm."[63] In this deep region, local differences (lungs, diaphragm, etc.) are paralleled by qualitative ones. There are "four kinds of breaths": the first "black, annoying, and disturbing"; the second "indifferent and low"; the third, of "elevation" with "peace"; the last makes one "majestically tranquil."[64] A subtle lucidity detects all these distinctions. It seeks to classify, name, and describe a confused movement to constitute a typology of breathing, a fundamental gamut of the relations to that primary form of space and to the *there is* constituted by *the air* itself. To this fine analysis intensified by pain, the deep body offers the wherewithal to establish a physiological grammar (or what should that science be named?) for the impalpable and necessary element that gives rise to all place, for "the milieu through and in which everything can appear"—that air that is openness itself, "the clearing of the opening."[65]

The intake of air recapitulates in Surin the first cry of the child and the longest voyage. It also gives the subject a space, and interiority an exteriority. Contraction is contrary to it. Contraction paralyzes the impetuosity, the warmth, the inability to bear being constrained—in a word, the energy characterizing the "nature," as it was expressed in those days, of Surin, or as Surin himself put it, his "instinct." It is probably to the violence of this contrast that the actual attempted suicide at Saint-Macaire in 1645 corresponds. Surin associates it with "the open window" onto the Garonne, that is, with the "precipice for which he had" at that time "a furious instinct." "He had no place," he said. He needed a space, and its condition, air. It is known that throwing objects is, in dreams or in reality, the means of giving oneself space. At Saint-Macaire, Surin is himself at once the object discarded—the "bundle" neither God nor man wanted anymore—and the thrown one that creates a space: "Without any view of what he was doing, he was launched out that window, and thrown."[66] He throws himself into the air. It is the gesture of his whole life, the very movement of *respir*.

The Nonplace: From Madness to Writing

By this first inventory, the journey made by Surin in his madness—or more precisely: what he does with the space into which his madness reduces him[67]—reveals the essential physical and symbolic conditions of all journeys. Reciprocally, the "illeity" of the regions traversed by a subject, their relation to the possible, their capacity for embodying an "I," the unveiling of the ordinary, the invention of a deep body in the course of itineraries supposedly geographical, the intake of air to which every departure aspires, etc., are aspects to be evoked in all journeys, whether those to distant seas and lands, or those remaining within the utopic in-between of the real and the dream.

The (quasi-phenomenological) glimpse that I have just provided of Surin's journey within his prison still leaves aside the two antinomic points around which, in madness itself, there emerges something that for Surin is not madness: damnation and speech. The one, cast in the setting of aphasia and paralysis, designates the "persuasion," the "belief," the "thought," or the "impression" (Surin uses these words interchangeably) of being *rejected*. The other, attempted first in the form of writing (this body of a voice expectant of another voice), refers to the "hope" or the "possibility" of being *awaited*. Both refer to what signal comes from the other. Both, also, are decided, in Surin, in that biological "nexus" in which the body seeks air, in which the "damned" is denied air, in which the writer begins to find a dilatation of his impetuosity. Indeed the physiology of *respir*, by all its traits, describes the strategic place, between aphasia and the abundance of "saying," in which communication with the other originates; it is a physiology of speech. Hence it is there as well that the journey begins to be written. In this respect, *La Science expérimentale* marks the coincidence between the account of a journey that the body itself is, and the one that writing is. In sum, this text, which tells how the relation to the other is decisive in the birth of a speaking body, is also the production of the body qua the account of a journey or qua writing.

Chapter Eight

Angelic Speech

On the horizon, the immense crowd of angels arises. "Two hundred million," said the Book of Revelation already in the first century;[1] "Three hundred million," in Athanasius Kircher's view, in his *Oedipus Aegyptiacus* (1652);[2] even more . . . The mathematician and calculator Gaspard Schott asserts, in his *Magia universalis* (1657), that he can "demonstrate with evidence" that "the number of all the angels" rises to a number whose order of magnitude is 10^{62}, which he writes out in full.[3] The number spins out of control. The letters as well: the combinatorics is on overload to form these names of angels that must be, according to Johann Reuchlin's *De arte cabalistica* (1517), "unknown, stupendous words, signifying nothing according to the normal use of language, but inducing us, by provoking the astonishment of our reason, to seek the intelligible ones assiduously, and then to venerate and love them."[4] To the prolixity of the numbers and letters, a simple indication of the angelic proliferation in the literatures and the historical experience, must be added an equally traditional and paradoxical note: if the angel is *number* ("myriads"), it is also the *singular.* Each angel is unique in his species; each human being is guided or "watched over" by an angel; and often the angel specifies the unusual, the "sudden," the particular event, the occurrence of the imponderable.

A strange subject, overflowing the fields of knowledge in both their extension and their comprehension. It is ungraspable. Yet this dream, or this music, haunted speculation and practice not only in the Middle Ages, or among so many "different" civilizations,[5] but in Western modernity, which has only superficially sublimated this fantastic. Thus, in Johann Georg Hamann, Rainer Maria Rilke, Franz Kafka, Paul Klee, Walter Benjamin, Antonin Artaud, and many others, the angel is for us the ghost of a poetics and a thinking. To restrict my attention to Western culture, I would be remiss not to also mention the renewal of angelology advanced by the monumental work of Henry Corbin, devoted to the Angel as "hermeneut of the divine Silence,"[6] and of which Christian Jambet has analyzed the philosophical givens.[7] To begin, it will suffice for me to quote René Char: "Communicating with the angel, our primordial care. (Angel, that part of man which safeguards from religious compromise, the language of highest silence, the meaning that is not measured out. Tuner of lungs who gilds the nutritious grapes of the impossible . . .)."[8]

This "madness" of the impossible even passes through the *Encyclopédie*: "It is madness to hear the concerts of the angels as do certain enthusiasts."[9] On this Monday, the day dedicated to the angels since the fifteenth century, I would like to say something about this musical theme. I will not venture to describe the singing, concerting, revealing, regulating, or law-upholding population, whose species have been multiplied and distinguished by so many speculations—gnostic and Dionysian in particular. I will leave aside the ontological or cosmological aspects. A preliminary selective framework, and only in the Western tradition, makes it possible to consider in that throng a long *theory of "saying"*: whether in the form of a hierarchy of the "speakers" (Seraphim, Cherubim, Thrones, Dominations, Virtues, Powers, etc., down to the Archangels and Angels); or in the form of the functions of speaking (praise, messages, orders, promises, judgments, etc., for example with the "psychopomps" who weigh souls,[10] or with "guardian" angels, whose main role, according to Thomas Aquinas,[11] consists in "illuminating" individual thought); or in the form of representations that portray angelic "styles" (for example, the "apteral" or wingless angels, the first to appear in the Christian catacombs, in the fourth century,[12] and still the only ones recognized by Jacob Boehme, with "hands and feet,"[13] whereas, in the continuity of a history going back to the ancient "victories" and "genies," Paul Klee gives them wings, particularly in the *Angelus Novus*, the inseparable companion of Walter Benjamin).[14] This vast panorama reveals, in the angelic mode, a sort of *ars dictandi* whose celestial and utopian tableau presents the possible modalities of enunciation, according to the threefold formality of the status of the speaker, of the illocutionary acts, and of the enunciative forms of rhetoric.

Of the immense literature devoted to them, poetic and/or rhetorical, I will look only at the Western and modern region, which is itself guarded by studious fortresses such as the *De angelis* of Francisco Suárez (1620), an in-quarto of 1,120 pages, or that of Denys Petau, in the third tome of his *Theologica dogmata* (1644). Behind that Great Wall of China, there is a world: a rustling of Angels. I would like merely to bring out a few general traits and a few figures of angelic speech. These passersby point us in the direction of the function and forms of a "saying" or, as Char put it, of "the word of the highest silence."

1. ENUNCIATIVE METAPHORS: "ANGELIZARE"

"Angelizare, to angelize," among so many other verbal inventions of which he holds the secret, is a creation of Nicholas of Cusa. Though he rejects the Angels qua rectors of medieval cosmology, he designates by this word an operation of the mind that leaves the night, which is subordinate to the principle of contradiction, and aims at the great solar light of the coincidence of opposites. This act of transfer, the angelic act, is, he says, "auroral."[15] In taking this beautiful verb as an emblem, my intention is not to expose the Cusan conception of the angelic in its relation to the nature of man and knowledge, but rather to take up the perspective, central to his work, of an "operating" or an "acting." I will begin with a phenomenology of the angelic act. The angel delineates the formality of an operation. My first question, then, is: "What is angelizing?" What kind of action does the angel outline? Within the framework I have set forth, a description begins by noting three characteristics.

The angelic passing. The angel cuts a zigzag path through the cosmic order. If we find in Saint Paul, as well as in certain texts of the early Christian tradition, a reserve with respect to angels in that they are the "rudiments of the world," or *stoicheia tou kosmou*, and impose their law on humans,[16] by and large the angel represents rather a transversality of communication. He takes his time and crosses through; he bypasses the hierarchies of beings and mediations. Like a crack in the metal of the universe, he marks direct circulations and communications across the established order. A transgression by shortcut, one might say. But the essential point is that these passages are in the form of a spoken word that challenges the order of things. Thus, in the book of Judges, the angel, that "divine man," announces a victory to the defeated and subjugated people: and to the barren woman, a birth.[17] A poetics defies ontological hierarchy and historical inevitability. The angelic word restores an eventalism and a possible. In this sense, it is "metaphorical": the passage to a different genre, the invention of a different space, the creation of a possible within what the facts posit as being impossible. In a dream, Jacob "sees" angels ascending and descending the steps of the ladder measuring the necessary distances and mediations between earth and heaven.[18] The space of the dream thus gives the angelic "metaphor" its fundamental figure: a word "passes" the frontiers of beings or things, paradoxically restores a historicity within the framework of the cosmic laws, and, beneath the sign of the sudden and unusual, opens up a field of possibility.

The double. In a more modern tradition, developing since the twelfth century and luxuriating since the fourteenth, the angel is a double who increasingly takes on the form of the "guardian angel." Like the word itself, this double is ambivalent. Sometimes he represents a utopia of perfection, a place/nonplace of meaning or of truth that contrasts with the transformations and contingencies of actual situations; analogous to the Platonic Idea, he "keeps" a model serving as a counterpoint to particular stories while at the same time being involved in them, like the angel struggling at night with Jacob, in a combat between the ideal and reality. In such cases he is thetic and assertive, but in the way a word or a song stands apart in relation to things in order to keep the reference to what should or can be. In this perspective, he ends up being, as in Kafka, the "guardian of the law," the incongruous presence of an impossible imperative of duty. At other times (and this has the appearance of being the opposite), he exudes an internal strangeness that disturbs the stability of places; he is the irruption of what one does not know of oneself (good or bad). This angelic "disquietude" is to being what etymology is to the word: a shadow come from afar, the advent of an unnamable origin in a passing sign, the "blur" of a movement coming from an unknown depth.

It is not surprising that guardian angels, figures of the double, experience an unprecedented boom beginning in the fifteenth century with the addresses and lyric mise en scènes of Denis the Carthusian[19] and of an entire "spiritual" literature. Echoing a new consciousness of the individual, they are also connected with the erosion of the great medieval syntheses in which heaven symbolized with earth in one sole speaking cosmos. They make up the thousand glittering bits—scattered fragments and "words"—of theological alliances broken by time. In these flamboyant angelologies shine forth from all directions the countless relics, living and evanescent, of "correspondences" that no longer possess cosmological guarantees and that proliferate in the interstices of a changed, modern society. A space between two worlds (celestial and terrestrial) and two ages (medieval and classical) fills up with angels, who, resistances or resurgences of a fundamental experience, "keep" a symbolism that is in the process of becoming individualized and culturally illicit.

Signs of enunciation. Angels, qua oscillations between the recall of an ideal or "imaginal" reference that opposes the compromises of history and the irruption of "something else" in a system of normalities, sustain a function of the spoken word, that is, a difference with respect to the observed world. But they exert this function in a most particular mode, consisting less in certifying true assertions than in vouchsafing the very existence of a spoken word. Its content is not the essential of the angelic message: that is already known; it often repeats a verse from Scripture, an article of faith, or an accepted truth. The angelic intervention transforms that common statement into a speech act that is addressed to you, singularly, here and now. The novelty consists not in corrections or supplements of assertions still unknown, but in the fact that the retained assertion is spoken, and therefore that there is speech. The angel *says that saying is.* This focal point organizes the rhapsodic, musical, vocal, and visual style of angelic apparitions. The message is its very enunciation.

This is why, in the Christian traditions, the angel is not an "object" of belief. Rather he traces, within a manifold of beliefs, the dimension of belief itself, if it is true that "belief" is sustained by the word of the other.[20] The sign of a "saying," it is the respondent of a "believing," and not its object. Therefore the "angelic" is that which speaks to us in a discourse, a body, or a landscape; that which "touches" like a word addressed to me in this instant; but also that which, of a truth, is not appropriable, to the extent that it is the saying of the other, and not an assertion subject to verification. The angel, if he says something, speaks it to the degree that it is believable, or, in other words, to the degree that it is word.

Whence the luxuriant ambiguity of angelic apparitions and messages. The "saying" does not hinge on truth values. It insinuates, between the false and the true, an uncertainty that is often emphasized by the accounts of angelic apparitions and connoted by the term "apparition" itself: an appearance, a seeming. In the name of what can we trust it? As in every trial of enunciation, a guarantee may be sought in the status of the speaker. "What is your name?" asks Manoah of "the divine man" who announces the birth of a son to his barren wife, and whose identity is unknown to him. The angel says: "Why do you ask me my name? It is wonderful"—a term (*fe li*) that also means "mysterious," "unintelligible."[21] No name will be given, or else it will be only the name that serves as an emblem of the unnamable, to which is added, as in Gideon's case, a sign, fire, which destroys signs.[22] By the thousands, modern stories of angels in turn relate these acts of enunciation characterized by effects of reception—esthetic impressions, inner feelings, stunning or tender touches—and generally put in the modality of "appearing." "It seemed to me that I heard," "presented itself," "appeared to me," "I thought I saw," etc.: a "seeming" modifies the event, not to minimize its certainty, but to localize its nature on the side on which the utterance is grasped in its echoing, and not abstractly isolated as an emission. Here, the saying is a phenomenon of reception and interpretation. Disappearing visibility, the angel has no "being there" that lends itself to objective verification. The credible word cannot be detached from what we believe about it, what we believe we see or hear in that respect. It is for this reason that the angel escapes the time of verification, the stability of a framework of criteria and the onomastic classification of status, at the same time as being the event-creator of temporality, the institution of possibles (whence its poetic function in epistemological matters) and manifestation of the unknowable peculiar to every name.

Last, if "angelizing" is being able to speak, if the angel is the unexpectedness of that which starts talking, anyone or anything can suddenly take on the angelic figure. An ancient Talmudic commentary already noted this. Whence the number—myriads—applied to that singular event. Who is my angel? What is it that suddenly "speaks to me"? You, perhaps, or that light, or that look from a female passerby. Because of this, the analysis must move toward the speaking subject, or toward the perception that receives here-now a message as "angelic." A long tradition asserts that the angel speaks but that we do not speak to him.[23] He says what we hear from him. This speaking, then, orients the research in the direction of a semiotics of listening, whereas our own semiotics is concentrated on the productions of language. It brings us back to the modalities of reception and the progress of attention (that is, to a whole philosophical lineage) and to the effects of interpretation induced by a "hermeneutics of silence." Ultimately, it assumes that language is first auditory, and that it is instituted once it is heard.

2. STYLES: BEING AND SAYING

In a history or historical phenomenology of angels in the West, periods and separations appear that must be recalled, however roughly, in order to situate the modern experience within that manifold. Perhaps, rather than a question of stages, it is a question of types, the recurrence and mixing of which, moreover, may be observed, and what characterizes a period is only the predominance of one of them. Among the criteria capable of generating a classification of the variants presented by the concept of the angel, I will retain only two, one of which refers to the "time" of the angel (is it an occasional mediator, or permanent?) and the other to its mode of intervention (vocal, musical, oral in short, or rather stigmatizing, touching and engraving the body, in short scriptorial). From these two criteria, two chronologies result.

Occasional versus permanent. According to this categorization,[24] a first period presents the conception of an occasional mediator, a "provisional and circumstantial emanation of the divinity": it is the "envoy," or *mal-'akh* of the tradition of Israel, until Philo of Alexandria. Mixed with Babylonian traits,[25] and Canaanite by the name itself, the angel appears as an ambassador charged with a mission in view of a particular situation, and carrying a message in the first person. Acting publicly or in secret ("the angel who spoke within me," says Zechariah),[26] he steps aside in deference to the word he transmits. More fundamentally, the "I" that he says is not his own, but God's. It is *the "speaking" of what it is not*, so that its interventions leave its nature in suspense: is it Yahweh or the angel that is manifested in "the angel of Yahweh"? Is it God, an intermediary being, an appearance, an image? The act of saying is a prophetic "phenomenon": it surprises, formidable or consoling, but it renders the identity of the speaker inaccessible. By his ephemeral status, his vanishing apparition, the angel creates an insurmountable frontier between the enunciative act and the speaking subject: the one is sure, the other uncertain.

A second period, especially Christian and medieval, is characterized by the movement that returns the act of speaking to the speaking subject (*actio sequitur esse*) and that inscribes the angelic interventions in the hierarchy of beings. Thus, this problematic, recognizable still today in the psychology that analyzes saying as the "expression" of a subject, has sought to classify ontological statuses in a world order and constructed an angelology that took for granted an overall adequation between the hierarchy of beings and the order of mediations. Already Philo of Alexandria integrated the occasional "verbs" with the Platonic structure of a universe in which everything is distributed by degrees of beings.[27] Dionysius the Areopagite reinforces the "thearchic" system of angelic intermediaries, so that, in his *Celestial Hierarchy*, the order of the mediations seems to exclude a direct relation of man with God,[28] according to the general principle, adopted by Thomas Aquinas, that "the inferior beings are administered by the superior beings."[29] In the vast architecture of these spiritual metaphysics, the initial givens of angelic experience become difficult speculative problems.

Thus Thomas Aquinas seeks to save the possibility, for man, of communicating directly with God (the very possibility that earlier implied the uncertain or transparent identity of the angel), and, on the other hand, he has to ensure a cosmological order. The angel is at the crossroads of this antinomy between the (theological) transversality of the word and the (metaphysical) hierarchization of beings. The Thomist speculation on angels, although it appeared "inept" to Descartes,[30] elucidates with rigor the consequences to be drawn from the philosophical option (an "undecidable" choice) that poses a metaphysical anteriority of being in relation to speaking. It inscribes in heaven, a space of theory, the (still-obtaining) implications of a thinking that functions on the postulate that it is necessary *to be* in order *to say*, or a thinking that, today, would presuppose an "experience" as the condition of its "expression." From being to saying, Thomas poses the mediation of a knowledge. The angel is a being who knows, but who may or may not "want-to-say." The "want to manifest" (*velle manifestare*), a transit from knowledge to *elocutio*, defends the thickness of an existence of its own against the identity between being, knowing, and showing: between being that knows and expression, the "want-to-say" (an "intention of communicating") or its opposite, the "want-to-conceal" (an "intention of keeping silence"), preserves a *secret* of existence; it dramatizes, so to speak, the very act of speaking.[31] The word becomes an event. A historicity, obliterated from heaven by the transparent order of beings, is reintroduced by the act of communicating and by all the intersubjective subtleties implied by the will to keep silent or the will to manifest. Because he speaks, the angel brings back into the metaphysical order the historical and theological "pathos" of a secret and its revelation. But he has had to pay a tribute to that order, since he is at first considered as mute being and knowledge. In this model, communication is a secondary phenomenon. In the beginning, there is a Verb that is the silent reason of the universe.

A third period may be envisaged, beginning with the Renaissance. Its specification would be the disjunction between being an angel and angelic saying. On the one hand, the angel, introduced into the field of the sciences of nature, represents intelligence regulating a class of phenomena, and, on the other hand, the angel, reduced to the occasional, represents the marvelous shards of a broken symbolic system. In the former category, we have the angel Johann Reuchlin speaks of in his *De arte cabalistica*, an "acting intelligence that moves the orbit" of each "celestial sphere" and is "delegated to that office."[32] This will be Kepler's "Angelus Rector," that of Gerolamo Cardano or of Giulio Cesare Vanini, later even those of Gustav Theodor Fechner. He will end up blending away into the regularity he upheld, except for his reappearance as the defender of occult or unknowable laws, as in the *Arcana Cœlestia* and the "speaking" heaven of Swedenborg[33] down to and including Balzac and Annie Besant. The other side (but the borders are not impermeable) teems with the colorful and marvelous population, now happy, now redoubtable, of angels, bearers of certainty, that no longer have a place in the physical or psychological universe. Whence, for example, in the sixteenth and seventeenth centuries, the immense literature, elitist and popular, dedicated to guardian angels. These are "words" that are displaced, out of the ordinary and migratory, authorizing a transnatural dimension, the language of which one no longer knows where to place.

The angel will disappear, either into the universal law of the stars, or into the singular event of the everyday. In the diverse functions he exercises, he no longer "dwells." But his absence is just as uncertain. Where he is assumed to be permanent, he fades away, and when he is thought to be ephemeral, he reappears. Certain modern theologians follow him in his evasions and withdrawals. Speculatively, it is moving to see Suárez, chapter after chapter, seeking that angel capable of proximity and of distance (*capax propinquitatis et distantiae*), beneath the banner of celerity (*celeritas*) and suddenness (*subito*). What is the angelic *ubi*, what is this place, as fugitive and fundamental as the "singular" that is the proper subject of angelic science?[34] The angel "dwells nowhere," and yet, not being infinite, he has a spatiality of his own. In the form of transit (*transitus*) and communication, he finally designates that which "binds" singularities: he corresponds to the most original contribution of the judicial and political thought of Suárez, which is concerned with instituting a system of civil obligations to counterbalance the disorder of the world.[35] The angel somewhere keeps the "presence" of that which *obliges*, in all senses of the term.

One might see in this persistence of the angel, combined with his self-effacement, the function of a postulate in the domain of speech. In language, the angel represents the necessity of postulating a credible "saying." Somewhere (but where? for it can only be outside our language), saying cannot be wrong. However misleading speech may be, it postulates an utterance "somewhere" that does not mislead and that the angel represents, lodged alternately in the will that moves the celestial spheres and in the shadow that doubles the everyday event, but vanishing from every place in which we would like to establish him as a guarantor. That is why the angel is inextricably bound up with the question of lying (or of the Liar, the deceiving angel), and not with that of error (which concerns the statement). He maintains a permanent and ever vanishing condition of the "saying"—a condition that is not localizable in a particular place in the world or in language.

In the stories, moreover, the angel is frequently presented in a threefold modality exempting him from the verification processes applying to constative assertions: (1) He is introduced, as *a quotation*, by textual authorities, by credible witnesses, or—and this institutes a different tradition of the believable—by the circumscription of an exempted space, that of the dream. (2) He appears beneath the sign of a captivating *beauty*, which pertains to an esthetic experience or a poetic imagination, and not to a rigorous logic. (3) He is the signature of an *excess* (even when it is the index of a different "order" of things), and by a "more" or a "too much," he opens a horizon of "sublime" that overflows, and must overflow, the common rules of veridiction. In these three modes, the angel is distinguished from the appropriable, the true, and the normal. Thus when, with the Renaissance, he escapes medieval speculations (which sought to guarantee his elocution by a status and that first committed him to silence, the better to ensure the privilege of a permanent being or knowledge), he begins once again to announce, as he did in his primitive manifestations, the postulate associating nondeception with the saying of ungraspable instants. In this form, as evanescent as irrefutable, he is responsible for speech, without being entirely either a speaker or a message.

Oral versus written. Another opposition makes a different distribution of the historical figures of the angel possible. Sometimes the angel speaks, sings, blows trumpets, or plays the viol; sometimes he writes, engraves, wounds (out of love or justice) with arrows, lances, and pointed standards. In reducing these differences to the anthropological and cultural binomial of an oral style and a written one, I am simplifying something nonetheless essential at stake here, whether it lies in the relationship of the angel with language, or in that of angelic performance with the trace, auditory or engraved, language leaves behind. The early angel tends to be rather vocal (albeit with a good many exceptions, such as "the man" who wrestles with Jacob and wounds him "in the hollow of the thigh").[36] A breath inhabits his body transformed into a cavern of winds. The air that animates him within, the movement of respiration, changes the atmosphere into a thousand and one exhalations of words and melodies. Like the voice, he articulates and transforms differences by the communications of a breath. This angel is armed, like the ancient Michael, only to strike the pagan nations with his thunderbolt. But essentially his power is that of the air. That is why he leaves after him the smoke of a fire, a smell, an echo, a benediction. This angelic race bespeaks a confidence in the breath that carries semantic messages and is, as it were, the winged body of the language.

While this crowd of angels orients us toward the vowel and vocalization, another one is manifested by inscription. He may have as his ancestor Ezekiel, the writing angel, probably originating in the scribe or Babylonian *nabu*: "a man clothed in linen, with a writer's inkstand on his side," is ordered to "set a mark upon the foreheads of the men that sigh and that cry" for the abominations committed in Jerusalem.[37] Thus, angelic writing has antecedents. One date, however, seems to mark the historical beginning of its great modern development: the "seraphic apparition" of Alverne, in 1224, that "marked the flesh" of Francis of Assisi "with the effigy of the crucified."[38] According to ancient accounts, at the same time that the vision disappears, the five wounds are marked on the flesh to constitute a "sign bearer" (*signifer*) and biblical (that is booklike) blazon of the Crucified. The ambivalence of the seraph (is it Christ or an angel?) is connected with the whole angelic tradition, but this seraphic writing is immediately considered as being "a mystery unknown to the prior centuries."[39] A writing born of the "disappearing vision" (*visio disparens*, says Bonaventure), the stigmata of Il Poverello do indeed inaugurate a body-memory. An inscription, and not a voice, answers for (and replies to) the vanished vision. This body, signed by the disappeared, a testamentary body, engraved and wounded by the moment of separation, forms a theater of memory, a new sacrament in which mourning is indissociable from love, in which the sign has the form of "cruelty" and bodily alteration. This sacrament is writing—a writing already close to the experience that Joyce or Artaud will have of it.

In the posterity of the seraph of Alverne—an innumerable population that develops angelic writing, even if it does not attain to the violent beauty of its first Franciscan moment—a different relation of the angel to language appears, organized by a new gravity of time. While the breath, or voice, crossed through the visible and invisible zones of the same world, while a musical animation was able to spread and cross the frontiers between diverse regions of a cosmic space, time begins to create insurmountable limits; it creates a break. Disappearance becomes the decisive event. The voice cannot pass through that division. The writing angel marks the progressive triumph of history over a space traversed by great speaking urges. The circulation of winds, breaths, and music is interrupted by the caesurae of a new order which is that of time, that is, by the successive coincidences between what disappears, a vision, and what is produced by that loss, a writing. Like a photograph, the angel henceforth marks instantaneous articulations between an evanescent vision (the *visio disparens*) and an extraneous place of recording. Indeed the body no longer preserves a voice or a breath that would insinuate a continuity from the angel to the soul; it is a place of inscription for the effect and the symptom of the vanished angel; it is a "book" in which the trace of what is disappearing stays, "a writing desk" "informed" by that which no longer speaks.

The angel withdraws into the field of the *visual* in which the instant of his apparition cannot be retained or certified; and the human gathers itself in the historical reality of a separation that scriptorial productions continually relate in bodily symptoms. The new face-to-face encounter of the writer-angel with the written body is not only the index of a rupture in the musical harmony between things and words, or in the conception of a cosmos that is "speaking" through and through. Between "seeing" and "writing" a mute relationship is instituted, and the dichotomy that disconnects a human writing from the fulgurating vision signals the power that a new consciousness of time attributes to death. Indeed it is time that suspends the word of the angel and retains no more than its vanishing glimmer, but it is already death that gives its intensity and insuperable nature to this moment of disappearance. Then an angelic writing makes the body the blazon of the disappeared and yields to the "flesh," to a human and terrestrial historicity, the privilege of being the sign bearer (*signifer*) of that which no longer speaks. The writer-angel attests the submission of the cosmic word to a historical struggle against death; it recapitulates (might this be a new symbol of language?) the coincidence between visionary instants that merely pass and the work of producing durable signs that such instants lead to in the body.

3. FIGURES OF EXCEEDANCE

These typologies are too loose to help us map the crowd of angels. We must get down to the singularity of performances and movements. No longer just styles, but, in dance terms, "figures." Three apparitions, drawn from a century particularly rich in angels (1550–1650), in Teresa of Avila, Jacob Boehme, and Angelus Silesius, will enable us to make a few supplementary notations on the excesses angels introduce into language.

The angel with the spear: Teresa of Avila. In his famous marble of Santa Maria della Vittoria, Bernini has caught the image of Teresa, ecstatic amidst the waves of her dress and struck by the amorous dart of a young cherub. The scene is related in the autobiography, the *Libro de la vida* (1562), in which the angel, however, appears only thirteen times—an austere Carmelite décor, compared with the baroque profusion of many contemporary texts. Generally, the references by Teresa relate to the traditional framework of an aura of "glory" surrounding God, Our Lady, or revered figures such as Father García of Toledo.[40] The angels form, in the background, homage to God who to them is "delight" (*regalo*). "Often," she says, they "are present, but without my seeing them."[41] She further specifies that she has a blind perception of them, a sense of presence that is not a vision or a representation but a sort of tactile intelligence,[42] as one might have an impression of air or sea. It is an element in which an experience unfolds. It is accompanied by a triple connotation: the indecision of an "appearing" (*parecer*) that leaves in suspense the exact nature of the phenomenon: a radiating beauty that describes an ambiance and not an object; an interrogation on that exquisite environment, in which a commenting word (but "from whom? I do not know") once suddenly emerges, explaining that "all one can do there is to understand that one can understand nothing."[43] In that indeterminate region, nothing objectively observable takes place: neither judgment of reality, nor assertion of truth, nor direction of meaning. A language will gradually articulate one or another of these. But first, as in the sonorous world in which the child is bathed and plays before speaking, there is a space of possibilities for movements in a different element and for a whole orchestration of kinesthetic impressions. That space is "angelic."

The "vision" of the angel—that of Bernini—stands as an exception in that experience of a different air. Repeated several times, it verges on the "marvel" (*maravilla*). In describing it, Teresa already sketches out an artistic composition: "I saw an angel close by me, on my left side, in bodily form. . . . He was not large, but small of stature, and most beautiful—his face so flaming (*encendido*), one of the highest angels, who seem to be all of fire: they must be those whom we call cherubim. Their names they never tell me. . . . I saw in his hand a long spear of gold, and at the iron's point there seemed to be a little fire. He appeared to me to be thrusting it at times into my heart, and to pierce my very entrails; when he drew it out, he seemed to draw them out also, and to leave me all on fire with a great love of God. The pain was so great, that it made me moan; and so surpassing was the sweetness of this excessive pain, that there was no longer any desire that it should stop, nor that the soul be satisfied with less than God."[44]

This transverberation evokes, by many of its traits, that of Francis of

Assisi. Early interpreters (and not the least among them Domingo Bañez, Luis de León) even hold that Teresa's "cherub" is in fact a seraph. In this they follow Bonaventure, taken up in the seventeenth century by Angelus Silesius, who considers mystic love to be "seraphic" and speculative contemplation "cherubic"; the seraph inflames; the cherub illumines.[45] In any case, Teresa is totally "dazed" or "stupefied" (*embobada*), she says: that there should be at the same time pain and pleasure "drives her crazy."[46] The Cherub that strikes her with its flaming spear upsets all the categories of that great classifier of perceptions and passions. The angel is the chaos she struggles against, like the God of the book of Genesis, by a tireless labor of distinction. It confuses everything in this fire that, so young and little, it thrusts into her body. And to crown it all for her, there is no longer, in that burning equivocation, even the desire "that it stop." But the disorder or madness is not what the angel-writer traces on her body with his spear; it is what it tears out of her. The movement is not of impression but of extraction, with those "entrails" that the arrow, in being pulled out, brings forth from their inner secrecy. The disorder was within, controlled by the bodily dispositive of appearance. The angel brings all that out, naked. Nameless, wordless, *infans*, he brings that madness, hitherto unknown, to light. He breaks through the borders of propriety, with the fire in which he is himself inflamed. The angelic is no longer an environment or an ambient space but, by the "deliverance" of an unknown interiority, by a poetics of madness, the burning fusion of the inner with the outer, or of the secret "entrails" with a new world. Hence the physical and intellectual apparatus of their separation falls inert, in "stupefaction," as if out of order. There remains, at the center of the scene, this "golden spear" that is neither the angel nor the "beast" but the very shard of the communication wrenching the one from heaven, the other from earth, and taking from Teresa all sense of limit: "nothing less than God."

The angelic limit: Jacob Boehme and Angelus Silesius. A half-century later, the German poetics of Jacob Boehme and of Johannes Scheffler (alias Angelus Silesius) organize around the angel the experience of a universe in which the divine does not cease distancing itself from the human. Assuming familiarity with the remarkable study Bernard Gorceix has devoted to these two angelologies,[47] I will begin by noting, as a starting point, the strange chiasmus that brings them together in setting them in opposition. Separated by some thirty years (Boehme wrote *Aurora* in 1612 and *Mysterium magnum* in 1623; Scheffler published his *Spiritual Aphorisms* in 1657), they envisage the angel in the formal structure of exceedance, but while in the first angelology the angel continually looks down on the human, in the second man must rise above the angelic. The angel spans an intermediary space that the two works seem to cross in opposite directions. In fact, these two movements are not as opposed as they appear; what they have in common, namely, the angelic delimitation of two regions of experience, is more essential to them.

In Boehme, there is salvation for men when the originary violence of God that is their being "speaks" in them. A "living death" must "blow up the solid lock of nature by applying the large charge of explosive (*die grosse Petarde*)" of the spiritual being, and "burn" everything that, in them, is "anything (*etwas*)," so that, "blind, deaf, and dumb," once the experience of the world is reduced to nothing, and reason to a "madness," they finally become "speaking beings"—an incandescence of Oneself: that is to say, angels.[48] An admirable conception of speech, angelic in its essence: to speak is to burn—just as, in the account of the Exodus,[49] the burning bush in which the Angel appears signifies by destroying signs, by devouring what has to do with being (a "being-there") or with state (a status), by an internal energy that manifests itself without depending on exteriority. This focal point unifies within itself the destiny of the angel and of man; in this accomplishment, they are "brothers." But while the angel is there by nature, man gets there only by a struggle against the opacity of the body and of reason, in uprooting himself from the ground of his assurances, in defying his metaphysical situation itself of being-in-the-world. Whence the difference between them.

A "putting into language" of the ineffable, a "putting into form" of the divine "energies" (*Kräfte*), a putting into "sound" (*Schall*) of the infinite virtualities of the unpronounceable Name (and even of its letters)—such is the threefold function of the angels.[50] They give body to divine Nature and constitute its oceanic concept. Each one of them is the "form" of a "force," the ambition, central to the sixteenth century, of instituting a "speaking" that articulates an "abundance,"[51] but each angel responds to it excessively. Indeed, its interminable beginning is the relation (mythical and founding, like all origin of language) between, on the one hand, the "choleric fire of the [divine] first person,"[52] a stormy "seething" in which the *bullitio* that characterized the deity in Meister Eckhart,[53] and on the other the transparency or even the "sweetness" of a "yes," a calm mirror in which the first principle can pass from its originary furor to self-knowledge. Therefore the angels, elements of this passage that defines speaking, "allow God to understand himself."[54] The same is true of men, when they become angelic by retrieving in the depths of themselves the fire that transforms them into words. But since the angel himself, proceeding from an inaccessible originary violence, is the mystery of language, he shows humans the necessity of forming the material "body" of the divine nature; the angels prophesy the construction of a *physical* language of God that man can realize better than they, to the point of ultimately making them jealous; they will fade away like a beginning, before the language they instituted.

From the start, for Silesius, the angel must be gone beyond, either because human silence pleases God more than all the songs of the angels,[55] or because the angelic life represents only one stage in the ascent of created being toward its election (or nomination) as "son of God," or as "divine" being. In *The Cherubic Wanderer*, the depreciation of angels ("the angels are of little value," "it is a lot to be an angel, but much more to be a man on the earth," etc.)[56] serves as a mainspring to an unlimited wanting to/being able to: "I want to be the son of God," "on earth I can become what I will, king, emperor, God."[57] The angel is the celestial mark of going beyond that never stops aiming at the extreme. All sorts of linguistic practices, then, impel language to its limit. Thus, the use of *über*, which throws the semantic units isolated in the spiritual world *beyond* themselves, as in the case of "superessence" (*Überwesenheit*), "supergod" (*Übergottheit*), "transformation" (*Überformung*), and also "superangelicity" (*Überengelheit*): "You ask what humanity is? I say: superangelicity, this one word suffices."[58] Thus, setting out from a binarity received from tradition (for example: God *versus* man, father *versus* son, angel *versus* man), Silesius's "aphorisms" carry out the inversion of the hierarchic relations, deny one after the other the principle of contradiction or the principle of identity, and posit the reciprocal inclusion of the terms. They torture the order of meaning. Everywhere the "objects" of thought are brought to a white heat and twisted by the fire of a strange exceedance.

While Boehme uses the angel to define a metaphysics of the spiritual language, Angelus Silesius makes the angel the counterpoint of an insatiable "it is not enough," "it is never enough." The former presents, in a constative mode, the production of a material manifestation by the advent of the Oneself; he contrasts an energy that asserts itself and dominates with the aberrations of consciousness: that, he says, is what happens (in this respect, his theosophy is still close to Jan van Ruusbroec or to Meister Eckhart). The latter submits his whole poem to the metamorphosis of the modalities, especially the deontic ones: "I must," "I should," etc. (*ich muss, ich soll*, etc.). His discourse is worked from within by the conditional, the optative, or the future, that is, by an assertion of desire and not of things. An irrepressible will incessantly creates a distance between the subject and his objects—"that's not it"—and its effect is the permanent torsion by which these objects are seized. The beyond the angel ("superangelicity") points to a desire that is instituted by its relation to the impossible, or (which amounts to the same thing) that emancipates itself from the real. It is the poetic figure of an ethics, if we take "ethics" to mean the procedure that does not conform to an order of things, and the criterion of which is no longer the law (tempestuous or clement) of reality. An irreducible exceedance pits a "will" that nothing can satisfy and that is animated by the "duty" for man to be "more than divine"[59] against the celestial hierarchy itself. Placed at the horizon of a cosmos, the angel withdraws, then, "obsolete."[60] It is even thrown out: "Out, out, seraphim. . . . out, out, angels, out, all of you. . . . I don't want you, I throw myself alone into the increate sea of pure deity."[61] A solitude of the superman: "It is beyond God (*über Gott*), toward a desert, that I must tend."[62] There is no longer any model or consolation or angelic message for that spiritual superhumanity which opens up, on the basis of its infinite future, a new conception of history, and which henceforth confronts language not with being but with the relation of a "should be" to the limits of the possible.

4. RETREATS BEFORE HISTORY

The angel, excluded from the arid space into which a superhuman will ventures, returns later, but in the suspect outskirts of the city, by illegitimate means, in the grotesque, animal, or monstrous form of a stranger who no longer has a place in the city of progress. Thus Edgar Allan Poe's "Angel of the Odd," a "Falstaffian" collage of bottles, canteens, and a rum-puncheon, appears like a "ruffian" in the study,[63] whose owner asks (once again): "Who are you, pray?" . . . "How did you get here?" But the Odd has no residence or life of its own. It presides over the *contretemps*. It zigzags with a grotesque derision through the narrator's resolution "to believe nothing henceforward that has any thing of the 'singular' about it."[64] This burlesque angel, a heteroclite phantasm introduced by accidents that perhaps are not accidents, is followed by a cohort of marginal beings, strange coded messages, now monstrous, now poetic. So "the ox," in Apollinaire's *Bestiary*:

> This cherub praises paradise,
> Where, near the angels,
> We will live again, dear friends,
> When the good Lord permits.[65]

Exiled from history, the "winged ox," illustrated by Raoul Dufy, "an unknown form" of "surprising beauty,"[66] is called back onto the stage by poetry. There, he goes on being the sign, ironic and light, impossible and necessary, of a different word—from Mallarmé, who kept only his wings, to Éluard, who gives the poem the "form" of angelic communication: "In the evening of madness, naked and clear / The space between things has the form of my words." Géo Norge transforms this reprise into a whim on the part of poet: "I have finally had enough of doing without seraphim, / Enough of getting bogged down in weeks disguised as reality."[67] The French angels flutter a bit. A more tragic tradition, more "catastrophic" even, captures the angel in his relation to the history from which he withdraws. It may be followed from Rainer Maria Rilke to Walter Benjamin, via Klee, the *doctor angelicus* in whom Paul Éluard, despite his distant relations, admired the ambivalent alliance of a blue ease, outside time, with the inscription of a mortal fatality.[68]

What is most striking in the angel of this tradition, in any case the only trait I would like to bring out as I conclude, is not that he is the "magician of insecurity" (a function reserved for the poet), but that his very disappearance organizes the intelligence of history. Driven out in the past in order for that history to be able to be born (perhaps, by the way, this "modern" gesture develops a reaction already perceptible in the first Christian developments of the incarnation), he becomes, by the void he leaves behind, by the deletion of that to which he gave rise, the means of measuring a history henceforth grown up and sure of itself. His absence speaks, so it seems, better than his manifestations ever did. He reveals that of which he is no longer a part. He furnishes a philosophy of history its sign.

Two examples will suffice, Rilke and Benjamin—two authors of that Germany in which the concept of the angel neither suffered nor benefited from the ostracism in which a French academic tradition long held him. Rilke seems to recapitulate the whole cycle of angelic history: from admiration—almost obsessive—for the perfect "beginner" (*das Beginnende*) that the angel is among beings,[69] to the revolt of the Seventh Duino Elegy, raising before the angel the works of human beings ("that *we* were capable of such") and pushing him back, with a gesture that appropriates that of the angel formerly righter of wrongs and giver of gifts: "Do *not* believe that I plead, Angel. . . . My call is like an outstretched arm."[70] But as intense as the work is throughout,[71] this cycle develops beneath the sign, inverted, of a perpetual lacking one, now terrible, now seductive or abandoned. "Angel, even though I should summon you, you will not come," adds the Seventh Elegy, taking up the famous inaugurating verse of the First Elegy, which comes in a voice carried by the wind of the sea: "Who of the angelic hosts would hear me, even if I cried out?"[72]

The angel does not hear. The smile on the statue at Chartres ignores human beings. "What do you know, stone angel (*Steinerner*), of our being?"[73] Elsewhere, the angel, a "calm, strong lantern," remains insensitive to the sound of the man who exists as well as to his last cry: "I am falling apart."[74] A question or an observation: "Have the angels turned discreet!"[75] For a long time, for Rilke, this withdrawal of the angels seemed to signify to the earth the absence of a reality that they took away with themselves, removing from history the weight of a higher existence. The revolution that is marked by the Seventh, Ninth, and Tenth Elegies unveils, on the contrary, the actual content of reality in human existence: "One thing grasped here on earth, once, has its price . . . . To be here is magnificent."[76] Without the need for angels, a density comes to this "house" we are in, and to "us," the most ephemeral of ephemeral things, precisely qua "perishable":

Once each; just *one* time. *Once*
and no more. And we, too,
once. Never more. But that,
to have been *once*, even if only *once*,
to have been of this earth,
that does not seem revocable.[77]

That the instant should have value forever founds "the expressible." Man can say his moment of existence and take advantage of it, without missing the angel. The instant of passage, which defined the angel in the past, henceforth sustains "the irrevocable" of the human risk and poem. Furthermore, by this reversal, our "fall," if it still troubles us, is no less "happy" than the ascension; while the old cosmology separated the good angels from the fallen ones, the history of "here" never stops producing the circle of a happiness in which "to rise" is indissociable from "to fall."[78] By its death, the ephemeral escapes the nostalgia of the angel, or becomes itself an angel who does not withdraw from time.

It was probably the rabbinic tradition that spared Walter Benjamin Rilke's protracted struggle with the immortal angel. Long before the Kabbalah, the Zohar held that "at each now God creates an infinity of new angels, all destined solely to sing for an instant the praise of God in front of his throne before melting into nothingness."[79] Thus Paul Klee's *Angelus Novus*, whose "traits have no human resemblance," appears to Benjamin in the "interrupted" moment of his disappearance.

Seen from the front, a bovine face (like that of Apollinaire's cherub) looking at what he is leaving, he is drawn into his future by a storm blown in from paradise: like the "Angel of history" in the *Theses on the Philosophy of History*.[80] This angel is withdrawing. By an ambivalence that runs through all angelology, he designates in turn, in the twofold meditation of 1933, the instance of a personal disappropriation, and in the *Theses* written in 1940 after the German-Soviet Pact, "the catastrophic instance" of a collective history in which progress changed into an accumulation of ruins. On the one hand, the angel is the movement of "the persons and things" that were taken away from Benjamin: "He dwells in the things I no longer possess. He makes them transparent, and behind each of them appears the figure of the person for whom they are destined."[81] On the other hand, he retreats, as if petrified by the "chain of past events" that form before him "one sole and unique catastrophe," a heap at his feet; while he would like to stop and "reawaken the dead and reassemble the defeated," the wind that has become caught up in his wings carries him "toward the future on which he turns his back." In this twofold retreat, Benjamin finally sees what takes his own name away from him, and from history its name of "progress." What recedes with the angel is identity reclaimed, the onomastic substitute of loss.

The angel, as if photographed at the moment he goes away, in that instant in which to appear is to disappear, bypasses at once the differences of time (the past and the future), of species (the bestial and the celestial), and of sex (he is bisexual, androgynous). Hence he is *novus*, as wild as an end of history. The lightning-like judgment, fulguration of an "interpretation" as understood by Jacques Lacan ("addition . . . that makes visible in a light of a thunderbolt what it is possible to grasp beyond the limits of knowledge"),[82] he has the form of a speech act, but without message or speaker. Outside time. His stupor alone, to which corresponds that of whoever sees him vanish into thin air, constitutes the exchange without duration, without identity and place, that is at the origin of Benjamin's writings on the impossibility of his own history and on the ruins into which the European ambition of the Enlightenment crumbles. An image that contradicts time, yet that comes from the night of the ages, that instantaneous angelic image seems, in Benjamin, to be the eschatological correlative of the Baudelairean scene that so prompted his pen: the look of a female passerby.

Chapter Nine

Biblical Erudition

1. *CHIAROSCUROS*: FROM CORRUPTION TO REFORM

The conception that French Catholics had of the translation of the Bible in the last third of the seventeenth century fits into a more general history in which the relation to Scripture plays a revelatory role in the Western world.[1] I cannot, as what I am presenting here is only a *note*, give these "ideas" of translation their proximate Christian environment.[2] Of their immediate context I will mention only one aspect, but a fundamental one: the contrast between *opaque institutions* and *clear* (*pervii*) *texts.* Thus for Luther, *claritas* is an inherent quality of Scripture.

In the sixteenth century, reformism plays on this tension between institutions, on the one hand, which are nearly universally considered *corrupt*, having been rendered opaque by decadence and the metamorphoses of history, and on the other hand a text whose literalness has kept the Word intact and that remains a clear "source" for new Christian beginnings. That which is no longer heard in the former continues to teach in the latter. If meaning is no longer visible in those timeworn Churches, it is clearly stated in the Bible. There it is audible. There it still has its power. Hence we must resume listening to this "document" (that is, to the Word that teaches)—both hearken to the *clarity* of its messages and open the will to their converting *power*. To lend an ear obedient to that force of meaning, that "power of the spirit"—such is the ambition that spurs an enormous labor of biblical publications, translations, and commentaries. The evidence of an institutional decadence (that haunts the visions of history during the sixteenth and seventeenth centuries) stands in opposition to the challenge of rediscovering, by a return to the primitivity of the Scriptures, their ability to enlighten and edify, today as yesterday, communities of believers.

Let it be said from the outset: the hope the reformers placed in the readability and power of the text was eroded, throughout the course of the seventeenth century, by the critique of the erudite. The work that went into the effort to restore the Word to its pristine clarity slowly brought about the opposite effect. It revealed the collapse that definitively compromised the *materiality* of the holy books (their dissemination through defective copies, the disappearance of texts, the relentless increase of error and deceit in the transmission, etc.) and the ambiguities that make *the meaning* hard to grasp (equivocal statements, stratification of contradictory interpretations, detachment from and hence ignorance of historical assumptions, etc.). Thus, through the meticulous fervor of erudite activity, the text appears just as *corrupt* as the institutions.

As a result, the basis of reformism was undermined. Richard Simon said this repeatedly to the Protestants, not without arrogance. But Catholic reformism was equally affected by this observation; its only recourse would be a return to the institution (whose teaching appeared henceforth clearer), in an apostolic quest for external assent (the "proof" of the "truth" came from the outside, by the increase in the number of conversions) or in a spiritual retreat inward (the mystic or prophetic attestation of the Word within the conscience). The idea of the Bible being a collapsed and opaque text was also the launch pad for Spinoza, when, from his position henceforth distant from those ambiguous ruins, he constructed his *historia Scripturae* or methodological and critical knowledge of the Bible. He established *common* rules making it possible to treat that particular object like others. He made an absolute distinction between the *truth* (*veritas*) and the organization of "sense" (what the text means: *sensus*) produced by a functioning of language, and he found in reason, outside these fissured texts, the unique principle fitting all these "senses" to a "truth."[3] If the Bible had ethical value, it could be translated only by a *speculative* discourse, differing from its letter and free from sectarian or ecclesial exploitation.

Of the transformations brought about by the change taking place in the seventeenth century in the status of the Bible (in short, the *Word* becomes a textual *object*) and the corresponding research in translation, two famous cases furnish examples: Louis-Isaac Lemaistre de Sacy and Simon.

2. THEORETICAL PRELIMINARIES

This research is framed within a set of "theoretical" assumptions; it will suffice to point out three traits of the epistemological space in which they develop.

1. On the one hand, *the absence of a theory of the biblical text qua text.* This void, which may be just the reverse side of a theological plethora, is already to be observed in the pioneer of Christian hermeneutics in the sixteenth century. Indeed, for Erasmus, restorer, editor, and commentator of the Book, which he considered to be the authority par excellence, Scripture was a collection of texts that varied (by language, style, content, etc.), and were united only by the *fact* of their having been received as such from tradition and by the theological *principle* affirming their inspired nature. These texts formed a unit only by virtue of a "canonic" circumscription guaranteeing their common privileged relation to one sole Author. Their material plurality was overcome by the doctrinal conviction that they all came from the same Word and that in it they formed a whole. But no literary theory of the corpus united that textual diversity. Perhaps that theory of the text became possible only when the theologies of Scripture, gradually losing their credibility, ceased ensuring that unification "from on high," extratextually as it were. In any event, the interventions of Erasmus in the letter or the meaning were based on very fluctuating criteria that referred, for each passage, to an exteriority essentially either before or after the book—for example to its sources, its historical presuppositions, or its ulterior (patristic) commentaries, its moral effects on the reader, or yet again to a "philosophy" of "evangelical" inspiration.[4]

An ethical and theological conception of the Book seems to dominate Erasmus from too great a height to truly regulate the choices that his immense knowledge in the areas of vocabulary, grammar, and rhetoric suggested to him. His decisions as editor or commentator are based on moral imperatives commanding his understanding of the text and on fields of knowledge called upon successively to fill in lacunae, but without any literary theory controlling his interventions and imposing a law *of* the text on them. Ultimately the Bible is the field in which a grammatical erudition and a religious ethics intersect. His critical edition will be the product of the former, and the representation of the latter, on a stage furnished and circumscribed by the Tradition of the Church. In this scheme of things, which continues into the seventeenth century in other modes, the truth *of* the text is decided *outside of* it, from above, that is, in the name of a "philosophy" of revelation, and from below, that is, by the multiform afflux of lexical, grammatical, and historical knowledge.

2. Later, in the seventeenth century and especially at Port-Royal, this work is structured by *a theory of language*. This theory conceives of language as a combination of *ideas* (or atoms of thought) prior to signifiers and presumed to belong to universal mental "language," and of *signifiers* (or *verba*, phonetic atoms) joined to one another and connected with ideas by sociolinguistic conventions, that is, by a language. The "ideas" are universal, even though the words designating them "are arbitrary" and belong to a kind of enunciative theater, since they are the effect of historical contracts and conventions.[5]

In principle, communication, the transfer of meaning or translation, is therefore always possible. Its difficulty does not assume the unsettling absence of a "conformity of ideas"[6] behind the décor of words. It may have several reasons: either the signifier is an inadequate match with the idea it represents (it is confused, obscure, etc.); or it is part of a system of conventions that we have not noticed or that we are unaware of (for example, the ambiguity of a word in the Bible might be due to the fact that we are wrong about the language it belongs to, or to our insufficient knowledge of that language); or there is not yet any signifier that corresponds to an idea in waiting (in which case we must find words for that slumbering idea, as in Sleeping Beauty). But in this way *obscurity* remains a surface phenomenon, and all ambiguity can be reduced to obscurity. A *translatability* is therefore guaranteed by a theory of language,[7] in which, incidentally, the projection of a theology is discernable.

3. Finally, a *rhetoric* (or rather "a thought of figuration,"[8] which replaces traditional rhetoric) reorganizes, in keeping with a distinction between the literal and the figurative, the questions—long crucial—relative to the *clear* and the *obscure*. This new rhetoric, or theory of representation—practicing a kind of witch hunt against the insinuation of figures of speech, metaphors in particular, into speculative discourse, and producing the protectionist artifact of a "literal" referential sense that ensures the adequation of word to idea—ends up considering the figurative as an effect of passion, and even more, as the instrument of a "belief-inducing" [*faire croire*] or "act-inducing" [*faire faire*] opera-

tion of the statement. Useful or necessary according to the case, the figurative [*le figuré*] appears wherever it is a question of convincing the receiver and of changing him through discourse. As the conveyance of meaning, the figurative is thus the characteristic proper to persuasion. It is indissociable from a *force*, or from a performativity of language. But this figuration of force comes at the price of a corresponding loss of clarity, since it assumes a drifting away and thus a pluralization of meaning.

Many Christian antecedents might be adduced, even if they do not belong to the same rhetorical formalization. Thus, apropos of lying, Saint Augustine divides truths into those that are "naked," therefore accessible to the mind, and those that, because "veiled" ("hidden beneath that sort of garment called figures"), appeal to a "desire" and bring about a "pleasure."[9] By contrast with the transparency that constitutes knowledge, the "hidden" introduces a libido. Whence, subsequently, the ambivalence of the "tra-vesty" [literally, change of clothing], which sometimes slips false ideas in, and at other times expresses and realizes the seduction of true ones. We should probably also connect to the attractive and persuasive power of discourse its musicality—"number"—which at once desemanticizes the text and "enchants" the reader. In *La Manière de bien traduire d'une langue en autre* [The Way to Translate Well from One Language to Another], Étienne Dolet gave the rule "the observation of oratory numbers is namely a liaison and assemblage of dictions with such sweetness that not only the soul is content, but also the ears are all delighted."[10] Number and penumbra hide the sense and represent the strength of what is meant.

However it may be with its antecedents, at Port-Royal the speculative is the analytic organization of a "literal"; oratory (poetry, preaching, etc.) is the play of an energy in the polysemic space of the "figurative." The former "paints" the idea; the latter, the effects that the idea generates. Hence there is no contradiction between the two—in principle at least. For Antoine Le Maistre, one can, in a translation, keep the ideas intact ("not add anything for the meaning") while at the same time augmenting their effects of seduction or persuasion ("add divers beauties for the style").[11] This was a dangerous problematics, since, from the beginning of the seventeenth century on, the attention given to matters of "color" and emotion becomes worldly or "mondaine" and detached from the truths it was supposed to "make people believe."[12] Between beauty and truth, a gap opens up, transforming the distinction between the figurative and the literal into an opposition between poetry (fable) and history (erudition). Hence translation, which owes allegiance to both, becomes the battleground of a war between muses.

3. LE MAISTRE DE SACY

Among the great French translations of the Bible (Olivetan, 1535–88; Diodati, 1644; etc.),[13] the one that Le Maistre de Sacy published little by little in separate books (1665–84)[14] has particular importance owing to its long career. It is positioned, moreover, at the moment when Scripture enters massively into the French language. In the Paris presses, for example, Bibles, the majority of which were published in ancient languages from 1640 to 1660 (thirty works out of forty from 1641 to 1645 or from 1655 to 1660), are subsequently, and increasingly, French translations (from 1695 to 1700, out of sixty editions, fifty-five were in French).[15] Translations were being undertaken on all sides at the time; Sacy began publishing in 1665; Samuel Desmarets published his translation in Paris in 1669; Henri Justel and the pastors of Charenton developed the project with which Richard Simon was associated and which did not come to fruition, despite seven years of collaboration; in 1672 François Turretini and his Genevan friends began preparing the French translation that Chouet published in Geneva at the end of 1678; etc. These fifteen years of translational effervescence (1665–80) constitute a high point in the theory and practice of our subject.

At the basis of Le Maistre de Sacy's conception of translation,[16] there is an option that distinguishes him from Richard Simon from the start: the former seeks a way to be the witness of a *Book-Subject*; the latter, how to treat a *book-object*. Sacy focuses on the "meaning" of the *Author*, that is, the Spirit of God; Simon the meaning of the *text*, that is, a literary and semantic organization. At the same historical moment, the same book elicits two different practices. These positions do not authorize, by the way, any conclusion about the authenticity of their Catholicism; they relate to different geographies of the faith that, in the one, is invested in the relation to the *Holy Scripture* and, in the other, is in the keeping of the oral and prophetic tradition of the *ecclesial institution*. Not placing the ideological and identificational stakes of *belief* in the same location or in the same way, they do not have the same *practices* as translators.

Sacy, to make sure he says and transcribes the meaning of the Author—a meaning that goes beyond man—disposes of two kinds of criteria:

1. A *mission* must qualify the translator. One cannot decide on it by oneself. The invariance of the meaning, a fundamental question the moment we are speaking of a truth (a revealed one), has as its condition of possibility a *place* specifically designated for the translator by the Church, as being the only "translational authority"[17] of the Holy

Spirit. It is therefore an *obedience* that connects the mediator to the meaning, introduces him into the place of its truth and authorizes him. Here it conforms to the Bérullian (and Dionysian) principle according to which "the Son intervenes in the production of the Holy Spirit," that is, in the manifestation of meaning, "only by the power he has received therefrom" through his Father.[18] No one is capable of saying the spirit of the letter without being "immediately sent." He breaks silence only "by force."[19] In the Bérullian perspective, still dominant in Sacy and Martin de Barcos, the ecclesial *institution* that gives access to the spirit has for its form an institution *of* the spirit, *spiritual direction*—a structure that avoids confusing the "mission" with the objective organization (increasingly worldly or "mondaine") of the ecclesiastic offices or, conversely, that avoids reducing the mission to a purely subjective exchange between the *oratio* that opens interiority to the Spirit (prayer) and the *oratio* that "produces" it outside (preaching, publishing, etc.). The translator is faithful to the spirit of the letter only if he has received the mission from his spiritual director.[20] It is the prerequisite of a *competency.*

The terms of the relation between the work of translation and the place that "authorizes" the access to meaning have varied since Sacy. But this relation itself remains. To be sure, the relevance of the *status* of the translator himself is often hidden, disguised, or denied by the text produced by the translational operation, but it remains no less fundamental, just like, in medical knowledge, "the status of the individuals who—alone—have the right, sanctioned by law or tradition, juridically defined or spontaneously accepted, to proffer such a discourse."[21] There is therefore good reason to analyze the history of what is stressed by Sacy, and since then acknowledged only indirectly—namely, the capacitation for meaning by inclusion in a milieu (assumed to be "neutral," scientific for example, and assuming this neuter has the capacity for truth) or by the social, linguistic, or ideological status of the speaker. In any case, an externality to the text (a mission, a place, a membership) serves to authorize translation and supports, as its postulate, a competency. It is also marked, in the translation, by a series of effects, such as, in Sacy, the privilege granted the Vulgate,[22] the "choices" between variants and versions,[23] the retention of the old division of chapters, the framing of the text within a discourse of titles, or the ontological options that orient the thousand and one details of translation in such a way as to make it into the story of a knowledge about being.

2. While the invariance of meaning has as its precondition a translator's mission, its nature has as its manifestation a *style* of the text. A way of saying (*modus loquendi*) represents a "want-to-say"/teaching of the

author (a *documentum*). This "manner" of God is indicated by a "proportion," internal to the text, between the intelligibility of the message and its obscurity. It is, in the writing, the visibility of that which, invisible, produces it: the mark of the utterer in the utterance. The spirit of the letter is no longer formulated, as in the Middle Ages, in "modes" of "readings" (literal meaning, allegorical meaning, tropological meaning, etc.), the hierarchizing of which corresponds to the successive treatments of the text along an *itinerarium* of the faith;[24] it is represented by the text, by its very contradictions, as disheveled tresses make visible the gesture of love. The relation between meanings and a disorder reveals the "want-to-say" of the recipient.

The letter is a combination of predicates and divine attributes among which, shrouding these revealed signifiers in darkness, the unthinkable Subject slips in, serving as their accomplice. Hence there is *nothing else* to think about except what the surface of the text states (only the "literal" sense is valid), but it is shot through with "dark shadows," with a zigzag of "disturbances,"[25] punctuated by incorrect expressions, "rough spots," and "bad sentences" through which the Exteriority of the speaker comes up into his statement itself and produces darkness there.

To translate is to maintain this relation, to navigate between lights and shadows, but without erasing the obscure traces of one's author. This spiritual respect for the letter is all the more difficult to maintain because an insuperable ambiguity is attached to the opaque spots in the text. On the one hand, there *must* be obscurity (a general principle relative to the nature of the author), but on the other hand, in each particular case, how can one know whether the obscurity comes from the principle or from a simple ignorance (grammatical, lexical, historical) of the letter? Is it not in fact the deficit of knowledge that localizes the marks of the Spirit in the text? Sacy's effort to surmount his instances of *technical* ignorance moves him, then, to suppress the indices of *divine* obscurity. Moreover, he is encouraged by the will to have the Bible understood by his addressees: we must, he says, write "for the others," and not "for ourselves."[26] He is always mindful (like many others, Spinoza first and foremost) of the problem posed by the status of the ignorant, the unlearned, in the history of biblical revelation. The "elegance" or the "purity" he seeks probably has, in his view, the value of seduction: it gives the power of attraction to the meaning of the discourse. But is it the power *of* the spirit?

The principles remain uncertain, then, in practice. As far as the translation of the text is concerned, they reduce to three:

1. There is no meaning except the literal one. 2. Without clarity,

there is no message. 3. Without obscurity, the message becomes insignificant. Relative to a quest for the Author, these principles ultimately deprive the translator of all surety of technique. This establishes him in fear: "I tremble," writes Sacy. His work itself has the effect of betraying the Holy Scriptures in making them attractive to those who "cannot suffer the obscure and embarrassed language used by the Holy Spirit."[27]

There is no solution (the translator is always guilty), but only palliatives. They consist in reintroducing obscurity on the borders of clarity, in creating a *trembling* of the translation itself. This will be in adding to the final translation the different meanings of which the original is capable, or in including a lamination of the original by translating Hebrew, Greek, or Latin variants of the same passage. In the page layout, a special combination of the *central* text and the *margins* (or notes) compensates for the excessive clarity of the continuous discourse by a proliferating semantic or critical pluralization. These microbic surroundings establish a "pluri-isotopy" of the text. They restore the inaccessibility of the "want-to-say" of the author. By the erudite framing of his translation, by these notes in the margins, Sacy adds an *indetermination*, but it is *secondary* in relation to the determination that he has forced on the text. The adjacent shadow of a polysemy thus replaces the obscurity belonging to the text itself. A too much meaning replaces a not enough of it. This is a compromise that simultaneously ensures everyone an ecclesiastic didactic of clarity and shifts readers "in the know" laterally toward its opposite. This almost plural structure orients the message toward a silence of the author. By its very framework, the body of the text flees discreetly toward an unknown.

4. RICHARD SIMON

If, for Sacy, polysemy has the positive value of extra meaning, it is, on the contrary, the principle of a vanishing of the text in Richard Simon.[28] A still more fundamental difference: while Sacy attempts to recognize the one sole author, Simon analyzes the organization and conditions of production of a diversity of books. He is interested in "the truth of the Text."[29] He inaugurates a "critique of Scripture."[30] His presupposition is the conviction that the Christian revelation is preserved by the oral tradition of the Catholic Church. Faithfulness to the institution, therefore, no longer has as its object, as in Sacy, to legitimate the translator; in mountain terms, it belays the climber, that is, it "ensures" the "certainty" of the believer, but it allows (and makes up for) the "uncertainty" of the critic.[31] This inverts the reformist problematics of the

Renaissance: it is now the ecclesial authority that decides in questions of "belief" and that, according to the theology of that century's end,[32] speaks the Christian truth clearly, whereas the textual truth, a place of suspicion, concerns defined autonomous *practices*, in keeping with the Cartesian schema, by the isolation of a field of its own, and (this is the essential point for Simon) by the construction of a "method."[33] The translation of the spirit belongs to the Church; that of the letter, to critical scholarship. In reality, the distinction is far from being that clear. The results of critical scholarship carry the trace of Simon's ecclesiological postulates—for example, that biblical texts come from groups rather than individuals, or that the inspired "public writers" who modified the original have "the same authority" as it, or that the historical transformation of the original has, in the end, more value than the Book itself, a result placed beneath the rubric of "the equivocal," etc.

For Richard Simon, translation is almost impossible, because criticism shows "how obscure the Scripture is."[34] Indeed, the biblical text comes apart by its two extreme poles: as a totality, it has been "altered," or even "purposely corrupted"; at its base, at the level of its elementary units, it is "equivocal." Thus, each semantic unity falls apart from within because of its ambiguity. Criticism exposes everywhere and brings out that defection. It cannot conclude, that is, stop the dissemination of meaning by setting a closure to it. Because "there are few words but what are equivocal,"[35] the text is on the contrary transformed by erudite labor into a multiplication of possibles. It cannot be published as *one* text, or articulated in *one discourse* of translation. The indefinite (encyclopedic) collection of textual or semantic variants makes the text itself ever more *innumerable* and *obscure*. It creates plurality and opacity. Hence, in order to say the truth that gets lost in it, contemporaries must replace this exploded text, either, like Spinoza,[36] with the clarity of a discourse of *reason*, or, like Fénelon, with the clarity of a preaching of the *Church*.

It is therefore interesting to follow R. Simon not only when he judges the translations of others,[37] but when he himself translates. His collaboration with Henri Justel and the reformed pastors of Charenton,[38] and even, for a time (1675–77), with the Genevan pastors for the French Bible of Turrentini,[39] led him to translate a chapter of Job and a chapter of Proverbs,[40] and to present the "so just idea" that he himself had "of a translation of the Bible."[41] This "project of a new version of the Holy Writ" is reprinted in *A Critical History of the Old Testament*,[42] in which is explained "the way which ought to be observ'd in the making of a Translation of the Bible; which may come nigher to a true one."[43] From this set of factors, a few points emerge.

All translation, being necessarily a *representation* of the original, faces a twofold difficulty: one, a textual one, concerning the material existence of the original; the other, semantic and literary, involving the organization of meaning. The originality of Richard Simon lies in his having attributed as much importance to literary as to textual criticism, and his having combined the two. Now, the observations he made and the representations resulting from them are parallel at these two levels (text and meaning). In one case as well as in the other, there is:

1. *Analysis of a loss* around which manifold remains, all defective or corrupt, nonetheless make possible a production of probabilities classifiable according to "the rules of criticism."

2. *The staging of a "body"* (textual body, that is, the "established" text, or body of meaning, i.e., the translation), but of a Harlequin-body, because for one thing it is made up of "pieces" taken from a stock of possibilities in which they appear to be the "best" and put together as hypotheses or conjectures, and for another because it is riddled with marginal notes that replace the parts retained in the "body" with other variants or other interpretations having, says Simon, "as much probability" and that annex to the space of a "representation" of the body another space representing its dissemination.

The edition (or edification) of the "version," already split between the establishment of the text and that of the meaning, thus has the look of a combat area. To the fabrication of a probable textual image, a combination of heterogeneous elements coming from earlier broken images, stand opposed *a thousand fragments* dispersed in the form of notes of a common origin, ready to replace the privileged elements and thus generate an indefinite series of other images. A body perpetually constructed out of ruins and reduced to ruins, a body made up of particles of dust, and to dust returning, the "version" oscillates, unstable, between the image, a provisional fiction, and the thousand fragments, the real effect of corruption.

The fact of the matter is that in this to and fro between the fiction and dissemination, the erudite history of a *struggle against time* follows its course, a struggle that has definitively "altered" the original ("the first Original . . . has been lost")[44] and produced "equivocations" in the language (we are speaking of a "Language . . . lost").[45] This struggle against the disastrous effects of time or against a destructive time—this is the very struggle of the Reformation since the sixteenth century. But in the field of writing, the struggle appears henceforth an uneven one, hopeless: while criticism, according to Simon, consists in "correcting,"[46] it must mourn the object it seeks to restore ("it is impossible to remedy that") and the certainty it aspires to ("there are always reasons to doubt"). Contrary to the Cartesian undertaking, the work of Criticism takes place entirely *within* loss and *within* the uncertain. It never leaves either of these. Giving up on primal "purity," it progresses within "corruption." It accepts this law of history.[47]

But criticism transforms its defeat into a force. Editing-translating is also a labor *of* suspicion and even a labor *of* loss, in that both are principles of operations. A certainty inhabits the *Critical History*, but in the form of a "method"; it is founded precisely on the mere probability of the image and the loss of the original. From this point of view, any theologian's intervention is suspect because ideological. Indeed, either it assumes that the image of the text has a value of truth as if the original were once again present in it: the theologian confuses the Book with the representation of its remains and thus falls into utter confusion; or (as Simon charges Sacy in the latter's translation of the New Testament) an ideological imperialism betrays itself in trying to surmount the "contrarieties" between lessons (for example, the Greek and Latin ones) as the result of compromises founded on a doctrinal conviction (then one no longer has "either the Greek or the Latin, under the pretext of reconciling them with each other") and in thinking it can clarify the text by additions or eliminations that make it conform to theological "prejudices" (it brings meanings that are "neither in the Greek nor in any version"). The theologian occults the scriptural plural (both) by the artifice of a neuter (neither the one nor the other) and hides, with his "particular" ideas, the Book he claims to represent.[48] On the other hand, the analysis of *loss* (loss of the origin and therefore loss of the voice that spoke in it) and the exercise of *doubt* (at work in and against "representations" that are all ersatz with respect to the lost text and meaning) produce rigor in the analytic and constructive operations.

In the workplace of the text and its production, there are "rules." They are essentially directed toward a *defense of the negative* and a *classification of the probable*: on the one hand, criticism refutes all "prejudiced" assertion, and on the other hand, it introduces distinction into the equivocal. These two movements sustain each other, since their combination makes it possible to cross over, classify, and order the uncertain without transforming it into the certain. They give rise to a succession of "reasonings" that all conform, more or less, to the same schema: (1) finding impossibilities (there are "lessons" and "interpretations" that are forbidden by the "facts"); (2) distinguishing and classifying probabilities; (3) deducing from these a plurality of conclusions circumscribed by hypotheses. This reasoning is almost the reverse of the form it received from Aristotle. It multiplies the probable within a field limited by the impossible.[49]

Pushed to the limit, translation becomes a workplace of the probable, a space devoted to the calculus of probabilities. All Richard Simon lacked was a modal logic that could supply him with an analytic instrument, but, before Leibniz,[50] it had not yet been developed. Such a reference is not arbitrary, however. The text "established" and translated according to Simon's norms already makes up a technical, but not yet a theoretical, theater of this logical work. In any case, what is represented there, in innumerable scenes throughout the "critical histories," is less the original than the erudite practice itself, combining with the exposition of its regulated choices ("the body") the encyclopedic and classified collection that makes other choices possible (the marginal annotations and the notes). It is not surprising that Richard Simon gave up translation, of which he had "such a just idea." To the production of instable and suspect images, he prefers treatises and, even better, notes, drafts, etc.—in a word, the representations of "Criticism." The theater of the Book is inverted into the theater of science.[51]

The relation of Scripture to a practice has always been decisive in a biblical hermeneutics. Richard Simon represents an important transformation of this relation. For others, as for Sacy, *the text precedes practice*; it calls for a work of understanding that is itself conditioned by a putting into practice of the text: one must obey the word in order to be able to understand it.[52] In Richard Simon, already *practice precedes the text*, and it is no longer the same practice; it "produces" the text as its transitory effect, always to be revised; it produces itself, tirelessly, in the textual space whose elements it broadens, manipulates, and orders; it suffices for it to represent itself on its own in commentaries or critical studies, in notes and drafts, that is, in a labor in the margins of a lost original. The representation of the disappeared is replaced by representation of the erudite production.

In order to tax Sacy with an essential lacuna in his translation, that is, with what it did not sufficiently show, Barcos has an expression that could express what Simon, by his critique, already makes too manifest: in the Bible, "God walks as if on the sea, without leaving footprints."[53]

Chapter Ten

The Strange Secret: Pascal

THE FOURTH LETTER TO MADEMOISELLE DE ROANNEZ

"Profoundly mystic,"[1] Pascal's fourth letter to Mademoiselle de Roannez is only an "excerpt."[2] This *fragment*, prepared for inclusion in the *Pensées* published in 1670 by Port-Royal,[3] also has the guise of a ruin.

This relic belongs to the correspondence that Pascal had with the young Charlotte de Roannez (she was twenty-three years old) during the seven months she spent in Poitou, at the Château of Oiron, following her "conversion" at the Church of Port-Royal de Paris (4 August 1656) before returning to Paris (in mid-March 1657) and precipitously entering the Abbey of Port-Royal (1 July 1657?) to be received as a novitiate. But however marvelously erudite and sleuth-like Jean Mesnard's critical and historical analysis of the nine "excerpts" is,[4] there remain traces of a story that *has withdrawn*. The intention of "bringing them to light" has slowly obliterated their particularities. The duke of Roannez (brother of the addressee and probably the first author of the cuts made in the original), Marguerite Périer, the Oratorians of Clermont-Ferrand, etc., have all in turn worked to hide the circumstances and publish "excerpts." The secrecy and the visibility of these letters grow concurrently, a paradox that is precisely the subject of the fourth one. Time has changed the personal correspondence into "thoughts"—precious stones from which the singularity of events has been expunged. Time has made the text visible and the author invisible: the one "uncovered" and the other "hidden" by the same process.

Excerpt 4 is indeed developed on "miracles." On 24 March 1656, in the Church of Port-Royal, Marguerite Périer, Pascal's niece and god-daughter, was cured of a lacrimal fistula by being touched with a "Sacred Thorn," a replica and fragment of the crown of thorns of Jesus. Five months later there occurred in the same church the "conversion" of Mademoiselle de Roannez ("blind" till then), and that "vocation" for the religious life occurred in such a way, as she wrote in 1657, "that there is perhaps no example in which he [God] has made it appear so clearly that he can, when it pleases him, make himself master of the heart without the intervention of the creatures."[5] But "these extraordinary feats" upon which the text was produced will not be sought here behind the text, as "experiences" or events that must be found below the discourse that hides them, as if the excerpt had to be turned back toward the referent that serves as a pre-text for it. I am assuming that "texts can no more be read than can objects of art," in the sense that they cannot be reduced to a *unity* capable of explaining *everything* and of defining *the* meaning: "They are objects."[6] Every explanation (of which there are as many as there are methods) will therefore be the result of questions asked and solutions proposed *qua* hypotheses interlocking with both "paradigms" (problematics sharing the same research environment) and procedures of analysis (practices subject to explicit rules). To go through a text in this way is to draw effects of commentary from it that can be considered one of the possible interpretations. This relation to Pascal's text is, moreover, homologous to the one he himself bears to the "extraordinary feats" that made it possible without his claiming to re-present them.

The examination of the pertinences created in this particular text by a rhetoric or a logic of argumentation brings out what Pascal calls the "way of writing"[7] and the ways of "turning things." "The ways of turning one selfsame thing are infinite."[8] Practices of transformations: "how one can vary statements" and "turn propositions in all directions."[9] Ways of saying and ways of doing make up a discourse that is new, even if their matter is old: "As if the same thoughts did not form a different discourse by being arranged differently, just as the same words form different thoughts by their being arranged differently!"[10] "Turns" multiply the possibilities, putting things in movement, making them turn and return to the instability of their equilibria. They belong to that problematic of the *modus loquendi* that characterizes all the processes productive of "mystic" language.[11] But in Pascal they have the mobile rigor of a style. The excerpt of the fourth letter to Mademoiselle de Roannez is the result of practices, of their combinations and their rapidity of sequence, far more than it is the reference to an object (the miracle is submitted to a series of transformations) or to a subject (the author is dispersed in a play of pseudonyms[12] and hides beneath his real name), that is, to one of the two forms of this "proper" that the text ruins.

TEXT AND PRE-TEXTS

The excerpt is not isolable from the "words" and "thoughts," from the circumstances and interests that it reworks in order to "arrange" them differently or that have made it possible. The elements it manipulates are pre-texts. The scriptorial operation would be unrecognizable without the exploration of the field in which it is carried out, the constraints to which it yields, and the situations it addresses. Given the generous proportions of the works already published on this subject and the exiguity of the analysis I am undertaking, it will suffice to mark the text with a few notes referring the reader to the historical space reconstituted by erudition and tracing on this fragment the place of its (broken) ties to the network from which it has been detached. Here, then, is the text such as it has come down to us, a body dismembered, a form drawn in upon itself:[13]

> It seems to me that you take sufficient interest in the miracle to send you particular notice that its verification is consummated by the Church, as you will see by this sentence of the Grand Vicar.[14] There are so few people to whom God manifests himself by these extraordinary feats that one really ought to avail oneself of these opportunities, since he leaves the secrecy of nature that covers him only to excite our faith to serve him all the more ardently that we know him more certainly. If God uncovered himself continually for men, there would be no merit in believing in him; and if he never uncovered himself, there would be little faith.[15] But he conceals himself ordinarily and discovers himself rarely to those whom he wishes to engage in his service. This strange secrecy, in which God has impenetrably withdrawn far from the sight of men, is a great lesson to betake ourselves to solitude far from the sight of men. He remained hidden beneath the veil of nature that hid him from us till the Incarnation; and when he *had to* appear, he hid himself even more in covering himself with humanity. He was far more recognizable when he was invisible than when he rendered himself visible. And in fine, when he wished to fulfill

> the promise that he made to his apostles to remain with men until his last coming, he chose to remain with them in the strangest and darkest secrecy of all, that of the species of the Eucharist.[16] It is this sacrament that Saint John calls in Revelation a hidden manna;[17] and I believe that Isaiah saw it in that state when he said in the spirit of prophecy: Truly thou art a God concealed.[18] This is the utmost secrecy in which he *can* be. The veil of nature that covers God has been penetrated by several of the unbelieving, who, as Saint Paul says,[19] have recognized an invisible God in visible nature. Heretical Christians have recognized him through his humanity and adored Jesus Christ God and man. But to recognize him under the species of bread is peculiar to Catholics alone: none but us are thus enlightened by God. One can add to these considerations the secrecy of the spirit of God concealed still in the Scripture. For there are two perfect meanings, the literal and the mystical;[20] and the Jews, stopping at one, do not even think that there is another and have no idea of searching it out, just as the impious, seeing the natural effects, attribute them to nature, without thinking that there is another author, and as the Jews, seeing a perfect man in Jesus Christ, did not think to seek in him another nature: We did not think that it was he, again says Isaiah[21]: and just as, in fine, the heretics, seeing the perfect appearances of bread, do not think to seek therein another substance.[22] All things cover some mystery; all things are veils that cover God. Christians ought to recognize him in everything. Temporal afflictions cover eternal goods to which they lead. Temporal joys cover the eternal ills that they cause. Let us pray God to make us recognize and serve him in everything. Let us give him infinite thanks that, having concealed himself in all things for others, he has uncovered himself in all things and in so many ways for us.[23]

THE STAGING OF THE ENUNCIATORY INSTANCE

Even reduced to an excerpt, this fragment remains a letter. From the beginning, it posits the terms of the relation it organizes: "It seems to *me* that *you* . . ." It belongs to what Benveniste called "discourse": "every utterance assuming a speaker and a hearer, and in the speaker, the intention of influencing the other in some way."[24] The *personal pronouns* (*I*, *you*, *he*) assure the placement of the "discourse," establishing a locus of enunciation (*I*), an addressee (*you/thou*), and, for the rest (*he*, *it*), a classification relative to the contract that the text produces between interlocutors. Here, the *I* and the *you* remain secondary. By contrast, a series of *we* forms a tight bond between the speaker and the addressee throughout the text, albeit in ambiguous modes: "we" Christians; "we" humans; "we" Catholics; "we" Christians attached to Port-Royal. One exception ("we did not think . . .") is from a quota-

Table 4. The topography of personal actors.

1st person singular	1st person plural	2nd person plural	2nd person singular
Seems to *me*	◄-----------► ▼▼▼ *Our* faith *We* know Carry *Us* Uncover for *Us*	*You* take To send *you* *You* will see	
I believe◄------	----------------	-----------►	"*You* are a hidden God"
	That *We* "*We*" [Jews] Make *Us* recognize Let *Us* give For *Us*		

tion that, biblical in origin and juridical in its functioning, introduces the Jews' admission of their ignorance.

This axis of the "we," which constitutes the structural framework of the text, is interrupted by the appearing of a modalized "I" ("I believe that Isaiah . . .") relative to a "you," but placed in quotation marks, the way a cloud opens the space of the painting onto an *other*, sacred;[25] "You are a hidden God." Normally Pascal quotes this expression in Latin,[26] thus reinforcing the gap distancing this liturgical and mystic "You." Hence the topography of the personal actors shown in table 4.

In "discourse," as Benveniste specifies, whether "explicit or not, the relationship of person is everywhere present. . . . The speaker opposes a non-person *it* to an *I/you* person."[27] Indeed, here, a large part of the figures occupying the place "they" (infidels, heretics, Jews, etc.) is ultimately recapitulated in the "for the others" that stands in opposition to the "for us," which ends the text. It does not designate the absence of anyone, but it designates opposed people. Thus there is a personalization of the pronouns in their relation to a central "we" in which the "not-I" ("you") and the speaking "I" are conjoined.

The importance of speech is also denoted in the frequency of "indicators" that send the named objects to the *present* instance of discourse.[28] Thus the demonstratives: "*this* sentence," "*these* extraordinary feats," "*these* opportunities," "*this* strange secrecy," "*this* sacrament," "*that* state" . . . The deictic proliferates. It is the index finger of the gesture of showing.[29] As that which is not said, but is seen from the place occupied by the sender, it reinforces the place of the speaker, postulating an adhesion on the part of the addressee, emphasizing the contract between them.

Another characteristic of "discourse": *tenses.* As opposed to "history" (specified by the use of the aorist, the imperfect, and the pluperfect), "discourse" has three fundamental tenses: the present, the future, and the perfect.[30] In the excerpt, the use of the present and the perfect is massive. The future occurs only once; the aorist, twice (creating in the text the pocket of a historical utterance). The imperfects, in principle common to the two levels (historical and discursive), are in part called for by the conditionals. Therefore we have here an "obstinate return"[31] of the same tenses. It ensures a stability of the text that will be in contrast with the rapidity of the logical movements. It establishes this stability within what Harald Weinrich calls "the world that is commented on" as opposed to the "world that is related" [or narrated];[32] the former corresponds to "discourse," which Benveniste distinguishes from "story" or "history." These "commentative tenses" consolidate the place in which the Pascalian argumentation of the miracle is played out.

This effect is further enhanced by the homogeneity of "temporal transitions" or passages from one verbal form to another in the course of the linear development of the text (for example, the passage from a present to the imperfect or to a *passé simple*). These passages can be counted up and classified in such a way as to show the variations, gaps, and sudden changes or, on the contrary, the holds (in the musical sense) presented by the subset of temporal forms.[33] The transition is "homogeneous" when it takes place within "commemorative tenses" (perfect or *passé composé*, present, future) *or* the tenses of "historical narration" (imperfect, *passé simple*, etc.); otherwise it is heterogeneous, coming and going from one level to the other. Excerpt 4, as shown in the table below,[34] has a remarkable homogeneity that is even immobilized, in the finale of the piece, on the repetition of the present: over eight successive transitions, the dominant note of the textual time is held.

In table 5,[35] A designates the *passé composé*, B the present, C the future, D the conditional II, E the conditional I, F the pluperfect, G the imperfect, and H the *passé simple*. The *passé antérieur*, which does not occur in the text quoted, is not represented in the table.

Temporal transitions: The two rectangles set off in dark lines represent homogeneous transitions, on the upper left for the commentative tenses, on the lower right for the narrative tenses. Out of 63 transitions, 55 are homogeneous, of which 51 are internal to the group of commen-

Table 5. Temporal transitions in commentative/narrative contexts.

	Ø	A	B	C	D	E	F	G	H
Ø			1						
A	1	4	6	1				1	1
B		8	31					2	
C			1						
D									
E			1					1	
F									
G		1	1			2		1	
H		1							

tative tenses (the square on the left). If it is true that to a maximum of homogeneous transitions there corresponds a maximum of "textuality" (i.e., of textual consistency) and a minimum of information—indeed, "the notion of textuality and that of information are in a relation of inverse proportion"—then this table indicates a reinforcement of the instance of discourse by textuality. This results in a stabilization of the place and contract of enunciation, and also a low permeability of this place by the alterations eventually introduced by information. Naked, narrow, closed—such is the setting in which Pascal's argumentation will be carried out in rapid gestures. It is a combat area. It excludes alibis and diversions.

TRIPARTITION OF MODALITIES

The modalities that affect the relation of the speaker to his or her utterances are also related to enunciation. Their occurrence is not limited to the use of modal verbs (such as "can," "must," "know," and "want"), for those verbs represent only a "lexical" aspect of modality. They include the characteristics that attach to propositions a value of truth or existence (*alethic*[36] modalities, modalities of necessity, impossibility, possibility, and contingency), a value of cognition or knowledge (*epistemic* modalities of the certain, of that which is "established"—the "ruled out," the plausible and the questionable), or finally a value concerning what should be done (*deontic* modalities of the obligatory, the forbidden, the permitted, and the optional).[37] If we believe, with Alan White, that these "modal concepts do not signify particular items either in the world or in our minds, but the relation of one item to others in a situation,"[38] if, then, they define not the status (objective or subjective) of the affected terms but *a particular relation* of *possible alternatives* to each other in a linguistic system, it becomes possible to specify the text itself by the modalities that articulate its statements in the field of saying (the type of affirmation), of knowledge (the degree of certainty), and of what should be done (the relation to rules of action)—questions of equal importance in Pascal. To simplify the analysis, I will limit myself to investigating the use of verbs and adverbs or adjectives.

The first thing to strike our attention is the contrast between the presence of the modalizers that relativize the utterance of the speaking "I" ("it *seems* to me that you . . . ," "I *believe* that Isaiah . . .")[39] and their absence in the group of (constative) propositions in which either the doings of God or the unknowing of the "others" is asserted. This disparity is of the *epistemic* sort. Everything happens as if the plausible affecting the saying of the "I" were situated *between two* self-evidences, one positive (the operations of the singular that is *God* or "he"), and the other negative (the drawbacks of a plural, the others or "they"). The *alethic* modalities intervene only apropos of the singular "he": "when he *had to* appear . . ." (the necessary), "the utmost secrecy in which he *can* be . . ." (the possible). By these modalities, also known as "traditional" or "Aristotelian," the propositions relative to the divine subject are set apart and placed beneath the sign of being or the true. It is an indication of the distinction that attaches the statement of/on God to the problem of truth, and the utterance of Pascal's "I" to the problem of certainty.

The "we," on the other hand, is uttered in the *deontic* mode. It is marked by obligation. An "ought to do" connotes, throughout the fragment, the series of propositions that end in concluding imperatives: "Let us pray," "Let us give him infinite thanks." Indeed the injunctives of that finale are prepared by the modalizers that affect the sentences in which the "we" appears progressively, first in the form of a neuter ("*one really ought to* avail oneself . . ."), and then of a plural ("*Christians ought to* recognize him"). Following this thread in the textual weave, we should probably recognize its allusive recurrence in the expression "we know him . . . with certainty," since, although epistemic, it transitions to the deontic by the augmentative of comparison ("all the *more* . . . that . . . *more* . . ."), a springboard positioned from place to place ("hid himself *even more*," "*far more* recognizable," etc.), an amplifier intended to pick up the pace and urge toward an ***obligation of*** passage. Even if the procedure already indicates a "***persuasive*** doing," it is still inscribed with the quasi-orchestral organization of the text in three interwoven modes: one epistemic, relating to the speaker; another alethic, relating to the referential (God and the typology of faith behaviors of which he is the criterion); and the last one deontic, relating to the enunciative contract between "us."

Beyond the modalizing evaluations constituted by certain adjectives ("extraordinary," "strange," "darkest," "last," "infinite," etc.) that have a classificatory value and distributive force, we may also mention the lexical elements (especially of adverbial form) that introduce a *quantification* of modal structures: playing on time ("ordinarily," "continually," "rarely," etc.) or on number ("sufficient," "so few," "several," etc.), they put frequency (little or much) at the service of the probable. But by a contradiction of the "natural" rules of the quantitative, diminishment increases value: the *less* there is, the *more* privileged it is. This relation of proportion regulates the relation of each mode with the next: the alethic to the epistemic (a truth all the more present for being less apparent) and the epistemic to the deontic (the less visible it is, the greater the obligation). It has the value of transversality. It ensures the transit between the modes, all of which it determines. But each time it is by the function of inversion, by a reversing of the quantitative increases proper to each. The text is unified by "turning" distinct intensities; it is woven together by manipulating them. This twisting structure, which incidentally brings the end back to the start, calls into question another level of analysis, that of argumentation.

THE RUSES OF ARGUMENTATION: A WAR OF MOVEMENT

The excerpt from the letter to Mademoiselle de Roannez, written at the same time as the last *Provincial Letters* (which become, beginning with the eleventh letter [August 1656] *Letters to the Reverend Jesuit Fathers*), is situated in the middle of a war, at the moment when the ironic mobility of the sniper changes into a more incisive and personal vehemence. Assimilable to a succession of feats, or of "moves" (in the sense in which, according to Stephen Toulmin,[40] an argumentation can take advantage of a situation to "make a move"), the entire series of the

Provincial Letters obeys, however, a principle that, according to Aristotle, already inspired the techniques of the Sophists and of Corax in particular: "to make *the stronger*" position "*the weaker*."[41] This is a principle of "reversal" thanks to which a way of using the occasional inverts an order and a "reason" of power. Since Socrates, accused of crimes of "sophism" and impiety for having changed the weaker discourse into the stronger, this *tactic* has developed in the margin of *strategies* that organize particularities into a rational system based on the strongest position—actually, theoretically, or utopically. The *Provincial Letters* participate in that same tactic whose Sophist referent remains today (for reasons that are too obvious) suspect of deviance or delinquency compared with "good" reason. Excerpt 4, too, bears testimony to this Sophist principle, outside the combat area of theological quarrels, it is true, but owing to fundamental concerns that call into question the relation of a contingent practice with a necessary truth.

It is true that the rhetoric of the excerpt, like all rhetoric, has as its object the *debatable*, not the true, and it aims at *effectivity*, not correctness (proper to grammar), or validity (proper to logic).[42] The argumentation must engender persuasion. It manufactures the credible. Here, it can already assume a certain adherence ("you take sufficient interest . . ."): we are thus dealing with an epidictic discourse, whose task is to reinforce that adhesion and, for Pascal, to "place" it otherwise. The tactic will use what is given by these premises—and also various forms of the plausible (handed-down truths, quotations, etc.)—in order to draw effects from them through a series of twists and turns. It leads the whole development, from the first page on, inaugurated by a constative ("there is"), but a development whose sinuosity springs forth, turns, and is propelled by a series of leverage points ("so few . . . that . . . ," "since," "only," "for," "all the more . . . that . . . more") to the finale, a repetition of short sentences in the present, a drumroll of the same words and the same sounds, a series of rapid moves, before the final proposition, ending with the "for us" whereon the text comes to rest.

The form of the discourse appears to belong to a *deductive* logic—that form which, on the basis of an assent given to premises, obligates us to accept the conclusion and does not allow for any escape if the premises are recognized as being right and if the reasoning is valid. The fact is that a *persuasive* argumentation subverts from within the order that follows first from the consequences (first part), then from variants ("One can add . . ."). It is all the more effective in that it thus makes its procedures almost invisible: the shifts it introduces from one proposition to the next, the elements it adds, each time assuming them to be taken for granted in the interval, the absence of localizable connecting links, or the velocity that hides the leaps performed in passing without leaving time for verification, etc.

Thus, from the start ("There are so few people . . . these opportunities"), the logical relation between (1) the rarity of the appearance of God, (2) the extraordinary nature of his "feats," (3) the "profit" attached to these last, furnishes the means for introducing *in addition* (4) the subtle slippage from the "few people" to the collective "one," (5) the passage from that constative to the ought (the text says, "one really ought to avail oneself," and not something like "there is therefore some profit," which would be valid), and (6) the metamorphosis of the "acts" (i.e., an in-itself) into "opportunities" (for us).[43] In each instance, anodyne in appearance, an increase slips in to which the reasoning serves as a support *and* as a veil. It is, moreover, entirely relative to the persuasion of the addressee, who is here encompassed in a *general* rule (surplus 4), bound by an *obligation* (surplus 5), and, as in present-day commercial publicity, seduced by an unexpected *opportunity* (surplus 6). The rest of the sentence—which interconnects (1) the fact of the "comings-out" of God, (2) the will that manifests itself in it (that is, the meaning of this fact), and (3) the "ardor" that must respond to it on our part (that is, the lesson that comes from the relation between the phenomenon and meaning)—surreptitiously doubles that logical sequence with persuasive adjuncts: (4) the creation of a "required passage" through the exclusive restriction ("only") that makes the addressee (embarked, moreover, with the speaker and by him: "our faith") the sole target and privileged object of a divine will (thus, in commercial ads, "it is just for you" that the product came out); (5) an equating of "faith" with "certainty," by a subtle shift to the ledger of "believed" opinion (distinct, as "plausible" or undecidable, from the "certain" or established proposition) of the affirmation that sustains it (we believe); (6) a relation of proportion ("all the more . . . that . . . more") between that "certainty" and the "ardor," or, in other terms, a performativity presupposing the saying to be obviously and necessarily bound to a doing.[44] These three adjunctions, slipped into the demonstration, charge it with a persuasive function that "passes" along with it and involves the addressee.

The same operation may be analyzed as a mixing of genres: on the one hand, *constative* elements (it is rare that God appears) or *explanatory* (he appears in order to . . .); on the other hand, exhortative elements ("one really ought to avail oneself," "to excite *our faith* all the more ardently").[45] The first serve as passports to the second: they authorize them, and they cover them. The impersonal nature of the first ensures a sort of incognito to the pressure exerted by the speaker (and by the place from which he speaks) on his partner. Whence a great persuasive efficacy. The addressee is affected without realizing it. The demonstration he thinks he is reading harbors an arrow that hits desire to the quick, a ruse that plays on the affects without warning, a passion that whips up ardor and stimulates (in simulating it?) certainty. Something *passes by*, with an incisive rapidity and penetration that changes the position of the reader *before* he gathers himself, and when he comes back to himself—more critical—*already* he is *altered*. The field of possibles has been modified by the persuasive *force* of the discourse. In the argumentation mode, and no longer that of "prophecy," this word has the character of brevity and lightning-like rapidity that, according to Saint-Cyran, would "ravish" the listener, without "slowing down the movement of the Spirit."[46]

By mandatory passages, by uncoupling or logical leaps, by accelerating ellipses that precipitate the pace, Pascal's modus operandi does not leave the reader time to regain his composure, or, therefore, the possibility of retaining his position. It calls him out. To be sure, it counts on an initial adhesion somewhere (it is epidictic), in the absence of which it would meet with a global refusal. But working with that given, it pushes it to the end it sets for it, by a method focusing on *movement* and not on an exhaustive treatment. Whereas a good mathematician examines all the cases of a figure to test the generality of his result—thus building a time and space of verification—Pascal makes his connections at a galloping pace, from one particular proposition to the next, a sequence made up of alternatives and detachments: "A or B, but A, therefore C. If C, then D or rather D′," etc. The celerity jumps across the gaps.[47] It thus creates something irreversible. One cannot ascend the stream of the time of the demonstration, because the latter produces, by its movements, a change of place whose trace it does not retain and which is external to it—that of the interlocutor.

It must be added that the ability to unseat the addressee is based not on the strength of the place in which the discourse is produced, but on the contrary on the very mobility of the pace, on the absence or refusal of a stronghold, in sum, on a kind of nonplace. A weakness here makes ruses possible, that is, the incessant shifts of the argumentation. Because there is no place to be defended, legitimated, or constituted, that persuasive logic presents the dual character of (1) a *presence*—violent but hidden—of the speaking *subject* in his text (in this respect, Pascal in his letter is like God in the Eucharist or in Scripture, all the more secret for being more present) and of (2) a *maneuvering* and manipulating *ability* that pulls the addressee away in his instability or escapes the grappling holds of a stable adversary. Such is precisely the place/

nonplace, nocturnal, solitary, mobile, doubling down at once on the subjective agency and the vanishing of the objective place, which, in the polemic mode, Pascal conveys to Father Annat: "From this world I have nothing to hope, nothing to dread, nothing to desire. Through the goodness of God, I have no need of any man's money or any man's patronage. Thus, Father, I elude all your attempts to lay hold of me. . . . I beg to inform you, in the plainest terms, that nobody is responsible for my letters but myself, and that I am responsible for nothing but my letters."[48] The addressee of the excerpt is also "stricken by an invisible hand."

MEANING: THINKING OF / PASSING TO / THE OTHER

To the procedure I have just analyzed on the first part of the fragment, and the functioning of which continues throughout, others must be added, concerning no longer the movement, but the alternatives it imposes, the space it constructs, and the principle to which it relates. The *alternative*, explicit or implied, organizes the text. But from the start it is inclined to the extreme, to go all out, and, constantly maintained at this level, it is diversified only by the fact of being directed onto several theological and historical fields. Placed beneath the sign of the "extraordinary," the argumentation creates the ultimate everywhere. It distinguishes and combines poles such as extreme rarity and extreme ardor or certainty, the "continually" and the "never," that which "reveals itself" the most and "covers itself up" even more, etc. The mode of exposition is the all or nothing. The stakes are advanced by frequent comparatives, and by superlatives (the strangest, the darkest, the ultimate secrecy, etc.). It is a rhetorical *hubris* in keeping, no doubt, with what is at stake, God, but technically characterizing that object by a passage to the extreme which is a passage to the other.

This "extremism" is a way of distributing the semantic matter by choices to be made, that is, by a logic of action. There is another consequence, also deriving from this passage to the other, in the way of divvying things up. Already the movement of almost the whole fragment comes from farther away (the greatest distance from God, his least visibility, the least recognition by human beings) and moves toward the closest, which is the strangest. It composes an itinerary. But this journey that from the depths of time leads to Port-Royal could be shown by particular points defined in an autonomous manner, like the advance of a march on a stationary map, a space constructed independently from the journey. There is nothing like this in the excerpt. The carving out of the units is itself often dictated by the argumentation—not received from outside, but decided by the argument. It is relative to the development of the reasoning and, more precisely, to what *it leaves* in its wake.

For example, the tripartite division "infidels" / "heretical Christians" / "Catholics alone" remodels the historical and orthodox geography that distributes the unities on the basis of a center (for example, Christians) and that forces on the entire discourse the law hidden within these named distributive unities. Pascal's gait is not in step with this law. It determines for itself the taxonomy by which its advance is marked. It partitions or "disposes" the theological matter otherwise. Thus, the "heretical Christians," placed *before* "Catholics alone" since the movement passes through the former and leaves them to go to the latter, receive an *autonomous* position due to their specific relation to the dialectic of occulting visibility. The unity, or the concept, is constructed here, the relation of the two terms ("Christians" and "heretics") designating an entity in its own right, identifiable with neither the one nor the other of the two but defined by what the argumentation *posits* and *passes* in advancing.

Whence the strange impression that the text gives of marking its progress only by what it abandons, and of furnishing, in the way of unities or semantic points of repair, only that which, remodeled by its passing, is always behind it. The walk and the path are produced at the same time. They are indissociable. This is why the reader is deprived of the possibility of measuring the one in terms of the other, by relating the walk to a geography of fixed elements. But the argumentation also loses that possibility since there is nothing immobile against which it can calculate its movement. It loses itself in its success, fragile precisely because of its ability to produce its own space, cornered into throwing itself forward or stopping, suspended, without rest.

The law of its own procedure is stated by the excerpt itself when it analyzes knowledge or the operation of thinking as a passage to the other. This piece of the fragment thus requires examination. After having traced out a phenomenology of the hidden according to the historical figures that correspond to the growth of the secret,[49] Pascal goes back to Scripture to sketch out a classification of contemporary figures pertaining to the reading of the secret or the intelligibility of its meaning.[50] The first moment is *alethic*; it articulates the relation between presence and visibility (being versus appearing). The second is *epistemic*, concerning the process of misunderstanding as the nonpassage of a meaning to the other (one versus the other). To the *Eucharistic* secret at which the progress of *visibility* ended and which commands the first series of figures "is added" the *scriptural* secret on which a parallel development on *readability* is based. To think the secret is to learn to read it. Hence, once again, to go from the "less" to the "more," and from insufficient but true positions to the right one, the reasoning that leads the epistemic moment first poses the principle of all reading (the "two perfect meanings") to then consider their applications ("just as," "and as," "and just as,") to the three levels—nature, humanity, and the Eucharist. The Jews, absent from the amplification on the hidden presence, have thus the twofold position of being (1) the key articulation of the principle of reading (Old and New Testaments, etc.) that organizes intelligibility, and (2) the central stage (humanity)[51] of its historical applications. They are at the junction of a structure of believing recognition (or thought) and a history of the divine secret.

Now, the schema, repeated four times (the scriptural principle and its three figures), and in the same terms, defines (negatively) the problematic of meaning and reading by a *passage* (or nonpassage) of "one" order to "another." The *one*, "perfect,"[52] is the object of a "seeing" that, in the scriptural model, is a "stop."[53] The lack, therefore, is due not to this level of experience (which is not an illusion and has an autonomy or "perfection" in its order), but to the fact of stopping at seeing, "*without thinking that there is another.*"[54] The visibility and the readability—or seeing and reading—are differentiated by the act of *passing to the other.* Thus thinking is put in opposition to stopping. It is a movement without rest ("continual reversal of for and against")[55] that is indicated in the formal ratio repeated here four times: *not the one without the other.*[56] But in thus giving thought the form of a faith (to pass to the other), this movement *makes us believe* that *thinking is believing.*

That *to think* means *to pass*, an excess toward the other, and ultimately a mortal ex-stasis of the identity: such is here the meaning[57]—the movement and the direction—of the procedure. Pascal's gesture is inscribed in the contents of the text. A religious semantic field is crossed by this way of thinking that produces, as its effect, "a lost God"[58] and a truth that "wanders unknown among men."[59]

"YOU": THE QUOTED GOD

The reversal of statements nonetheless supposes, as we have seen, an enunciating agency as strong and hidden in the text as Port-Royal is "far from the view of men" and privileged by the presence (the miracle). It destroys the assurances based on visible localizations of a knowledge, or of a power, but in view of constructing the invisible point at which God uncovers himself "for us."

The quotations come to authorize this "strange secret." True, they introduce a plurality of voices and a form of dialogue, but they lend volume to the text only by opening the distance of an echo. The two literal quotations, from Isaiah, repeat the statement in the letter: "He has remained hidden—Truly thou art a hidden God"; "The Jews . . . did not think to seek in him another nature—We did not think that it was him." The discourse quoted duplicates the epistolary one. It gives it the semblance of a body. This fragment of a mirror creates an effect of depth in the fragment of correspondence. But this effect has two important functions: on the one hand, it introduces a referentiality and participates in a persuasive doing; and on the other hand, the statement that is reproduced by the quotation comes back transformed, since the mirror placed at the center of the text makes the divine *you* appear in the image.[60]

The "alleged" quotations, as they said in the seventeenth century, that is, deputized, placed front stage, are all biblical, two from the Old Testament (Isaiah), the only ones haloed by quotation marks and located far away, and two from the New (Saint Paul, the object of a paraphrastic rewriting, and the Revelation of Saint John, one "word" of which is recategorized by the excerpt). Each of them is put in relation to an act of locution ("says," "calls") that the addressor-author alleges from his place, to his place, and that he thus uses as a device of enunciation. But at the discursive level, they make up an exteriority. They increase the number of proper names, inflating the illusion of realism.[61] They are accompanied, though discreetly, by a paraphrase, which always produces a descriptive expansion on the circumstances, in this case attached to the speaking subject: "Isaiah saw it in that state when he said. . . ." But does the summoning of a biblical fragment make the citing text travel? Does it supply it with an elsewhere? Rather it serves to furnish it with "references" (in the social sense of the term). Generally speaking, "the quotation is the referentially opaque context *par excellence*,"[62] an effect of perspective and horizon. Furthermore, it stands as a shard of the broken Great Text, the Bible. A quoted discourse, far from opening up a crack in the epistolary discourse or eliciting a commentary, comes in only as a piece that has been torn away. Its role here is to manifest the presence of an "authority" all the more "opaque" and referential for being in pieces (therefore "quotable"), and thereby at once manipulable and accrediting—a "nucleus" inductive[63] of the text that is constructed by making it [the quoted discourse] "turn," and a source of credibility for the result of this treatment. The quoted allows a production and authorizes it. It comes to reinforce the persuasive action of the argumentation.

More surprising is the *Thou* that becomes visible in the brightness of the mirror. A twofold withdrawal ("I believe / that Isaiah saw it . . . / when he said . . .") precedes the apparition. A reciprocal movement of the one described in the text: the secret of God increases with his approach. Here, a distancing of the speaker goes together with the manifestation of *Thou*.[64] In reality, it is a question no longer of vision, but of writing. Visibility, mediated by a believing ("I believe"), is only the locus of the other's saying ("Isaiah saw it . . . when he said . . ."), a saying addressed to the true Other. The *I* and the *thou* answer each other only across that distance—the *I* affected by noncertainty and the *thou* beaming behind the veils of a saying that hides a vision and of an ancient Scripture that holds at a distance, undecidable, the prophetic speech. Yet it is here, and not apropos of the close miracle (which is, by contrast, the index of the *we* binding speaker to addressee), that—separated *and* posited by the scriptural difference, anonymous, without proper names, stripped therefore of all "proper" and of even the possibility of ever being a *we*, the contracting parties of the alliance knotted through time—*I* and *Thou* are uttered.

THE APPROACH CONCEALS[65]

From the excerpt of a letter to Mademoiselle de Roannez, that fragment, that fallout, nothing can be concluded in general concerning the relation between rhetoric and mystics. Perhaps only the style of an intensity. The effective *ruses* of the argumentation are tied to a *contradiction* internal to the text, to an impossibility or a despair that sustains them: a deictic from one end to the other,[66] the discourse *shows* everywhere what it asserts to be *invisible*. Like the guide who leads visits to Port-Royal des Champs today, it says, "Here is . . . ," but nothing can be seen. Once, perhaps, Isaiah saw it; at least it is permissible to believe so on the basis of what is written. What, then, does such a persuasive virtuosity relate to, if it loses, if it even makes an effort to lose, the object it is capable of imposing?

This tension probably opens up a freedom for the addressee captivated by the logic of Pascal. But it indicates rather what falls and is lost here: the alliance between seeing and saying, the ancient contract between things perceived and linguistic nomination. Writing replaces a "prose of the world." That prose is no longer adequate to it, it no longer expresses it; it establishes itself in an insurmountable difference. The readability is produced as loss of visibility: "The fall and the look, the fall of the look. . . . What has fallen is that which, of the body, is knowledge: the eye."[67] Ruin, not of sight (which has its "perfect" order), but of representation: mystic remarks, the effect of a rhetoric.

Moreover, if all the strength of Pascal's reasoning bears on a misunderstanding that grows as one sees it closer and closer, how is it—barring a "miracle" that cannot be presumed—with my own approach to this excerpt? My ana-lysis comes under what Pascal says of the town: "From afar a town, a farmland, is a town and a farmland; but as you approach, there are houses, trees, tiles, leaves, grass, ants, ant legs, to infinity."[68] So it is with commentary. The approach conceals. However partial, it calls once again for a distance, the marker of a modesty and a silence, the renunciation of an impossible appropriation—something that might be said as a corollary to this text: I must back off for it to become once again a text.

The Opera of Speech: Glossolalias

"Glossolalia: A class of similar deviant linguistic behaviors, characterized by a fluent, anarthric, segmentable speech in terms of phonemic units, and consisting entirely or almost entirely of neologisms."[1]

"The French authors consider *glossolalia* (or *speaking in tongues*) to be a tendency to forge a new language that becomes fixed and is progressively enriched. In the formation of such a language, a lucid consciousness and reflective will are largely present (Cénac, Teulié). The German authors, on the contrary, departing less from tradition, consider that glossolalia, in multiple verbal manifestations, is no more than the automatic explosion of intense affective processes, with diminution of lucid consciousness (Berze, Gruhle)."[2]

FICTIONS OF SPEECH

The authorities in the field repeat it tirelessly: glossolalia resembles a language, but really isn't one. It looks like one, but it does not have the structure of a language. It is only a "façade."[3] In every case, "we can distinguish between glossolalic speech and a language that we do not know."[4] This semblance, which can be produced artificially if we know its phonetic rules, is an aural illusion, just as there are visual illusions. It speaks "to say nothing," precisely to avoid being fooled by words, to escape the traps of meaning, to be a pure *fable* (*fari*, to speak) and get back to primary *speech* in its anteriority. This is at least the *prima facie* fact, in forms now infantine ("am stram gram . . ."), now "pathological" (neologisms, alliterations, etc.), now literary (Dadaist, for example) or religious ("gift of tongues," "ecstatic utterances," etc.): a fictive discourse orchestrates the act of saying but states nothing; it is also an art of saying within the enclosure of a semblance.

Is the phenomenon so exceptional? A glossolalia is already instituted, in dotted lines so to speak, in ordinary conversation: bodily noises, quotes of delinquent sounds, fragments of foreign voices punctuate the order of sentences with unguarded outbursts and surprises. Said by whom to whom? A secondary, disseminated vocalization crosses the stated discourse, cutting through or paralleling it. The major voice that becomes the messenger of meaning appears caught up in a twinning that compromises it. It frees itself from this unsettling doppelgänger only in the functions in which it is farthest from interlocution. The political, professorial, or predicatory discourse, for example, becomes increasingly less permeable to the vocal irruptions and interruptions that the presence of the other induces in a series of propositions. A fragility disappears from it. The erasure of the occasional stuttering, hesitations and verbal tics, slips of the tongue or derivative sounds coincides with the distancing of the interlocutor, who is transformed into a public.

On the other hand, conversation restores the porosity of discourse to these *noises of the other*. Proximity fragilizes the spoken word with respect to the addressee. Different voices then strew the organizing system with meaning. Weeds growing between the paving stones. Like the voodoo *loas*, "voices" momentarily seize the discourse. They "straddle" it. They snatch it away from me in some spots, without my knowing where they come from, or which "spirits" they are. They come from something else in me and respond to . . . what other? This piecemeal "possession" disturbs, breaks, or suspends the autonomy of the speaker. The parallel noises that people ordinary conversations represent an interlocutionary and vocal tattooing on discourse. They indicate the workings of language when it is spoken. This vocal vegetation also crops up in interviews, but the transcriptions that clean up their sentences wash away the traces relative to a status of the spoken word—an essential element. Strewing the field of statements with excess or suspensions, a *coven of voices* murmurs something that escapes the control of the speakers and does not obey the presumed division between speaking individuals. It fills that interval with the plural and diffuse act of communication. It forms, *mezza voce*, an opera of speech on the stage of verbal exchange.

Glossolalia *isolates* an opera of speech and *authorizes it*. It organizes a space in which the ability to speak unfolds for itself. To explain how he speaks in tongues, one glossolal says that instead of forming words, "I can concentrate on the *communication* itself, rather than on the *mode* of communication."[5] The fiction of language is the stage on which a *fiction of speech* appears. It is located beyond the reach of truth or error. Outside the walls of a language. It no longer (or not yet) articulates semantic units. An abjectness of meaning serves as a precondition for this *vocal utopia* of speech. But this ersatz, a stranger to all possible language, gives voice to something that, in every language, concerns its ability to be spoken. The semblance-statements constitute the theater in which the veri-similitude of speech conducts its trial run. As in the "fictions" of lunar landings, speakers play out separately, in a linguistic simulation, the real passage from mutism (*not being able* to say) to the spoken word (*being able* to say). Circumscribed and authorized like scripted laboratory scenarios, the glossolalic fiction makes it possible to experience this passage.

A "BELIEVING"

Not only does the glossolalic fiction make such a passage possible, it even forces it, on the twofold basis of a "must say" and a belief in the word. It thus deploys, around saying, the whole spectrum of modalities: can, must, and know/believe. Indeed, on the one hand, glossolalia is buttressed by a need to speak, which pressures it, before furnishing it with an escape valve. There is glossolalia only when a value, an obligation, or a constraint (cultural, religious, or psychological) is attached to the spoken word; when there is a "you should have said"; when *that* has to come out because it is speaking inside of me. Orality is gold. It is aurum-ality. The act is more important in this case than the content. The act is brought forth the moment the meaning of statements falls away. It arises as an imperative or a need, like a cry or a confession. Tearing its way through patience and ritualized silence, stimulated by the playful, religious, medical, or literary circle authorizing it, a *must say* demands the passage from the *unable* to the *able to say*. It calls for it, a legitimate and necessary transgression in relation to the order that forces us to keep quiet or control our voices by articulating sentences.

But this transition also assumes that there is, somewhere, a reservoir of voices ready to speak. An expectation focuses on that still distant Other—some speech, an indecipherable oracle, a vocal liquidity from which a mutism separates us. A *belief* is waiting for these waters of a primal orality capable of passing through the walls of our languages. If only there were a Word! We await the Fable itself. It would suffice for our mouths to open, emptied of words, and "let themselves be taken over" by the "torrents" of these passing voices. But where are they, these rushing streams? Where do they come from? To believe in them is not to know the answer. In the religious domain, the non-place of "that which speaks" is, moreover, emphasized by the term that designates, in many traditions, the act and the actor of saying: *the Spirit*. After and before many others, John of the Cross calls the "spirit" *el que habla*, that which speaks.[6] The belief that subtends the expectation of a *saying* also results in the *atopia* of the scene in which it appears. To it there corresponds a glossolalic utopia—"utopia" because it is neither one nor the other of the positive languages, neither this one nor that one, but a linguistic neuter.[7] It takes on a semblance that escapes localization to ask a question that is universal (what is "saying" without saying something?) and by definition deprived of its own place. The semblance (the fiction) is the place/nonplace of the theoretical question. The saying postulated by belief can be lodged only in a *fiction of spirit*, at once scientific simulation and poetic production. What utopia is to the social space, glossolalia is to oral communication, in circumscribing in a linguistic simulacrum everything else that the voice realizes besides language when it speaks the language.

TWO TYPES

To schematize the process, a first type of glossolalia ensures the passage from the cannot say "~c (S)" to the can say "c (S)" by a can not say "c (~S)" that is supported by a must say "m (S)" and a believing in saying "b (S)," as if obligation and belief compensated for the absence of statements and allowed the utopian space offered to voices (see figure 8).

There is a second glossolalia that follows the reverse path. It moves in the opposite direction. Based on articulate speech, it proceeds to deconstruct it by a play on phonemes and/or by deriding the spoken word. Thus, Christian Morgenstern and Hugo Ball in Germany, or Raoul Duguet and Claude Gauvreau in Quebec. Or this poem, by Pastor Paul:

Schua ea, Schua ea
O tschi biro tira pea
akki lungo ta ri fungo
u li bara ti ra tungo
latschi bungo ti tu ta.[8]

|vocal utopia|
b (S)
m (S)
~c (S) ——→ |c (~S)| ——→ c (S)

Figure 8. Glossolalia type 1.

|vocal utopia|
~b (S)
~m (S)
~c (S) ←—— |c (~S)| ←—— c (S)

Figure 9. Glossolalia type 2.

Literary, playful, or infantine, sometimes pathological as well, this glossolalic figure goes beyond the bounds of statements to try out the potentialities of the vocal palette before falling into silence and to fill an enunciative space with polyphonic rumors. Its locus is no less utopic and circumscribed than that of the first figure, but it is based on an absence of obligation (a permission to play with the language) rather than on a duty (to say), and on an incredulity (a lucidity about the madness of meaning) rather than on a belief (in the word). The formula for this reverse process is given in figure 9.

If the first type (religious) makes saying play a role analogous to *tears* (there are extensive analogies between the "gift of tongues" and the "gift of tears"), and if the second type (poetic) bears a greater resemblance to *laughter* ("glossolalia comes over me like laughter," said an English glossolal woman who believed neither in "spirits" nor in the Spirit), both put into question, in a semblance of language, the modalities of can, must (obligation or permission), and know (or believe) that pertain to *saying*. They are equally fictions of saying.

This particular phenomenon, moreover, has a universal ambition. To the exclusion of all actual languages, it is the *saying* of every language, or that without which no language is spoken. It has a metalinguistic value, but in relation to speech. Glossolalia isolates the speaking of all speaking. In that theoretical space of the vocal genus, saying can say itself. The problem of the beginning and the end is therefore central to it. How do we begin speaking? "Glossolalia" means "to babble," or even to stammer, to stutter (*lalein*) in or with the tongue (*glōssēi*). It is therefore not astonishing that we should find glossolalic traces or moments in children as well as in countless literary texts (see Rabelais, Cyrano de Bergerac, etc.) that take an interest in the nature, conditions, and beginnings of the Word. But the question of the end or of the *lapsus* of the word is linked to that of the beginning. How does speech fall apart? The passion of the fall intensifies that of birth. The one can, moreover, be the very locus of the other. Hence the two figures are often intermingled. Furthermore, in every glossolalia, there is a combination of something prelinguistic, relative to a silent origin or to the "onset" of the spoken word, and something postlinguistic, made up of excess, of overflows, or of leftovers of language. Like myth, these fictions cobble together the before and after of saying to construct the artifact in which saying plays itself out.

THE ILLUSION OF MEANING

It is an odd fact that this fiction of language keeps being taken as a language and treated accordingly. It is constantly required to "mean" something. It excites an indefatigable drive to decrypt and decipher that always assumes, behind the series of sounds, an organization of meaning. The history of glossolalia is almost entirely that of interpretations that want to make it say sentences and that claim to reduce vocal delinquency to the order of the signified. Restricting our focus to our Western era, from the interpretation given by the Acts of the Apostles to the glossolalia of the Pentecost ("devout men from every nation" understood "in [their] tongues")[9] to the Saussurean or psychoanalytic analyses, the serious and jubilatory play of speech receives in response a hermeneutics, always clever enough to reduce the "want-to-say" to a "want-to-say-something."

The history of this equivocation sends us back to the relations that, since Greek and Roman times, Reason has maintained with the Fable, in taking its place. Indeed, learned hermeneutics manages a substitution of bodies, replacing the made-up tale with a semantic content, but in the very place that was founded by the Fable. Western modernity developed this switch in all the forms of ethnological, psychiatric, and pedagogical exegesis, as if it had to write in the space in which *that* speaks. Wild voices and voices of the people, mad voices and infantile voices define the spaces in which it becomes possible and necessary to write. They furnish hermeneutics with its condition of production, that is, the spaces it occupies to turn them into pages.[10] Before the glossolalic chain, the hermeneutic work thus mobilizes its scientific apparatus. But in doing so, it exposes its motivating belief. While glossolalia claims that somewhere there is the spoken word, interpretation assumes that *somewhere there must be meaning.* It seeks that meaning, and finds it, because it expects it to be there, because it meshes with the conviction that surely, especially where meaning seems absent, it is hidden somewhere, present "nonetheless." Hermeneutics goes to any lengths, then, in these "mad" places of saying, claiming the presence of "secret languages" there. It favors what it constitutes by making them into challenges for meaning. And ultimately, because it believes in meaning, it falls into the trap of a semblance of language.

The functioning of this equivocation thus teaches us something about the glossolalic voice. In this respect, it would be tempting to follow the exegesis—tenacious and resourceful in maintaining a revelation of meaning—of the first Christian texts that mention cases of glossolalia, an exegesis more flourishing still since the "Pentecostal" and "charismatic" movements have given new relevance to the "gift of tongues."[11] But two more recent cases, Saussure's analysis and the psychoanalytic study by Oskar Pfister, will suffice to show how the madness of glossolalic discourse sets its trap and drives interpretation to raving.

PFISTER: THE EQUIVOCATION OF COMMUNICATION

Oskar Pfister, who, as a friend and scientific associate of Freud, maintains a faithful correspondence of almost thirty years (1909–38),[12] was very interested in glossolalia. He devoted two studies to it,[13] which were, moreover, the object of epistolary exchanges with Freud[14] and Jung. The "psychoanalytic method," exposited in the second, consists in transcribing a fragment of glossolalic discourse, segmented into phonetic units (*Esin gut efflorien meinogast schinohaz* . . . , etc.), and, through associations, in groping toward a corresponding signified for each of these units. The association of ideas is the roundabout way that furnishes a substitute for etymology and that makes it possible, as in etymology, to find a meaning by going back to a childhood: in the beginning there is meaning. Indeed, for Pfister, glossolalia is a regression to infantile states. Through the return to the child's affects, mad vocalization is transformed into a coherent discourse.

A start that sets the tone: "*Estin* means 'a meaning' (*ein Sinn*)." A brilliant onslaught: from the first "word" on, the interpretation poses its postulate. The rest follows, by means of a to-and-fro between German and English. ("*Si wo* means: *see* (English), where (German *wo*) are you!") and frequent appeals to proper names drawn from the most heterogeneous traditions (*Efflorien* means Florence). A key to the exegesis also appears with the fourth "word," *Meinogast*, which apparently means "my (*mein*) Oskar": the interpreter (Oskar Pfister) is written into the discourse itself, which declares in advance that it cannot be separated from this "dear friend." No, says the vocal narration, I will not be taken away, neither from you nor from meaning; seek, and ye shall find. And in fact Pfister does discover that hidden "friend," meaning, which speaks, out of the mouth of a "religious fanatic aged twenty-four," of the anxiety of practicing the profession of pastor (Pfister is himself a Swiss pastor). The analytic operation, treating seriatim the fragments of this piecemeal speech, reduces each bit of it to meaning and to the same by a series of connections: this "signifies," that "means," this "refers to," etc. In the end, the exegete can "assume the right to formulate the meaning" and give in decoded form the *written translation* of the voice, which is assimilated to a "secret speech."

What comes with this victory of interpretation? "The pious," writes Freud, "are not usually as generous as that in their ravings."[15] Nor are the scholars. The hermeneutic operation yields a revenue. The semblance of meaning, torn away, like a confession, from the fragmented (tortured?) voice, allows the conservation of two *general* characteristics of all language, namely (1) that it organizes some *meaning*, and (2) that it articulates some *real*. Pfister succeeds in obtaining as much by the conversion of "fanatic" speech, first into a series of quotations relative to stories involving the childhood of the speaker (each phonetic unit becomes a little piece of an absent narrative), then by a group of "complexes" going back to those first years. Finally, it is the system of "complexes" (i.e., a speech of the real) that makes it possible to construct meaning out of quotations. The fiction produced by this twofold passage from the vocal to the narrative and from the narrative to the structural (a passage that corresponds to the program Freud set out for his friend),[16] guarantees the possibility of "hearing" the speaking body like a language. In it, exegesis produces its own postulates. It is repeated in the semblance it produces.

Freud, with a word he later also used to define *Moses and Monotheism* ("a historical novel"), designates Pfister's *Glossolalieversuch* as a "novel" that is "awfully amusing," to boot.[17] A detective novel indeed—that series of twists and turns intended to give form and feature to coherent and real actors (complexes) behind the mad voices that, as in the ethnography of the voodoo *loas*, are assumed to be just "masks." The ruses of reason struggle against these voices in order to change them into a décor determined by the "work" that takes place in the hidden corridors. But that "behind the scenes" is also a theater, a sort of scientific hallucination. The system of interpretation enacts there a representation of the values it favors—*meaning*, a *reality*, *work*. These thus replace the "masks" (gods, principles, or values) that the glossolalic opera authorizes—the mad (an excess), *fiction* (an atopia), and pleasure (a game). It tells itself its own history when Pfister's exegesis has the "secret speech" say of his young "fanatic": "You possess the necessary religious, moral, and intellectual qualifications to be able, with God's help, to become a minister in spite of persecution and misfortune."[18] You can still become the apostle of a meaning, a real, and a productive ascesis. This hermeneutic "morality" is drawn from its opposite, the fable, and it converts it: the voice can become the "minister" of meaning.

But the explanation, foreign to glossolalic saying, is at the same time necessary to the latter: foreign because in denying itself all real language, this saying turns the whole burden of meaning over to commentary; it no longer controls it, and thus lets the hermeneutic task change into a raving that can do no more than repeat the presuppositions of the interpretation. On the other hand, the stage on which saying isolates itself in an enunciative "song" can be constituted only if there is meaning *besides*. The semblance of language presumes the existence of positive languages and envisages a possibility of speaking them. It already implies the exteriority of a commentary, a foreignness necessary to its own becoming autonomous. In other words, *a reciprocity* links glossolalia and interpretation to each other, but *in the mode of the equivocal*. The one cannot be without the other. The former is all the more misleading to the latter in that it needs this reference point to exile itself from meaning. As for explanation, it uses glossolalia to steady itself in its own principles. Illusion is the mainspring of the necessary relations between these two figures: each generates itself on the basis of the other, which it transforms into a simulacrum of its own aim—language becomes a semblance for the "nonetheless" of an enunciative act, and saying furnishes material for the fiction that "in spite of everything" asserts meaning.

This problematic of the mix-up (one in the place of the other) and of illusion (one is the semblance of the other) characterizes the relation (necessary, in this case) between two positions of language. It involves not the organization of statements but the functioning of the speech. It is developed on the basis of the moment when it is a question of communication and not of its content, therefore of saying and hearing—*in fine*, of speaking: of being to, and for, the other. This question, posed by glossolalia, generates its hermeneutic reciprocal. It brings out the illusion of the relation. In this way we are led to wonder whether the content is not here just to hide the illusion of communication and whether, reciprocally, the perception of an illusion camouflaged by the organization of meaning might not be at the origin of the vocal utopia that, by destroying the possibility of articulating meaning, is attempting to restore a speaking.

SAUSSURE: A SPEAKING TAKEN FOR A LANGUAGE

No less typical is the analysis Saussure carried out, between 1895 and 1898, of the speech of a young medium and glossolal dubbed Mademoiselle Hélène Smith by the Genevan psychologist Théodore Flournoy, a tireless observer of the "case."[19] The lady in question spoke Martian, but also a language that seemed to be Sanskrit (which she did not know). In order to judge what he refers to as "Sanscritoid," Flournoy appeals to specialists, among others Ferdinand de Saussure, a "professor of Sanskrit," of whom he quotes many letters and whom he depicts transcribing the sounds "quite near Hélène who sang seated upon the ground." A learned council surrounds the voice. Noting the "grammatical nullity" of Hélène's Sanskrit, Saussure makes the following diagnosis: (1) this speech "resembles" Sanskrit, it "reminds one" of the Sanskrit words and contains "fragments" that have meaning; (2) the other fragments, unintelligible, "never have an anti-Sanskrit character," that is, they do not present "groups materially contrary or in opposition to the general figure of the Sanskrit words"; (3) in particular, this speech is characterized by a greater frequency of the vowel *a*[20] and by an absence of the consonant *f*, as in Sanskrit.[21] Furthermore, he makes the hypothesis that beneath this discourse, there is a syntactic "weft" of French words, and that, for these already-constituted semantic units, the medium seeks other sounds, "exotic-sounding substitutes" of heteroclite origin (English, German, etc.). The whole, on this hypothesis, obeys one essential rule: "It is essential above all, and only, that it should not seem French."[22]

In omitting the *f*, Hélène obeys this rule: "The word 'French,' as Victor Henry notes, begins with an *f*; for this reason the *f* must appear as the 'French' letter par excellence, and therefore she avoids it as much as she can." As Todorov notes, a symbolic system (*F* symbolizes "French") reorganizes the spoken language.[23] By a series of coincidences (the frequency of *a*, the disappearance of *f*, etc.), Hélène's speech is ***understood*** as being Sanskrit, which probably leads the speaker to develop that resemblance as much she can. But that supposed identity, the result of a listening that creates the erudite mobilization (and its lure), must not lead us to forget the essential, which is the will of a saying that is *other.* The illusion has to do with the equivocation between a speaking that wants to be other (not French) in order to say, and its reception, which identifies it with a positivity that is foreign but knowable (Sanskrit). It involves not the content but, here too, a process of communication: a speaking taken for a language.

How, then, does it come about that it must not seem French, an auditory illusion that leads the learned listeners to think it must be Sanskrit (or Sanskritoid)? Mademoiselle Smith's sincerity is not in question. All the witnesses agree in recognizing her loyalty. She probably started speaking "Sanskrit" and developing its sonorous landscapes because her listeners were awaiting her and hearing her there, a bit the way children begin to speak the language with which their parents, *by their listening*, engage their vocal simulation by distinguishing their "first words." True, Mademoiselle Smith is leaving a language (French) rather than entering it, but that "departure" might also have been the learning of Sanskrit if the learned circle of her examiners had thought to respond to her rather than observing her, and sought communication (a speaking) rather than the existence of a knowledge (a language). Nevertheless, her gibberish ["charabia"], as Saussure calls it, is focused not on a language, but on something like the institution of a speaking.

THE VOCAL INSTITUTION

Glossolalia involves a particular form of being able to say: its foundation. It brings onto the stage that which makes it possible to say. That stage is first of all psychic. The glossolals tell the story: it is "an event in my throat," and often, at the first stages, without phonation; a glossolabial movement, "a warmth in my tongue and lips," etc. A glottal movement sets off a speaking. Little by little rough phonations come, then a more structured articulation. The beginning is modeled in the course of a progressive apprenticeship, until it becomes a "glossopoiesis."[24] The "vocal miracle" is narrativized. The threshold that leads from mutism to speech seems susceptible of extension and orchestration so as to be constituted, like a no-man's-land, into a space of vocal manipulations and jubilations, already having emerged from silence and not yet pressed into the service of any particular language.

Games along the border. Intoxicating beginnings. Analogous, in their technical aspect, to the work of inversion, stretching, and variation that is practiced at the "onset" of a vocal or instrumental piece. Comparable rather to what began one day with a verse that came to Dante on the bank of a clear stream: "my tongue spoke as if moved of its own accord," "These words I laid up in my mind with great joy, thinking to take them for my beginning," then, "after some days of thought I began a canzone with this beginning, arranged in the mode which will be seen below in its division."[25] But the beginning that induces the song is not, in the glossolal, a verse; it is only an "air" of beginning.

In this place in which there is not yet the production of phrases, the foundation of a theater of action permitting such a production is played out. In the not so distant past, in ancient Rome, it was the role of the *fetiāles* priests to open a legitimate space (*fās*) for warlike, military, or commercial actions that one wanted to attempt outside the city. Their ritual procession, which went from the center to the exterior of the city, did not ensure the success of these actions, but it authorized their theater by a *repetitio rerum*, which consisted in repeating the stories of the origins in a new space, and also, as a general rehearsal, in "opening" the scene of future activities on foreign territory.[26] Similarly, glossolalia "repeats" infantile phonation, that is, the beginnings of speech, but with the intention of establishing a theater for linguistic operations to come.

The first vocal narrations hold that space: predominance of the vowels *a* and *i*, then *ū*, labials and dentals, then velars. These songs made up of primitive phonemes in many languages,[27] hence "repetitions," sometimes designated as "regressive languages," create, by their return to the originary, the authorization of a new beginning, as if to begin to speak it were necessary each time to go back to that *arkhē*, that "principle" of speech which is constituted by the initial Fable. A place of ease and playfulness as well, because it is not yet subject to the technical and tactical constraints imposed by the linguistic articulation of communication. The place of a jubilant indetermination, "laid up in my mind with great joy."

This moment of openness corresponds to the one the poet refers to (already within the enclosure of the poem, but still on its threshold) when he says: "Come, O Muse . . ." The invocation, an inaugural sacrifice on the verbal stone of a proper name, calls on an "inspirational" Voice that speaks and causes to speak, instituting the area of a language. The Muse, a doppelgänger of the Mind, allows the passage from one space to another. It founds the possibility of the poem, and one must be possessed by it to be introduced into the song. For the "charismatics," by the way, who call their glossolalia a "song," there is but one preparation: "to abandon oneself," "to let oneself go," to offer oneself "as a child" to that which speaks. From the beginning, with the baby, it is indeed the voice that opens up (and circumscribes) for it a sphere of communication in preparation for the word. Invoked here as Spirit, it defines the function of glossolalia, which is to *institute a space for speech.*

Attached to this instituting function are the social and/or psychological circumstances that characterize the periodic recurrences of glossolalia. These apparitions fall within the precinct of a question that has a history, if not a historiography: the institution of the spoken word. Normally, in a society, institutions found, guarantee, and distribute the space of speaking. They owe this role not to the meaning-capital they supposedly preserve (this is only what they would have us believe), but to their capacity to organize a checkerboard of places that at once authorizes and delimits a verbal circulation, distributing and controlling it. Family, profession, and public function—each of these defines *topics of illocutionary acts*, that is, networks of places in which the word is permitted (founded), but in a system of conventions that fix its conditions and relevance: one speaks here, but not there; that is said here, but not in such and such circumstances, and not elsewhere, etc. Countless rites and gestures thus mark, in each case, the act of beginning to speak. The instituting of speech is thus treated in the mode of a spatial, complex, and stratified distribution that disseminates its interrogation and even masks it behind the intense game of usage and custom.

THE SENSELESS AND REPETITION

In this subtle functioning, two curious traits must be commented on because they are found in exaggerated form in the extraordinary phenomena (glossolalic in particular) that tend to compensate for that regular institution of speech when it is lacking or when (in poetry, for example) it loses its relevance. In current usage, what authorizes speech is very often on the order of the *senseless* and *repetition.* On the one hand, as Jakobson noted (in a study devoted to glossolalia),[28] incomprehensible "words," received from the tradition and that "transcend your reason," are precisely those which make you speak. The word seems to be reborn ceaselessly from these "ancient words" that are "wise words" because they have *no meaning* and because, like the institution, they objectify the blind origin (the "fable") from which all meaningful discourse emanates. From the ordinary conversation to the psychoanalytic experience, thousands of examples would show this relationship of the articulate word to "voices," devoid of meaning, that have made it possible.

Furthermore, in all the stereotypes, proverbs, and all the everyday equivalents of these nursery rhymes [*comptines*], which have mistakenly been made into the specialty of children, *repetition* is also the mainspring of speech: the already said authorizes new words, just as the *repetitio rerum* of the *fetiāles* priests once sanctioned undertakings outside the "received" place. All conversation is punctuated by "beginnings," that is, places in which the experience of being *in-fans*, without speaking, is reiterated, and in which it revives the process of "allowing" the transition to speech by verbal stereotypes and rhymed or even, more elementarily, by glottal sounds, sounds alien to meaning, by means of vocal citations, etc. These sonorous tics are repetitions that "raise" the word from its sonorous origin. Despite their dispersion, they hark back to the vocal institution of speech.

By the preceding phenomena we are already able to recognize an autonomy, and also an instability, of the voice in relation to the articulation of meaning. The speech act, fragile amid circumstances, subject to the difficulty of beginning and the risk of falling, introduces flaws and dissension within the perfect harmony (assumed by language) between sound and sense. While a language has neither beginning nor end, speech bestows the pathos of time—that is, the vagaries of beginnings, of returns to originary meaninglessness, of falls and defections—on the voice, on its troubles, on its jubilations. Voice is the dramatic or comedic history of those deaths and births that speech must play and parry, though language, in eliminating them, does not prepare it to do so.

Why is it that at certain moments (historical, sociocultural, psychological), this disparate play in the everyday exercise of speech focuses on vocal utopias? How is it that the "vocal institution" thus backs up in an eddy, in the form of glossolalia, for example? These moments are localizable and typical: devaluations of the institutions (ecclesial or social) of speech, deterioration of usage and custom, degradation of the conventions of language, etc. There are also psychological equivalents of these social phenomena. Thus glossolalia presents itself as an auxiliary process. It takes charge, vocally, of that "art of nonsense"[29] which is, in sum, the art of beginning or resuming speech in *saying*.

The ideologies that surround glossolalia only orchestrate that function. In glossolalia it is a question of the *primitive* or pre-Babelic *language* (the origin) or what replaces it; a question of *unity* surmounting the breaking up into languages or speakers (a point zero, or "neutral," or divine point of speech); of *inspiration* that is precisely the being-there of the originary and that triumphs over the uncertainty of the beginning; of *angelic language* in which the transparency of the content leads to a privileged status for the "want-to-say" and the audition that characterize a pure act of speaking;[30] of *infantile* babble especially, a passage (ever to be resumed) from mutism to language, a risky and creative between-the-two, the production of the space of speaking.

EBRIETAS SPIRITUALIS: AN OPERA

Thus glossolalia, before being exploited by the institutions that retrieve it and reduce it to being no more than the "illustration" of doctrines written in books and taken possession of by clerics, has the aspect of a *joy of origin.* "Ebrietas spiritualis," as one said in the Middle Ages, a spiritual intoxication, the jubilation of a beginning of speech: "that . . . the boundless extent of joy may have no limits of syllables," said Saint Augustine.[31]

Indeed glossolalia, the invention of vocal space, increases the possibilities of saying. It is not maintained, or held back, by any determination of meaning. The decomposition of syllables and combination of elementary sounds by the play of alliteration create *an indefinite* that is no longer subjected to the legality of a language. An artificial and bewitching immensity, this vocal virgin forest is assumed to have "meaning" globally, as a totality, but one can circulate freely within it without encountering the limits that condition all articulation of meaning. On this privileged stage, this ephemeral artifact, it is a question no longer of statements but of an opera made up of the vocal modalizations of which the former are capable. There is no longer effectuation of language but, on the stage of a semblance of language, *vocalization of the subject.*

"A flowerbed of colored vowels,"[32] this garden of rich sounds drifting playfully through many pathways soon disappears. Then perhaps there is the return, all the more strict, of the law of a linguistic and semantic order from which the voice chose exile to find autonomous spaces. The dichotomy between voice and language would allow only ephemeral "excursions" relative to a reinforced system. But that is another aspect—social and political—of glossolalia.

Notes

Presentation

1. I have explained my approach to this topic in the discussion on Michel de Certeau, "Feux persistants" [Persistent Fires], *Esprit* (March 1996): 131–54. The other participants were Jeremy Ahearne, Dominique Julia, Pierre Mayol and Olivier Mongin.

2. Luce Giard, "Bibliographie complète de Michel de Certeau," in *Le Voyage mystique. Michel de Certeau*, ed. L. Giard (Paris: Recherches de science religieuse and Éditions du Cerf, 1988), 191–243. It contains 422 entries.

3. For these collections, as well as for prior, reedited works, of which I will say more presently, I furnish in parentheses, in the text, the date of the first publication instigated by me, and in the notes the reference for the most recent edition.

4. *Histoire et psychanalyse entre science et fiction*, new edition, revised and enlarged, coll. "Folio Histoire" (Paris: Gallimard, 2002).

5. *La Faiblesse de croire*, corrected edition, coll. "Points" (Paris: Éd. du Seuil, 2003).

6. *La Prise de parole et autres écrits politiques*, republished in coll. "Points" (Paris: Éd. du Seuil, 2008).

7. *Le Lieu de l'autre: Histoire religieuse et mystique*, Coll. "Hautes Études" (Paris: Gallimard and Éd. du Seuil, 2005).

8. *L'Étranger ou l'union dans la difference*, new edition, coll. "Points" (Paris: Éd. du Seuil, 2005).

9. *L'Invention du quotidien*, new edition, revised and enlarged, coll. "Folio Essais" (Paris: Gallimard, 1990). Vol. 2 had been written in collaboration with Pierre Mayol and me.

10. *La Culture au pluriel*, new edition, coll. "Points" (Paris: Éd. du Seuil, 2003).

11. *L'Écriture de l'histoire*, Coll. "Folio Histoire" (Paris: Gallimard, 2002).

12. *Une Politique de la langue. La Révolution française et les patois: L'Enquête de Grégoire*, new edition, revised and enlarged with a new postface by Dominique Julia and Jacques Revel, co-authors of the work, coll. "Folio Histoire," (Paris: Gallimard, 2002).

13. *La Possession de Loudun*, revised edition, coll. "Folio Histoire" (Paris: Gallimard, 2005).

14. See the work published in 1988, cited in note 2, above; *Michel de Certeau*, Centre Georges-Pompidou, coll. "Cahiers pour un temps," 1987; *Histoire, mystique et politique. Michel de Certeau*, with the collaboration of Hervé Martin and Jacques Revel (Grenoble: Jérôme Millon, 1991).

15. My work of verification was limited to four languages: German, English, Spanish, and Italian.

16. Blessed Pierre Favre, *Mémorial*, translated with commentary by Michel de Certeau, coll. "Christus" (Paris: Desclée de Brouwer, 1960).

17. *La Fable mystique, XVIe–XVIIe siècle*, vol. 1, coll. "Bibliothèque des histoires" (Paris: Gallimard, 1982), 411; trans. *The Mystic Fable*, vol. 1: *The Sixteenth and Seventeenth Centuries* (Chicago: University of Chicago Press, 1992), 299.

18. See above, note 17. Michael B. Smith was later to translate *The Possession at Loudun* (Chicago: University of Chicago Press, 2000).

19. Here I faithfully copy the author's handwritten document with respect to quotation marks, italics, parentheses, and punctuation.

20. François Dosse, *Michel de Certeau. Le marcheur blessé* (Paris: La Découverte, 2002), 559n10.

21. I chose to include it in the book *Le Lieu de l'autre* (see above, note 7), 239–48.

22. "Le Corps folié. Mystique et folie aux XVIe et XVIIe siècles," in *La Folie dans la psychanalyse*, ed. Armando Verdiglione (Paris: Payot, 1977), 189–203.

23. Simplified Italian version published in 1977. The full French text, which remained unpublished, has been included in *Le Lieu de l'autre*, 115–34.

24. Like the preceding text, this one, too, has been included in *Le Lieu de l'autre*, 265–99.

25. Jean-Joseph Surin, *Guide Spirituel pour la perfection*, edited and with an introduction by Michel de Certeau, coll. "Christus" (Paris: Desclée de Brouwer,

1963); id., *Correspondance*, edited and with an introduction by Michel de Certeau, preface by Julien Green, coll. "Bibliothèque européenne" (Paris: Desclée de Brouwer, 1966).

26. "La Folie de la vision," *Esprit*, issue devoted to Merleau-Ponty (June 1982): 89–99; "The Madness of Vision," trans. Michael B. Smith, *Enclitic* (Minneapolis, MN) 7/1 (Spring 1983): 24–31.

27. *La Faiblesse de croire*, 315–18.

Mystic Historicities

1. By "historiography" I mean the historical study, "the writing of history," to distinguish between its object (history) and our analysis of it.

2. Dan. 5: 24–28.

3. See Michel de Certeau, *The Mystic Fable*, "The Substantive of a Science," 1: 101–12.

4. [For reasons I state in my "Translator's Note" to *The Mystic Fable*, 1: ix–x, I used the italicized term *mystics*, to translate Certeau's "la mystique," reserving the English "mysticism" for his "mysticisme." In the present (second) volume, however, as the analyses concern the metamorphoses of "la mystique" in nineteenth-century psychotherapy, for example, I have had to abandon that neat system of equivalence and to use *mystics* only when it is clear from the context that it is specifically Christian mysticism of the sixteenth and seventeen centuries that is under discussion.]

5. For this rapid panoramic overview I will abstain from citing the archival collections and "series" involved: the mention of just a few sources would be derisory.

6. The pejorative nature of this term, in the documents, is not a late phenomenon, due to an "antimysticism" of the end of the seventeenth century. Already in the sixteenth, measures taken against the "alumbrados," the placing of works of spirituality on the Index, debates on the Rheno-Flemish, etc., attest everywhere to the suspicion directed toward anything that can be characterized as "mystic." If, for a time, the Neoplatonic reference lends this term a prestige in various alchemist or hermetic sciences (see Wayne Shumaker, *The Occult Sciences in the Renaissance* [Berkeley: University of California Press, 1973]), the autonomization of the "mystic science" continually gave rise (like a new state that did not succeed in becoming recognized) to attempts to excommunicate it or bring it back to theology. Henri Bremond has already mentioned that history (*Histoire littéraire du sentiment religieux en France*, vol. 11, *Le Procès des mystiques*, Paris, 1933) [available online at http://jesusmarie.free.fr/henri_bremond_tome_11.html (accessed 2/5/14)]. But it is not just the backlash to a mystic "invasion"; it dominates and envelops mysticism.

7. See for example Alvaro Huerga, *Historia de los Alumbrados (1570–1630)*, 2 vols. (Madrid, 1978); Antonio Márquez, *Los Alumbrados (1525–1559)* (Madrid, 1980), etc.; see also Louis Cognet, *Crépuscule des mystiques* (Tournai, 1958); Jacques Le Brun, *La Spiritualité de Bossuet* (Paris, 1972), "La querelle du quiétisme," 439–695; etc.

8. What they waken around them is also what they experience in themselves: a primal "passion" that they call "anger," "furor," or "hatred" and that overflows the individual scene, like an originary "excess" also attested in social relations. The alternation between defiance (a risk) and dolorism (a suffering) points to a primal, underlying sadomasochism. They are the results of a "descent" into the roots of existing and attest to a nonidealist vision of human life.

9. See for example Jacques Le Brun, "L'Institution et le corps, lieux de la mémoire," *Corps écrit* 11 (1984): 111–21.

10. Suffice it to mention the impassioned debates of which the classic works were both the object and the expression, Teresa of Avila, John of the Cross, Benet Canfield, etc. See Enrique Llamas Martínez, *Santa Teresa de Jesús y la inquisición española* (Madrid, 1972); Jean Krynen, *Le Cantique spirituel de saint Jean de la Croix commenté et refondu au XVIIe siècle* (Salamanca, 1948); Jean Orcibal, "La Montée du Carmel a-t-elle été interpolée?," *Revue de l'histoire des religions* 166 (1964): 171–213; Roger Duvivier, *La Genèse du "Cantique spirituel" de saint Jean de la Croix* (Paris, 1971); Jean Orcibal, *Benoît de Canfield. La Règle de perfection* (Paris, 1982); etc.

11. So, among others, the anonymous manuscript presented by Jean Guennou (*La Couturière mystique de Paris* [Paris, 1959]). But the work of Marie of the Incarnation, that French Teresa of Avila who left for Quebec, has not even been completely published.

12. Is this the explanation of the incredible fact that there still is no truly critical edition of Teresa of Avila or John of the Cross? And what are we to make of so many others, such as Jeanne de Chantal, known only by an edition that is incomplete and "retouched by pious hands"?

13. See a microanalysis performed on a letter of Surin's, in Certeau, *Mystic Fable*, "Textual Histories (1630–90)," 1: 211–25.

14. See Pierre Delooz, *Sociologie et canonisations* (Liège and The Hague, 1969); André Vauchez, *La Sainteté en Occident aux derniers siècles du Moyen Âge* (Rome, 1981).

15. See, for example, Jean-Louis Fabiani, "Enjeux et usages de la 'crise' dans la philosophie universitaire en France au tournant du siècle," *Annales ESC* 40 (1985): 377–409.

16. Edmund Husserl, *The Crisis of the European Sciences and Transcendental Phenomenology*, trans. David Carr (Evanston: Northwestern University Press, 1970), 4–5.

17. Ibid., 5.

18. Flaubert to Louise Colet, 8 May 1852, *Correspondance*, ed. Jean Bruneau, vol. 2 (Paris, 1980), 88.

19. Particularly in the *Glaubenslehre.*

20. Ernest Renan, "L'Avenir religieux des sociétés modernes," *Revue des Deux-Mondes*, 15 October, 1860, reprinted in his *Œuvres complètes*, ed. Henriette Psichari, vol. 1 (Paris, 1947), 273.

21. Michel de Certeau, "Henri Bremond et la Métaphysique des Saints" [1966], reprinted in *Le Lieu de l'autre. Histoire religieuse et mystique* (Paris, 2005), 59–88; Émile Goichot, *Henri Bremond historien du sentiment religieux* (Paris, 1982), 209–33.

22. Marie Cariou even says "a great treatise on the social order." *Bergson et le fait mystique* (Paris, 1976), 236.

23. Bergson, *The Two Sources of Morality and Religion*, trans. R. Ashley Audrea and Cloudesley Brereton (London: Macmillan, 1935), 200.

24. A felicitous expression by M. Cariou, *Bergson et le fait mystique*, 239, 239, etc. For this analysis, Bergson is in large part indebted to Henri Delacroix, *Études d'histoire et de psychologie du mysticisme* (Paris, 1908), "a book," he said, "which deserves to become a classic" (*Two Sources*, 194n2.) The work remains essential: specifically, it strongly emphasizes that the nature of the mystic experience is to be an "acting" even if it is not that of the subject (*Études*, 235, apropos of Madame Guyon).

25. Émile Poulat provides a panoramic view of this scientific literature on mysticism, from 1895 to 1935, in *Critique et mystique* (Paris, 1984), 254–306.

26. Jules Sagerat, *La Vague mystique* (Paris, 1920); see É. Poulat, *Critique et mystique.*

27. See David James Fisher, "Sigmund Freud and Romain Rolland," *American Imago* 33, no. 1 (1976): 1–57.

28. For example in the letter of 15 November 1920 to Georg Groddeck: "Now every clever person comes to a point where he starts to turn mystical, where his most personal thinking begins." Georg Groddeck, *The Meaning of Illness*, trans. Gertrud Mander (New York: International Universities Press, 1977), 54. See Michel de Certeau and Mireille Cifali, "Entretien: Mystique et psychanalyse," *Le Bloc-notes de la psychanalyse* 4 (1984): 135–61.

29. Freud to Romain Rolland, 19 January 1930, quoted by Fisher, "Sigmund Freud and Romain Rolland," 38.

30. On this second point, see Serge Moscovici, *Essai sur l'histoire humaine de la nature* (Paris, 1968), a critical examination of the division that has long separated the social history of class or political power conflict from natural history.

31. See Fabiani, "Enjeux et usages," 38.

32. Stephen Sharot, *Messianism, Mysticism and Magic* (Chapel Hill, NC, 1982), 13–16, 20, 255. And already, apropos of the religious phenomenon, the more general reflections of Norman Birnbaum, "Beyond Marx in the

Sociology of Religion," in *Beyond the Classics? Essays in the Scientific Study of Religion*, ed. C. Y. Glock and P. E. Hammond (New York, 1973), 3–70, or of Clifford Geertz, *The Interpretation of Cultures* (New York, 1973), "Religion as a Cultural System," 87–125.

33. Ernst Troeltsch, *Social Teaching of the Christian Churches* (London, 1931), 734–36, 743–49, 795–900, etc.; Max Weber, *Economy and Society* (New York, 1968), 544–51, etc.

34. A constant, spiritual, and literary theme that shifts toward the prince the allegiance or protests earlier addressed to the pope. Teresa of Avila testifies to this only when her ambition, little woman [*femmelette*] that she is, is to "speak to those who govern" (*Libro de la vida*, 21). See Steven Ozment, *Mysticism and Dissent* (New Haven, 1973), a theme that goes back to Engels (*The Peasant War in Germany*) and Ernst Bloch (*Thomas Münzer as Theologian of the Revolution*) and is found as late as Perez Zagorin, *Rebels and Rulers, 1500–1660* (Cambridge, UK, 1982).

35. There is an entire literature on the subject, including one that makes the royal person the theater par excellence of a confrontation between "the soul" and power. See J. G. A. Pocock, *The Machiavellian Moment* (Princeton, 1975); Hans Blumenberg, *The Legitimacy of the Modern Age* (Cambridge, MA, 1983), 123–226.

36. See Marc Bloch, *The Royal Touch: Sacred Monarchy and Scrofula in England and France* [1924], trans. J. E. Anderson (London: Routledge and Kegan Paul, 1973), 186–213.

37. See her letter of 18 September 1577 to Philip II, and *Las Fundaciones*, chap. 29.

38. See Jean-Louis Thireau, *Les Idées politiques de Louis XIV* (Paris, 1973), 33–56.

39. One might extend to the mystics the (too unilateral) thesis of Michael Walzer, *The Revolution of the Saints* (Cambridge, MA, 1965). David Hume, moreover, in his *History of England*, had already analyzed that political significance—and for him, the danger—of "enthusiasm." See Laurence L. Bongie, *David Hume: Prophet of the Counter-Revolution* (Oxford, 1965), xii–xiii.

40. Dr. Michéa, "Extase," in *Nouveau Dictionnaire de médecine et de chirurgie pratique*, ed. Dr. Jaccoud (Paris, 1871), 14: 337–347. In particular, he targets the *Nosologie méthodique* of F. Boissier de Sauvages (trans. Gouvion [Lyon, 1772], 10 vols.).

41. "Our predecessors (*Vorgänger*) in psychoanalysis, the Catholic directors of conscience," he wrote to Pfister on 18 March 1909. Sigmund Freud and Oskar Pfister, *Briefe, 1909–1939*, ed. Ernst-L. Freud and Heinrich Meng (Frankfurt am Main, 1963), 18.

42. Pierre Janet, *De l'angoisse à l'extase* [1926], 2nd ed., 2 vols. (Paris, 1975).

43. William James, *The Varieties of Religious Experience* [1902] (New York, 1958), "Mysticism," 292–328.

44. James Leuba, *The Psychology of Religious Mysticism* (London, 1925), who had the honor of being translated into French by Lucien Herr. Prior to that, "Les Tendances fondamentales des mystiques chrétiens" [Fundamental Tendencies of the Christian Mystics] had been published in French in the *Revue philosophique* in July and November 1902. Henri Delacroix (*Études*, 381–97) held, on that basis, the "theory" of Leuba to be "the most penetrating and the most broad," but, more the philosopher, he replaced "the unconsciousness" that the American placed at the center of his "theory" with "the irrational apperception of an essential will, distributed throughout nature, and which nature repeats in innumerable variations, in the way music chants the movements of a soul" (389). It is Leuba, rather than William James, whom Joseph Maréchal attacks (*Études sur la psychologie des mystiques*, vol. 2 [Paris, 1937], 383–407), scandalized particularly by the assimilation of "the lofty Christian contemplation" to "the trance of savages."

45. Robert Charles Zaehner, *Mysticism, Sacred and Profane* [1957] (Oxford, 1978). The work was inspired by Aldous Huxley (*The Doors of Perception* [London, 1954]) and Jung.

46. Rudolf Otto, *Mysticism East and West*, trans. Bertha L. Bracey and Richenda C. Payne (New York, 1932), esp. 139–64, on the "differentiation of mystical feeling" and the "differences" between mystics, apropos of Śankara and Meister Eckhart. A great text, still to be meditated on.

47. Walter T. Stace, *The Teaching of the Mystics* (New York, 1960), and especially *Mysticism and Philosophy* (Philadelphia, 1960). See already Evelyn Underhill, *Mysticism* (London, 1911), who popularized an entire trend.

48. Ninian Smart, "Interpretation and Mystical Experience," *Religious Studies* 1, no. 1 (1965). From the same author, "Mystical Experience," in *Art, Mind and Religion*, ed. William H. Capitan and Daniel D. Merrill (Pittsburgh, 1967), 133–58; and "History of Mysticism," in *Encyclopedia of Philosophy*, ed. Paul Edwards (New York), vol. 5.

49. Otto, *Mysticism East and West*, 139.

50. Steven Katz, "Language, Epistemology and Mysticism," in *Mysticism and Philosophical Analysis*, ed. Katz (New York, 1978), 22–74. From the same author, *Jewish Ideas and Concepts* (New York, 1977).

51. See M. de Certeau, *Mystic Fable*, 1: 113–50.

52. Leszek Kolakowski, *Chrétiens sans Église. La conscience religieuse et le lien confessionnel au XVIIe siècle*, trans. Anna Posner (Paris, 1969). [This work, *Swiadomosc religijna i wiez koscielna: studia nad chrzescijanstwem bezwyznaniowym siedemnastego wieku* (Religious Consciousness and the Church: Studies in Seventeenth-Century Nondenominational Christianity), has not yet been translated into English.]

53. Ibid., 1–68.

54. On the innovative points and the weak ones of this historical interpretation, see Michel de Certeau, *L'Absent de l'histoire* (Paris, 1973), "La mort de l'histoire globale: Leszek Kolakowski," 109–14.

55. Gilles-Gaston Granger, *Essai d'une philosophie du style* (Paris, 1968), 13–16, 187–216.

Chapter One

1. [*The Collected Poems of Octavio Paz, 1957–1987*, trans. Eliot Weinberger (New York: New Directions, 1987), 435.]

2. The *De icona* or *De visione Dei* has unfortunately not yet appeared in the large edition of *Opera Omnia* of Nicholas of Cusa, published by the Academy of Heidelberg, Leipzig, and then Hamburg (F. Meiner, 1932–), or in his *Philosophische Schriften*, 2 vols., ed. Alfred Petzelt (Stuttgart: W. Kohlammer, 1949), but it does appear in the *Philosophisch-theologische Schriften*, ed. Leo Gabriel, 3 vols. (Vienna: Herder, 1964–67), with a German translation, 3: 94–219. Therefore I refer to the Viennese edition (referred to as Vienna) for *De icona*, and to that of Heidelberg (hereafter Heid., with indication of the volume and fascicule) or to that of Stuttgart (hereafter Stutt.) for the other works. I have also availed myself of the *Opera*, ed. Jacques Lefèvre d'Étaples (Paris: J. Bade, 1514) in the Basel edition (Henri Petrus, 1565) (hereafter Basel), and several translations: *Traité de la Vision de Dieu*, trans. Sieur de Golefe (Paris: C. Chappelain, 1630); *La Vision de Dieu*, trans. E. Vansteenberghe (Louvain: Museum Lessianum, 1925); *The Single Eye*, trans. Giles Randall (London, 1646); *The Vision of God*, trans. E. Gurney Salter [1928] (New York: F. Ungar, 1960); as well as of the German translation of Vienna. See also Eduard Zellinger, *Cusanus-Konkordanz* (Munich, 1960), the doctrinal classification of which makes it hardly consultable. Nicholas of Cusa himself, when he subsequently cites his treatise, refers to *De icona* (for example *De possest* 58, Heid., XI, 2, pp. 69–70), whereas the old editions all bear the title *De visione Dei sive De icona*.

3. *De pace fidei*, Praefatio editorum (R. Klibansky and H. Bascour), Heid., VII, pp. ix–xiii; text, esp. chaps. 1–6 and 19, pp. 1–17, 61–63.

4. Thus, on 14 July 1454, Geissenfeld (of Tegernsee) wrote to Weilhaim (in Melk) on the topic of the treatise: "J'en ferai une copie pendant les heures qui me restent pour écrire et je vous l'enverrai au moment des vendanges" [I will make you a copy of it during my remaining hours to write and I will send it to you during the wine harvest]; a text published by Edmond Vansteenberghe, *Autour de la Docte Ignorance*, Beiträge zur Geschichte der Philosophie des

Mittelalters 14.2–4 (Münster, 1915),. That work supplies a large portion of the documents pertaining to the debate on *De icona*; see 105–220.

5. On Marquard Sprenger, see Vansteenberghe, *Autour de la Docte Ignorance*, 66–77.

6. See Edmond Vansteenberghe, *Le "De ignota litteratura" de Jean Wenck de Herrenberg contre Nicolas de Cues*, Beiträge zur Geschichte der Philosophie des Mittelalters 8.6 (Münster, 1910). [See, in English, Jasper Hopkins, *Nicholas of Cusa's Debate with John Wenck: A Translation and an Appraisal of* De Ignota Litteratura *and* Apologia Doctae Ignorantiae (Minneapolis: A. J. Banning Press, 1981)]; Rudolf Haubst, *Studien zu Nikolaus von Kues und Johannes Wenck*, Beiträge zur Geschichte der Philosophie des Mittelalters 38.1 (Münster, 1955), 118–36. Haubst ascribes the date 1542 to *De ignota litteratura*; G. Ritter, etc., give it the date 1548: see Robert E. Lerner, *The Heresy of the Free Spirit in the Later Middle Ages* (Berkeley, 1972), 168–74.

7. *Apologia doctae ignorantiae*, Stutt., 1: 274 [trans. Jasper Hopkins, in *Complete Philosophical and Theological Treatises of Nicholas of Cusa*, vol. 1 (Minneapolis: A. J. Banning Press, 2001), 460].

8. Vansteenberghe, *Autour de la Docte Ignorance*, 15, 104, etc. This is to borrow the expression already used by Bernard of Waging (from Tegernsee) in his *Defensorium Laudatorii Docte Ignorancie* [1459]: the Cusan literature was for him a "mystic theosophy" (text edited by Vansteenberghe, 175).

9. Jacques Ridé, *L'image du Germain dans la pensée et la littérature allemandes, de la redécouverte de Tacite à la fin du XVIe siècle*, vol. 1 (Lille and Paris, 1977), 79–191; and Robert Folz, *L'idée d'Empire en Occident du Ve au XIVe siècle* (Paris, 1953), 160–84.

10. See the preface of *De concordantia catholica*: "I have collected with great care a large number of originals (*originalia*) in the stock (*armaria*: chests and libraries) of old monasteries where they were lost for having been long mistreated. . . . Everything, here, is drawn from ancient originals" (Heid., XIV, 1, p. 3).

11. Ludwig Pralle, *Die Wiederentdeckung des Tacitus. Ein Beitrag zur Geistengeschichte Fuldae und zur Biographie des jungen Cusanus* (Fulda, 1952). See Poggio's letters, in Phyllis W. G. Gordan, *Two Renaissance Book Hunters* (New York, 1974): Poggio is particularly excited by the unpublished Plautus manuscripts that Nicholas of Cusa is to take to Rome (135, 138, 160); he also notes how hurt and ill-received the latter was by the pontifical court at the end of 1427 (115). On the exaggerated hopes raised in Rome by the "discoveries" of Nicholas of Cusa in the library of the cathedral of Cologne, see Paolo Botta, *Il cardinale Niccolò di Cusa* (Milan, 1928).

12. *De concordantia catholica*, II, 29, and III, 39.

13. See Edmond Vansteenberghe, "Quelques lectures de jeunesse de Nicolas

de Cues," *Archives d'histoire doctrinale et littéraire du Moyen Âge* 3 (1928): 275–84; Rudolf Haubst, "Die Thomas—und Proklos—Exzerpte des 'Nicolaus Treverensis' in codicillo Strassburg 84," *Mitteilungen und Forschungsbeiträge der Cusanus-Gesellschaft* 1 (1961): 9–11.

14. *Apologia doctae ignorantiae*, Stutt., 1: 291. See Herbert Wackerzapp, *Der Einfluss Meisters Eckharts auf die ersten philosophischen Schriften des N. von K. (1440–1450)*, Beiträge zur Geschichte der Philosophie des Mittelalters 39.3 (Münster, 1962).

15. *De conjecturis*, II, 15, Stutt., 1: 188.

16. *De concordantia*, preface, Heid., XIV, 1, pp. 2–3 (my emphasis) [English trans., *The Catholic Concordance*, ed. and trans. Paul E. Sigmund (New York: Cambridge University Press, 1992), 3 (trans. modified).] *De docta ignorantia* begins the same way. Nicholas of Cusa stresses the "barbarous clumsiness" (*ineptiae barbarae*) that, as a "German" (*Germanus*), he addresses to Giuliano Cesarini (1398–1444), the cardinal of Saint-Ange, an Italian legist and humanist (see DHGE, vol. 12, cols. 220–49), but he asserts "the immense labor" (*labor ingens*), the result of which was "the way of reasoning" (*ratiocinandi modum*) he presents him with (*Apologia doctae ignorantiae*, Stutt., 1: 1).

17. See Erich Auerbach, *Literary Language and Its Public in Late Latin Antiquity and in the Middle Ages*, trans. R. Manheim (London, 1965), 25–81.

18. Bernard Guenée, *L'Occident aux XIVe et XVe siècles. Les États* (Paris, 1971), 117 (concerning the end of the Middle Ages) and 299: "In the forming of the German national feeling, language is what played the essential role."

19. See Paul E. Sigmund, *Nicholas of Cusa and Medieval Political Thought* (Cambridge, MA: Harvard University Press, 1963).

20. See the pioneer work by Ernst Cassirer, *The Individual and the Cosmos in Renaissance Philosophy* [1927], trans. Mario Domandi (Chicago: University of Chicago Press, 2010).

21. Ibid., 9, on "the general picture of the *Stufenkosmos*, a *graduated cosmos*" in the Middle Ages.

22. *De conjecturis*, II, 8, Stutt., 1: 173, in which he is clearly speaking of his own experience.

23. One of the first, Johannes Wenck (*De ignota literature*, text in Vansteenberghe, *Le "De ignota litteratura,"* 22), reproves Nicholas, to whom the "rare" is rather a stimulant to thought ("Rara quidem, et si monstra sint, nos movere solent," he says apropos of his Germanisms at the beginning of *De docta ignorantia*, Heid., I, 2, p. 4), or a cause of admiration ("Pulchra atque rara narras," says the interlocutor of the *Idiota*, I, Heid., V, 14, p. 16). On the pejorative sense of *rarus*, see Wackerzapp, *Der Einfluss Meisters Eckharts*, 14n71.

24. Pierre Francastel, *La Figure et le lieu. L'ordre visuel du Quattrocento* (Paris, 1967), 230. And Bruno Zevi, "L'operazione linguistica di Leon Battista Alberti," *L'Architettura* 18 (1972): 142–43. Thomas Cajetan will develop this

problematics of the "speech in several senses" (*diversi modo loqui*), which attempts to multiply the semantic potentiality of words on the basis of linguistic unity.

25. There is an entire research project to be carried out on the *plays of meaning* suggested to Cusa by the proximity of sounds, a very fifteenth-century poetic "art" (see below, note 71). The same is true of the *plays on letters:* for example on *i* and *n* in "in," or on the repetition of the *e* in "posse," "esse" and "nexus," the "e" being to language what God is to the world, in *De possest*, 54, Heid., XI, 2, pp. 65–69.

26. Cassirer, *Individual and the Cosmos*, 19 (Cassirer's emphasis).

27. See the remarks of Raymond Klibansky and Hans Gerhard Senger, "De latinitate Cusani," Praefatio editorum, *De venatione Sapientiae*, Heid., XII, pp. xxi–xxii; and Hans Gerhard Senger, "Die Sprache der Metaphysik," in *Nikolaus von Kues* (Fribourg in B. and Münster, 1979), 95–97. I do indeed interpret the Cusan *asperas compositiones* as the effects of a German speech pattern on Latin.

28. Cassirer, *Individual and the Cosmos*, 20.

29. "Beryl stones are bright, white, and clear. To them are given both concave and convex forms." (*De beryllo*, 2) [*Complete Philosophical and Theological Treatises of Nicholas of Cusa*, trans. Jasper Hopkins (Minneapolis: A. J. Banning Press, 2001), 792]. Like the picture for *De icona*, it is the object that leads to the treatise bearing its name (1458). The same holds for the game of bowling, in *De ludo globi* (1463); for the top (*trochus*), in *De possest* (1460), or for the spoon made by the "profane," in the *Idiota* (1450). On the clock, see *De icona*, 11: in Italy, public clocks had just begun to be installed everywhere (Paul Lawrence Rose, *The Italian Renaissance of Mathematics: Studies on Humanists and Mathematicians from Petrarch to Galileo* [Geneva: Droz, 1975], 7).

30. *Idiota*, III, 2 and 5 [trans. Hopkins, 150].

31. Maurice de Gandillac, *La Philosophie de Nicolas de Cues* (Paris, 1941), 446. Giordano Bruno, a fervent reader of Nicholas, will explicate the distinction between these two "sights": *Des fureurs héroïques*, trans. Paul-Henri Michel (Paris, 1954), 218 (dialogue 4).

32. *De docta ignorantia*, III, 12, Peroratio [trans. Hopkins, 151]. On Cesarini, see above, note 16.

33. See Gandillac, *La Philosophie de Nicolas de Cues*, 111.

34. *Apologia doctae ignorantiae*, Stutt., 1: 282–83 [trans. Hopkins, 467, modified].

35. *De conjecturis*, I, 11–12, Stutt., 1: 140.

36. Torquato Tasso, *Del giudizio sovra la sua gerusalemme da lui medesimo reformata*, in *Le prose diverse*, ed. C. Guasti (Florence, 1875), vol. 1.

37. *De possest*, Heid., XI, 2, p. 54. *See De docta ignorantia*, 1: 11, etc.

38. *De Possest*, Heid., XI, 2, p. 71: "mathematice aenigmatizare."

39. *De non aliud*, Basel, p. 189, on the meaning of *videre.*

40. See Erwin Panofsky, *Early Netherlandish Painting* (New York, 1971), 149–204, and especially his beautiful analysis of the *Virgin in the Church* by Van Eyck as presence of the immaterial, 144–48.

41. 1 Corinthians 13: 12. See *De docta ignorantia*, I, 11: "quasi in speculo et in aenigmate"; *De beryllo*, 1, etc. Nicholas of Cusa frequently associates these words.

42. Moritz Cantor, a good judge, quoted by Cassirer, *Individual and the Cosmos*, 59 [trans. modified]. Pierre Duhem, to the contrary, devotes a hundred pages to explaining the "verbal juggling" of the Cusan, his plagiary and mathematical errors: he concludes by recognizing in him the worthy precursor "of Fichte and Hegel": *Le Système du monde*, vol. 10 (Paris, 1959), 247–347. It is well known that for Giordano Bruno, Nicholas is "il divino Cusano," "the author of the most beautiful secrets of geometry" (*De la causa*, 5th dialogue), and, for Kepler, "divinus mihi Cusanus" (see Alexandre Koyré, *Études d'histoire de la pensée scientifique* [Paris, 1973], 336).

43. Cassirer, *Individual and the Cosmos*, 31, 33, 36–37. See the remarks of Mariano Alvarez-Gómez, *Die verborgene Gegenwart des Unendlichen bei Nikolaus von Kues* (Munich and Strasbourg, 1968), 59ff., on the pivotal importance of *De icona*.

44. *De beryllo*, 1; *Idiota*, I, 1.

45. *Apologia doctae ignorantiae*, Stutt., 1: 288.

46. Certeau, *Mystic Fable*, 1: 188, 200.

47. The Van der Weyden painting, a self-portrait, has disappeared, but there is a copy of it (a tapestry conserved in the Berne Museum). See Erwin Panofsky, "Facies illa Rogeri maximi pictoria," in *Late Classical and Mediaeval Studies in Honor of Albert Mathias Friend Jr.*, ed. Kurt Weitzmann (Princeton, 1955), 392–400; id., *Early Netherlandish Painting* (New York, 1971), 248. The self-portrait was in the right-hand part of one of the *Examples of Justice* (*Justice of Trajan and Herkinbald*).

48. The paintings from Nuremberg, Koblenz, and Brixen have not been identified. As for the all-seeing "figure" he may have had at his disposal, Nicholas of Cusa wrote to Tegernsee on 14 September 1453 that he "has a painting of it at home" and that he "has a painter" he will ask to make a copy of it for the addressees of the treatise (text published by Vansteenberghe, *Autour de la Docte Ignorance*, 116).

49. *De icona*, "Praefatio," Vienna, 94–98 [trans. Hopkins, 680–82, modified].

50. Hildegard of Bingen, *Scivias*, ed. A. Fürkötter and A. Carlevaris, Corpus Christianorum, CM, vols. 43–43 A (Turnhout, 1978): Pars prima, visio prima, pp. 7 and 9; Pars tertia, visio octava, p. 481. See Josef Schomer, *Die*

Illustrationen zu den Visionen der hl. Hildegard als künstlerische Neuschöpfung, dissertation, Bonn, 1937.

51. See [Jacques de Voragine], *Legenda aurea Sanctorum*, ed. P. Lopez (Madrid: J. Garcia, 1688), 241 (legenda 64); and, in Teodor de Wyzeva's translation (though a bit approximate) *La Légende dorée* (Paris, 1929), 310–11.

52. In Nuremburg, Nicholas obtained manuscripts and astronomical instruments from Prague (see Barbara Obrist, *Les Débuts de l'imagerie alchimique du XIVe au XVe siècle* [Paris, 1982], 282). There he met the astronomer Georg Peurbach (see below, note 108). Thus it is a city placed beneath the sign of the zodiac.

53. Thus the *Crucifixion* by Rogier Van der Weyden in the Kunsthistorisches Museum in Vienna contains (left panel of the triptych) a Veronica holding the linen on which a *Holy Face* of Jesus looks at the viewer (see also *Veronica's Veil* by Quentin Metsys, or the reproductions of the *Volto sancto* distributed by the merchants of Lucca). We also have, from the same Van der Weyden, women's faces fixed on the onlooker (see *Portrait of a Woman*, Museum of Berlin). Nordic painting presents numerous cases of "all-seeing": during this period, it generally seeks "an impression of including the beholder within the represented space" (E. Panofsky, *Perspective as Symbolic Form*, trans C. S. Wood [New York: Zone Books, 1991], 81).

54. Further on (chap. 9, etc.), he invokes "that painting of your Face," in speaking of Jesus, but that specification seems to be a result of the discursive development (which runs through the forms of the divine look successively) rather than concerning the painting itself.

55. *De icona*, foreword.

56. Text edited by Vansteenberghe, *Autour de la Docte Ignorance*, 116.

57. Ibid., for the letter to Aindorffer. On this aspect of Nicholas V (1447–55), see Rose, *Italian Renaissance of Mathematics*, 36–44.

58. *Complementum theologicum*, 1, Basel, p. 1107 [trans. Hopkins, modified, 747].

59. Michael Baxandall, *Painting and Experience in Fifteenth Century Italy* (Oxford, 1974), 41ff.; Daniel Arasse, "Fonctions de l' image religieuse au XVe siècle," *Faire croire* (Rome, 1981), 131–46.

60. Since the tenth century, the novices of Tegernsee performed jugglery (*joci*), mimicked animals, and told the content of fables. See a poem by Fromond on them, in Edgar de Bruyne, *Études d'esthétique médiévale*, vol. 1 (Bruges, 1946), 179.

61. Buffon, *Œuvres complètes*, 4: 73, quoted and commented on, without specification of the edition consulted, by Jean Petitot, "Psychanalyse et logique: plaidoyer pour l'impossible," in *Le Lien social, Confrontation*, ed. René Major (Paris, 1981), 171–234 (a study the perspectives of which might shed much

light on the Cusan preface). See also Gilles Deleuze, *Différence et répétition* (Paris, 1969), 309–11.

62. *Complementum theologicum*, 9. See on this point Gandillac, *La Philosophie de Nicolas de Cues*, 156, 159, 405–7, 420–21, etc.

63. Henri Rey-Flaud, *Le Cercle magique. Essai sur le théâtre en rond à la fin du Moyen Âge* (Paris, 1973), 44–50, 299–301.

64. See S. Münster (the German Strabo), "Germaniae atque aliarum regionum . . . Descriptio" (Basel: Andreas Cratander, 1530).

65. See the famous texts of *De docta ignorantia*, II, 11–12 [trans. Hopkins, 161–62].

66. See E. H. Gombrich, "Light, Form and Texture in Fifteenth Century Painting," *Journal of the Royal Society of Arts* 112 (1964): 826–49. A medieval Dionysian tradition, however (for example Ulrich de Strasbourg, known to Nicholas of Cusa), defines beauty by its luminosity: see Bruyne, *Études d'esthétique médiévale*, 3: 262–77.

67. William of Conches (d. 1154), *De philosophia mundi*, IV, 25, "De oculis" (Migne, PL 172, cols. 95–96): "Visualis spiritus usque ad rem pervenit," etc. This text was endlessly recopied during the Middle Ages and published by the fifteenth century in Nuremberg, under the name of Honoré d'Autun, whom Nicholas quotes, for example in his *Apologia doctae ignorantiae*, Stutt., 1: 294. On William of Conches, see Bruyne, *Études d'esthétique médiévale*, 2: 112–13 and 255–79, particularly on the ability of the "eye" to recognize abstract "forms": "Formae vero oculis possunt discerni in opere" (quoted 262). The School of Chartres, moreover, played a decisive role in the Cusan's thought, as did Thierry de Chartres, even more than did William of Conches; see Duhem, *Le Système du monde*, 10: 269–72. The Euclidian conception was opposed by the Stoic theory (it is the forms of things that come to the eye) mentioned and rejected by William of Conches. The Stoic theory, adopted by Ibn al-Haytham (Alhazen), translated into Latin at the end of the twelfth century by Gérard de Crémone (*Opticae thesaurus Alhazeni Arabi libri VII*), will slowly win out in the sixteenth century, starting with *De artificiali Perspectiva* (Toul, 1505) by Jean Pèlerin, called "the Viator" (see Liliane Brion-Guerry, *Jean Pèlerin Viator* [Paris, 1962]). Nicholas of Cusa also knew Alhazen: *Apologia doctae ignorantiae*, Stutt., 1: 282–83.

68. "Les objets de la vue peuvent être sentis, non seulement par le moyen de l'action qui, étant en eux, tend vers les yeux, mais aussi par le moyen de celle qui, étant dans les yeux, tend vers eux" (*Dioptrique*, Discours 1er, ed. André Bridoux (Paris, 1953), 183). ["The objects of vision can be sensed not only by means of the action which, being within them, tends towards the eyes, but also by means of that which, being in the eyes, tends towards them." http://science.larouchepac.com/fermat/Descartes%20--%20Dioptrique.pdf, pp. 3–4, accessed 3/8/14.]

69. Marsilio Ficino, *Commentaire sur le Banquet de Platon* [1469], VII, 10, éd. Raymond Marcel (Paris, 1956), 254–56. [See Sears Reynolds Jayne, *Commentary on Plato's Symposium on Love* (Dallas: Spring Publications, 1985), 113 for the Latin and 228 in English. As the French trans. followed by Certeau remains very close to the Latin, I have chosen to translate the former here.—Trans.]

70. See Francastel, *La Figure et le lieu*, 244–45.

71. See Paul Zumthor, *Langue, texte, énigme* (Paris, 1975), 25–88; id., *Le Masque et la lumière* (Paris, 1978), 244–81.

72. See Petitot, "Psychanalyse et logique," 201.

73. "I exist because You look upon me" (*De icona*, chap. iv) [trans. Hopkins, 685]. See the analyses of Jacques Lacan, *The Four Fundamental Concepts of Psychoanalysis*, ed. Jacques-Alain Miller, trans. Alan Sheridan (New York: Norton, 2005), 67–119 "Of the Gaze as Objet Petit *a*."

74. "Landscape" in the broad sense of a reciprocity between places, and not in the strict sense of an autonomization of the background in relation to the figures of the painting, which is a later, originally Nordic phenomenon, analyzed by E. H. Gombrich, *Norm and Form* (London, 1966), 107–21.

75. There is, he says, masculinity in femininity and vice versa, even in what involves the signs of sexual difference. By his *nature*, the individual is a sort of monad. See *De conjecturis*, II, 8, Stutt., 1: 172.

76. *De icona*, 10 [trans. Hopkins, 698, modified].

77. Such as Thomas de Verceil: see Bruyne, *Études d'esthétique médiévale*, 3: 58ff.

78. See Petitot, "Psychanalyse et logique," 209.

79. E. H. Gombrich, *Art and Illusion* (London: Phaidon Press, 1969), 222, etc.

80. These "imaginary experiments" practiced by Galileo, Descartes, etc., have "a role that is intermediary between mathematics and reality." See Koyré, *Études d'histoire de la pensée scientifique*, 224–71, on Galileo, and the reservations of Maurice Clavelin, *La Philosophie naturelle de Galilée* (Paris, 1968), 389–459.

81. See for example Geissenfeld's letter (from Tegernsee) to Weilhaim (in Melk), on 15 July 1454, text published by Vansteenberghe, *Autour de la Docte Ignorance*, 219.

82. In this paragraph, I am quoting from and commenting on *De icona*, 1, at the beginning. My emphases. [Trans. Hopkins, 682, modified].

83. This etymology is also found in *De icona*, 8, in *Complementum theologicum*, 13 (Basel, 1119), in *De quaerendo deum* (Heid., IV, 1, p. 22, or in the form of an alternative between a "seeing" and a "running" God: "Theos dicitur a theōrō sive theō, quod est video et curro," ibid., p. 15), in *De Deo abscondito*,

14, 1 (Stutt., 1: 207), etc. See Dionysius the Areopagite, *On the Divine Names*, XII, 2 (Migne, *PG* 3, col. 969 C).

84. The treatise is punctuated with returns to the painting (chaps. 4, 9, 10, 15, 22, etc.) of the type: "as is befigured by this painted image that I look upon," etc. (chap. 9). This movement corresponds not only to the ability of the image to "cause to speak" and induce developments, but also to the need for discursive expression to retrieve within the figure *the unity* of these developments and their intuitive totalization.

85. See above, note 58.

86. Latin text edited in Vansteenberghe, *Autour de la Docte Ignorance*, 113. The letter uses expressions from the *Apologia doctae ignorantiae*: "Testimonium de visu esse certius," etc. (Stutt., 1: 283).

87. Psalm 33: 9 (Vulgate). Oddly (or lucidly?), J. Wenck had taken the verse as the epigraph of his pamphlet (*De ignota litteratura*) against Nicholas: see above, note 6.

88. *De icona*, 5 ("Quod videre sit gustare . . ."), Vienna, 108ff. [trans. Hopkins, 686ff.]; *De icona*, 17 [trans. Hopkins, 713–17].

89. *De icona*, 12 [trans. Hopkins, modified, 701ff.]

90. See above, note 8.

91. See above, note 16.

92. *Apologia doctae ignorantiae*, Stutt., 1: 282–83: moreover, Cusa speaks there of what he has *not seen*, and not of what he has *seen*; letter to G. Aindorffer, text edited in Vansteenberghe, *Autour de la Docte Ignorance*, 116.

93. *Apologia doctae ignorantiae*, dedication, Stutt., 1: 1. Maurice de Gandillac (in Nicolas de Cues, *Œuvres choisies* [Paris, 1942], 66–67) euphemizes the text inordinately, in translating *barbaras ineptias* as "approximations sans élégance" and in omitting the other occurrence of *ineptus* (Louis Moulinier, in his translation *De la docte ignorance* [Paris, 1932], translated "extravagances maladroites"). On the other hand, Gandillac's translation rendering of *suscipere* ("croire" [believe] instead of "adopter" [adopt], "accueillir" [welcome, receive]) does much to clarify the text.

94. See Michel de Certeau, "L'institution du croire," in *Recherches de science religieuse* 71 (1983): 61–80.

95. See above, note 6.

96. "Le silence éternel de ces espaces infinis m'effraie." *Pensées*, Brunschvicg frag. 206; and Louis Marin, *La Critique du discours* (Paris, 1975), 215–38, 343–51.

97. See Tzvetan Todorov, *The Fantastic: A Structural Approach Introduction to a Literary Genre*, trans. Richard Howard (Ithaca, NY: Cornell University Press, 1975), 107–23.

98. *De docta ignorantia*, I, 8 [trans. Hopkins, 14–15].

99. On zero, "une chiffre donnant umbre et encombre" [a figure causing confusion and difficulty], as Nicolas Chuquet [1484] says, see Florian Cajori, *A History of Mathematical Notations* (La Salle, IL, 1928), 1: 124–139 (on the authors of the fifteenth century); Geneviève Guitel, *Histoire comparée des numérations écrites* (Paris, 1975), 653–706; Karl Menninger, *Number Words and Number Symbols*, trans. P. Broncer (Cambridge, MA, 1969), 396–406, 420–24, etc.

100. *De icona*, 14.

101. See *De conjecturis*, I, 11: "De unitate et alteritate."

102. Plotinus, *Enneads*, VI, IX.

103. Spinoza, letter 50 (to Jarig Jelles, 2 June 1674), *Œuvres complètes*, ed. Roland Caillois et al. (Paris, 1962), 1230 (translation modified, my emphasis); and Stanislas Breton, *Unicité et monothéisme* (Paris, 1981), 19–35.

104. See, in another context, the suggestions of Petitot, "Psychanalyse et logique," 214–25, on the Lacanian "signifier." There are, incidentally, pages in Jacques Lacan on the look that are very close to Cusa's analysis (see above, note 73).

105. *De Icona*, 3.

106. Ibid. In this text, "view" or "sight" (*visus*) participates in the ambiguity of the "one": the term sometimes designates the "look" (the principle, which is *videre*) and sometimes one of the "points of view" (*rationes*) on the principle, such as hearing, taste, etc.

107. See Rudolf Wittkower and B. A. R. Carter, "The Perspective of Piero della Francesca's *Flagellation*," *Journal of the Warburg and Courtauld Institute* 16 (1953): 292–302.

108. See, for example, Rose, *Italian Renaissance of Mathematics*, 91–94.

109. See Gandillac, *La Philosophie de Nicolas de Cues*, 91–94.

110. See above, note 58.

111. See above, note 42.

112. *De icona*, foreword, in which Cusa explains his project.

113. In *Art Press*, issue titled "Audiovisuel," 1982.

114. To characterize "learned ignorance," Cusa reuses with insistence the Dionysian vocabulary of "dark shadows," "cloud," etc.; he himself points out, in his *Apologia*, his indebtedness and admiration for the Areopagite.

115. "The necessary impossible," a formality of coincidence. See *De icona*, 9, 13, 17; letter to Aindorffer, in Vansteenberghe, *Autour de la Docte Ignorance*, 115: "goûter la nécessité dans l'impossibilité" [to savor the necessity in impossibility]; etc.

116. At the end of the *Apologia*, Nicholas mentions, scattered through Italy (*per Italiam*), a few "studious spirits" among whom his "fervent" interlocutor seems to have, with "much fruit," cultivated "the admirable seed" of learned

ignorance (Stutt., 1: 299). A rare case, and one that remains the accomplishment of an Italian intermediary.

117. See Joseph M. Victor, *Charles de Bovelles (1479–1553)* (Geneva, 1978), 15–25; M. de Gandillac, "L'art bovillien des opposés," *Charles de Bovelles en son 5e centenaire (1479–1979)* (Paris, 1982), 157–70; Guy Bedouelle, *Lefèvre d'Étaples et l'intelligence des Écritures* (Geneva, 1976), 60–70; Frances A. Yates, *Giordano Bruno* (London, 1971), 124, 244, etc.

118. Text edited in Vansteenberghe, *Autour de la Docte Ignorance*, 163–88.

119. See above, note 6.

120. Text edited in Vansteenberghe, *Autour de la Docte Ignorance*, 189–201 (I quote from p. 195). See also E. Vansteenberghe, "Un Écrit de Vincent d'Aggsbach contre Gerson," *Studien zur Geschichte der Philosophie* 1 (1913): 357–64.

121. *De icona*, 6.

122. See Sigmund, *Nicholas of Cusa and Medieval Political Thought*; and the index of *De concordantia* for the word *consensus* (Heid., XIV, 4, p. 509).

123. *De concordantia catholica*, II, 19, Heid., XIV, 2, p. 205.

124. Sigmund, *Nicholas of Cusa and Medieval Political Thought*, esp. 226–28, on Cusa's faithfulness to his principles. See Erich Meuthen, "Nikolaus von Kues in der Entscheidung zwischen Konzil und Papst," in *Nikolaus von Kues als Promoter der Ökumene, Mitteilungen und Forschungsbeiträge der Cusanus Gesellschaft* 9 (1971): 19–33; James E. Biechler, in "Nicholas of Cusa and the End of the Conciliar Movement: A Humanist Crisis of Identity," *Church History* 44 (1975): 5–21.

125. *De icona*, 22, on the coincidence of opposites in Jesus Christ.

126. In this paragraph, I quote and comment on *Idiota*, III, 1, Stutt., 1: 321–22. This third book is devoted to "thought" (*mens*).

127. This "famous philosopher" is probably George of Trebizond, "the prince of Aristotelians," as he was called, who, that year, was living in Bagno di Romagna until July, and then in Florence: see John Monfasani, *George of Trebizond* (Leiden, 1976), 36ff. Later, in Rome, Nicholas, who had met him in Florence, will protect him and order several translations of Plato from him: *Parmenides* and *Laws* (ibid., 321–29).

128. *Idiota*, I, 1.

129. The *Idiota* is presented as a dialogue between three "interlocutors" (books I and II), and then four (book III). Among them, there is the "I" of "the author" (*auctor*), but, as in *De icona*, it serves as the introducer to the word of the "idiot," in whose name Cusa addresses the readers. On the history (which is Rhenish) of the "Friend of God" or *idiotus* in the fifteenth century, see Certeau, *Mystic Fable*, 1: 234–40.

130. *De icona*, 6.

Chapter Two

1. [The French term is "s'entre-tiennent" (hyphenated, exceptionally, to bring out the etymology of "holding one another"), and can mean "speak to each other" as well as "maintain each other."]

2. See especially, besides a classic, Dámaso Alonso, *La poesía de san Juan de la Cruz* [1942], 5th ed. (Madrid, 1962), a few recent works: Eulogio de la Virgen del Carmen, *San Juan de la Cruz y sus escritos* (Madrid, 1969); Roger Duvivier, *La Genèse du "Cantique spirituel" de saint Jean de la Croix* (Paris, 1971); id., *Le Dynamisme spirituel dans la poésie de Jean de la Croix. Lecture du "Cántico spiritual"* (Paris, 1973); Colin P. Thompson, *The Poet and the Mystic: A Study of the "Cántico espiritual" of Saint Juan de la Cruz* (Oxford, 1978). For the texts, see *Obras de san Juan de la Cruz*, ed. Silverio de Santa Teresa, vol. 3: *Cántico espiritual* (Burgos, 1930); *Le Cantique spirituel de saint Jean de la Croix*, ed. Dom Chevallier (Bruges, 1930); *Vida y obras de san Juan de la Cruz*, ed. Lucinio del Santo Sacramento, Biblioteca de autores cristianos, 3rd ed. (Madrid, 1955) (hereafter BAC). For the French translations, see *Œuvres complètes*, trans. Cyprien de la Nativité, ed. Lucien-Marie de Saint-Joseph, 4th ed. (Paris, 1967). Unless otherwise indicated, I quote version A of the *Cántico*.

3. Juan de la Cruz, *Cántico espiritual*, str. 1 [trans. in *Complete Works of Saint John of the Cross, Doctor of the Church*, trans. E. Allison Peers, 3 vols. [London: Burns, Oates & Washbourne, 1934–35], 2: 26].

4. Louis Massignon, *Parole donnée* (Paris, 1962).

5. Didier Anzieu, *Psychanalyse du génie créateur* (Paris, 1974), 3.

6. Dominique Rouche, *Huilques copules* (Paris, 1973). [What have I been, in this pale and consequent trembling: what awaiting and emptiness without name? / Nothing unless it be nothing, office of One lacking to the letter. Think / And that which still I have been able to say, or To Say, will be erased like the rest, / That I happen to be able to announce some time. In Ecstasy.]

7. Christiane Rabant, "L'Enfer des musiciens," in *Musique en jeu* 9 (1972): 30. See also Reinhord Hammerstein, *Die Musik der Engel* (Berne and Munich, 1962), on the Middle Ages; Ernst Benz, *Die Vision. Erfahrungsformen und Bilderwelt* (Stuttgart, 1969), 418–40, "Die himmlische Musik."

8. *Cántico*, str. 14 [trans. Peers, 2: 27]. In Hölderlin, the peaceful nomination also comes "before the morning illuminates" (the elegy *Return*). The "silent music" resumes the "silent concert" of Ruusbroec (*Book of the Twelve Beguines*, 14). Poetic continuities. On John of the Cross and Ruusbroec, see Helmut Hatzfeld, *Estudios literarios sobre mística española* (Madrid, 1955), 33–143.

9. Martin Heidegger, *Elucidations of Hölderlin's Poetry*, trans. Keith Hoeller (Amherst, NY: Humanity Books, 2000), 218, 211, resp.

10. *Cántico*, Prólogo, ed. Silverio, 3; BAC, 901.

11. Hölderlin, "Am Quell der Donau" [At the Source of the Danube], trans. Michael Hamburger, in *Hyperion and Selected Poems*, ed. E. L. Santner (New York: Continuum, 1990), 197.

12. Mallarmé, put on the spot to define poetry, responds: "Je balbutie meurtri" [I stutter wounded] (letter to Léo d'Orfer, 27 June 1884, in *Correspondance*, ed. Henri Mondor and Lloyd James Austin, vol. 2 [Paris, 1965], 266).

13. On this drawing, see Michel Florisoone, *Esthétique et mystique* (Paris, 1956), 94–113.

14. *Obras*, BAC, 1315 [trans. Willis Barnstone, in *The Poems of Saint John of the Cross* (New York: New Directions, 1972), 71].

15. See, on the subject of Benveniste, Certeau, *Mystic Fable*, 1: 162–63.

16. Joë Bousquet, *Mystique* (Paris, 1973), 33.

17. Magdalena del Espíritu Santo relates this response from John of the Cross: "Unas veces me las daba Dios, y otras las buscaba yo" (*Obras*, ed. Silverio, 10: 323). See Duvivier, *La Genèse du "Cantique spirituel,"* 127–29.

18. Paul Valéry, "Au sujet d'Adonis," in *Œuvres*, ed. Jean Hytier (Paris, 1959), 1: 482: "Les dieux, gracieusement, nous donnent pour rien tel premier vers, mais c'est à nous de façonner le second, qui doit consonner avec l'autre et n'être pas indigne" [The gods, mercifully, give us some first verse for nothing, but it is up to us to form a second one that must suit the other, and not be unworthy].

19. Dante Alighieri, *Vita nuova*, XVIII–XIX, ed. M. Barbi (Florence, 1932), 24–25; English trans., *The New Life of Dante Alighieri*, trans. C. E. Norton (Boston: Houghton, Mifflin, 1895), 33–34. Teresa of Avila relates a parallel scene at the beginning of *Las Moradas*. See Certeau, *Mystic Fable*, 1: 193–97.

20. *Subida del Monte Carmelo*, II, 19, a fundamental text on the *manera de entender* [way to understand] biblical words, or inner words and visions.

21. On this chapter of the *Subida*, Jean Baruzi has emphasized that John of the Cross proposes "on the subject of the entire Bible, and of any texts whatsoever, a spiritual method" (*Saint Jean de la Croix et le problème de l'expérience mystique*, 2nd ed. [Paris, 1931], 507).

22. What Bergson's philosophy of the "moving" owes to Marey's depictions is well known.

23. *Cántico*, Prólogo. In quoting the Hymn to Wisdom ("Attingit ergo a fine usque ad finem," Sagesse 8, 1), John of the Cross transforms "to reach" to "to touch," a pivotal term in his mystic language.

24. See Emilio Orozco Días, *Poesía y mística* (Madrid, 1959), 77–78.

25. [My God! What sweetness, what comfort and pleasure / The soul receives as it feels itself seized by the gesture, and sound and voice all together.] Ronsard, "Hymn to the Cardinal of Lorraine," in *Oeuvres complètes*, ed. Prosper Blanchemain, vol. 5 (Paris, 1866), 96. See Gilbert Rouget, *La Musique et*

la transe (Paris, 1980), 317–48; Angel C. Vega, *Cumbres Místicas* (Madrid, 1963), "Misticismo y música," esp. 250–52.

26. See Max Milner, *Poésie et mystique chez Jean de la Croix* (Paris, 1949), 61–75.

27. Testimony of Ana de San Alberto, cited by Duvivier, *La Genèse du "Cantique spirituel,"* 11.

28. Baruzi, *Saint Jean de la Croix et le problème de l'expérience mystique*, 352.

29. Thus, Mother Francisca relates in her deposition (the Beas trial) that John of the Cross, overjoyed ("arrobado y elevado") during a sermon given to the Carmelites (in Granada?), said, once he had come back to himself: "¿Han visto que sueño me ha dado?" (BN Madrid, MS 12738, p. 427; see Duvivier, *La Genèse du "Cantique spirituel,"* 107).

30. See below.

31. *Subida del Monte Carmelo*, II, 4. John of the Cross wrote the *Subida* at the same time that he was finishing the first commentary of the *Cántico*, in 1584.

32. See Certeau, *Mystic Fable*, vol. 1, chap. 2.

33. *Las Moradas*, conclusion, in *Obras completas*, ed. E. de la Madre de Dios (Madrid: BAC, 1954), 2: 494.

34. Meister Eckhart, *Sermons*, trans. Jeanne Ancelet-Hustache (Paris, 1974), 1: 47–48, etc.

35. The *Anotación*, which occurs only in version A, appears at the head of the "declaración" of strophes 13 and 14 (*Cántico*, ed. Silverio, 63; BAC, 964–65). See also, in version B, the "anotación" that connects the "declaraciones" of strophes 27 and 28 (*Cántico*, ed. Silverio, 356–57; BAC, 1052). As in Ignatius Loyola, the "anotación" is a "notice," a "user instructions," addressing the reader's use and not the actual content of the text.

36. In Church Latin, *declaratio* means not only the manifestation or the exposition, but the revealing and even the festival of the Epiphany: "festivitas declarationis ejus," says Léon le Grand. I will translate *declarar* with "explicate": what is involved is an unfolding for an other. In a proximate sense, John of the Cross also uses "to manifest."

37. See Eulogio de la Virgen, *San Juan de la Cruz y sus escritos*, 207–18.

38. BN Madrid, MS 12738, cited by Baruzi, *Saint Jean de la Croix et le problème de l'expérience mystique*, 191n1.

39. Redacted in 1577, *Las Moradas* were at first kept secret; then, in 1580, censured by Gracián and Diego de Yenguas in order to spare the author the inquisitorial trial that the *Vida* had already brought upon her.

40. See *Cántico*, ed. Silverio, 3–5; BAC, 901–2. The title of the book, in the Sanlucar MS, "Declaración de las Canciones que tratan del ejercicio de amor entre el Alma y el Esposo Cristo . . . , a petición de la Madre Ana de Jesús, priora de las desclazas en San José de Granada." [Here Certeau supplies

his own, original translation in French. I substitute that of Peers, in *Complete Works of Saint John of the Cross*, 2: 23–25; but in order to provide an accurate reflection of Certeau's interpretation, I have modified the Peers translation accordingly.—Trans.]

41. Wisdom of Solomon 8: 1.

42. Romans 8: 26.

43. The Song of Songs, in the Bible.

44. A reference to the doctrine and vocabulary of Dionysius the Areopagite themselves, on the "difformity of signs." See *La Hiérarchie céleste*, II, 1 and 3, ed. René Roques et al., 2nd ed. (Paris, 1970), 75 and 77: the Word of God uses "very holy poetic fictions" that go so far as "to the height of implausibility and absurdity."

45. Subida, II, 22; BAC, 535.

46. Hans Urs von Balthasar, *La Gloire et la Croix. Aspects esthétiques de la révélation*, II, 2, trans. Robert Givord and Hélène Bourboulon (Paris, 1972), 11.

47. Such as the art of the medieval Calculatores in measuring the "proportions" between terrestrial misdeeds and purgatorial punishments (see Jacques Le Goff, *The Birth of Purgatory*, trans. Arthur Goldhammer [Chicago: University of Chicago Press, 1984], 227–30), or the techniques developed by the pioneers of the merchant economy of Salamanca, when John of the Cross was a student there (see Pierre Vilar, "Les Primitifs espagnols de la pensée économique," in *Mélanges Marcel Bataillon*, ed. Maxime Chevalier et al. [Bordeaux, 1962], 261–84).

48. More than in Nicholas of Cusa, in whom the comparatives tend toward the coinciding of the maximum and the minimum (see *De docta ignorantia*, I, 4), Dionysius the Areopagite has frequent recourse to the relation of disproportion (see *Celestial Hierarchy*, II, 2–3). This usage is also found, by the way, in Thomas Aquinas.

49. For example *Subida*, II, 16: "That which in God is supreme light and refulgence is to man blackest darkness"; also II, 8, etc.

50. The *Anotación*, which is placed at the head of the "declaración" of strophes 13 and 14 and which plays, within the commentary, a role analogous to that of the prologue, points out in turn that in the poem "se contiene lo más" and "se comprende todo."

51. See Roman Jakobson, *Essais de linguistique générale*, trans. Nicolas Ruwet (Paris, 1963), 213–14.

52. End of the prologue, not translated above.

Chapter Three

1. The numbers in parentheses refer to the numbering of *Dichos* in the translation of Bernard Sésé (Jean de la Croix, *Les Dits de lumière et d'amour* [Paris,

1985]). I refer to the Spanish text of the seventy-eight *Dichos* contained in the autograph manuscript of Andújar, the only ones whose authenticity is certain, and to the editions published by Jean Baruzi (*Aphorismes de Jean de la Croix* [Paris, 1924]), José Vicente Rodríguez (*Dichos de luz y amor*, transcription and facsimile [Madrid, 1976]), and Lucinio Ruano de la Iglesia (*Obras completas*, 11th ed. [Madrid: BAC, 1982]). The critical work of Dom Chevallier (*Les Avis, sentences et maximes de saint Jean de la Croix* [Paris, 1933]) concerns the historical constitution of a Sanjuanist corpus or "chain" by the Carmelite tradition (the text is given, pp. 166–217, in keeping with a classification specific to Dom Chevallier).

2. Jean Baruzi used this term to translate *Dichos.*

3. See for example Crisógono de Jesús, *Jean de la Croix. Sa vie*, trans. Pierre Serouet (Paris, 1982), chaps. 10–12, pp. 151–209.

4. *Cántico espiritual*, Prólogo, 1.

5. Paralleling this, in the prologue of the *Cántico*, the words or "dichos" ally "intelligence" with "love": "los dichos de amor en inteligencia mística" (ibid.).

6. *Subida del Monte Carmelo*, Prólogo, 2.

7. See John of the Cross, *Escritos breves*, ed. José Vicente Rodríguez, 5th ed. (Madrid, 1983); Dom Chevallier, *Les Avis*, 111–14.

8. Teresa of Avila, *Libro de la vida*, 5 and 13, etc.; *Way of Perfection* (Escorial), 3 and 8; *Interior Castle*, IV, 1, and V, 1; etc.

9. Dom Chevallier, *Les Avis*, 113. In his view, these heterogeneous addresses could not therefore be part of one sole collection, despite their coexistence in the autograph.

10. See Baruzi, *Aphorismes de Jean de la Croix*, xiff., etc.

11. Dámaso Alonso, *La Poesía de San Juan de la Cruz* [1942], 3rd ed. (Madrid, 1958).

12. Teresa of Avila, *Libro de la vida*, 11–21. Teresa repeats on several occasions that she uses a "comparison" (*Libro de la vida*, 11, 6, in *Obras*, ed. Silverio de Santa Teresa, vol. 1 [Burgos, 1915], 77) to develop her theoretical distinctions. It is also a "comparison" (the castle of crystal) that supplies the "foundation" for the entire treatise of *Las Moradas* (I, 1, in *Obras*, ed. Silverio de Santa Teresa, 2: 341). See Certeau, *Mystic Fable*, 1: 188–200.

13. *Ascent of Mount Carmel*, prologue, 3.

14. "Rendimiento" (39) is the behavior of the woman who "abandons herself" to her suitor. "Recogimiento" (51), which Cyprien de la Nativité felicitously translates as "la sainte introversion" (*Les Œuvres spirituelles du B. Père Jean de la Croix* [Paris: Chevalier, 1652], 576), designates "meditation," silence of the heart and emptiness of the mind ("no pensar nada"): this was the way of the "recogidos" (French *recueillis*), a tendency suspected at the time of deviationism. See Melquíades Andrés, *Los Recogidos* (Madrid, 1976).

15. This break separates even 32 from 33, and 43–44 from 45, although each of these two groups seems to constitute a semantic unit.

16. Dicho 18: Matthew 11: 18; Dicho 74: Matthew 22: 14 and 7: 14; Dicho 78: Matthew 16: 26. Dicho 4 already refers to Matthew 11: 18. The usual protocols for quotation in John of the Cross are found only in 18 ("que dice") and 78 ("porque"). The references are obviously not given by the autograph.

17. Usually John of the Cross writes a text citing just one book of the Bible, as if he were writing one and reading the other. See Jean Vilnet, *Bible et mystique chez saint Jean de la Croix* (Paris, 1949), 34–38. The Gospel of Matthew is particularly quoted in *Ascent of Mount Carmel*, in which, incidentally, we find two of the four verses quoted in the Dichos: Matthew 7: 14 (*Ascent of Mount Carmel*, II, 7) and Matthew 16: 26 (*Ascent of Mount Carmel*, III, 18).

18. Évagre le Pontique [Evagrius Ponticus], *Traité pratique ou le Moine* [*Praktikos*], ed. A. and C. Guillaumont (Paris, 1971). These "maxims," a literary genre that Evagrius is the first Christian author to use, already combine statements of various types—general aphorisms, addresses to God, to the soul, or to the reader, exclamations—into a coherent treatise of spirituality.

19. See above, note 14.

20. This is the first title (1657) of what was later called *The Cherubinic Wanderer* [1675]: see the edition by Eugène Susini (Paris, 1964).

21. [The French term here is *langagière*, for which "linguistic" is an inadequate translation because the former evokes the full "languagey" language-likeness of language, and not those formal elements that are the object of the "linguistic" study.]

Chapter Four

1. P. Pacheu, "Les Mystiques interprétés par les mystiques," *Revue de philosophie* 21 (1913): 616–60.

2. On the life and teachings of Surin (1600–1665), see Jean-Joseph Surin, *Guide spirituel pour la perfection*, ed. Michel de Certeau (Paris, 1963), "Introduction," 7–61.

3. Jean Orcibal, "Les Débuts de la spiritualité carmélitaine à Bordeaux," *Bulletin de la Société des bibliophiles de Guyenne*, no. 89 (1969), offprint, 15 pp.

4. Michel Olphe-Galliard, "Le P. Surin et saint Jean de la Croix," *Mélanges . . . Cavallera* (Toulouse, 1948), 425–39. See also, apropos of a long discussion between Surin and Father Bastide on the way to interpret certain texts in *Ascent of Mount Carmel*, the data already furnished by Ferdinand Cavallera, "Une Controverse sur les grâces mystiques," *Revue d'ascétique et de mystique* 9 (1928): 163–96 (to be completed by Jean-Joseph Surin, *Correspondance*, ed. Michel de Certeau [Paris, 1966]).

5. Olphe-Galliard, "Le P. Surin et saint Jean de la Croix," 433–35.

6. Jean de la Croix, *Œuvres complètes*, trans. Cyprien de la Nativité de la Vierge, ed. Lucien-Marie de Saint-Joseph, 4th ed. (Paris, 1967). For the publication of Surin's *Correspondance*, see above, note 4.

7. Jean Krynen, *Denys le mystique et saint Jean de la Croix* (Doctorat d'État, Paris, Sorbonne, 1955); id., "Du nouveau sur Thomas de Jésus. L'avènement de la mystique des lumières en Espagne (1601–1607)," in *Mélanges Marcel Bataillon*, ed. M. Chevalier et al. (Bordeaux, 1962), 113–35.

8. See the introduction, concerning "a child's secret," in Surin, *Correspondance*, 42–51.

9. J. Orcibal, "La Montée du Carmel a-t-elle été interpolée?," *Revue de l'histoire des religions* 162 (1964): 171–213.

10. Surin, *Correspondance*, 658, 663, etc.

11. *Œuvres spirituelles pour acheminer les Âmes à la parfaite union avec Dieu, Du bienheureux Père Jean de la Croix* (Paris: Sonnius, 1621). This translation is not to be confused with that of the *Spiritual Canticle*, also published by Sonnius, the following year (five years before the Spanish publication of the *Cántico*): *Cantique d'amour divin entre Jésus-Christ et l'Âme dévote* . . . , trans. René Gaultier (Paris, 1622).

12. See the dedication to the Queen Mother, in the *Œuvres spirituelles.*

13. "Je propose aux amateurs des beautés de notre langage de considérer désormais l'un des plus parfaits poètes de France dans le R. P. Cyprien de la Nativité de la Vierge" [I propose to lovers of the beauties of our language that they consider henceforth one of the most perfect poets of France in the Reverend Father . . .]: Paul Valéry, *Variété V* (Paris, 1944), "Cantiques spirituels," 165–96.

14. Bordeaux, Bibliothèque municipale, MS 832, p. 129 (French texts). On Surin, there is the *Catéchisme*, 1657 edition (ibid., p. 115) and the two-volume 1663 edition (ibid., pp. 147 and 152); the *Dialogues*, Nantes edition, 1700 (ibid., p. 119) and the *Lettres spirituelles sur les mystères*, Nantes edition, 1700 (ibid., p. 132).

15. See texts excerpted by Orcibal in "La Montée du Carmel a-t-elle été interpolée ?," 179–83.

16. On this muffled yet fundamental elaboration, see Michel de Certeau, "Crise sociale et réformisme spirituel au début du XVIIe siècle," *Revue d'ascétique et de mystique* 41 (1965): 339–86.

17. See Orcibal, "Les Débuts de la spiritualité carmélitaine à Bordeaux," 8–12.

18. Robert Mandrou, *Introduction à la France moderne* (Paris: Albin Michel, 1961), 117.

19. [This term, in use in both France and England in the seventeenth century, designates a part of the bedroom in which ladies received visits.]

20. See Michel de Certeau, "Mystique au XVIIe siècle. Le problème du langage mystique," *L'Homme devant Dieu. Mélanges Henri de Lubac* (Paris, 1964), 2: 267–91. The saints, Surin writes, "are the conquerors who invite us to take part in their conquest" (*Correspondance*, 1256, letter of 1 November 1661).

21. Surin, *Guide spirituel*, 185.

22. Ibid., 246.

23. Ibid.

24. Certeau, "Crise sociale et réformisme spirituel," 357n76.

25. See the works of Michel Florisoone, a curator at the Louvre Museum, on the portraits of John of the Cross.

26. Surin, *Guide spirituel*, 150. See José de Jesús María (= Quiroga), *La Vie du Bienheureux Père Jean de la Croix* (Paris, 1638), part 2, p. 74. It happened in Segovia in spring 1591 (*Vida y obras de San Juan de la Cruz*, 3d ed. [Madrid: BAC, 1955], 403).

27. *Correspondance*, 1560, letter to Mother Anne Buignon, 8 August 1664; see also 1368, 1542–43, 1554–55, etc.

28. Ibid., 1554, letter of 1 August 1664.

29. Ibid., 1508–9, letter of 3 January 1664.

30. Ibid., 1256, letter of 1 November 1661.

31. "Les trois Pères carmes déchaux, savoir est le bienheureux Jean de la Croix, Thomas a Jesu, Joannes a Jesu Maria" (Surin, *Guide spirituel*, 181–82, etc. I correct the edition of 1963, the MS folio 187 bearing the words "Thomas a Jesu"). Surin's *Les Fondements de la vie spirituelle* (Paris, 1930), 81, speaking of several "mystic doctors," mentions only two Carmelite friars by name, "the Blessed John of the Cross, Joannes a Jesu Maria, and several others."

32. Thomas de Jésus, *De contemplatione divina* (Antwerp, 1630), and *Opera omnia*, 3 vols. (Cologne, 1632). Jean de Jésus-Marie, *Opera omnia*, 3 vols., (Cologne, 1622), then a more complete edition (4 vols., 1650).

33. See above, first reference in note 20. While this triangular construction is new and in the seventeenth century accompanies the elaboration of a modern status for what is designated as "scientific," the discussions on the relations between a "spiritual" language and a "theological" one are much older. See Y. M. J. Congar, "Langage des spirituels et langage des théologiens," *Situation et tâches présentes de la théologie* (Paris, 1967), 135–58; and the works of Marie-Dominique Chenu, Jean Leclercq, François Vandenbroucke, etc., on this subject. Since the thirteenth century, that great debate has been linked to the tensions between clerics and laymen.

34. See Jean Dagens, "La Résistance à l'introduction des termes de la mystique germanique en France au XVIIe siècle," *Langue et littérature* (*Actes du VIIIe Congrès de la Fédération internationale des langues et littératures modernes*) (Paris, 1961).

35. Jean Orcibal (in *Problèmes et méthodes d'histoire des religions. Mélanges publiés . . . par l'EPHE* [Paris, 1968], 256–57) stressed the lack of these systematic surveys of words and images and pointed out several fields of investigation.

36. An entire lexographic literature is devoted to spiritual vocabulary, born of the necessity that mystic discourse have a language of its own. Along with the classic work of Maximilianus Sandaeus, *Pro theologia mystica clavis* (Cologne, 1640), it will suffice to cite, since it is governed by the same preoccupations but in a totally different perspective, the precious *Index anagogicus seu contemplativus* at the end of *Anatomia totius doctrinae sancti Augustini*, 2 vols. (Liège, 1643–45), by Mathias Hauzeur. At the end of the century, Honoré de Sainte-Marie will have the same concern: see his note "De plusieurs comparaisons touchant l'union mystique et la contemplation," *Tradition des Pères sur la contemplation* (Paris, 1708), 2: 532–42.

37. J.-J. Surin, *Catéchisme spirituel* (Rennes: J. Durand, 1657), 231.

38. On Sanjuanist symbols, see Georges Morel, *Le Sens de l'existence selon saint Jean de la Croix*, vol. 3: *Symbolique* (Paris, 1964). I leave till later the exposition of my too thick file on the symbolic system and symbols of Surin.

39. See for example Jean Rousset, "Les Images de la nuit et de la lumière chez quelques poètes religieux," *Cahiers de l'Association internationale des études françaises* 10 (May 1958): 58–68, or the fine analysis by R. Virolle, "Deux Aspects romantiques du thème de la nuit dans la poésie du XVIIe siècle," *L'École*, esp. the issue of 12 November 1955.

40. See for example *Les Fondements de la vie spirituelle*, 317–18; *Guide spirituel*, 310; *Dialogues spirituels* (Nantes, 1700), 1: 205–6.

41. E.g., *Guide spirituel*, 309.

42. *Catéchisme spirituel*, 39–40.

43. *Cantiques spirituels* (Bordeaux: G. de la Court, 1660), 164–68 (canticle 39).

44. For embroidering, see *Correspondance*, 1111; the *Dialogues spirituels*, private MS, f. 119–25, speak at length of the "height" of the stars due to the parallaxes; for weaving, for example, *Guide spirituel*, 311.

45. Prologue to *Cantique spirituel*: see *Vida y obras de San Juan de la Cruz* (Madrid, 1955), 902.

46. *La Vive Flamme d'amour*, stanza 3, verse 4, in *Œuvres spirituelles . . . du bienheureux Père Jean de la Croix*, trans. René Gaultier (1621), part 3, p. 48.

47. See for example *La Science expérimentale*, III, 2 (the part published in J.-J. Surin, *Lettres spirituelles*, vol. 2 [Toulouse, 1928], 82).

48. Thus the canticle "Je veux aller courir parmi le monde" [I want to run through the world], often quoted (Surin, *Cantiques spirituels*, 21–26). There is, moreover, some of everything in Surin's poetry, including catechetical primers in doggerel. His intent is not to create a poetic work. He jots down on paper what comes to him or what seems to him to be useful, mixing the

outpourings of a man afflicted with love with the pastoral objectives of the missionary.

49. See the texts quoted by Orcibal, "La Montée du Carmel a-t-elle été interpolée ?," 182–83.

50. *Correspondance*, 1005, 1402, etc.

51. MS de Chantilly, Archives SJ, 17th cent. [henceforth Archives SJ, Vanves]. See Michel de Certeau, "Les Œuvres de Jean-Joseph Surin, I," *Revue d'ascétique et de mystique* 40 (1964): 457.

52. MS de Chantilly, inside cover.

53. [Abbreviation for the Jesuit "Assemblée," a secret pious association founded around 1630. Such assemblies existed in many French cities, some remaining active into the nineteenth century. See René Pillorget and Suzanne Pillorget, *France baroque, France classique, 1589–1715*, vol. 2: *Dictionnaire* (Paris: Robert Laffont, 1995), 1–2.]

54. MS de Chantilly, f. 91. *The Living Flame of Love*, as opposed to all the other canticles, does not bear the instruction "to the tune of."

55. See for example the prologue to the *Cántico.*

56. *Correspondance*, 1368.

57. Ibid., 1197–98.

58. Certeau, "Mystique au XVIIe siècle. Le problème du langage mystique."

59. *La Vive Flamme*, stanza 2, verse 3, in *Œuvres*, trans. Cyprien de la Nativité (1665), 364. See Surin, *Correspondance*, letter of 27 Jan. 1660, p. 905.

60. Piero Scazzoso, *Ricerche sulla struttura del linguaggio dello Pseudo-Dionigi Areopagita* (Milan, 1967).

61. See Jean Starobinski, "Kierkegaard et les masques," *Nouvelle revue française* 148 (1965): 607–22, and 149 (1965): 819–25.

62. See for example, apropos of mystic "terms," J.-J. Surin, *Questions importantes à la vie spirituelle sur l'amour de Dieu* (Paris, 1930), 136.

63. Translation by René Gaultier, inserted at the end of the *Œuvres spirituelles* of John of the Cross (1621), part 3, pp. 147–229. This translation has already been "revised" and reedited.

64. To the text of Diego, Cyprien de la Nativité adds his translation of the *Éclaircissement théologique des phrases et propositions de la théologie mystique contenues ès livres du R. P. Jean de la Croix*, by Father Nicolas de Jésus Maria: a volume in itself, nearly 300 pages in-octavo, a discourse more scholastic, more apologetic, and less colorful than that of Diego.

65. See Certeau, "Mystique au XVIIe siècle. Le problème du langage mystique," 289–91.

66. Jean Baruzi, "Recherches sur le langage mystique," *Recherches philosophiques* 1 (1931–32): 66–82; H. Chandebois, "Lexique, grammaire et style chez saint Jean de la Croix," *Ephemerides Carmeliticae* 3 (1949): 543–47.

67. Jacques [Diego] de Jésus, *Notes et remarques en trois discours*, translation revised by Cyprien de la Nativité (1641), 280.

68. *Raideur* "is said of the violence of movement," of its impetuosity (Furetière).

69. Surin, *Questions importantes à la vie spirituelle*, 118–19.

70. Surin, *Correspondance*, 518ff.

71. Surin describes at length this "discrepancy" in parts 1 and 2 of *La Science expérimentale* [1663].

72. Surin, *Correspondance*, 638.

73. Ibid., 749.

74. Ibid.

75. Ibid., 638.

76. Ibid., 687.

77. *Ascent of Mount Carmel*, II, 22. [I quote the English translation by E. Allison Peers, *The Complete Works of Saint John of the Cross*, vol. 1 (London: Burns, Oates & Washbourne, 1935), 184.—Trans.].

78. See Jean Orcibal, *La Rencontre du Carmel thérésien avec les mystiques du Nord* (Paris: Presses Universitaires, 1959), 24.

79. See, in Surin, *Correspondance*, "Une campagne contre Surin et la Nouvelle spiritualité," 433–60; in Surin, *Guide spirituel*, "Réponse à l'Examinateur de la théologie mystique," 39–50; or Certeau, "Crise sociale et réformisme spirituel," 353–86.

80. The evolution analyzed by Henri de Lubac, *Augustinisme et théologie moderne* (Paris, 1965), 135–257, appears singularly hardened in the theological and moral teaching of Bordeaux in the middle of the seventeenth century. See, on Father Champeils (an extreme case, to be sure), Surin, *Correspondance*, 444–48. On the positions of the Carmelites of the Mitigated Rule in the sixteenth century, see L. M. Poliseno, "I Carmelitani e la certezza dello stato di grazia nel Concilio Tridentino," in *Carmelus* 1 (1954): 111–45.

81. For example, *Correspondance*, 1679, referring to *Ascent of Mount Carmel*, II, 7.

82. For example, *Guide spirituel*, 267, which refers to *Ascent of Mount Carmel*, II, 11.

83. *Guide spirituel*, 303.

84. *Correspondance*, 1236.

85. Ibid., 1653, referring to the *Spiritual Canticle*, 17, 6, and to *Dark Night of the Soul*, II, 2 and 14.

86. *Guide spirituel*, 312.

87. For example, *Correspondance*, 1171–74.

88. Ibid., 1546.

89. The Carmelites of Bordeaux did the same, between 1610 and 1620, and

the Bordeaux "ecclesiastics" who were the first translators of *The Living Flame*. See above, section 2, "Surin, Reader of John of the Cross through R. Gaultier," and the studies of J. Orcibal cited in notes 3 and 9.

90. *Les Œuvres spirituelles . . . du bienheureux Jean de la Croix*, trans. René Gaultier (1621), part 3, pp. 101–2. [Since the discussion turns on Surin's reading of Gaultier's "transcription," I translate that document, rather than John of the Cross's original.—Trans.].

91. André Rayez, "Gaultier (René)," in *Dictionnaire de spiritualité*, vol. 6 (1967), cols. 144–47.

Chapter Five

1. Abundant literature since Jehan de Cuchermoys, *Petit traité du Voyage de Hierusalem* (Paris, 1530?); Henry Castela, *Le Guide et adresse pour ceux qui veulent faire le S. Voiage de Hierusalem* (Paris, 1604); Yves Dugué, *Brief Discours de la manière de voyager* (Bourges, 1638); François Du Soucy, *L'Art de voyager utilement* (Paris, 1650); S. Sorbière, *De l'utilité des grands voyages* (Paris, 1660); etc. See N. Doiron, "De la manière de voyager," *Dérives* (Montreal) 41 (1984): 3–16.

2. The term seems to appear for the first time in Bartolomeo Ricci, *Instruttione di meditare* [1600], 2nd ed. (Rome, 1602), 216–20; Latin trans., G. Busée (Mainz, 1605), 185–91. See Hermann Josef Sieben, "De la *lectio divina* à la lecture spirituelle," *Dictionnaire de spiritualité*, vol. 9 (Paris, 1976), col. 494.

3. See for example Elizabeth L. Eisenstein, *The Printing Press as an Agent of Change* (New York: Cambridge, 1979), 453–88, on this dichotomy ("books versus Nature") among the humanists, whose intellectual impact, however, as the author rightly emphasizes, is contingent on their activity as writers, and as public ones, too.

4. John of the Cross, *La Subida del Monte Carmelo*, prologue, etc.

5. Teresa of Avila, *Libro de la vida*, 4, etc.

6. See Eisenstein, *Printing Press as an Agent of Change*, 3–42.

7. Dante, *De vulgari eloquentia*.

8. Frances A. Yates, *The Art of Memory* (Chicago, 1960), 1–128.

9. See Certeau, *Mystic Fable*, 1: 157–205.

10. François Rabelais, *Quart livre*, chaps. 55–56. See, among numerous other studies, Michel Jeanneret, "Les Paroles dégelées," *Littérature* 17 (1975): 14–30.

11. Hans Robert Jauss, *Toward an Aesthetic of Reception*, trans. Timothy Bahti (Minneapolis: University of Minnesota Press, 1982), 14ff.; Tzvetan Todorov, *Théorie de la littérature. Textes des formalistes russes* (Paris, 1965).

12. Maurice Merleau-Ponty, *Phenomenology of Perception*, trans. Colin Smith (London: Routledge, 1962), 330ff.

13. Particularly since John J. Gumperz and Dell Hymes, eds., *Directions in Sociolinguistics: The Ethnography of Communication* (New York: Holt, Rinehart and Winston, 1972).

14. Roland Barthes, "Sur la lecture," *Le français aujourd'hui* 32 (January 1976): 11–18.

15. Gérard Genette, *Figures* (Paris, 1966), 123ff.

16. See Certeau, *Mystic Fable*, vol. 1, chap. 4, "Manners of Speaking."

17. Guillaume de Saint-Thierry, *Lettre aux frères du Mont-Dieu* (*Lettre d'or)*, ed. J. Déchanet (Paris: Sources chrétiennes, 1975), 240–41, §124.

18. Ibid.

19. *Instructions spirituelles aux bonnes âmes* (Paris: Jacques de Laize-de-Bresche, 1674), notice to the reader, unpaginated.

20. Throughout this volume, the French term *vouloir-dire* (sometimes unhyphenated), will be translated as "want-to-say."

21. *Libro de la vida*, chap. 4.

22. Ibid.

23. Ibid., chap. 9.

24. See the texts cited by Sieben, "De la *lectio divina* à la lecture spirituelle," cols. 487–96.

25. See for example J. Álvarez de la Paz, *De exterminatione mali et promotione boni libri quinque* (Mainz, 1614), book 3, part 5, section 2, 2 ("De lectione spirituali"), cols. 1173–76.

26. Teresa of Avila, *Primera Relación* [1560], 7, in *Obras completas* (Madrid: BAC, 1954), 2: 505–6.

27. *Libro de la vida*, chaps. 1, 2, 4, 6, 8, etc.

28. Ibid., chap. 40.

29. See Terry Comito, *The Idea of the Garden in the Renaissance* (New Brunswick, NJ, 1978), chaps. 2–4.

30. Émile Benveniste, *Problems in General Linguistics*, trans. Mary E. Meek (Coral Gables: University of Miami Press, 1971), 217–30.

31. See J. Álvarez de Paz, *De vita spirituali* (Mainz, 1614), book 2, part 4, 31, col. 379.

32. Guillaume de Saint-Thierry, *Lettre aux frères du Mont-Dieu*, 240, §122.

33. Jean-Joseph Surin, *Catéchisme spirituel*, IV, 2 (MS of Bordeaux, 1654).

34. See for example Allen G. Debus, *The Chemical Philosophy*, 2 vols. (New York, 1977).

35. *The Way of a Pilgrim*, translated from Russian by R. M. French (Pasadena: Hope, 1989), 66.

36. Jean-Joseph Surin, *Guide spirituel*, ed. Michel de Certeau (Paris, 1963), IV, 3, p. 183.

37. Louis Guespin, Introduction, *Langages* 74, "Dialogue et interaction verbale" (1984): 7.

38. Marguerite Duras, *The Vice-Consul*, trans. Eileen Ellenbogen (New York: Pantheon Books, 1987), 158 (trans. modified).

39. An expression from *Speculum inclusorum*, written at the end of the fifteenth century by a disciple of Richard Rolle.

40. Juan de Avila, *Audi filia*, trans. J. Cherprenet (Paris, 1954), 2: 195.

41. Ibid.

42. J. Álvarez de Paz, *De exterminatione mali et promotione boni*, col. 1175: a classic, often repeated expression, dating back at least to Guillaume de Saint-Thierry, *Lettre aux frères du Mont-Dieu*, §123.

43. Gaston Brillet, "La Bible et la lecture spirituelle," *La Vie spirituelle* 73 (1945): 498.

44. Tony Duvert, "La Lecture introuvable," *Minuit* 1 (November 1972): 11.

45. Sigmund Freud, *Der Mann Moses*, in *Gesammelte Werke* (London, 1950), 16: 239.

46. Quoted by Fidèle De Ros, *Un Maître de sainte Thérèse, le P. François d'Osuna* (Paris, 1936), 396.

47. Rainer Maria Rilke, *From Rilke: Selected Poems*, trans. C. F. MacIntyre (Berkeley: University of California Press, 1957), 92.

48. Dom Augustin Baker, *La Sainte Sapience* (translation of *Sancta Sophia* [Douai, 1657]) (Paris, 1953), 1: 68.

49. See Jean Leclercq, *L'Amour des lettres et le désir de Dieu* (Paris, 1957).

50. Luis de Granada, *Œuvres complètes*, ed. J.-F. Bareille, vol. 2 (Paris, 1863), 143–44.

51. Maximilianus Sandaeus, *Pro Theologia mystica clavis* (Cologne, 1640), 263–64.

52. See Pierre Kuentz, "Le tête à texte," *Esprit* (December 1974): 946–62.

53. Claude Rabant, *Délire et théorie* (Paris, 1978), 99.

54. Maurice Blanchot, *The Space of Literature*, trans. Ann Smock (Lincoln: University of Nebraska Press, 1982), 194–96; my quotation is from p. 195 ["Lazare, veni foras": John 11: 44].

Chapter Six

1. On the French vocabulary of "tourment," "supplice," etc., the importance of which diminishes and the proper or strict meaning of which disappears during the second half of the seventeenth century (the end of the "mystic" period), see Pierre Dumonceaux, *Langue et sensibilité au XVIIe siècle* (Geneva, 1975), 25–71.

2. Descartes, *The Passions of the Soul*, I, 31–32, and II, 53.

3. Michel de Certeau, *The Possession at Loudun*, trans. Michael B. Smith (Chicago: University of Chicago Press, 1996).

4. Sandro Sticca, *The Latin Passion Play* (Albany: SUNY Press, 1970).

5. Basil Smallman, *The Background of Passion Music: J. S. Bach and His Predecessors*, 2nd ed. (New York: Dover, 1970).

6. Michel de Certeau, "Mystic Speech," trans. Brian Massumi, *Heterologies: Discourse on the Other* (Minneapolis: University of Minnesota Press, 1986), 80–100.

7. See the article "Passions," in Frédéric Godefroy, *Dictionnaire de l'ancienne langue française et de tous ses dialectes du IXe au XVe siècle* [1881–1902], vol. 6 (Paris, 1936).

8. Stillman Drake, "Galileo's New Science of Motion," in *Reason, Experiment and Mysticism*, ed. Maria Luisa Righini Bonelli and William R. Shea (New York: Science History Publications, 1975), 131–56.

9. Teresa of Avila, *Las Moradas*, I, 1.

10. Ibid.

11. See for example Teresa of Avila, *Libro de la vida*, 16ff.

12. See for example John of the Cross, *Cántico Adónde te escondiste.*

13. See the articles by A. J. Greimas (pp. 90–107) and Jean-Claude Coquet (pp. 64–70) in *Langages* 43, "Modalités" (September 1976).

14. Including "must/should" among the modalities, as Michael Rengstorf proposes (pp. 71–77, in the issue of *Langages* cited in the preceding note), with analogous hesitations but different hypotheses.

15. See Raymond Lull, *Libro de Contemplación*, which proposes replacing the knight's *lance* with *tears* [*larmes*].

16. Teresa of Avila, *Libro de la vida*, 18.

17. Jacob Boehme, *Mysterium magnum*, 3, 11, etc.

Chapter Seven

1. Louis Cognet, in *Recherches de science religieuse* 54 (1966): 162–63, and 56 (1968): 269–81; Jean Orcibal, in *Revue d'ascétique et mystique* 42 (1966): 385; Julien Green, preface, in Jean-Joseph Surin, *Correspondance*, ed. Michel de Certeau (Paris, 1966), 7–23.

2. I have published this historical dossier in the *Correspondance.*

3. These two parts form a whole, which, moreover, is distinguished as such by all the old manuscripts. They were, I think, later framed by parts 1 and 4 on Loudun and demonology. I quote from the following edition: Jean-Joseph Surin, *Lettres spirituelles, II, 1640–1659*, ed. Louis Michel and Ferdinand Cavallera (Toulouse, 1928), 1–151, correcting and completing it with the best

old copy (Paris BN, fonds fr., 14596); I refer to it as *La Science*, specifying the part by a Roman numeral and the chapter by an Arabic numeral. Unless otherwise indicated, the quotations are from Surin's text.

4. *Lucida Intervalla: Containing Divers Miscellaneous Poems, Written at Finsburg and Bedlam* (London, 1679). See for example Lillian Feder, *Madness in Literature* (Princeton: Princeton University Press, 1980), 155–61.

5. See Michel Foucault, *Madness and Civilization: A History of Insanity in the Age of Reason*, trans. Richard Howard (New York: Pantheon Books, 1965).

6. See Michael MacDonald, *Mystical Bedlam* (Cambridge: Cambridge University Press, 1981).

7. See John Saward, *Perfect Fools* (Oxford: Oxford University Press, 1980), mainly 118–46.

8. *La Science*, II, 4.

9. Shakespeare, *King Lear*, act 4, scene 5.

10. *La Science*, III, 9.

11. "Je veux aller courir parmi le monde / Où je vivrai comme un enfant perdu / J'ai pris l'humeur d'une âme vagabonde / Après avoir tout mon bien répandu." [Jean-Joseph Surin], *Cantiques spirituels*, 2nd ed. (Bordeaux, 1660), 25, canticle 5. Some old versions have "dépendu" instead of "répandu."

12. Ibid., 26. "la folie / De ce Jésus qui sur la croix un jour / Pour son plaisir perdit honneur et vie."

13. See for example Michel de Certeau, *The Writing of History* (New York: Columbia University Press, 1988), 209–43, on Jean de Léry.

14. See Michel de Certeau, *Heterologies: Discourse on the Other*, trans. Brian Massumi (Minneapolis: University of Minnesota Press, 1986).

15. See François Hartog, *The Mirror of Herodotus: The Representation of the Other in the Writing of History*, trans. Janet Lloyd (Berkeley: University of California Press, 1988).

16. *La Science*, II, 10; II, 15; III, 10; III, 16.

17. Ibid., III, 9–10. On this imagery of the storm at sea, see Robert Myle, *De la symbolique de l'eau dans l'œuvre du Père Surin* (Louvain, 1979), 51–87.

18. See Michel Thévoz, *L'Art brut* (Geneva, 1975); W. Morgenthaler, *Adolf Wölfli*, trans. Henri-Pol Bouché (Paris, 1964).

19. *La Science*, II, 14–15; III, 4; II, 10; II, 13; III, 6; III, 4.

20. Ibid., II, 7, etc.

21. See Ross Chambers, *Gérard de Nerval et la poétique du voyage* (Paris, 1969), esp. 343–98; Shoshana Felman, *La Folie et la chose littéraire* (Paris, 1978), 67ff.

22. *La Science*, II, 13.

23. Ibid., II, 8; see II, 4.

24. Ibid., II, 3.

25. Ibid., II, 11; II, 4.

26. *La Science*, II, 1, first sentence.

27. The beginning of *Aurelia* presents a similar structure (Gérard de Nerval, *Œuvres*, ed. Albert Béguin and Jean Richer [Paris, 1974], 359ff.). See Felman, *La Folie et la chose littéraire*, 67–68.

28. *La Science*, II, 7 (my emphasis). See, on the blows and insults he received: "mad, as I truly was in what *appeared*, but *at bottom* no more so than now" (ibid.); "Our Lord left me reason and heedfulness as great as I have at this hour" (ibid.); "I was never more serious in my thinking or more attentive to God in my reason, or more desirous of satisfying him, but never less capable, on the contrary mad, in everything I did by a disorder of the imagination that I could neither say nor hold back" (ibid.).

29. For example in Jean de Léry: see Certeau, *Writing of History*, 218–26.

30. The present act of writing: for example, "when *I* am at present writing this" (*La Science*, II, 4, first return of the "I"), "at present *I* am here" (II, 4), "*I* do not claim" (II, 6), "what *I* must say" (II, 7), "*I* said that" (II, 8), etc. The present act of remembering: for example, "at this hour when *I* remember it" (II, 5), "the memory of which touches *me*" (II, 8), etc. My emphases.

31. *La Science*, III, 14. My emphasis.

32. Ibid., II, 1; II, 6; II, 7; etc.

33. "I must give a remarkable example," "I must tell another story" (*La Science*, II, 14); etc.

34. See Eugenio Costa, "La tromperie, ou le problème de la communication chez Surin. Note sur quelques textes de *La Science expérimentale*," *Revue d'ascétique et de mystique* 44 (1968): 413–23.

35. *La Science*, II, 12.

36. Ibid., II, 12–13.

37. "Produce" means "bring forth, make manifest outside."

38. *La Science*, II, 16.

39. Ibid., II, 17.

40. "I remember," Surin repeats (*La Science*, II, 8), an expression to be understood as meaning "*It* comes back to *me*" [*Il me* revient], the return of the "he" [*Il* means both "he" and "it"] to the "I."

41. *La Science*, II, 4.

42. See, in the introduction" to the *Correspondance*, "the secret of a child," pp. 42–51, and, in the same work, the appendix on "Jean-Joseph Surin's family," pp. 1685–1720.

43. See, in *Correspondance*, the appendix on "Jeanne des Anges," pp. 1721–48; and Michel de Certeau, *The Possession at Loudun*, trans. Michael B. Smith (Chicago: University of Chicago Press, 1996), 200.

44. "Some went so far as to look into a race and a horoscope, and by observations taken on what had happened in my youth . . ." (*La Science*, II, 11). In 1639, a colleague, Léonard Champeils, invokes the following against Surin:

"a melancholy spirit who has already led several of his relatives to madness" (*Correspondance*, 454).

45. See Michel de Certeau, *The Practice of Everyday Life*, trans. Steven F. Rendall (Berkeley: University of California Press, 1984), 115–21.

46. *La Science*, II, 4 and 9.

47. Ibid., II, 17: "I suffered so extremely from this change of undershirt that sometimes I spent almost the entire night between Saturday and Sunday taking off my undershirt and putting on another one, with extreme pain, so much so that it was a normal thing for my soul that I always thought I was joyful when it was before Thursday, and very anxious when it was Thursday, or the following day, because this change of linen tormented me." But it was a "trial nothing could spare me, so great was my desire to stay neat and clean."

48. *La Science*, II, 9.

49. Ibid.

50. G. E. Moore, "Wittgenstein's Lectures in 1930–1933," in *Classics of Analytic Philosophy*, ed. Robert R. Ammerman (New York, 1965), 284.

51. *La Science*, II, 5.

52. Ibid., II, 4.

53. Ibid., II, 9; II, 13; III, 2; etc.

54. Ibid., III, 5.

55. See Jean-Joseph Surin, *Questions importantes à la vie spirituelle sur l'amour de Dieu*, ed. Aloys Pottier and Louis Mariès (Paris, 1930), III, 2, pp. 116–17.

56. *La Science*, II, 11.

57. Ibid.

58. *La Science*, II, 10.

59. [Surin], *Cantiques spirituels*, 15.

60. *La Science*, III, 9. The theory of "spirits" still prevails from Robert Burton (*The Anatomy of Melancholy* [1621], ed. H. Jackson (New York, 1977), part 1, pp. 375ff.) to Thomas Willis (see M. Foucault, *History of Madness*, trans. Jean Khalfa [London: Routledge, 2006], 299–317, 327).

61. See, on Descartes himself, Sylvie Romanowski, *L'Illusion chez Descartes* (Paris, 1974), 83–95.

62. See Burton, *Anatomy of Melancholy*, part 2, pp. 34–69, 235–36, etc.

63. *La Science*, II, 11.

64. Ibid., III, 3; see III, 6.

65. Luce Irigaray, *The Forgetting of Air in Martin Heidegger*, trans. Mary Beth Mader (Austin: University of Texas Press, 1999), 8–9, 41–42.

66. *La Science*, II, 4.

67. See already in the reflections of M. T.-L. Penido, "Grâce et folie. À propos du P. Surin," *Études carmélitaines* 24.1 (1939): 176: "La folie peut être instrument de la grâce."

Chapter Eight

1. Revelation 9:16.

2. Athanasius Kircher, *Oedipus Aegyptiacus* (Rome, 1652).

3. Gaspard Schott, *Magia universalis naturae et artis* (Würzburg, 1657), part 3 ("Mathematica"), p. 598.

4. Johann Reuchlin, *La Kabbale* (*De arte cabalistica*), intro. and trans. François Secret (Paris, 1973), 234.

5. See *Génies, anges et démons* (Paris, 1971).

6. Henry Corbin, *Avicenna and the Visionary Recital*, trans. Willard R. Trask (New York: Pantheon Books, 1960), 55. See esp. "Nécessité de l'angélologie" in *L'Ange et l'homme* (Paris, Cahiers de l'hermétisme, 1978), 15–79. To this must be added the sumptuous iconography gathered by Peter Lamborn Wilson (*Angels* [New York, 1980]) and dedicated to Henry Corbin.

7. Christian Jambet, *La Logique des Orientaux* (Paris, 1983).

8. René Char, *Furor and Mystery and Other Writings*, translated and edited by Mary Ann Caws and Nancy E. Kline (Boston: Black Widow Press, 2010), 139.

9. *Encyclopédie ou Dictionnaire raisonné des sciences, des arts et des métiers*, s.v. "Folie."

10. See H. Leclercq, "Anges," in *Dictionnaire d'archéologie chrétienne et de liturgie* (Paris, 1907), vol. 1.2, cols. 2080–2161.

11. Thomas Aquinas, *Summa Theologica*, Ia, quest. 113, art. 5, ad secundum.

12. See André Grabar, *Le Premier Art chrétien* (Paris, 1966), 225, 230–31, etc.

13. Jacob Boehme, *Aurora*, 12, 83. See Bernard Gorceix, "L'Ange en Allemagne au XVIIe siècle," in *L'Ange et l'homme*, 141.

14. See Christine Buci-Glucksmann, "Walter Benjamin et l'Ange de l'histoire," *L'Écrit du temps* 2 (1982): 45–85.

15. See Maurice de Gandillac, *La Philosophie de Nicolas de Cues* (Paris, 1941), 443–44.

16. Galatians 4:3, 9; Colossians 2: 8, 20. The argument of J. Turmel was that "during the first five centuries, the Doctors of Christianity condemned all angel worship" (in *Revue d'histoire et de littérature chrétiennes* 3 [1898]: 550). See G. Bareille's clarification, under the article "Anges" in *Dictionnaire de théologie catholique*, vol. 1.1 (Paris, 1923), cols. 1192–1222.

17. Judges 6: 11–23 (call to Gideon); 13: 2–22 (announcement of the birth of Samson).

18. Genesis 28: 12. On the "*meta* function" of the angel, a void "between beings," see Stanislas Breton, "Faut-il parler des anges?," *Revue des sciences philosophiques et théologiques* 64 (1980): 225–40.

19. Denis the Carthusian, *Opera omnia*, vol. 15 (Tournai, 1902), commen-

tary on the "Celestial Hierarchy" of Dionysius the Areopagite); vol. 21 (1903), commentary on the Sentences, book 2, dist. 2–11); vol. 23 (1906), Sermons on the Angels; etc. See Anselme Stroelen, "Denys le Chartreux," in *Dictionnaire de spiritualité*, vol. 3 (Paris, 1957), cols. 430–49; Joseph Duhr, "Anges," ibid., vol. 1 (1937), cols. 580–625.

20. See Michel de Certeau, "Une Pratique sociale de la différence: Croire," in *Faire croire. Modalités de la diffusion et de la réception des messages religieux du XIIe au XVe siècle* (Rome, 1981), 363–83; id., "L'Institution du croire," *Recherches de science religieuse* 71 (1983): 61–80.

21. Judges 13: 16–18. The same question in the account of Jacob's struggle with the angel (the unknown "man"): "Jacob questioned him and said: 'Tell me your name.' He said: 'Why do you ask me my name?'" (Genesis 32: 30).

22. Judges 13: 20; see also 6: 21.

23. "In the ancient traditions, the angel does no more than transmit the divine command; he does not bring man's prayers to God" (André Caquot, "Anges et démons en Israël," in *Génies, anges et démons*, 123).

24. See the notes of Étienne Souriau, *L'Ombre de Dieu* (Paris, 1955), 126–72.

25. See Marcel Leibovici, "Génies et démons en Babylonie," in *Génies, anges et démons*, 85–112.

26. Zechariah 1: 9, 2: 2, 4: 1, 4: 4–5, 5: 5, etc.

27. See Souriau, *L'Ombre de Dieu*, 137.

28. See René Roques, introduction, in Dionysius the Areopagite, *La Hiérarchie céleste*, ed. R. Roques et al., 2nd ed. (Paris, 1970), lxxvi–lxxx.

29. *Summa Theologica*, Ia, quest. 112, art. 2, resp.: "Hoc habet ordo divinae providentiae, non solum in angelis, sed etiam in toto universo, quod inferiora per superiora administrantur."

30. Descartes, *Conversation with Burman*: "Bien qu'il ne se soit peut-être nulle part ailleurs donné plus de mal, nulle part il n'est plus inepte" (*Œuvres*, ed. André Bridoux [Paris, 1953], 1370). ["Though perhaps on no other subject did he take greater pains, on no other is he more inept." My translation.—Trans.]

31. *Summa Theologica*, I a, quest. 107, art. 1 et 2, on the language between angels. See A. Vacant, "Anges" (la scolastique), in *Dictionnaire de théologie catholique*, vol. 1.1 (1923), cols. 1222–48; and Jean-Louis Chrétien, "Le Langage des anges selon la scolastique," *Critique* 387–88 (1979): 674–89.

32. Reuchlin, *La Kabbale*, 300–301.

33. See Pierre Demange, "Swedenborg, l'homme qui s'entretenait avec les anges," in *L'Ange et l'homme*, 157–70.

34. Francisco Suárez, *De angelis* IV, 1–12, on the "ubi angelicum" (angelic place—angelic where), in *Opera omnia*, ed. Vivès, vol. 2 (Paris, 1856), 419–78.

35. See Vidal A. Castello, "L'Obligation politique chez Suarez," *Archives de philosophie* 42 (1979): 179–203, and that whole special issue devoted to Suárez.

36. Genesis 32: 26, 33.

37. Ezekiel 9: 2–4.

38. Saint Bonaventure, *Legenda minor*, 6, 2, in *Analecta franciscana* (Quaracchi) 10 (1926–41), 673.

39. Saint Bonaventure, *Legenda major*, 13, 10, in ibid., 620.

40. Teresa of Avila, *Libro de la vida*, 8, 6; 19, 2; 30, 21; 33, 14; 33, 16; 34, 18; 38, 20; 39, 26; etc. (in *Obras completas* [Madrid: BAC, 1951], vol. 1).

41. *Libro de la vida*, 29, 13 (*Obras completas*, 1: 775).

42. Ibid., 9, 6 (*Obras completas*, 1: 644). See Michel Florisoone, *Esthétique et mystique* (Paris, 1956), 38–48.

43. *Libro de la vida*, 39, 22 (*Obras completas*, 1: 866).

44. *Libro de la vida*, 29, 13 (*Obras completas*, 1: 775; see also ed. Silverio [Burgos, 1915], 1: 234). [Here as elsewhere for this work, I have followed the David Lewis translation, making a few minor changes to remain as close as possible to Certeau's interpretation of the text—Trans.]

45. See Saint Bonaventure, *Itinerarium*, 4; and Bernard Gorceix, *Flambée et agonie. Mystiques du XVIIe siècle allemand* (Sisteron, 1977), 246.

46. *Libro de la vida*, 29, 14 and 30, 1 (*Obras completas*, 1: 775–76).

47. Gorceix, "L'Ange en Allemagne au XVIIe siècle."

48. *Epistolae Theosophicae* 56, 12, etc. See Heinz R. Schmitz, "La Visée de l'expérience boehmienne. Faire de l'homme un ange," *Nova et vetera* 49, no. 4 (1974): 252–89; id., " L'Expérience mystique de Jacob Boehme et son projet philosophique," in *Jacob Boehme ou l'obscure lumière de la connaissance mystique* (Paris, 1979), 9–29.

49. Exodus 3: 2–14.

50. At each of these levels, Boehme develops a kind of fundamental generative grammar analyzing the rules obeyed by the articulation of a language with the ineffable, of a form with a force, and of "sounds" or "chords" with the letters making up the divine tetragram, so that the angels constitute the "branches of the great trees of divine names, on which celestial fruit grows."

51. See Terence Cave, *The Cornucopian Text* (Oxford, 1979).

52. Gorceix, "L'Ange en Allemagne au XVIIe siècle," 138–41; see Pierre Deghaye, "J. Boehme ou de la difficulté du discours sur Dieu," in *Jacob Boehme*, 31–59.

53. Meister Eckhart, *Expositio Libri Exodi*, 3, 16, in *Die lateinischen Werke*, vol. 2 (Stuttgart, 1954), 21.

54. Gorceix, "L'Ange en Allemagne au XVIIe siècle," 135.

55. Angelus Silesius, *Cherubinischer Wandersmann*, II, 32.

56. Ibid., II, 21; III, 107; etc.

57. Ibid., II, 236; IV, 146; etc.

58. Ibid., II, 145; I, 15; II, 256; II, 44.

59. Ibid., I, 4.

60. Gorceix, "L'Ange en Allemagne au XVIIe siècle," 149.

61. *Cherubinischer Wandersmann*, I, 3.

62. Ibid., I, 7.

63. Edgar Allan Poe, "The Angel of the Odd," in *Complete Stories and Poems of Edgar Allen Poe* (Garden City, NY: Doubleday, 1966), 366–67. [The author cites the famous French translation by Charles Baudelaire in 1856.]

64. Ibid., 367.

65. Guillaume Apollinaire, "The Ox," in *Bestiary, or, The Parade of Orpheus*, trans. Pepe Karmel, woodcuts by Raoul Dufy (Boston: D. Godine, 1980), 60. See also p. 48, the quatrain "Orpheus," contrasting the sirens, "these wretched birds," with the "Angels of paradise."

66. Apollinaire, "Le Bestiaire," in *Alcools* (Paris, 1978), 177, note by Apollinaire.

67. Géo Norge, *Eux les anges* (Paris, 1978), 137.

68. Paul Éluard, "Paul Klee," in *Œuvres complètes*, ed. Marcelle Dumas and Lucien Scheler, vol. 1 (Paris, 1968), 182; and Jean-Charles Gateau, *Paul Éluard et la peinture surréaliste* (Geneva, 1982), 133–38.

69. Rainer Maria Rilke, *Sämtliche Werke*, vol. 1 (Frankfurt am Main, 1955), 409 ("Verkündigung," in *Das Buch der Bilder*, II, part 1).

70. Ibid., 713; see Rilke, *Duinesian Elegies*, German text with English translation and commentary by Elaine E. Boney, 2nd ed. (Chapel Hill: University of North Carolina Press, 1977), 43, 107–8.

71. See J.-F. Angelloz, *Rainer Maria Rilke. L'évolution spirituelle du poète* (Paris, 1936), 339–48.

72. Rilke, *Duinesian Elegies*, trans. Boney, 43, 3, resp.

73. "L'Ange du méridien," in Rilke, *Sämtliche Werke*, 1: 497; *Rainer Maria Rilke: Selected Poems*, trans. A. E. Flemming (New York: Methuen, 1986), 116.

74. "À l'ange," in Rilke, *Œuvres*, vol. 2: *Poésie*, ed. Paul De Man (Paris, 1972), 417–18 [my trans.—Trans.].

75. "Vergers" (poems written in French), ibid., 477; trans. A. Poulin Jr., *The Complete French Poems of Rainer Maria Rilke* (Saint Paul, MN: Graywolf Press, 1986), 151.

76. Rilke, *Sämtliche Werke*, 1: 710; *Œuvres*, vol. 2: *Poésie*, 333, 364 [my trans.—Trans.].

77. Rilke, *Sämtliche Werke*, 1: 717; *Œuvres*, vol. 2: *Poésie*, 337–38, 369.

78. Rilke, *Sämtliche Werke*, 1: 726; *Œuvres*, vol. 2: *Poésie*, 343, 375.

79. I quote the text of Walter Benjamin, "Agesilaus Santander," two versions dated from Ibiza, 12 and 13 August 1933, in *Zür Aktualität Walter Benjamins*, ed. Siegfried Unseld (Frankfurt am Main, 1972), 94–102. Benjamin refers to "the Kabbalah." It is true that Reuchlin, for example, quoted this opinion in his *De arte cabalistica* (see his translation, *La Kabbale*, 301). But it comes from the Zohar (*Beresh. Rabb.*, section 78), which spoke of a creation "every day,"

while Benjamin writes "in each now" (*in jedem Nun*). See Benjamin, *Selected Writings*, vol. 2: *1927–1934*, trans. Rodney Livingstone et al., ed. Michael W. Jennings et al. (Cambridge, MA: Belknap Press, 1999), 712 [trans. modified].

80. Walter Benjamin, *Selected Writings*, vol. 4: *1938–1940* (Cambridge, MA: Harvard University Press, 2003), 392–93. See Christine Buci-Glucksmann, "Walter Benjamin et l'Ange de l'histoire," *L'Écrit du temps* 2 (1982): 45.

81. Benjamin, "Agesilaus Santander," version of 13 August, *Selected Writings*, 2: 715.

82. Jacques Lacan, seminar on anxiety, session of 21 November 1962.

Chapter Nine

1. See for example E. A. Nida, "Principles of Translation Exemplified by Bible Translating," in *On Translation*, ed. Reuben A. Brower (Cambridge, MA: 1959), 11–31. There the author considers the possibilities of translating the Bible into all languages in their relation to the cultural specificity of the text. See, by the same author, "Linguistics and Ethnology in Translation Problems," *Word* 2 (1945): 194–208. The fundamental work of Georges Mounin, *Les Problèmes théoriques de la traduction* (Paris, 1963), unfortunately does not analyze the historical role played by the Bible in the theories of translation. Recognition must also be given to the importance of the exegetic tradition of medicine (W. Fulbecke, P. J. Toletus, C. Martinengus, C. Guarinonius, etc.), to the *hermeneutica juris* until Leibniz, and to the theories involving a *hermeneutica generalis* (J. C. Dannhauer, J. Clauberg, etc.), all areas of research that, in the sixteenth and seventeenth centuries, often include and pass through the particular field of biblical exegesis.

2. See Jacques Le Brun et al., *Histoire du texte. Recherche sur la place du livre dans le christianisme*, Université de Paris XII, UER de Lettres et Sciences humaines, 1974.

3. Particularly in "De interpretatione Scripturae," chap. 8 of *Tractatus theologico-politicus* [1670].

4. See Olivier Fatio and Pierre Fraenkel, eds., *Histoire de l'exégèse au XVIe siècle* (Geneva, 1978).

5. *Logique de Port-Royal*, part 1, 1. See Louis Marin, "La Critique de la représentation classique. La traduction de la Bible à Port-Royal," in the collective work *Savoir, faire, espérer. Les limites de la raison*, vol. 2 (Brussels, 1976), 549–75. The *Logique* should also be set within a history that goes back to the Hermogenes of Plato's *Cratylus*.

6. Pascal, *Pensées*, Lafuma frag. 213; *Pensées*, trans. Roger Ariew (Indianapolis, IN: Hackett, 2004), 30.

7. On the contemporary conceptions of the relationship between a theory

of language and the principle of translatability, we have the example of two contrary positions with Louis Hjelmslev, "Existe-t-il des catégories qui soient communes à l'universalité des langues humaines?" [Do categories exist that are common to the universality of human languages?] in *Actes du Congrès international des linguistes* (Paris, 1949), 419–30, and James Barr, *The Semantics of Biblical Language* (London: Oxford University Press, 1961), esp. "Problems of Method," 21–45, and "Languages and the Study of Theology," 288–96.

8. Gérard Genette, *Figures III* (Paris, 1972), 23. On the attrition and metamorphoses of traditional rhetoric, shared in the seventeenth century between logic and grammar, see Michel Foucault, introduction, in [Antoine] Arnauld and [Claude] Lancelot, *Grammaire générale et raisonnée* (Paris, 1969), iii–xxvii, and esp. Pierre Kuentz, "Le Rhétorique ou la mise à l'écart," *Communications* 16 (1970): 143–57.

9. Saint Augustine, *Contra Mendacium*, X, 24. See Tzvetan Todorov, *Theories of the Symbol*, trans. Catherine Porter (Ithaca, NY: Cornell University Press, 1982), 76–77.

10. Étienne Dolet, *La Manière de bien traduire d'une langue en autre* (Lyon, 1540), text republished in *Babel* 1, no. 1 (1955): 18–19 [my trans.—Trans.].

11. Antoine Le Maistre, *Règles de la traduction* (in Nicolas Fontaine, *Mémoires pour servir à l'histoire de Port-Royal*, 1736), quoted by Marin, "La Critique de la représentation classique," 557. The fact is, Antoine Le Maistre's translations were judged grandiloquent at Port-Royal and he did not pursue them. See Basil Munteano, "Port-Royal et la stylistique de la traduction," in *Actes du VIIe Congrès de l'Association internationale des études françaises* (Paris, 1955), 151–72.

12. Apropos of the paraphrases and translations of the Psalms, Michel Jeanneret, *Poésie et tradition biblique au XVIe siècle* (Paris, 1969), has analyzed the evolution that leads from transpositions modeled on a respect for the spirit of the text (first half of the sixteenth century) to a second stage of erudite faithfulness to its letter (see Baïf, Vigenère, etc.) and comes out, at the threshold of the seventeenth century, on works of personal creation for which Scripture is no more than the pretext.

13. For the New Testament, we have, before the translation of Sacy (1667), or contemporary ones, those of J.-C. Deville (1613), P. Frizon (1621), P. de Besse (1631), J. Corbin (1643), F. Véron (1647), M. de Marolles (1649), P. Amelotte (1668), etc., to mention only the most important.

14. These translations, which are in fact the work of a sort of collective (Sacy, Antoine Le Maistre, Antoine Arnauld, Pierre Nicole, the duke of Luynes) and of numerous consultations (with Martin de Barcos, in particular), appeared in an order and with lacunae (Ezekiel, Jeremiah, the Song of Songs, etc.) in which ecclesiastic and pastoral preferences are discernable: *Psaumes* in 1665, *Nouveau Testament* in 1667 (the edition known as "de Mons," 5,000 copies of which

sold in six months), *Proverbes* in 1672, *Ecclésiaste, Sagesse et Isaïe* in 1673, *Livre des Rois* I and II in 1674, the twelve *Petits Prophètes* in 1679, *Genèse* in 1682, *Exode* and *Lévitique* in 1683, *Ecclésiastique* in 1684.

15. See Henri-Jean Martin, *Livre, pouvoirs et société à Paris au XVIIe siècle* (Geneva, 1969).

16. We find this especially in his "Préface à la traduction du Nouveau Testament" (in *La Bible de Mons* [Paris, 1696]), in the *Choix de lettres inédites de Louis-Isaac Le Maistre de Sacy (1650–1683)*, ed. G. Delassault (Paris, 1959), and in Nicolas Fontaine, *Mémoires pour servir à l'histoire de Port-Royal* (Cologne and Paris, 1753), in particular 2: 385ff. and 4: 322ff.

17. Marin, "La Critique de la représentation classique," 555.

18. Pierre de Bérulle, *Discours de controverse* [1609], I, 24–28, in *Œuvres complètes*, ed. Migne (Paris, 1856), cols. 673–81. See Jean Orcibal, "L'Idée d'Église chez les catholiques du XVIIe siècle," *Relazioni del Xmo Congresso internazionale di scienze storiche*, vol. 4 (Florence, 1956), 116–17.

19. See Jean Orcibal, "Martin de Barcos (1600–1678), abbé de Saint-Cyran, et sa correspondance," *Revue d'histoire ecclésiastique* 52 (1957): 892.

20. A doctrine in conformity with the position of Saint-Cyran, whose "first maxim," in matters of writing, was "never to write except when under engagements coming from God." See Claude Lancelot, *Mémoires touchant la vie de M. de Saint-Cyran* (Cologne, 1738), vol. II, part III, 13, pp. 127–32: "De la manière dont M. de S. Cyran voulait que l'on se comportât dans les ouvrages qu'on entreprenait pour la défense de la vérité" [On the way in which M. de St. Cyran wanted one to comport oneself in works undertaken for the defense of the truth].

21. Michel Foucault, *The Archeology of Knowledge*, trans. A. M. Sheridan Smith (New York: Vintage Books, 2010), 50.

22. The title of the complete edition of 1704, for example, emphasizes in red capital letters that the Bible is "translated into French, ON THE BASIS OF THE VULGATE" (*La sainte Bible* . . . , [Brussels: H. E. Frick, 1704], in-folio). This heading has the force of a post-Tridentine blazon: it signals an ecclesiastic option. But it also has the ritual value of a mask: it says something other than what Sacy does, since in fact (Richard Simon will reprove him for it in his *Histoire critique des versions du Nouveau Testament* [Rotterdam, 1690], 396–447) his translation often gives preference to the lessons of the Septuagint over those of the Vulgate, and thus, given this mixture, it "represents" neither the Greek nor the Latin.

23. On the "choices" Sacy makes between variants and versions furnished by the different versions of the same text and that he himself adjudges to be doubtful, see his preface to the *Épîtres de saint Paul* cited in Geneviève Delassault, *Le Maistre de Sacy et son temps* (Paris, 1957), 155.

24. See Michel de Certeau, "Exégèse, théologie et spiritualité," *Revue*

d'ascétique et de mystique 36 (1960): 357–71; James J. Murphy, *Rhetoric in the Middle Ages* (Berkeley: University of California Press, 1974), 238, 327, 353, etc. (the four meanings constitute the "modes" of exposition in an *ars dictaminis* or in an *ars concionandi*; they modalize and hierarchize at the same time the relation of the speaker to his theme, of his discourse to its recipients, and of these last to the *res* by the *significatio*).

25. See the remarks by Sacy as transmitted by Fontaine, *Mémoires*, 4: 325, 331, etc. This position should be connected with the theory of the mystics on the *modus loquendi*, characterized by the *coincidatio oppositorum*, "incorrectness," and the mad. See above, chapter 4, sections 4 and 5.

26. Letter to his brother Antoine Le Maistre, quoted in Fontaine, *Mémoires*, 1: 386: Sacy rejects "that rigorous exactitude" that would have specialists be the only addressees of the Bible.

27. Quoted in Fontaine, *Mémoires*, 4: 325 and 322.

28. On the conception of translation of Richard Simon (1638–1712), the most synthetic elements may be found in his *Histoire critique du Vieux Testament* (Rotterdam: R. Leers, 1685) [*A Critical History of the Old Testament*, translated "by a Person of Quality" (London: Walter Davis, 1682)]; in his *Réponse au livre intitulé Sentimens de quelques théologiens de Hollande* . . . (Rotterdam: R. Leers, 1686); and in *L'Histoire critique des versions du Nouveau Testament* . . . (Rotterdam: R. Leers, 1690), translated as *A Critical History of the TEXT of the New Testament* (London: R. Taylor, 1689). See also Paul Auvray, *Richard Simon* (Paris: PUF, 1974); and Richard Simon, *Additions aux Recherches curieuses sur la diversité des langues et religions d'Edward Brerewood*, ed. Jacques Le Brun and John D. Woodbridge (Paris: PUF, 1983).

29. See for example Simon, *Histoire critique du Vieux Testament*, 364 [trans. *A Critical History of the Old Testament*, book 3, chap. 3 (16) (the translation is not paginated; reference is to the sixteenth page of chap. 3)].

30. Simon, *Histoire critique du Vieux Testament*, preface, unpaginated [translated as *A Critical History of the Old Testament*, unpaginated preface, with a definition of "the word Critick, which is a term of Art": "The aim of those which practice that Art, is not to destroy, but establish"].

31. On this relation between the "certainty" received from the Church and the "uncertainty" of the Bible, see *A Critical History of the Old Testament*, "The Author's Preface, translated out of French," fourth point.

32. This will be the position of Fénelon, for whom, ultimately, the Christian meaning of Scripture is as the priest explains it to be. See the "Lettre à l'évêque d'Arras sur la lecture de l'Écriture sainte en langue vulgaire" [1707], in *Œuvres complètes*, vol. 2 (Paris: Gaume, 1848), especially 194–95, 200–201.

33. On this turn, see Michel de Certeau, *The Writing of History*, trans. Tom Conley (New York: Columbia University Press, 1988), chap. 4, "The Formality of Practices," pp. 147–205.

34. *Critical History of the Old Testament*, title of book 3, (1). Simon adds: "we have at present no exact Translation of the Holy Scriptures. If we consider the difficulties which have already been observed, it seems impossible for us to succeed."

35. Ibid., book 3, chap. 4, (22).

36. Richard Simon did not read Spinoza until approximately 1674–75, when he had almost completed his *Histoire critique du Vieux Testament.* See Paul Auvray, "Richard Simon et Spinoza," in *Religion, érudition et critique à la fin du XVIIe siècle et au début du XVIIIe* (Paris, 1968), 201–14.

37. In particular the French translations, in his *Histoire critique des versions du Nouveau Testament*, chaps. 27–39, 311–483.

38. On this subject, Simon writes to D. H. in 1699: "M. Justel who was persuaded that his Ministers were not capable of such a great undertaking consulted me to find out how to proceed" (*Lettres choisies de M. Simon* [Amsterdam: Pierre Mortier, 1730], vol. 3, supplement, p. 274) [my trans.—Trans.].

39. The first Genevan translations (Genesis 3; 2 Corinthians 7) were not appreciated by Richard Simon and the Charenton pastors (beginning of 1677). The French Bible of Geneva in preparation by 1672 at the instigation of François Turrentini, the rector of the Academy, appeared at the end of 1678 from the publisher Chouet.

40. See *Réponse au livre intitulé Sentimens de quelques théologiens de Hollande*, 77–78. These translations have disappeared. Jean Le Clerc claimed that a "reformed Doctor," after having examined them, considered them to be a plagiarism of the Protestant erudite Samuel Bochart (J. Le Clerc, *Défense des sentimens de quelques théologiens de Hollande sur l'Histoire critique du Vieux Testament* [Amsterdam: H. Desbordes, 1686], 54).

41. *Réponse au livre intitulé Sentimens de quelques théologiens de Hollande*, 24. That translation, still announced as forthcoming soon by Justel in 1676, unfortunately never appeared.

42. *Critical History of the Old Testament*, book 3, chaps. 1 and 2, (1–14): "A Project for a new Translation of the Scripture, where the faults of other Translations are also shewn."

43. Ibid, (1–2).

44. Ibid., (2).

45. Ibid., (10).

46. "The Hebrew Text may be corrected," *Critical History of the Old Testament*, book 3, chap. 1, (5); "reestablish a language that has been lost" (10), etc. These terms specify the definition given to "Criticism": to "correct the Bibles" (preface). See also, on Erasmus, *Histoire critique des versions du Nouveau Testament*, 252.

47. There is probably a key, here, to Richard Simon's behavior toward the Protestant churches and the Catholic Church: the former, reformist at the price

of too many illusions (about the Bible, etc.), and the latter, more conformist ("worldly"), or even more corrupt, than it admits. Allergic to revolutionaries, he accepts an actual (Catholic) given that permits critical labor over the long haul. See Miriam Yardeni, "Richard Simon et la Réforme," in *Historiographie de la Réforme*, ed. Philippe Joutard (Geneva, 1977), 60–70.

48. Simon, *Histoire critique des versions du Nouveau Testament*, 434–64.

49. This is already the case with the *word*, a unit of the signifier in which the meaning vanishes and proliferates in turn: it is an *uncertain* on which *limits* are placed (there are unacceptable meanings) and within which hypotheses to be classified are produced.

50. See Hidé Ishiguro, *Leibniz's Philosophy of Logic and Language* (London: Duckworth, 1972), 119–45, "Necessity and Contingency."

51. To this effect produced, in Richard Simon, by the vanishing of meaning, we should compare the famous theses of W. V. Quine on the indetermination of translation and the myth of meaning (see W. V. Quine, *Word and Object*. [Cambridge: Technology Press of the Massachusetts Institute of Technology, 1960], chap. 2; Paul Gochet, *Quine en perspective* [Paris, 1978], chap. 4, etc.). For Quine, if translations that are incompatible with one another and yet equally correct are possible, it is because they cannot be based on a true synonymy, because the "verbal envelopes" are in reality empty, and because meaning is societal, inseparable from contacts and occasions, in sum, from a historical intersubjectivity. See also Jacques Bouveresse, *La Parole malheureuse* (Paris, 1971), chap. 2.

52. Pascal is situated beyond this position, in a "modern" in-between: the insurmountable distance of Scripture makes possible a way of "getting around" its internal *differences*, so that this movement of opposites constantly provides a passage to faith—the analysis of texts being inscribed in a logic of believing. See below, chap. 10.

53. *Correspondance de Martin de Barcos*, ed. Lucien Goldmann (Paris, 1956), 372; see Marin, "La Critique de la représentation classique," 569.

Chapter Ten

1. Jean Mesnard, *Pascal et les Roannez* (Paris, 1965), 542. See p. 545, on the nine letters: they "bear close similarities to the writings of Pascal that may legitimately be described as mystic, the *Memorial*, the *Mystery of Jesus*."

2. The oldest manuscript is a copy by P. Guerrier (G [2], n. 100, from the Oratoire de Clermont-Ferrand) and established in 1734. It is titled *Extraits de quelques lettres de M. Pascal à Melle de Roannez*. On the history of the text, see Mesnard, *Pascal et les Roannez*, 463–97, and Blaise Pascal, *Œuvres complètes*, ed. J. Mesnard, vol. 1 (Paris, 1964), 135–69 (Pierre Guerrier coll.) and

45–46 (the projected edition of these letters by Guillaume Desprez, in 1664). In Guerrier's copy, the "letter" on "the strange secret" bears the number 2; since the study and edition of Charles Adam (1891), it bears the number IV. With other papers of Port-Royal, the autograph was thrown into the fire by its addressee (who had become the duchess of La Feuillade) at the order of her husband in 1683, a few days before her death: see Mesnard, *Pascal et les Roannez*, 934–46.

3. *Pensées chrétiennes* (Paris: Desprez, 1670). Chapter 27 ("Pensées sur les miracles") contains, excerpted from this letter, a passage that was numbered 18 in the reprinted edition of 1678.

4. Mesnard, *Pascal et les Roannez*, 463–546.

5. Letter to her mother, the marquise de Boissy (July 1657), in Blaise Pascal, *Œuvres complètes*, ed. Louis Brunschvicg et al., Les grands écrivains de France, vol. 5 (Paris: Hachette, 1914), 400. I will refer to this edition of Pascal by the sole mention: Pascal, *Œuvres*, with indication of volume and page number. [My trans.—Trans.]

6. Jean Molino, "Lire Racine," in *Actes du second colloque de Marseille. État présent des études concernant le XVIIe siècle* (Marseille, 1973), 21 and 29. See also, by the same author, "Structure et littérature," *Archives européennes de sociologie* 14 (1973): 106–25.

7. *Pensées*, Lafuma frag. 745. *Pensées*, trans. Roger Ariew (Indianapolis, IN: Hackett, 2005), 184 [references to this work will be indicated hereafter as Ariew, and followed by page number.]. See Pierre Kuentz, "Un Discours nommé Montalte," *Revue d'histoire littéraire de la France* 71 (1971): 195–206, and "La Main de Pascal," in *Histoire littéraire de la France, 1600–1660*, ed. Anne Ubersfeld and Roland Desné (Paris, 1975), 200–205, studies of an incisive and innovative rigor.

8. Pascal, *Traité des ordres numériques*, in *Œuvres complètes*, ed. Louis Lafuma (Paris, 1963), 65.

9. Ibid. See *Pensées*, frags. 784, 789, etc.; trans. Ariew, 192, 193, etc.

10. *Pensées*, frag. 696. Trans. Ariew, 173.

11. Michel de Certeau, "L'Énonciation mystique," *Recherches de science religieuse* 64 (1976): 183–215.

12. "Louis de Montalte" is the author of the *Provinciales*; "Amos Dettonville," that of *Diverses inventions en géométrie*; "Salomon de Tultie" (at once wise and foolish—*Stultitia*), that of the *Apologie*.

13. I reproduce the text of Pascal, *Œuvres*, 6: 87–90; trans. O. W. Wight, *The Thoughts, Letters, and Opuscules of Blaise Pascal* (Boston: Houghton Mifflin, 1858), 443–44 [trans. modified.].

14. The *Sentence* is that of 22 October 1656, signed by Alexandre de Hodencq, vicar general of the archbishop of Paris, the cardinal de Retz, who is at the time "distanced from his diocese" (text in Pascal, *Œuvres*, 6: 65–70).

It was immediately printed. At the time of the solemn office of the prayers of thanksgiving celebrated in the Church of Port-Royal, on Friday, 27 October, by the same "Grand Vicar," "such a great number of sentences of Monsieur the Grand Vicar were sold that it is estimated to have amounted to one hundred francs at one sou apiece, in the courtyard in front of the church door alone" (Jacqueline Pascal to Madame Périer, 30 October 1656, in Pascal, *Œuvres*, 6: 98). Hence the date of the fragment: either *Sunday, 29 October*, after the ceremony of the 27th and the day of the normal post for Poitou (Mesnard, *Pascal et les Roannez*, 471–72), or more likely *Thursday, 26 October* (feast of the Holy Sacrament and anniversary of the inscription of the Religious of Port-Royal as "Daughters of the Holy Sacrament," in October 1647), given the absence of references to the 27th and especially the very probable allusions in the excerpt to the hymn and litanies of the Holy Sacrament (see Philippe Sellier, *Pascal et la liturgie* [Paris, 1966], 68–70).

15. See *Pensées*, frags. 149, 835, etc.; trans. Ariew, 49–50, 116, etc.

16. See a parallel passage in the sixteenth *Provinciale* (written during the same period and published on 4 December 1656, in Pascal, *Œuvres*, 6: 275–76).

17. Revelation 2:17. "Vincenti dabo manna absconditum." The eighteenth litany of the Holy Sacrament also calls the Eucharist *Manna absconditum* (see Sellier, *Pascal et la liturgie*, 69).

18. Isaiah 45: 15. "Vere tu es Deus absconditus." This text, often quoted in the *Pensées* (frags. 427, 781, 921) is also found (see Sellier, *Pascal et la liturgie*, 69) in the ninth litany of the Holy-Sacrament: "Deus absconditus et Salvator."

19. Romans 1: 20. "Quod notum est Dei manifestum est in illis, Deus enim illis manifestavit. Invisibilia enim ipsius a creatura mundi, per ea quae facta sunt intellecta, conspiciuntur." See *Pensées*, frag. 275; Ariew, 83.

20. On the two meanings, see *Pensées*, frags. 252, 274, etc.; trans. Ariew, 73, 82, etc.

21. Isaiah 53: 3. "et quasi absconditus vultus ejus et despectus, unde nec reputavimus eum."

22. See *Pensées*, frag. 733; trans. Ariew, 181.

23. [Since the use of tenses differs substantially in French and English, I include here Pascal's original French text—without which the analysis in table 5 would not be fully intelligible.—Trans.] "Il me semble que vous prenez assez de part au miracle pour vous mander en particulier que la vérification en est achevée par l'Église, comme vous le verrez par cette sentence de M. le Grand Vicaire. Il y a si peu de personnes à qui Dieu se fasse paraître par ces coups extraordinaires, qu'on doit bien profiter de ces occasions ; puisqu'il ne sort du secret de la nature qui le couvre que pour exciter notre foi à le servir avec d'autant plus d'ardeur que nous le connaissons avec plus de certitude. Si Dieu se découvrait continuellement aux hommes, il n'y aurait point de mérite à le croire ; et, s'il ne se découvrait jamais, il y aurait peu de foi. Mais il se cache

ordinairement, et se découvre rarement à ceux qu'il veut engager dans son service. Cet étrange secret, dans lequel Dieu s'est retiré, impénétrable à la vue des hommes, est une grande leçon pour nous porter à la solitude loin de la vue des hommes. Il est demeuré caché sous le voile de la nature qui nous le couvre jusques à l'Incarnation ; et quand il a fallu qu'il ait paru, il s'est encore plus caché en se couvrant de l'humanité. Il était bien plus reconnaissable quand il était invisible, que non pas quand il s'est rendu visible. Et enfin quand il a voulu accomplir la promesse qu'il fit à ses Apôtres de demeurer avec les hommes jusques à son dernier avènement, il a choisi d'y demeurer dans le plus étrange et le plus obscur de tous, qui sont les espèces de l'Eucharistie. C'est ce Sacrement que saint Jean appelle dans l'Apocalypse une manne cachée; et je crois qu'Isaïe le voyait en cet état, lorsqu'il dit en esprit de prophétie : Véritablement tu es un Dieu caché. C'est là le dernier secret où il peut être. Le voile de la nature qui couvre Dieu a été pénétré par plusieurs infidèles, qui, comme dit S. Paul, ont reconnu un Dieu invisible par la nature visible. Les Chrétiens hérétiques l'ont connu à travers son humanité et adorent Jésus-Christ Dieu et homme. Mais de le reconnaître sous des espèces de pain, c'est le propre des seuls Catholiques : il n'y a que nous que Dieu éclaire jusques-là. On peut ajouter à ces considérations le secret de l'Esprit de Dieu caché encore dans l'Écriture. Car il y a deux sens parfaits, le littéral et le mystique: et les Juifs s'arrêtant à l'un ne pensent pas seulement qu'il y en ait un autre, et ne songent pas à le chercher ; de même que les impies, voyant les effets naturels, les attribuent à la nature, sans penser qu'il y en ait un autre auteur ; et comme les Juifs, voyant un homme parfait en Jésus-Christ, n'ont pas pensé à y chercher une autre nature : nous n'avons pas pensé que ce fût lui, dit encore Isaïe; et de même enfin que les hérétiques, voyant les apparences parfaites du pain, ne pensent pas y chercher une autre substance. Toutes choses couvrent quelque mystère; toutes choses sont des voiles qui couvrent Dieu. Les Chrétiens doivent le reconnaître en tout. Les afflictions temporelles couvrent les biens éternels où elles conduisent. Les joies temporelles couvrent les maux éternels qu'elles causent. Prions Dieu de nous le faire reconnaître et servir en tout. Rendons lui des grâces infinies de ce que s'étant caché en toutes choses pour les autres, il s'est découvert en toutes choses et tant de manières pour nous."

24. Émile Benveniste, *Problems of General Linguistics*, trans. Mary Elizabeth Meek (Coral Gables, FL: University of Miami Press, 1971), 209.

25. See Hubert Damisch, *Théorie du nuage* (Paris, 1972), 65–67.

26. *Pensées*, frags. 427, 781, 921; trans. Ariew, 216, 191, 279.

27. Benveniste, *Problems of General Linguistics*, 209.

28. Ibid. 218.

29. It is accompanied by the sending of documents *to look at*: *Sentence* of the Grand Vicar (excerpt 4), or, later (December 1656), quite probably, the *Remonstrance* of the parish priests and the attached documents given to the

Assembly of the Clergy (see Mesnard, *Pascal et les Roannez*, 485). To send, "to summon" (excerpt 4), to show—these three gestures reinforce *physically the demonstrative* adjective and give it an *injunctive* value rendered more explicit by the future-imperative "you will see."

30. Benveniste, *Problems of General Linguistics*, 206–7, 209–10, and 211.

31. Harald Weinrich, *Le Temps. Le récit et le commentaire*, trans. Michèle Lacoste (Paris, 1973), 34.

32. Ibid.

33. Ibid., 198–205.

34. This is an application of a matricial representation of Weinrich, *Le temps*, 203. In keeping with his conventions, the subjunctives, infinitives, imperatives, and participles are not counted. The beginning tenses are represented in columns, and the ending tenses in rows. The initial and final transitions are included, i.e., the one starting at zero (Ø →), and the one ending at zero (→ Ø).

35. Weinrich, *Le temps*, 205.

36. *Alethic*, from *alēthes*, "true." They are also called "ontological," relating to being.

37. See for example Herman Parret, *La Pragmatique des modalités* (Urbino, 1975).

38. Alan R. White, *Modal Thinking* (Ithaca, NY: Cornell University Press, 1975), 176. See whole chapter "The Nature of Modality," 165–79.

39. There is also the ambiguous case of "one *can* add to these considerations . . ." Here, as is frequent, *possible* is opposed to *certain*, rather than to *necessary*. It therefore has an epistemic, not an alethic value. Further, the *one* refers to the "I/we" of the enunciative contract and, secondarily, to the collective neuter (not appropriable by a "we") of a traditional, theological, and prior self-evident assumption. The impersonal is strategic.

40. See Stephen Toulmin, *The Uses of Argument* (Cambridge: Cambridge University Press, 1958).

41. Aristotle, *Rhetoric* II, 24, 1402a: "making the worse argument seem the better," in Aristotle, *Rhetoric*, trans. W. Rhys Roberts, and *Poetics*, trans. Ingram Bywater, Introduction by Friedrich Solmsen (New York: Modern Library, 1954), 160. Plato attributes the same "find" to Tisias (*Phaedrus* 273b–c, in *Plato's Phaedrus*, trans. R. Hackforth [Cambridge: Cambridge University Press, 1952], 153). See also W. K. C. Guthrie, *The Sophists* (Cambridge: Cambridge University Press, 1971), 178–79. On the *techne* of Corax, mentioned by Aristotle in connection with the "apparent enthymemes," see Charles Perelman and L. Olbrechts-Tyteca, *Traité de l'argumentation* (Brussels, 1970), 607–9. But here I retain only the principle, and not the particular procedure, in which Aristotle detects it. See Jean-François Lyotard, "Que le signe est hostie, et l'inverse," *Critique* 342 (November 1975): 1118–20.

42. See Charles Perelman and L. Olbrechts-Tyteca, *Rhétorique et philosophie* (Paris, 1952), 12 and 38.

43. In Pascal's vocabulary, the "acts" are related to chance, to *sortis eventus*; the "opportunities," to grace, to the *tempus opportunum*, or *kairos*.

44. On the performative, see J. L. Austin, *How to Do Things with Words* (Cambridge: Harvard University Press, 1962).

45. The whole fragment presents an analogous but more visible mixture by a series of loops leading from the general (a truth) to the "we" (a doing). We have a series of segments. In A ("There is . . . certainty"): *first segment*, from the general to "us," here. In B ("If God uncovered himself . . . his service"): *second segment*, a general truth commenting on the premise of A (hidden God) and coming out at C. In C ("That strange secrecy . . . far from the sight of men"): commentary on B, but "for us." In D ("he remained hidden . . . the species of the Eucharist"): *third segment*, explication of the "secrecy" taken in C as self-evident. In E ("It is this sacrament . . . in which he can be"): a scriptural illustration of the starting premise (A: hidden God) and of its Eucharistic explication (D)—a time of recapitulation. In F ("The veil of nature . . . thus enlightened by God"): *fourth segment*, repetition of A ("the secrecy of nature that covers him") but in the general mode, with substitution (and erasure) of the "we" by the impersonal "Catholics" before the ending on "none but us." In G ("One can add . . . another substance"): intensification of F; here the scriptural principle founds a typology of believing behavior parallel to the historical development of F. In H ("All things cover . . . for us"): *fifth segment*, which recommences from the general to go to the particular. The end ("to make us recognize and serve him") is a return to the beginning (A: "to serve him all the more ardently that we know him").

46. That is what Lancelot says about it in his *Mémoires touchant la vie de M. de Saint-Cyran*. See Marc Fumaroli, "Jésuites et Gallicans. Recherches sur la genèse et la signification des querelles de rhétorique en France sous les règnes d'Henri IV et de Louis XIII," State Doctoral Thesis, Université de Paris IV–Sorbonne, 1976, pp. 751–68.

47. This modus operandi has a more general significance. It relates to a remark by Louis Brunschvicg: Pascal "does not try to transform his *tactical procedure* into a *strategic instrument*" (quoted by Jean Beaufret, *Dialogue avec Heidegger* [Paris, 1973], 2: 63). It is at once a *condensation* of the reasoning, an *ellipsis* of meditations, and an *absence of a space of unfolding* or of generalization.

48. Seventeenth Provincial Letter (23 January 1657), in Pascal, *Œuvres*, 6: 344–47. *The Provincial Letters of Blaise Pascal*, trans. Thomas M'Crie (New York: Hurd and Houghton, 1866), 422 and 424.

49. Infidels, heretical Christians, the Catholics alone. This is segment F: see above, note 45.

50. The impious, the Jews, the heretic. It is segment G: see above, note 45.

51. While all the rest of the piece (G) is in the present, the second mention of the Jews is in the past (they "did not think"), perhaps by the attraction of the quotation from Isaiah ("we did not think"): that historical deviation in a present typology of the figures of religious knowledge seems to anchor in a past event (the Incarnation) the structure that it constituted.

52. The "*perfect* meaning" that is the "literal" one, the "*perfect* man," and "the *perfect* appearances of the bread." There is a coherence and a closure proper to this level, and not destruction of the letter, humanity, or the appearances by what else must be "thought" there.

53. "*Stopping* at one" (of the two meanings), "*seeing* the natural effect," "*seeing* a perfect man," "*seeing* the appearances . . ."

54. The Jews "*do not* even *think that there is another*" (mystic); the impious see "*without thinking that there is another* author" (the pressure of the opposition *one* versus *other* is so strong that it elicits the doublet "an other" and "an author"); the Jews "did *not think* to seek in him *another* nature"; the heretics "*do not think* to seek therein *another* substance."

55. *Pensées*, frag. 93; trans. Ariew, 27. See the whole series titled "Cause of the Effects," ibid., frags. 89–103; trans. Ariew, 26–30.

56. This formal ratio is posed by the relation that *one* Testament bears to the *other*, or *one* meaning to the *other*. But it corresponds to the gesture of thinking itself, in the way it goes to work, already in the *Entretien avec M. de Sacy* (this last being very "surprised to see how he [Pascal] could turn things"), on two isolated terms, healthy nature (Epictetus) and disabled nature (Montaigne): "they cannot subsist alone because of their flaws, or unite because of their oppositions . . . they break," and "a totally divine art" alone "harmonizes the contrarieties" by the play, and not the suppression, of their difference (*L'Entretien de Pascal avec M. de Sacy*, ed. Pierre Courcelle [Paris, 1960], 59–61).

57. [The French word is *sens*; it denotes either meaning or direction, or exceptionally (as in this case) both.]

58. *Pensées*, frag. 449, 471, etc.; trans. Ariew, 226–28, 237.

59. Ibid., frag. 840; trans. Ariew, 117.

60. On quotation, see, in addition to Kuentz, "Un Discours nommé Montalte": M. Metchies, *Zitat und Zitierkunst in Montaignes Essais* (Geneva, 1966), and the collective work *Signe, langage, culture* (The Hague, 1970), with contributions by M. R. Mavenova, "Expressions guillemetées. Contribution à l'étude de la sémantique du texte poétique"; S. Morawski, "The Basic Functions of Quotation" (including his definition of the quotation, p. 691); and A. Wiersbicka, "Descriptions or Quotations." Louis Panier's dissertation, "Récit et commentaires. Tentation de Jésus au désert. Approche sémiotique du discours interprétatif" (Université de Paris–Nanterre, 1976), places his analyses of the biblical quotation (pp. 202–18) in a rather different perspective.

61. See Philippe Hamon, "Un Discours contraint," *Poétique* 16 (1973): 426–27, on the "realist" novel.

62. W. V. O. Quine, *From a Logical Point of View* (New York: Harper & Row, 1953), 67.

63. The biblical quotations in this letter, like those of casuistry in the *Lettres provinciales*, "function as a nucleus generative" of the text (see Kuentz, "Un Discours nommé Montalte," 205–6). The historical analysis seems, moreover, to show that the excerpt on the hidden God is born of scriptural and liturgical words (see Sellier, *Pascal et la liturgie*, 68–70).

64. Something takes place that is analogous to what Jean-François Niceron (*La Perspective curieuse* [Paris, 1638]) expected from catoptric anamorphoses produced by mirrors in the form of columns: "This will be a new marvel when, after having seen the body of these columns bursting with light by their beautiful shine, and *without* any image or painting, *as one approaches one will see appearing inside them little by little the images* or representations" (quoted in Jurgis Baltrušaitis, *Anamorphoses* [Paris, 1969], 156; my emphasis). But in Pascal it is "from afar" or *in going away* that one sees.

65. "L'approche dérobe," an expression of Louis Marin, *La Critique du discours. Sur la "Logique de Port-Royal" et les "Pensées" de Pascal* (Paris, 1975).

66. "Deictic," from the Greek *deiktikos*, "that shows or serves to show." See, for example, on the demonstratives, pp. 198–99 above, the text completed by notes 28 and 29.

67. Michel Serres, *Hermès III. La traduction* (Paris, 1974), 209 (in the remarkably acute chapter "La Tour traduit Pascal," [203–31]).

68. *Pensées*, frag. 65; trans. Ariew, 21. See the thoughtful commentary of Marin, *La Critique du discours*, 113–46.

The Opera of Speech

1. André Roch-Lecours, "La glossolalie dans l'aphasie de Wernicke, dans la schizophasie et dans les états de possession," lecture, Centro internazionale di Semiotica e di Linguistica, Urbino, 11 July 1978.

2. Jean Bobon, *Introduction historique à l'étude des néologismes et des glossolalies en psychopathologie* (Liège, 1952), 62. The works of Jean Bobon follow a remarkable series of studies on the "pathology" of language at the end of the nineteenth century and at the beginning of the twentieth. Remarkable for the clinical description of the avatars of language (which fascinated enlightened science), these studies are today without equivalent. From this dossier I retain above all: A. Kussmaul, *Les Troubles de la parole*, trans. A. Rueff (Paris, 1884); Émile Lombard, "Essai d'une classification des phénomènes de glossolalie," *Archives de Psychologie* 7, no. 1 (1908): 1–51; A. Maeder, "La Langue

d'un aliéné. Analyse d'un cas de glossolalie," *L'Encéphale* (1910): 208–16; P. Quercy, "Langage et poésie d'un aliéné," *L'Encéphale* (1920): 207–12; Michel Cénac, *De certains langages créés par des aliénés. Contribution à l'étude des "glossolalies"* (Paris, 1925); the series of research projects of C. Pfersdorff, in *Travaux de la clinique psychiatrique de la Faculté de médecine de Strasbourg* 5 (1927): 1–157; 7 (1929): 241–362; 10 (1932): 260–366; 11 (1936): 43–182; Guilhem Teulié, "Une Forme de glossolalie. Glossolalie par suppression littérale," *Annales médico-psychologiques* 96, no. 2 (1938): 31–51.

3. William J. Samarin, *Tongues of Men and Angels* (New York: Macmillan, 1972), 128.

4. Roch-Lecours, "La glossolalie dans l'aphasie de Wernicke."

5. Quoted by William J. Samarin, *Requirements for Research on Glossolalia*, Centro internazionale di Semiotica e di Linguistica (Urbino, 1978), 14.

6. *Subida del Monte Carmelo*, prologue. The Sanjuanist definition of the Spirit as "he who speaks," far from being exceptional, is found in a whole "spiritual" tradition, and joins the tradition, which is even broader, that makes the voice the very act of the *spirit* (good or evil).

7. On the "neuter" of utopia, see Louis Marin, *Utopiques. Jeux d'espaces* (Paris, 1973), chap. 1.

8. Quoted by H. Rust, *Das Zungenreden. Eine Studie zur kritischen Religionspsychologie. Grenzfragen des Nerven- und Seelenlebens* (Munich, 1924). This poem sometimes plays on proper names used in spiritual lieder: thus "Schua ea" or, in the second stanza (not quoted above), "Ea Tschu," for *Iesu* or *Iešuah*. On these poetic phenomena, see also Leo Navratil, *Schizophrenie und Sprache. Zur Psychologie der Dichtung* (Munich, 1966), 24–158, esp. 57ff.

9. Acts of the Apostles, 2: 5 and 11. See Francis A. Sullivan, "Langues (don des)," *Dictionnaire de spiritualité*, vol. 9 (Paris, 1976), cols. 223–27.

10. See Michel de Certeau, *The Practice of Everyday Life*, trans. Steven F. Rendell (Berkeley: University of California Press, 1984), chap. 11, "Quotations of Voices," 154–64.

11. Acts of the Apostles 12: 10 and 19 (case of "speaking in other languages"); 1 Corinthians 14 (which envisages rather a language spoken "with the spirit," "manifestation of the Spirit," inspired therefore, but bereft of intelligible meaning, although verifiable by the speakers). See Gerhard Kittel, ed., *Theologisches Wörterbuch zum Neuen Testament* (Stuttgart, 1933),1: 721–26 ("glôssa, Die Glossolalie") and 10, no. 2 (1979): 1025–26 (recent bibliography).

12. *Psychoanalysis and Faith: The Letters of Sigmund Freud and Oskar Pfister*, trans. Eric Mosbacher (New York: Basic Books, 1964). See Sigmund Freud and Oskar Pfister, *Briefe, 1909–1939* (Frankfurt am Main, 1963). The only letter dating from 1939 was written by Pfister to Mrs. Freud.

13. Oskar Pfister, *Die psychologische Enträtselung der religiösen Glossolalie*

und der automatischen Kryptographie (Leipzig and Vienna, 1912); id., *Die psychoanalytische Methode* (Leipzig, 1913), which includes a chapter on "religious glossolalia" (see *The Psychoanalytic Method*, trans. Charles Rockwell Payne [New York: Moffat, Yard, 1917], 230–40 in particular).

14. Freud to Pfister, 27 September 1910, 18 June 1911, 14 December 1911, etc.

15. Freud to Pfister, 18 June 1911.

16. On 27 September 1910, Freud wrote on glossolalia: "I expect you will soon be in a position to reveal (*entlarven*) all the so-called involuntary actions as the work of complexes." *Psychoanalysis and Faith*, 44; *Briefe, 1909–1939*, 43.

17. Freud to Pfister, 18 June 1911. *Psychoanalysis and Faith*, 52; *Briefe, 1909–1939*, 51–52.

18. Pfister, *Psychoanalytic Method*, 238.

19. Théodore Flournoy, *Des Indes à la planète Mars. Étude sur un cas de somnambulisme avec glossolalie*, 3rd ed. (Paris and Geneva, 1900). *From India to the Planet Mars: A Study of a Case of Somnambulism with Glossolalia*, trans. Daniel B. Vermilye (New York: Harper & Brothers, 1901). On the same case, Flournoy also publishes "Nouvelles Observations sur un cas de somnambulisme avec glossolalie," *Archives de psychologie de la Suisse romande* (December 1901): 102–55 (devoted mainly to the "signs" or "ultra-Martian hieroglyphics" of Mademoiselle Smith); and a linguist, Victor Henry, publishes *Le Langage martien* (Paris, 1901). See also Tzvetan Todorov, *Theories of the Symbol*, trans. Catherine Porter (Ithaca, NY: Cornell University Press, 1984), "Saussure's Semiotics," 255–70.

20. This is rather a characteristic trait of glossolalic speech.

21. Saussure, quoted in T. Flournoy, *From India to the Planet Mars*, 329. [Saussure's observation on the absence of the consonant *f* in Sanskrit, added at the last minute to the third edition (p. 315; see above, note 19), is not contained in Vermilye's 1901 translation.]

22. *Des Indes à la planète Mars*, 305 [passage not contained in English translation].

23. Henry, *Le Langage martien*, 23; Todorov, *Theories of the Symbol*, 259–60.

24. See Docteur Madeleine Masure, *Le Parler en langues* (Nice, 1974).

25. Dante, *The New Life of Dante Alighieri*, trans. Charles Eliot Norton (Boston: Houghton, Mifflin, 1895), 33 [chap. 19].

26. See Georges Dumézil, *Idées romaines* (Paris, 1969), 61–78; and Certeau, *Practice of Everyday Life*, 98–101.

27. These primitive phonemes are also, as Jakobson notes, the last to be lost.

28. Roman Jakobson, *Selected Writings*, vol. 4 (The Hague: Mouton, 1966), 637–44.

29. The expression is from Elizabeth Sewel, quoted by Jakobson, *Selected Writings*, 4: 642.

30. See Jean-Louis Chrétien, "Le Langage des anges selon la scolastique," *Critique* 387–88 (August–September 1979): 674–89.

31. *Enarratio in Ps. 32, 8* (CCL, 38: 254), trans., *Expositions on the Book of Psalms* (Oxford: J. H. Parker, 1847), 317. See Sullivan, "Langues (don des)."

32. Francis Ponge, "La Promenade dans nos serres," included in his collection *Le Parti pris des choses suivi de Proêmes* (Paris, 1967).

Index of Names